India in the Arctic

Nikhil Pareek

India in the Arctic

Geopolitical and Economic Engagements

Nikhil Pareek
Chandigarh, Punjab, India

ISBN 978-981-97-3639-3 ISBN 978-981-97-3640-9 (eBook)
https://doi.org/10.1007/978-981-97-3640-9

© The Editor(s) (if applicable) and The Author(s), under exclusive license to Springer Nature Singapore Pte Ltd. 2024

This work is subject to copyright. All rights are solely and exclusively licensed by the Publisher, whether the whole or part of the material is concerned, specifically the rights of translation, reprinting, reuse of illustrations, recitation, broadcasting, reproduction on microfilms or in any other physical way, and transmission or information storage and retrieval, electronic adaptation, computer software, or by similar or dissimilar methodology now known or hereafter developed.

The use of general descriptive names, registered names, trademarks, service marks, etc. in this publication does not imply, even in the absence of a specific statement, that such names are exempt from the relevant protective laws and regulations and therefore free for general use.

The publisher, the authors and the editors are safe to assume that the advice and information in this book are believed to be true and accurate at the date of publication. Neither the publisher nor the authors or the editors give a warranty, expressed or implied, with respect to the material contained herein or for any errors or omissions that may have been made. The publisher remains neutral with regard to jurisdictional claims in published maps and institutional affiliations.

This Palgrave Macmillan imprint is published by the registered company Springer Nature Singapore Pte Ltd.
The registered company address is: 152 Beach Road, #21-01/04 Gateway East, Singapore 189721, Singapore

If disposing of this product, please recycle the paper.

Contents

1	Introduction	1
2	Geopolitical and Economic Significance of the Arctic Region	41
3	India's Involvement and Engagement with the Arctic Region	101
4	Unravelling Challenges in the Arctic and India's Response Strategy	199
5	Conclusion and Recommendations	301
Annexure A: Republic of India's Observer Report		329
Annexure B: Select Questions in the Parliament on India's Polar Research		335
Annexure C: Engagement of Indian Leaders with Arctic Leaders on Arctic Issues		347

Annexure D: Memorandum of Understanding (MOU) Signed with Arctic Countries   371

Annexure E: Emails by Various Working Groups/PPs   425

Bibliography   433

Index   445

Abbreviations

A5	Arctic 5 (USA, Canada, Russia, Denmark/Greenland, Norway)
A8	Arctic 8 (A5 plus Sweden, Finland, Iceland)
AAC	Arctic Athabaskan Council
AANDC	Aboriginal Affairs and Northern Development Canada
AC	Arctic Council
ACAP	Arctic Contaminants Action Program
ACIA	Arctic Climate Impact Assessment
AEPS	Arctic Environmental Protection Strategy
AHDR	Arctic Human Development Report
AMAP	Arctic Monitoring and Assessment Programme
AMSA	Arctic Marine Shipping Assessment
AMSP	Arctic Marine Strategic Plan and Cooperation
ANWR	Arctic National Wildlife Refuge
AOR	Arctic Ocean Review
ASEAN	Association of Southeast Asian Nations
ASSW	Arctic Science Summit Week
AWPPA	Arctic Waters Pollution Prevention Act
BAM	Baikal-Amur Mainline
BAT	Best Available Techniques
BCFG	Billion Cubic Feet of Natural Gas
BEAC	Barents Euro-Arctic Council
BEAR	Barents Euro-Arctic Region
BEP	Best Environmental Practice
BIS	Department for Business, Innovation and Skills (UK)
BOE	Total Barrels of Oil and Oil Equivalent Natural Gas
BP	British Petroleum

ABBREVIATIONS

CAA	Chinese Arctic and Antarctic Administration
CAFF	Conservation of Arctic Fauna and Flora
CARC	Canadian Arctic Resources Committee
CBD	Convention on Biological Diversity
CBSS	Council of the Baltic Sea States
CCGS	Canadian Coast Guard Ship
CFP	Common Fisheries Policy
CITES	Convention on International Trade in Endangered Species
CLCS	Commission on the Limits of the Continental Shelf
CNRS	Centre National de la Recherche Scientifique (France)
COP25	255th Conference of Parties (to the Kyoto Protocol)
CORE	Centre for Offshore Research & Engineering
CP	Le Cercle Polaire
CPAR	Conference of Parliamentarians of the Arctic Region
DC	Davis Corridor
DECC	Department of Energy and Climate Change (UK)
DEFRA	Department for Food and Rural Affairs (UK)
DFAIT	Department of Foreign Affairs and International Trade (Canada)
DfT	Department for Transport (UK)
DND	Department of National Defence (Canada)
DWT	Dead Weight Tons
EBM	Ecosystem Based Management
EC	European Commission
EEZ	Exclusive Economic Zone
EFTA	European Free Trade Agreement
EIA	Environmental Impact Assessment
ENGO	Environmental Non-governmental Organizations
EP	European Parliament
EPPR	Emergency Prevention, Preparedness and Response
EU	European Union
FC	Fram Corridor
FCO	UK Foreign and Commonwealth Office
FPSO	Floating Production Storage and Offloading
GBP	Great Britain Pound
GDP	Gross Domestic Product
GEGA	Groupe d'Etude sur la Gouvernance Arctique (France)
GPS	Global Positioning System
HDI	Human Development Index
IASC	International Arctic Science Committee
IASSA	International Arctic Social Science Association
ICC	Inuit Circumpolar Council
IEA	International Energy Agency

IGO	Intergovernmental Organisation
ILO	International Labour Organisation
IMO	International Maritime Organisation
INSROP	International Northern Sea Route Programme
IPCC	Intergovernmental Panel on Climate Change
IPEV	Institut Polaire Français
IPS	Indigenous Peoples' Secretariat
IPY	International Polar Year
IR	International Relations
ISA	International Seabed Authority
ITC	Inuit Tapirisat of Canada
ITK	Inuit Tapiriit Kanatami
IUCN	International Union for the Conservation of Nature
JAMSTEC	Japan Agency for Marine-Earth Science and Technology
JANSROP	Japan Northern Sea Route Programme
JARE	Japanese Antarctic Research Expedition
JAXA	Japan Aerospace Exploration Agency
JCAR	Japan Consortium for Arctic Environmental Research
JOGMEC	Japan Oil, Gas, and Metals National Corporation
LNG	Liquefied Natural Gas
MARPOL	Convention on the Prevention of Pollution by Ships
MCA	Maritime and Coastguard Agency (UK)
MEP	Member of European Parliament
MEXT	Ministry of Education, Culture, Sports, Science and Technology
MFA	Ministry of Foreign Affairs
MLIT	Ministry of Land, Infrastructure, Transport and Tourism (Japan)
MMBNGL	Million Barrels of Natural Gas Liquids
MMBO	Million Barrels of Oil
MMPA	Marine Mammals Protection Act (USA)
MoES	Ministry of Earth Sciences
MoFA	Ministry of Foreign Affairs (Japan)
MOU	Memorandum of Understanding
MP	Member of Parliament
MPA	Maritime and Port Authority (Singapore)
MT	Metric Tons
NAFO	Northwest Atlantic Fisheries Organization
NAFTA	North American Free Trade Agreement
NASA	National Aeronautics and Space Administration
NATO	North Atlantic Treaty Organisation
ND	Northern Dimension (EU)
NDFP	Northern Dimension of Canadian Foreign Policy

NEAFC	North-East Atlantic Fisheries Convention
NEP	North-East Passage
NERC	Natural Environment Research Council (UK)
NGO	Non-Governmental Organisation
NIPR	National Institute of Polar Research (Japan)
NMC	Northern Maritime Corridor
NORA	Nordic Atlantic Cooperation
NORAD	North American Air Defence Command
NORDEFCO	Nordic Defence Cooperation
NORDREG	Northern Canada Vessel Traffic Services
NORDSUP	Nordic Supportive Defence Structures North-East Atlantic
NPC	Northern Pacific Corridor
NQA	Not Quantitatively Assessed
NSIDC	National Snow and Ice Data Center
NSPD	National Security Presidential Directive
NSR	Northern Sea Route
NUS	National University of Singapore
NWP	Northwest Passage
NWT	Northwest Territories
OME	Offshore and Marine Engineering
OPRC	International Convention on Oil Pollution Preparedness, Response
OPRF	Ocean Policy Research Foundation (Japan)
OSPAR	Convention for the Protection of the Marine Environment of the
PA	Polar Ambassador
PAME	Protection of the Arctic Marine Environment
PAP	People's Action Party (Singapore)
PAS	Polish Academy of Science
PM	Prime Minister
PMO	Prime Minister's Office
POPs	Persistent Organic Pollutants
PP	Permanent Participants
PRS	Stanislaw Siedlecki Polish Research Station
PRU	Polar Regions Unit (UK)
PSA	Port of Singapore Authority
RAIPON	Russian Association of Indigenous Peoples of the North
RCMP	Royal Canadian Mounted Police
RFE	Russian Far East
RFMO	Regional Fisheries Management Organization
SAO	Senior Arctic Official
SAON	Sustaining Arctic Observation Network
SAR	Search and Rescue

SCPAR	Standing Committee of Parliamentarians of the Arctic Region
SDF	Japan Maritime Self-Defense Force
SDWG	Sustainable Development Working Group (Arctic Council)
SIPRI	Stockholm International Peace Research Institute
SMC	Singapore's Maritime Cluster
SNP	Scottish National Party
SOE	State Owned Enterprises
SOF	Ship and Ocean Foundation
SOLAS	Safety of Life at Sea (IMO)
STCW	Standards of Training, Certification and Watchkeeping for Seafarers
TNC	Transnational Corporations
TPP	Trans Polar Passage
TSR	Transpolar Sea Route
UDHR	Universal Declaration on Human Rights
UK	United Kingdom
ULCC	Ultra Large Crude Carrier
UN	United Nations
UNCCD	United Nations Convention to Combat Desertification
UNCED	United Nations Conference on Environment and Development
UNCLOS	United Nations Convention on the Law of the Sea
UNCTAD	United Nations Conference on Trade and Development
UNDP	United Nations Development Programme
UNDRIP	United Nations Declaration on the Rights of Indigenous Peoples
UNECE	United Nations European Economic Commission for Europe
UNEP	United Nations Environmental Programme
UNFCCC	United Nations Framework Convention on Climate Change
UNIS	University of Svalbard
USA	United States of America
USGS	United States Geological Survey
USSR	Union of Soviet Socialist Republics
VLCC	Very Large Crude Carrier
WCED	World Commission on Environment and Development
WDGF	Walter and Duncan Gordon Foundation
WMD	Weapons of Mass Destruction
WMO	World Meteorological Organization
WWF	World Wildlife Fund
WWII	World War II

List of Figures

Fig. 1.1	Arctic Council showing 8 member states, 6 working groups, 6 permanent participants (*Source* https://Arctic-council.org/index.php/en/about-us)	12
Fig. 1.2	Offshore extent of maritime zones recognised under international law (*Source* https://thewire.in/diplomacy/maritime-territory-continental-shelf-unclos-india)	28
Fig. 2.1	Arctic share of global petroleum production (*Source* Lindholt. L, Arctic natural resources in a global perspective, The Economy of the North, p. 27, 2006)	42
Fig. 2.2	Arctic share of proven petroleum reserves (*Source* Lindholt. L, Arctic natural resources in a global perspective, The Economy of the North, p. 28, 2006)	43
Fig. 2.3	Undiscovered hydrocarbon reserves among the Arctic coastal states (*Source* Russian strategies in the Arctic: Avoiding a new cold war, Heinenen, Sergunin, Yarovoy, September 2014, Valdai Club)	46
Fig. 2.4	Arctic share of global non-ferrous minerals and precious metals ore extraction (percent) (*Source* Lindholt. L, Arctic natural resources in a global perspective, The Economy of the North, p. 30, 2006)	56
Fig. 2.5	Arctic share of global wood volume of forests (*Source* Lindholt. L, Arctic natural resources in a global perspective, The Economy of the North, p. 35, 2006)	57

Fig. 2.6	Cargo forecast for NSR (*Source* Pham Thi Bich Van, Miltiadis Aravopoulos, Feasibility Study on Commercial Shipping in the Northern Sea Route, p. 15)	68
Fig. 2.7	Northwest passage transits (*Source* Scott Polar Research Institute, SPRI, 2019, https://www.spri.cam.ac.uk/resources/infosheets/northwestpassage.pdf)	70
Fig. 3.1	Indian Arctic programme (*Source* NCPOR Annual Report 2018–2019)	108
Fig. 3.2	Indian Antarctic programme (*Source* NCPOR Annual Report 2018–2019)	109
Fig. 3.3	Resource allotment for polar programme (*Source* Annual Reports NCPOR, compiled by author)	109
Fig. 3.4	Various sensors on IndARC (*Source* ncaor.gov.in/pages/display/398indarc)	111
Fig. 3.5	Global Natural Gas Consumption growth 2017–2023 (*Source* GAS 2018, Analysis and Forecasts to 2023, IEA, pp. 12, www.iea.org)	154
Fig. 3.6	India's Natural Gas Demand 2003–2023 (*Source* GAS 2018, Analysis and Forecasts to 2023, IEA, pp. 23, www.iea.org)	155
Fig. 3.7	Top 10 Sources of Import During April-September 2019 (*Source* Directorate General of Foreign Trade, Ministry of Commerce, 2019, Monthly Bulletin on FTS, DGFT, October 2019, DGCIS, Kolkata, pp. 29 accessed on 01 December 2019 from https://dgft.gov.in/more/data-statistics)	169
Fig. 3.8	Polar expenditure (*Source* NCPOR Annual Report 2018–2019)	173
Fig. 3.9	Country-wise Scholarly Output on the Arctic (*Source* Dag Aksnes, Igor Osipov, Olga Moskaleva, Lars Kullerud, Arctic Research Publication Trends: A Pilot Study)	187
Fig. 3.10	Arctic publications: Indian authors (*Source* Stensdal Iselin, Asian Arctic Research 2005–2012: Harder, Better, Faster, Stronger, Fridtjof Nansen Institute, May 2013)	188
Fig. 4.1	Ice cover in the Arctic on 2 January 2019 (*Source* NOAA)	201
Fig. 4.2	Ice cover in the Arctic on 8 October 2019 (*Source* NOAA)	202
Fig. 4.3	Arctic Sea Ice minimum volumes 1979–2018 (*Source* AMAP, AMAP climate change update 2019, An Update to Key Findings of Snow, Water, Ice and Permafrost in the Arctic [SWIPA] 2017)	203
Fig. 4.4	Summer minimum sea ice extent	206

Fig. 4.5	Feedback loop (*Source* https://climatetippingpoints.info/2016/10/21/Arctic-sea-ice-and-positive-feedback-loops/)	207
Fig. 4.6	Projected ice loss till 2030 and 2080 (*Source* AMAP, AMAP climate change update 2019, An Update to Key Findings of Snow, Water, Ice and Permafrost in the Arctic [SWIPA] 2017)	210
Fig. 4.7	Arctic shipping accidents, 2005 to 2017 (*Source* PAME: Hjalti Hreinsson, Fishing vessels in the Arctic polar code area)	263
Fig. 4.8	Comparison of oceans depths (*Source* AMSA, Arctic Marine Shipping Assessment report 2009)	267
Fig. 4.9	Arctic countries scorecard on environmental conservation (*Source* WWFARCTIC.ORG, 2019, Arctic council scorecard 2019)	273
Fig. 4.10	Global gas prices, 2012 to 2018 (*Source* Annual Report, ONGC, 2018–19, p. 148)	279
Fig. 4.11	Emissions by India, projection up to 2050 (*Source* https://climateactiontracker.org/countries/india/)	293
Fig. 4.12	NCPOR, income, and expenditure account (*Source* NCPOR Annual Report, 2018–2019)	298

List of Maps

Map 1.1	Map showing the Arctic Circle at 66° 34′ North, 10 °C/ 50 °F Isotherm and Arctic boundaries (*Source* National Snow and Ice Data Centre https://nsidc.org/cryosp here/Arctic-meteorology/Arctic.html)	7
Map 1.2	Map showing Arctic by AMAP and AHDR definitions (*Source* UiO, University of Oslo, accessed on 12 October 2019 from https://www.duo.uio.no/bitstream/handle/ 10852/42108/5071.pdf)	8
Map 1.3	Map showing the Arctic by High Arctic, Low Arctic, and sub-Arctic definitions (*Source* Dag Aksnes, Igor Osipov, Olga Moskaleva, Lars Kullerud, Arctic Research Publication Trends: A Pilot Study)	10
Map 1.4	International Maritime Organisation's Arctic Polar Code area (*Source* PAME: Hjalti Hreinsson, Fishing vessels in the Arctic Polar Code area)	30
Map 2.1	Location Map of large mineral and hydrocarbon deposits in the Russian Arctic and sub-Arctic areas (*Source* Russian strategies in the Arctic: Avoiding a new cold war, Heinenen, Sergunin, Yarovoy, September 2014, Valdai Club)	48

Map 2.2	Circum Arctic Resource Appraisal (CARA) provinces abbreviations (*Source* United States Geological Survey, Circum-Arctic Resource Appraisal: Estimates of Undiscovered Oil and Gas North of the Arctic Circle, 2008, accessed on 01 December 2019 from https://pubs.usgs.gov/fs/2008/3049/)	49
Map 2.3	Map showing Central Arctic Ocean (CAO) boundary (*Source* https://www.sciencedirect.com/science/article/pii/S0308597X15002997)	54
Map 2.4	North East Passage and North West Passage shipping routes	60
Map 2.5	Potential Arctic routes (*Source* Emmanuel Guy, Frédéric Lasserre, Commercial shipping in the Arctic: new perspectives, challenges, and regulations, Cambridge University Press, accessed on 01 December 2019 from https://www.cambridge.org/core/journals/polar-record/article/commercial-shipping-in-the-Arctic-new-perspectives-challenges-and-regulations/24D92421C2024E93D8C48EF29FBAFCEA)	61
Map 2.6	Map showing NSR transit points (*Source* Pham Thi Bich Van, Miltiadis Aravopoulos, Feasibility Study on Commercial Shipping in the Northern Sea Route, p. 13)	64
Map 2.7	Key straits in Russian Arctic Seas (*Source* Gao Tianming & Vasilii Erokhin, Arctic yearbook 2019)	65
Map 2.8	NSR shipping traffic: Start of summer navigation/activities in July 2019 (*Source* https://Arctic-lio.com/nsr-shipping-traffic-start-of-summer-navigaton-period-activities-in-july-2019-2/)	66
Map 2.9	Transit voyages on the NSR in 2021 (*Source* Arcticlio.com. Accessed at https://arctic-lio.com/transit-voyages-on-the-nsr-in-2021-the-results-as-of-the-current-date/)	68
Map 2.10	North West Passage with its straits and variations (*Source* Scott Polar Research Institute, SPRI, 2019, https://www.spri.cam.ac.uk/resources/infosheets/northwestpassage.pdf)	70
Map 2.11	Bering Sea and USA-Canada maritime boundary (*Source* https://en.wikipedia.org/wiki/USSR%E2%80%93USA_Maritime_Boundary_Agreement)	74
Map 2.12	Svalbard Islands and adjoining seas (*Source* Arctic office, www.arctic.ac.uk)	79

Map 3.1	Map showing Sakhalin Islands (*Source* https://www.res earchgate.net/figure/Map-of-Sakhalin-Island-showing-offshore-oil-and-gas-blocks-and-study-locations-Okha_f ig1_248393621)	145
Map 3.2	Map showing locations of Taas-Yuryakh and Vankor oilfields (*Source* https://www.telegraphindia.com/bus iness/oil-trio-buy-stake-in-russia/cid/1462355)	146
Map 3.3	Map showing sourcing of hydrocarbons by India (*Source* http://petroleum.nic.in/sites/default/files/internati onal_coopJul2019.pdf)	147
Map 4.1	Map showing Beaufort dispute between USA and Canada (*Source* Dovile Petkunaite, City University of New York)	214
Map 4.2	Map showing the location of Hans Island (*Source* Nikoleta Maria Hornackova, Hans Island Case, A territorial dispute in the Arctic, accessed on 1 October 2019 from https://projekter.aau.dk/projekter/files/281 245824/Master_Thesis_2018_Nikoleta_Maria_Hornack ova.pdf)	215
Map 4.3	Arctic territorial claims (*Source* https://www.researchg ate.net/figure/Lomonosov-Ridge-donut-hole-and-nat ional-exclusive-economic-zones_fig3_259694535)	218
Map 4.4	Map showing Bastion and extended Bastion (Map: Kauko Kyöstiö. *Source* House of Commons Defence Committee 2018)	251
Map 4.5	Map showing the North Pole and Lomonosov Ridge (*Source* Congressional Research Service, Changes in the Arctic: Background and Issues for Congress)	271

List of Tables

Table 1.1	Arctic chairmanship 1996–2023	20
Table 1.2	Memberships and groups' active in the Arctic region (*Source* Arctic Portal, 2019, accessed on 01 July 2019 from https://Arcticportal.org/Arctic-governance/Arctic-cooperation)	21
Table 2.1	Province wise oil and gas reserves in the Arctic Region: Summary of results of the circum-arctic resource appraisal	50
Table 2.2	Marine fisheries in the Arctic (Million Tons)	52
Table 2.3	Estimated Arctic share of global production of some raw materials	55
Table 2.4	Distances between places by various passages	63
Table 2.5	Number of transit voyages on NSR	67
Table 3.1	Supply/demand of petroleum products (in MMT)	147
Table 3.2	Supply/demand natural gas (MMSCMD)	148
Table 3.3	Re-gasification terminals in India (MMTPA)	151
Table 3.4	Top Ten sources in respect of LNG Liquefied Natural Gas	152
Table 3.5	Top ten sources in respect of petroleum and bituminous crude oils	153
Table 3.6	India's exports: export by region x countries	159
Table 3.7	Total trade: top countries (2018–2019)	167
Table 3.8	Import by India (April to September 2019) from Arctic Countries (Rs in crores)	168
Table 3.9	Questions on the Arctic in the Indian Parliament	177
Table 3.10	Discussion on Arctic Issues in Indian Parliament	177

Table 3.11	Engagement of Indian Leaders/Bureaucrats with Arctic countries	179
Table 3.12	Outgoing visits to Arctic countries by Indian leaders	182
Table 3.13	Arctic countries on India's inclusion in UNSC	183
Table 3.14	Incoming visits to India by Heads of Arctic Countries	184
Table 3.15	Population of Overseas Indians (compiled in December 2018)	188
Table 3.16	Observers from Non-member Parties at NAMMCO Council Meetings	193
Table 4.1	Summary of submissions to CLCS	219
Table 4.2	Status of Arctic observers	237
Table 4.3	Inclusion of Arctic observers	239
Table 4.4	Ship casualties in Arctic waters 2005–2014	262

CHAPTER 1

Introduction

The Arctic is a unique region among the Earth's various ecosystems which is composed of glaciers, ice sheets, sea ice, and permafrost making it stand out from other terrestrial forms. The Arctic region, including sub-Arctic, has more than 50% of the world's wetlands, and it is home to more than 21,000 species of wildlife. The landmass, ocean, flora, and fauna in the Arctic are a critical intersection of economic, environmental, political, and security interests of the major global powers of today. This region which has acquired global recognition and limelight in recent times is a place with distinct characteristics. The region with an area of 32 Million Square Kilometres (14.5 million square kilometres within Arctic Circle) is about 6% of the globe's (about 2.8% of territories inside Arctic Circle) surface. The region's strategic importance also lies in the fact that it connects three continents, which are the power centres of the global economy, trade, and military. This region is undergoing unprecedented and hastened, and a rather discursive transformation from being a desolate place to a region, keenly watched by the global power states and non-states actors.

Lately, there are three prominent themes which have emerged threatening to disrupt the current structures in the region namely a resurgent Russia which has perceptibly reignited the post-cold war geopolitics between the West and Russia, increasing focus on climate change amidst growing voices from increasingly militant young activists and general population and emergence of China as a global power with high aspirations. Among these global agendas, climate change has assumed the zenith due to wide and cross-cultural and universal support demanding urgent government action. The impacts of global climate change are being experienced throughout diverse regions from Australia to Haiti, yet the most visible effects are being presented in the Arctic region, with the region showing instantly recognisable signs of an increasingly warming planet. The alarming loss of ice cover, permafrost, and glaciers is pushing the world on an edge, forcing abrupt climate changes, denuding ice levels, inundating coastal areas, changing monsoons, and other sudden calamities leading to immense socio-economic suffering, migration, water stress, food shortages and so on. The year 2007 saw a record low in the extent of summer sea ice and a similar situation was again encountered in 2012 and there are different predictions that the Arctic will be ice-free by 2044 or by 2067 based on various studies. "According to research published in the journal Nature Climate Change, the Arctic could be "functionally ice-free" by September 2044—and no later than 2067—assuming no changes to global carbon emissions."[1]

The Arctic region can also pride itself with no civil unrest, no civil wars, or any violent anti-government movements, and hence the states' sovereign ownership is supreme. The region is also a depository of immense hydrocarbon and mineral resources and there is a scramble between the littoral states to claim territories to commercially exploit these. Some sections of the press and think tanks have likened this to the 'Gold Rush' of the sixteenth century thereby painting an alarming picture. Surprisingly the vocal discussion among players far away from the region has also been a factor leading to some alarm. Though the political voices in the Arctic are dominated by the five coastal Arctic states (Russia, USA, Greenland, Canada, and Norway called the Arctic5) and other three states lying within the Arctic Circle (Sweden, Iceland, and Finland) constituting the eight-member states of the Arctic Council (AC), yet China, EU, India, Spain, Germany, Netherlands have also voiced opinions on a fast-changing Arctic. The thinning of ice is also opening new sea routes, cutting transit distance between Europe and Asia by around 40%. The advent of double-acting tankers and ice breakers is already changing the

---

[1] CBC News, 2019, accessed on 01 December 19 from https://www.cbc.ca/news/canada/north/ice-free-Arctic-this-century-1.5370504.

face of shipping in the Arctic and transit and destination voyages trespassing the Arctic Ocean are already a reality. However is the scramble for the resources the cause for international and regional attention or is there something more than meets the eye here? As per Michael Byers, "We're talking about the centre of a large, inhospitable ocean that is in total darkness for three months each year, thousands of miles from any port. The water in the North Pole is 12,000ft [3,650 meters] deep and will always be covered by sea ice in the winter. It's not a place where anyone is going to be drilling for oil and gas. So it's not about economic stakes, it's about domestic politics."[2]

The powers, even far away from the Arctic, both politically and geographically have been making calls citing their stakes in the Arctic region for reasons of either their self-interests or for expressing concerns over the wider global implications of climate change. The increasingly assertive geo-economic and geostrategic role of China is already raising eyebrows in the USA and other Arctic states and some quarters are even warning of a likelihood of a conflict in the future. Russia has already revived most of its once defunct and dilapidated military assets near the Kola Peninsula and maintains a sizeable submarine force around the Arctic coastline. The threats of the militarisation of the region present a security dimension of unprecedented nature.

Though certain hypotheses have hounded that the rush for resources will push the region to the brink of conflict yet the precedent indicators testify to the mature and peaceful resort among the eight Arctic states (Arctic 8) to resolve differences among them. In any case, given physical difficulties and other reasons, the exploration of Arctic hydrocarbons appears to be a long drawn gradual process. In any case, the businesses flourish under regimes of political stability and the experience with the institution of AC in the last 23 years has shown that established legal procedures will be complied with in earnest. There are several well-defined international law mechanisms like United Nations Convention on the Laws of the Sea (UNCLOS), Commission on the Limits of Continental Shelf (CLCS), International Convention for the Prevention of Pollution from Ships (MARPOL), and so on to define and demarcate limits between the nations, and Arctic countries seem to affirm their collective resolve to peacefully resolve issues.

---

[2] The Guardian.com, accessed on 02 July 2019 from https://www.theguardian.com/world/2013/dec/10/russia-military-Arctic-canada-north-pole.

The Arctic region has been viewed differently by the Realists and the Constructivists and several thoughts are running in between these two opposing themes. The realists include Blunden, Howard, Huebert, and others who view that the region's unravelling economic and strategic potential with the involvement of China and the resurgence of Russia will render the region to great power competition, which it is unequipped to respond to. The constructivists like Young, Koivurova, and others view that there are common interests and organisations which bind the players together in international, regional, inter-regional/bilateral rules, and a functional cooperative framework to address issues. One of the middle ground views is that of the Arctic is an International Society (Exner-Pirot & Murray, 2015) which they say is composed of members united and governed by common norms, rules, and institutions, especially in environment and ocean management.

The indigenous people of the Arctic have a distinct and historical connection of livelihood wherein they have traditionally lived and sustained by ancient and ecologically friendly ways for the economic and social development of their communities in a sustainable manner. Since hunting, fishing, and resource gathering by adopting centuries-old customs is the practice, they also consider maintaining the pristine environment of their natural habitats a part of their way of life. A rewarding and commendable feature of the Arctic governance is the co-opting of these indigenous people in the AC and governance issues. Yet since there are calls for reforming the Arctic governance, the ability of these indigenous communities to influence the future discourse is also worth serious consideration.

India is a consultative member of the Antarctic Treaty and has responsibly associated herself with scientific research activity with established and entrenched credentials. In the Arctic domain, India had signed the Spitsbergen Treaty in 1920, accepting Norwegian sovereignty over Svalbard Islands. There was a belief in some sections of India's academic community that the Spitsbergen Treaty had conferred certain rights on India however they discounted the fact that there are concerns and disputes between the interpretation of the treaty between Norway and certain other Arctic nations including Russia. By the mere signing of this treaty, some Indian scholars feel that India is a full-fledged player in the Arctic,[3] a view which will be clarified in further pages in light of legal provisions and international norms. India had established its research presence in the Arctic since 2007 and established research station Himadri in 2008. India had obtained observer status in the Arctic Council in 2013 along with China and three other Asian countries. India has relied on its Antarctic experience for formulating a vision for the Arctic which perhaps partly justifies the reason for certain lacunae in her position. India enjoys special collaborative and friendly relations with Russia, Norway, and a rapidly growing and mature association with the USA. India also has highly influential Diaspora in Canada and the USA which has been actively pursuing its national interest's agenda. Though India is yet to formally chart out its Arctic Policy Framework for greater and transparent conduct of bilateral and multilateral structures, yet it enjoins goodwill and trust to proactively and constructively chart out its national interest objectives in the region. Select Indian thoughts have called for declaring the Arctic as global commons, a view which has found less traction among the international fora as well as the Arctic states. This reasoning was specifically expressed by the notion of the Arctic as a "common heritage of mankind"—a vision that some Arctic rim states might have found both ill-conceived and misinformed.[4]

India is concerned about the negative impacts of reduction in ice caps in the Arctic which will have a devastating corresponding effect on the Indo-Gangetic plains and disrupt agricultural production and trigger natural calamities and disasters. Concurrently, India is a major energy consumer and is keenly awaiting the development of the potential of Arctic in this direction and opening of new, shorter passages connecting Asia to Europe.

Other than a small village by the name of the Arctic, there is no legal political entity/unit called the Arctic. It is a peripheral region for the littoral states surrounding the Arctic Ocean which comprises the Arctic Region. Geographically speaking, the Arctic Region contains areas North of the Arctic Circle which has territories of 5 Arctic coastal nations (Arctic

---

[3] Sakhuja, V, The Arctic Council: Is There a Case for India? Voice of India, URL: http://www.voiceof.india.com/in-focus/the-Arctic-council-is-there-a-case-for-india/996/2.

[4] Chaturvedi, S, India's Arctic Engagement: Challenges and Opportunities. Asia Policy, Number 18, July 2014, pp. 73–79 (Article) https://doi.org/10.1353/asp.2014.0037.

5) and Iceland, Sweden, and Finland, thus making these 8 nations as stakeholders in the Arctic. These eight nations also make up the member states of the Arctic Council (AC), other than the Permanent Participants and the Working Groups.

Most commonly, scientists define the Arctic as the region above the Arctic Circle, an imaginary line that circles the globe at approximately 66° 34′ N. The Arctic Circle marks the latitude above which the sun does not set on the summer solstice, and does not rise on the winter solstice. The Arctic Circle is an imaginary line that circles the globe at approximately 66° 34′ N like the other imaginary lines of the Equator, Tropic of Capricorn, etc. The region lying to the North of this line is termed as the Arctic. Due to the tilt of the earth and the location of this region at the fringe, there are six months of continuous daylight and six months of the continuous night in this region making it unique from the other parts of the globe. At lower latitudes, but north of the Arctic Circle, the duration of continuous day and night is shorter.[5] (See Map 1.1).

As marked on the Map 1.1, the distinction based on 10 °C (50 °F) July isotherm roughly corresponding to the tree line in most of the Arctic is another definition. However, the Arctic Monitoring and Assessment (AMAP), one of the 6 Working Groups, adopts a differing definition that has portions of North Atlantic Ocean too, which was adopted by it in 1998 with the concurrence of the Arctic states. The other working groups have their definitions, based on their respective areas of work. The Map 1.2 shows the extent of difference in definitions given by Arctic organisations.

Functional definitions spring from the usage of the region rather than specific boundaries. Areas located south of the Arctic Circle but with Arctic-like operating conditions are sometimes included in a functional definition of the region. The United States Geological Survey (USGS) report published in 2000, included the East Siberian Basin in its estimates of Arctic undiscovered oil and gas resources, although the entire province lies south of the Arctic Circle. Because this area is covered by ice

---

[5] National Snow and Ice Data Center, All About Arctic Climatology and Meteorology, 2019, accessed on 29 November 2019 https://nsidc.org/cryosphere/Arctic-meteorology/Arctic.html

1 INTRODUCTION 7

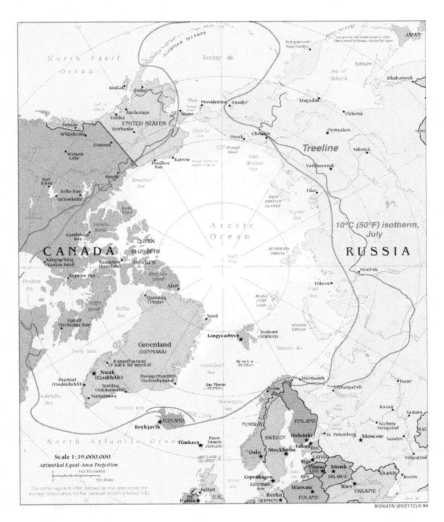

Map 1.1 Map showing the Arctic Circle at 66° 34′ North, 10 °C/50 °F Isotherm and Arctic boundaries (*Source* National Snow and Ice Data Centre https://nsidc.org/cryosphere/Arctic-meteorology/Arctic.html)

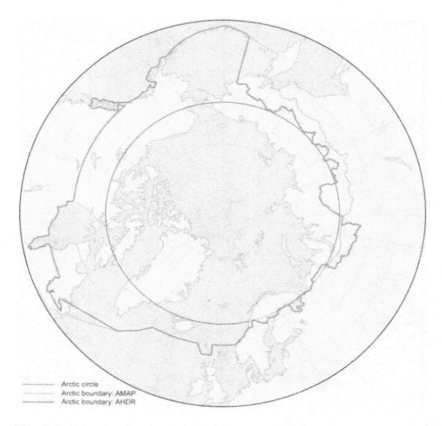

Map 1.2 Map showing Arctic by AMAP and AHDR definitions (*Source* UiO, University of Oslo, accessed on 12 October 2019 from https://www.duo.uio.no/bitstream/handle/10852/42108/5071.pdf)

for large parts of the year, it may make sense to include it in a functional definition of the Arctic.[6]

There are other definitions like the European Arctic (region extending from Greenland to Northwest Russia), the Russian Arctic and American

---

[6] Tamnes Rolf, Offerdal Kristine, Geopolitics and Security in the Arctic, Regional Dynamics in a Global World, 1st Edition, Routledge, London, 11 July 2014 https://doi.org/10.4324/9781315813455.

Arctic, and so on, which are based on the political delineation of national boundaries. Another definition of Arctic can be based on its indigenous communities having a great geographical, ethnic, and cultural divide. All the 6 Permanent Participants are composed of various communities, with differing political-ethno-socio-cultural characteristics with each other belonging to a localized community. However, the AC in its deliberations to the Arctic implies the circumpolar Arctic which is facing the brunt of climate change and worsening environmental conditions. At this point, it is also vital to define sub-Arctic as in many contexts; the sub-Arctic is also included in many references to the Arctic. The sub-Arctic is a region in the Northern Hemisphere immediately south of the true Arctic and covering much of Alaska, Canada, Iceland, the North of Scandinavia, Siberia, the Shetland Islands, and the Cairngorms.

As seen by the Map 1.3, the geographical coverage of sub-Arctic, i.e. areas South of High and Low Arctic, is wider than these two. These definitions are based on Arctic landmass with the variation in climate and vegetation as the dividing parameter. The above mentioned 10 °C isotherm works as the demarcation between sub-Arctic and low Arctic.

It was the eight Arctic states' 1991 adoption of the Arctic Environmental Protection Strategy (AEPS) and the fleshing out of environmental policies for six priority environmental problems confronting the region that initiated the gradual emergence of the Arctic as a distinct place for international policy and law.[7] The cooperative frameworks for participative governance in science and environmental issues were a precursor to the formation of the AC in 1996. The International Arctic Science Committee (IASC) was created in 1990 which was followed by the 1991 Arctic Environmental Protection Strategy (AEPS). The prelude to these measures is the 1987 Murmansk Speech by the USSR statesman, Mikhail Gorbachev calling the Arctic as a 'zone of peace.' This was later followed by the constitution of the Arctic Council at Ottawa Declaration in 1996.[8] It was after that the institutions formed in the last decade of the twentieth century which proved to be sturdy and functional, despite some quarters warning on their longevity that the AC was formed at the

---

[7] Koivurova, Timo, The Arctic Council: A Testing Ground for New International Environmental Governance, Brown Journal of World Affairs, vol. 19, issue 1 (Fall/Winter, 2012), pp. 131–144.

[8] Arctic Council, Declaration on the Establishment of the Arctic Council, accessed on 02 October 2019 from https://oaarchive.Arctic-council.org/handle/11374/85.

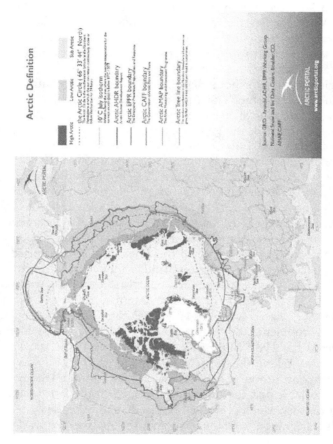

Map 1.3 Map showing the Arctic by High Arctic, Low Arctic, and sub-Arctic definitions (*Source* Dag Aksnes, Igor Osipov, Olga Moskaleva, Lars Kullerud, Arctic Research Publication Trends: A Pilot Study)

Ottawa Declaration in 1996 leading to greater role and participation of the Arctic states as a combined entity to occupy its place in international law. The onset of the cooperative framework was focussed on environmental protection, socio-economic welfare, and several organisations that were established like AEPS, Barents Euro-Arctic Cooperation (BEAC), etc., which later transformed into Arctic Council. The period after the end of the cold war brought in a changed dimension to the Arctic, which witnessed the relaxation of geopolitical tensions. In 1993, the International Conference of Arctic Parliamentarians was held in Iceland which was a regular feature earlier too. The declaration on the establishment of AC was signed on 19 September 1996 at Ottawa, Canada, by the eight Arctic states (Arctic 8). The AC is the leading intergovernmental forum promoting cooperation, coordination, and interaction among the Arctic States, Arctic indigenous communities, and other Arctic inhabitants on common Arctic issues, in particular on issues of sustainable development and environmental protection in the Arctic (Fig. 1.1).[9]

The AC's full membership to the eight nations with territory north of the Arctic Circle (Arctic 8) is—Canada, Russia, Norway, Denmark, the US, Finland, Sweden, and Iceland. There are two more variations with the Arctic Ocean littoral countries termed as Arctic 5. As given out in subsequent paragraphs, though there is presence Permanent Participants, Working Groups, Observers, etc., yet the decision-making authority rests entirely with the Arctic Eight, as they discuss and chart out AC policy and direct the working groups. Each member state is represented by a Senior Arctic Official (SAO), who is usually drawn from that country's foreign ministry. The SAOs meet at least twice per year.[10]

As per the Arctic Council Rules of Procedure, 6 Permanent Participants though are not granted voting privileges but they can participate in all meetings and can offer full consultation. Their names along with the dedicated web sites are as follows:-

(a) Aleut International Association (AIA): The Aleut have been the indigenous communities residing near the Bering Sea for millennia. A key feature of the Aleut people is that they are spread in

---

[9] Arctic Council, Fram Centre, Tromsø, Norway, accessed on 01 December 2019 from https://Arctic-council.org/index.php/en/about-us.

[10] Arctic Council, Frequently Asked Questions, updated 6 June 2018, accessed 30 July 2019, from https://Arcticcouncil.org/index.php/en/about-us/Arctic-council/faq.

Fig. 1.1 Arctic Council showing 8 member states, 6 working groups, 6 permanent participants (*Source* https://Arctic-council.org/index.php/en/about-us)

both the USA and Russia and governed by a Board of Directors comprising of four Alaskan and four Russian Aleut and one President. It was formed to preserve centuries-old cultural, economic, and environmental concerns that are connected to the Bering Sea for sustenance. Before the formation of the AIA, the natives of Alaska were governed by the Alaska Native Settlement Claims Act of 1971, while the Russian Aleut organised under the Association of the Indigenous Peoples of the North of the Aleut District of the Kamchatka Region of the Russian Federation (ANSARKO). AIA was admitted as a PP in the AC in 1998, and the same year the AIA was registered as a not for profit corporation with its Headquarters at Alaska. The AIA offers a remarkable collaborative and cooperative arrangement between the USA and Russia, which were divided over other issues/regions but stood side by side in the AIA. The website of the AIA is https://aleut-international.org/.

(b) Arctic Athabaskan Council (AAC): The AAC is a treaty organisation representing the indigenous peoples of Athabaskan descent spread across America and Canada. It is estimated that these people are spread over Yukon, Alaska, and Northwest Territories. Similar to other indigenous groups in the Arctic region, the Athabaskans are believed to have continuously occupied the regions for over 10,000 years and include three of North America's largest river systems (Mackenzie, Yukon, and Churchill Rivers). Like all indigenous people, they were reliant on fishing and hunting as traditional forms of staple diets with a nomadic lifestyle. The AAC has issued its AAC Arctic Foreign Policy and Arctic Resilience Action Framework. The website of the AAC is https://Arcticathabaskancouncil.com/wp/.

(c) Gwich'in Council International (GCI): The GCI is identical to the AAC as its indigenous population is native to Alaska, Yukon, and Northwest territories. However, the population of GCI is around 10,000, while that of AAC is around 45,000. The GCI Board Directors is composed of two members from the Northwest Territories, two members from the Yukon, and four members from Alaska. GCI is also formed as a, not for profit and non-governmental organisation. There is one village named Arctic Village which is situated 100 miles north of Fort Yukon, and the Neets'aii Gwich'in are the residents thereof. The website of the GCI is at https://gwichincouncil.com/.

(d) Inuit Circumpolar Council (ICC): One of the oldest Inuit bodies in the world, the ICC, was founded in 1977 by the late Eben Hopson of Barrow, Alaska. Today it represents around 180,000 Inuit of Alaska, Canada, Greenland, and Chukotka, Russia. The ICC has been celebrating 07 November (birth date of Eben Hopson) as Inuit Day. Presently ICC is working as 04 chapters of ICC as ICC Greenland, ICC Alaska, ICC Chukotka, and ICC Canada with the central role assigned to ICC chair. The Presidents of the chapters work as Vice-Chairs to the ICC. Inuit consider themselves as one people and have a single homeland, Inuit Nunaat, and do not consider the political boundaries as borders between the Inuits. Like other indigenous organisations, the Inuit live a traditional lifestyle where hunting is a source of food and part of the culture. The permanent participants view their membership in the AC as a forum to air the Inuit voices in the Arctic and globally. The website of the ICC is https://www.inuitcircumpolar.com/.

(e) Russian Association of Indigenous Peoples of the North (RAIPON): The RAIPON was founded on 31 March 1990 and represents 41 indigenous natives of North, Siberia, and the Far East. The association has been striving to protect the rights of indigenous peoples and support the traditional subsistence lifestyles while preserving the environment and protection of the original habitat and traditional image. The website is at http://www.raipon.info/en/.

(f) Saami Council (SC): The Saami Council has a membership of Saami member organisations in Finland, Russia, Norway, and Sweden. The members of the SC are Reindeer Herders Association of Sweden, Kola Saami Association, Saami Association of the Murmansk Region, Reindeer Herders Association of Norway, Saami Association of Norway, National Association Sáme Ätnam of Sweden, Saami Peoples Union of Norway, National Union of the Swedish Saami People, and Central Saami Association of Finland. The website of SC is at http://www.saamicouncil.net/en/.

The unique structure of the AC with the PPs accorded a seat at the high table along with the member states was made possible in the Arctic region, which had a restricted and limited number of states. The restriction on granting full membership and later refined criteria for entry of observers has preserved and enhanced the mechanism of the AC to address the regional issues under its mantle. The AC can be said to be found on liberal internationalist values and is forward-looking in its approach and such a mechanism cannot be replicated elsewhere, making it truly unique. The many observers in the AC have recourse to various multilateral institutions in which they enjoy a full membership to raise and address the issues of Arctic having international repercussions. The present observers of the AC are a mixed lot possessing huge economic, diplomatic, and political clout on the world stage and can adequately address the concerns at suitable international bodies.

Other than the Permanent Participants, there are 6 Working Groups in the Council, which are:-

(a) *Arctic Contaminants Action Program (ACAP)*: The ACAP was formed to prevent, reduce, and eliminate pollutants from the Arctic environment. Initially, it was part of AMAP wherein the AMAP was identifying the pollutants. It became a working group in 2006. It has four ACAP expert groups, namely POPs and Mercury, Hazardous Wastes, Indigenous People Contaminant Action Programme, and Short-lived climate pollutants.
(b) *Arctic Monitoring and Assessment Programme (AMAP)*: AMAP is responsible to measure pollutants in the Arctic and recording the pollution statistics and the impact of the same on Arctic flora and fauna. It also provides scientific advice to support Arctic governments to take preventive actions relating to contaminants. AMAP precedes the AC as it was established in 1991 and later ACAP was carved out of it in 2006.
(c) *Conservation of Arctic Flora and Fauna (CAFF)*: It is the biodiversity working group consisting of national representatives of the Arctic 8 and other stakeholders. It works by sharing information on species and habitat management so that informed decisions are taken. A common and calculated response is drawn by regarding the CAFF inputs for the sustainable preservation of the Arctic ecosystem.
(d) *Emergency Prevention, Preparedness, and Response (EPPR)*: One of the six working groups of the Arctic Council, EPPR, is earmarked to contribute to the prevention, preparedness, and response to environmental and other emergencies, accidents, and Search and Rescue (SAR).
(e) *Protection of the Arctic Marine Environment (PAME)*: There are some overlaps and similarities in the tasks of PAME and ACAP as both deal with threats due to pollution. As the name suggests, PAME is primarily concerned with preserving the Arctic marine environment with the swift changes in economic structures and also due to the effects of climate change.
(f) *Sustainable Development Working Group (SDWG)*: Among the groups, the SDWG addresses the human element in Arctic affairs. This group has a direct bearing and correlation with the work and sustainability of the Arctic indigenous population and communities.

Other than the aforesaid, **38 entities have been granted observer status, wherein there are thirteen** Intergovernmental and Inter-Parliamentary Organisations having an approved observer status, which are as under:-

(a) *International Council for the Exploration of the Sea (ICES)*: ICES is a marine science organisation, promoting the sustainable use of the marine assets, i.e. seas and oceans. It studies and provides inputs on the study of marine ecosystems so that these are managed efficiently.

(b) *International Federation of Red Cross & Red Crescent Societies (IFRC)*: IFRC is a major humanitarian organisation guided by the seven principles of humanity, impartiality, neutrality, independence, voluntary service, universality, and unity. It works through volunteer service and aims to work without any discrimination whatsoever.

(c) *International Maritime Organisation (IMO)*: IMO is a UN specialized agency that has been assigned responsibility for the safety and security of shipping. It is also assigned the role of preventing pollution by ships.

(d) *International Union for the Conservation of Nature (IUCN)*: IUCN is a membership organisation comprising both government and civil society organisations. Its prominence can be gauged that species are generally identified by the IUCN codes allotted, making it an authority of the natural world and the measures needed to safeguard it.

(e) *Nordic Council of Ministers (NCM)*: NCM was founded in 1971 and is the intergovernmental forum for Nordic Cooperation. It has members from Nordic countries as well as from the autonomous areas of the Faroe Islands, Greenland, and the Åland Islands.

(f) *Nordic Environment Finance Corporation (NEFCO)*: Like NCM, NEFCO is also a Nordic forum to finance environmental and climate projects in a cost-efficient way.

(g) *North Atlantic Marine Mammal Commission (NAMMCO)*: NAMMCO accepts that hunting is an essential part of the ecosystem and looks holistically at the marine ecosystem and provides inputs for sustainable methods for resource exploitation.

(h) *OSPAR Commission*: OSPAR is named after two cities of Oslo and Paris at which the agreement was signed by which 15

Governments & the EU cooperate to protect the marine environment of the North-East Atlantic. The principles applicable under the OSPAR commission are—Ecosystem Approach, Precautionary Approach, Polluter Pays principle, and Best Available Techniques and Best Environmental Practices.

(i) *Standing Committee of the Parliamentarians of the Arctic Region (SCPAR)*: SCPAR is a conference for parliamentarians from the Arctic 8 and also the European Parliament. Its first Conference on Arctic cooperation was held in Reykjavik, Iceland in 1993.

(j) *United Nations Development Programme (UNDP)*: Another of the UN bodies, UNDP, has a special focus on developing countries, and it strives to build better lives for the inhabitants.

(k) *United Nations Environment Programme (UNEP)*: UNEP is considered the champion of the global environmental agenda and a watchdog of the global environment.

(l) *World Meteorological Organisation (WMO)*: WMO is a UN body on Earth's atmosphere and its interaction with the land and oceans. There are profound impacts of the weather and climate produced by the interaction between the atmosphere and water bodies which manifests in the distribution of water resources.

(m) *West Nordic Council (WNC)*: A deviation of the Nordic Alliance was formed in 1985 as West Nordic Parliamentarian Council of Cooperation, and its present name was adopted in 1997. It has three members,' i.e. Greenland, Iceland, and the Faroe Islands.

There are Twelve Non-governmental Organisations approved as Observers in the Arctic Council, namely:-

(a) *Advisory Committee on Protection of the Sea (ACOPS)*: ACOPS was established in 1952 by Lord Callaghan as one of the world's first environmental NGOs. It is currently engaged in reducing marine oil pollution and land-based sources of marine pollution, as well as other aspects of degradation of the coastal and marine environment.

(b) *Arctic Institute of North America (AINA)* (Formerly Arctic Cultural Gateway (ACG)): AINA was instituted by a Parliamentary Act of Canada in 1945 as an NGO working as an Arctic research institute. Since 1976, AINA has been a part of the University of Calgary.

(c) *Association of World Reindeer Herders (AWRH)*: AWRH works with the Arctic states in the field of world reindeer husbandry. It has also decided to work with observers like China and the UK as they too have a small number of the reindeer population.

(d) *Circumpolar Conservation Union (CCU)*: CCU is dedicated to preserving the ecological and cultural integrity of the Arctic in the areas of health and medicine, human rights and civil liberties, and environment and sustainability.

(e) *International Arctic Science Committee (IASC)*: IASC was established in 1990 and is an NGO composed of international science groups participating in Arctic science research. India is also a member of IASC.

(f) *International Arctic Social Sciences Association (IASSA)*: IASSA deals with social sciences disciplines like cultural, behavioural, anthropological, psychological, etc., in respect to the Arctic and sub-Arctic populations.

(g) *International Union for Circumpolar Health (IUCH)*: IUCH is an international NGO with membership across the circumpolar regions.

(h) *International Work Group for Indigenous Affairs (IWGIA)*: IWGIA is a global human rights organisation that promotes and advocates the rights of indigenous people.

(i) *Northern Forum (NF)*: The members of NF include the Gangwon Province, Kamchatka Krai, Lapland, Magadan Oblast, Alaska, Primorsky Krai, Nenets Autonomous, Akureyri, Chukotka Oblast, Khanty, and Yamalo Nenets and are assigned the well-being of Northern populations.

(j) *Oceana*: Oceana was established to advocate ocean preservation after learning that funds directed to this field of study were minuscule. It is committed to protecting and restoring the world's oceans.

(k) *University of the Arctic (UArctic)*: UArctic is a knowledge organisation having a network of universities, colleges, research institutes, and other organisations working in the field of education and research in and about the North.

(1) *World Wide Fund for Nature-Global Arctic Programme (WWF)*: The WWF programme, especially for the Arctic, is made to combat threats to the Arctic and to preserve its rich biodiversity sustainably.

International Maritime Organisation (IMO) was added to the list of intergovernmental and inter-parliamentary observer organisations in 2019. AC is different than other international organisations as it was created as an informal cooperative forum, not a binding "intergovernmental organisation." Rather, the Arctic Council is a "soft law" institution—it "creates norms [and] standards of behaviour without creating legally binding obligations on [its] member states."[11]

The AC addresses the contentious issues by constituting Task Forces which operate within the framework of the Arctic Council and submit their report for further action by the AC. On submission of the report, the task forces become operational and inactive. The Task Forces are appointed at the Ministerial meetings to work on specific issues for a limited amount of time. The Task Forces are active until they have produced the desired results, at which point they become inactive.[12] Till December 2019, there were eleven Task Forces who have completed their work and are no longer functional. Other than task forces, there are expert groups that are constituted to study and advise the AC on specific issues.

Though the AC has come to be a phenomenally successful mechanism, for the few years till 2013, it was working without a permanent secretariat. Then, the secretariat functions were managed by the respective chairs, rotated every two years. For around 15 years that is till May 2011, the AC was functioning without a permanent secretariat, and the decision to establish it was taken at the Nuuk Ministerial Meeting in May 2011 and the Secretariat was made operational on 01 June 2013 at Tromso, Norway. The council has a two-year chairmanship that rotates among the eight-member states. The current Chair is Russia which assumed it in 2021.

The Table 1.1 provides the duration of AC Chairmanship held by the Arctic 8, beginning with Canada in 1996 after the Ottawa declaration. As is evident by the table, the first round of chairmanship concluded in 2013

---

[11] Alison Ronson, Political Climate Change: The Evolving Role of the Arctic Council, Northern Rev., 2011, vol. 33, issue 95, p. 100.

[12] Arctic Council, Task Forces, accessed on 27 July 2019 from https://Arctic-council.org/index.php/en/about-us/subsidiary-bodies/task-forces.

Table 1.1 Arctic chairmanship 1996–2023

S.No	Nation	Period
1	Canada	1996–1998
2	United States	1998–2000
3	Finland	2000–2002
4	Iceland	2002–2004
5	Russia	2004–2006
6	Norway	2006–2009
7	Denmark	2009–2011
8	Sweden	2011–2013
9	Canada	2013–2015
10	United States	2015–2017
11	Finland	2017–2019
12	Iceland	2019–2021
13	Russian Federation	2021–2023

with Sweden at the helm and it is during this chairmanship that observer status was granted to India and five other non-Arctic states at Kiruna Ministerial Meeting. The changes in the nature of deliberations, content, and modus-operandi during the second and more mature second round of chairmanship has been covered in 'Role of Arctic Council Chairmanship' by P Kankaanpaa and M Smieszek in Arctic Year Book 2015. The details of chairmanship held in the past are as under:-

Since AC works on the principle of cooperative arrangements, its decisions are taken by consensus of the eight Arctic Member States. Though the PPs are involved in the decision-making process, the rights and responsibilities for the decisions rest with the member states alone in the AC governance scheme. More specifically, the council states that "Decisions at all levels in the Arctic Council are the exclusive right and responsibility of the eight Arctic States with the involvement of the Permanent Participants."[13] The Arctic Council works on multilateralism and all its decisions are made by consensus among the members.

The AC in its Rules of Procedure had kept observer status in the AC open to non-Arctic States: global and regional intergovernmental and inter-parliamentary organisations and non-governmental organisations. As set out in the Declaration on the Establishment of the AC and governed

---

[13] Arctic Council, Observers, updated 23 May 2019, accessed on 30 July 2019 from https://Arctic-council.org/index.php/en/about-us/Arctic-council/observers.

Table 1.2 Memberships and groups' active in the Arctic region (*Source* Arctic Portal, 2019, accessed on 01 July 2019 from https://Arcticportal.org/Arctic-governance/Arctic-cooperation)

by the AC Rules of Procedure, observer status in the AC is open to non-Arctic States; intergovernmental and inter-parliamentary organisations, global and regional; and non-governmental organisations that the Council determines can contribute to its work.[14]

Originally, non-Arctic states were given observer status: Germany, the Netherlands, Poland, and the United Kingdom in 1998, and later, these were joined by France in 2000 and Spain in 2006. China applied for permanent observer status in 2007 and by 2009, Italy, South Korea, and the European Union (EU) had submitted applications, followed shortly thereafter by India, Japan, and Singapore. In 2007, the one-time observer status was given to China, Korea, the European Commission, and Italy. A remarkable feature of the status of observers is that all five permanent members of the United Nations Security Council (UNSC) are now either the members or observers in AC. India was accorded observer status at Kiruna Ministerial Meeting in May 2013 along with Japan, Singapore, China, ROK, and Italy. Many Indian experts called this foreign policy step an "Arctic victory" and a "major diplomatic achievement" for the Ministry of External Affairs of India.[15]

The AC mentioned in its rules of procedure that enunciated that anybody or nation desirous of obtaining observer status in the Council will accede to certain conditions and fulfilling some criteria. These rules have the effect of asserting the Arctic States' sovereignty, sovereign rights, and jurisdiction in the Arctic as also compliance with the Law of the Sea in the Arctic Ocean. Further, the law of the sea principles was to provide for a solid foundation for responsible management of the Arctic Ocean. Broadly the criterion for admitting observers was a re-assertion of the principles of the formation of the AC and commitment by the signatory to adhere to these objectives. In the determination by the Council of the general suitability of an applicant for observer status, the Council will, inter alia, take into account the extent to which observers:

- Accept and support the objectives of the Arctic Council defined in the Ottawa declaration.

---

[14] Ibid.

[15] India's Arctic Victory: A Major Diplomatic Achievement, DNA, 21 May 2013. URL: http://www.dnaindia.com/analysis/column-india-s-Arctic-victory-a-major-diplomatic-achievement-1837429.

- Recognise Arctic States' sovereignty, sovereign rights, and jurisdiction in the Arctic.
- Recognise that an extensive legal framework applies to the Arctic Ocean including, notably, the Law of the Sea, and that this framework provides a solid foundation for responsible management of this ocean.
- Respect the values, interests, culture, and traditions of Arctic indigenous peoples and other Arctic inhabitants.
- Have demonstrated a political willingness as well as financial ability to contribute to the work of the Permanent Participants and other Arctic indigenous peoples.
- Have demonstrated their Arctic interests and expertise relevant to the work of the Arctic Council.
- Have demonstrated a concrete interest and ability to support the work of the Arctic Council, including through partnerships with member states and Permanent Participants bringing Arctic concerns to global decision-making bodies.[16]

Practically, the role of observers is quite limited as they don't enjoy any voting rights or the authority to make any decisions. The former rights remain with the eight Arctic States with the involvement of the Permanent Participants. The observers can observe the working of the Council and can make relevant contributions at the level of Working Groups. There are limitations also laid down on observers' funding to various projects as the funding cannot exceed that of a member state. The observers can offer projects through the member states or a PP. The observers can though make written submissions at Ministerial meetings and also in meetings of subsidiary bodies with the permission of the Chair. Decisions at all levels in the Arctic Council are the exclusive right and responsibility of the eight Arctic States with the involvement of the Permanent Participants.

- Observers shall be invited to the meetings of the Arctic Council once observer status has been granted.

---

[16] Arctic Council, Supra Note 9.

- While the primary role of observers is to observe the work of the Arctic Council, observers should continue to make relevant contributions through their engagement in the Arctic Council primarily at the level of Working Groups.
- Observers may propose projects through an Arctic State or a Permanent Participant but financial contributions from observers to any given project may not exceed the financing from the Arctic States unless otherwise decided by the SAOs.
- In meetings of the Council's subsidiary bodies to which observers have been invited to participate, observers may, at the discretion of the Chair, make statements after Arctic states and Permanent Participants, present written statements, submit relevant documents, and provide views on the issues under discussion. Observers may also submit written statements at Ministerial meetings.[17]

The Observers are denied voting rights and there is a curb on their financing too, wherein their financial contributions are prohibited from exceeding those of the Arctic Eight. This means that the presence of observers in AC is symbolic of the AC efforts to make the body inclusive, though the privileges and rights extended to them are curbed. The entry of observers, though with restricted powers to modulate the discussion or alter the course, still can't affect decisions to incorporate their perspectives in the AC.

The issue of governance among a disparate set of political entities with each one having a different policy, vision, and strategy and compounded by the presence of diverse indigenous people having diverse economic, social, and cultural parameters is in itself is a mammoth task. The AC is hailed as a uniquely successful body, depicting a model of regional cooperation in the Arctic Region. The AC lacks any formal authority to ensure adherence to regulatory regimes in the region, yet is highly effective despite its weak and informal arrangement. The AC also lacks the authority to make formal decisions and to implement/enforce decisions. The Arctic region is bereft of many international institutions/organisations excluding the observer nations/organisations and the scope of further adding observers later remains open. It is unclear whether

---

[17] Ibid.

the expansion of the roster of Council observers will affect the decision-making capabilities of the Council, given that only the initial eight Arctic states retain voting rights, and decisions within the body continue to be made by consensus.[18]

Though there were some apprehensions raised on the issue of expansion of the AC by inducting observers however since the voting rights have not been extended to the observers, their capacity to mould the discussion or issues remains restricted. Also, the procedure requiring the acceptance of certain conditions before granting entry and periodic review of observer status by the AC ensures that AC maintains the direction and moderates the proceedings in the Arctic.

The soft law regime and the multilateral governance arrangements with an overlap of political, institutional, and legal mechanisms provide sound support and backing to the AC. The adherence to the international law in marine affairs by laws like UNCLOS, CLCS and others like MARPOL and IMO's Polar Code ensures that the operations are governed by prevalent statutory and legally binding laws and the absence of any formal treaty is thus not felt and no hindrance is encountered in governance. Several other conventions and agreements regulate specific aspects of Arctic problems, such as fisheries, land and marine mammals, energy resources, and pollution.[19] Since all the Arctic member states, as well as admitted observer states, have already affirmed that they accept and abide by the international legal structures, there is an explicit undertaking in complying with the provisions. The applicable laws and provisions are covered in subsequent paragraphs.

Arctic governance invariably draws parallels with the Antarctic which possesses a developed legal regime. However, a key difference is that with the 1959 Antarctic Treaty, there are no sovereigns in the Antarctic, while there are claims and counterclaims based on international law in the Arctic. The Antarctic Treaty also opens the membership to any countries which are members of the UN, while the AC consists of only Arctic states

---

[18] Lanteigne Marc, The Role of China in Emerging Arctic Security Discourses, Sicherheit und Frieden (S+F)/Security and Peace, vol. 33, issue 3, Themenschwerpunkt: Die Arktis: Regionale Kooperation oder Konflikt? / The Arctic: Regional Cooperation or Conflict? 2015, pp. 150–155.

[19] Helga Haftendorn, The Case for Arctic Governance: The Arctic Puzzle, Institute of International Affairs, University of Iceland, 2019, accessed on 22 October 2019 from http://ams.hi.is/wp-content/uploads/2014/04/thecaseforArcticgovernance.pdf.

as its members. Even for the grant of status of observer, the decision is taken based on acceptance of certain criteria by the AC and is subject to periodic review. Also, there is no treaty binding the Arctic members unlike the Antarctic Treaty, which entails the fulfilment of treaty obligations. The Arctic Council is not based on an international treaty with the statute of international law like is the case with the Antarctic Treaty.[20]

The member states in the AC are represented by the Senior Arctic Officials, SAO, which was previously termed Senior Arctic Affairs Officials, (SAAO), as they represent their governments and attend the Ministerial meetings and also follow up the progress. They also discuss ongoing actions and approve or comment on future projects and thus stake out a role as dynamic movers in Arctic affairs.[21] They chart out the goals for future projects and discuss and strategize the ongoing projects.

The Arctic Council is a forum; it has no programming budget. All projects or initiatives are sponsored by one or more Arctic States. Some projects also receive support from other entities. The Arctic Council does not and cannot implement or enforce its guidelines, assessments, or recommendations. That responsibility belongs to each individual Arctic State. The Arctic Council's mandate, as articulated in the Ottawa Declaration, explicitly excludes military security.[22]

There have been discussions on having an Arctic Treaty and the role and responsibility of the international response to enforce a developed legal apparatus. However to prevent any outside interference in Arctic affairs, the Arctic 8 had unequivocally rejected the idea of an Arctic treaty. "as an example, outside voices often advocated a comprehensive Arctic Treaty, which all eight AC members had rejected".[23] The European Parliament in 2008 had made a controversial statement, calling for an international environmental treaty to be made applicable to the Arctic. This was the time that few scholars, NGOs, and environmental groups

---

[20] Ibsen Thorir, The Arctic Cooperation, a Model for the Himalayas—Third Pole? Science and Geopolitics of the white world, Springer International Publishing AG 2018, https://doi.org/10.1007/978-3-319-57765-4.

[21] Ibid.

[22] Arctic Council, The Arctic Council: A Backgrounder, updated 13 September 2018, accessed on 30 July 2019, from https://Arctic-council.org/index.php/en/about-us.

[23] Piotr Graczyk and Timo Koivurova, A New Era in the Arctic Council's External Relations? Broader Consequences of the Nuuk Observer rules for Arctic Governance. Polar Record, 2013, pp. 1–12, Cambridge University Press.

supported the same and made a voice for a firm legal framework. This call angered the Arctic 5, who out rightly denied the same by making the 2008 Ilulissat Declaration by citing sovereign rights, sovereignty, and UNCLOS provisions empowering them as stakeholders to guard the Arctic ecosystems. Thus, a curtain was drawn on efforts of non-Arctic on governance in the Arctic by the 2008 Ilulissat Declaration by the Arctic 5, wherein adherence to rules of the law of the sea was quoted as sufficient for the resolution of Arctic international legal issues. The preamble to this declaration states that by their sovereignty, sovereign rights, and jurisdiction in large areas of the Arctic Ocean, the Arctic states are "in a unique position to address these possibilities and challenges." The declaration cited that the law of the sea provides for important rights and obligations concerning the delineation of the outer limits of the continental shelf, the protection of the marine environment, including ice-covered areas, freedom of navigation, marine scientific research, and other uses of the sea. We remain committed to this legal framework and the orderly settlement of any possible overlapping claims.[24] Similar views were also aired in the 2010 Chelsea Ministerial Meeting wherein the Arctic 5 reconfirmed the adequacy of the UNCLOS and no requirement of any new international legal regime to settle any disputes between the littoral states.

As per the declaration, the faith in the existing mechanism of AC is reaffirmed as adequate to address all issues of governance. However, a direct reference to the 1982 UN Convention on the Laws of the Seas (UNCLOS) was not made to, presumably to accommodate the USA, which is NOT a signatory thereof. This declaration also debunked the myth of Arctic being a terra nullius and also the Arctic Ocean with its coastal countries forming the core of the Arctic. The exclusion of Iceland, Finland, and Sweden from the treaty also unequivocally showed that the sovereign rights of the littorals will form the basis to resources. The action obviously had the impetus to re-territorise the region. The concept of the freedom of the sea was initiated in Holland in the seventeenth century and was termed as *mare liberum*. Till the period up to World War II, there was no clarification and definition of the concept and even the League of Nations had failed to reach any consensus solution. With 320 Articles

---

[24] Rothwell Donald R, The Law of the Sea and Arctic Governance, Proceedings of the Annual Meeting, International Law in a Multipolar World, 2013, vol. 107, pp. 272–275.

and nine annexes, UNCLOS has a very wide scope. In 1945, US President Truman had unilaterally declared US control over all resources on its continental shelf and it was in 1956 that the first convention for codifying laws of the seas was convened by the United Nations. The UNCLOS III was convened in 1982 and came into force in 1994. The UNCLOS has a very wide scope and contains 320 Articles, and as on 08 April 2019 there were 168 nations as a party to the convention. However, the terrestrial claims are not covered by UNCLOS and also it does not apply to waterways, not part of the Arctic Ocean. The governance of these may still demand more clarity from the AC. The authorized and legal position on the resources as defined and approved in the UNCLOS is as under (Fig. 1.2).

As depicted in the figure above and convened under UNCLOS, the territorial seas of nations extend 12 nautical miles (NM) from the shoreline. These form the part of the sovereign territory of the controlling

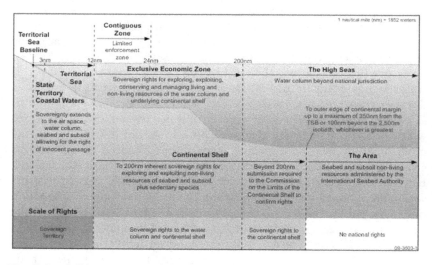

Fig. 1.2 Offshore extent of maritime zones recognised under international law[25] (*Source* https://thewire.in/diplomacy/maritime-territory-continental-shelf-unclos-india)

[25] Wire. In, accessed on 22 December 19 from https://thewire.in/diplomacy/maritime-territory-continental-shelf-unclos-india.

nation. The Contiguous Zone which extends from the limits of territorial seas (12 NM) to another 12 NM and offers limited enforcement zone. The exclusive economic zone (EEZ) extends from the country's shore up to 200 NM. The EEZ provide the nation's access to natural resources, primarily fisheries and seabed resources, such as oil and gas. Since the EEZ provide a vast area to a sovereign nation for resource exploitation, the same is being actively pursued to increase the area under the same. India by having a large coastline is in a geographic advantage as the sea bed resources can be legally extracted.

UNCLOS was adopted in 1982 as the "culmination of more than 14 years of work involving participation by more than 150 countries representing all regions of the world, all legal and political systems and the spectrum of socio/economic development.[26] As of April 8, 2019, 168 nations were party to the treaty."[27] The Continental Shelf is the submerged prolongation of land territory beyond its territorial waters to the outer edge of the continental margin, or 200 NM, whichever is greater. Certain conditions have been specified when a state's continental shelf may exceed 200 NM up to 350 NM. The States have the right to harvest mineral and non-living material in the subsoil of their continental shelf to the exclusion of other states.

Under Article 76 of UNCLOS, the nations can extend their Continental Shelf beyond the 200NM limit provided certain laid down conditions are met. A specific body, CLCS—Commission on the Limits of the Continental Shelf, has been set up to receive and analyse the claims by nations for extension of their continental Shelf which has to be supported by marine geoscientific data. However, even the CLCS ruling is not binding and definite as states may choose to accept it or dispute it. CLCS can offer advice and recommendations only. It does not make legal rulings, nor does it have the mandate to settle disputes.[28] The states are free to make new or revised submissions. Also, the opaqueness of the CLCS process, wherein the CLCS does not publicly explain

---

[26] United Nations, United Nations Convention on the Law of the Sea of 10 December 1982, Overview and full text, updated 28 June 2019, accessed 2 August 2019, from https://www.un.org/depts/los/convention_agreements/convention_overview_convention.htm.

[27] Chronological lists of ratifications of, accessions and successions to the Convention and the related Agreements as of 3 February 2017, accessed on 13 December 2018, from http://www.un.org/Depts/los/reference_files/chronological_lists_of_ratifications.htm#.

[28] Michael Sheng-ti Gau, The Commission on the Limits of the Continental Shelf as a Mechanism to Prevent Encroachment upon the Area, Chinese Journal of International Law, 2011, vol. 10, pp. 3–33.

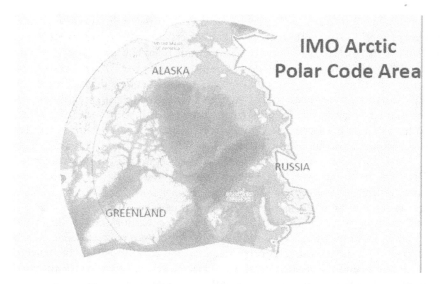

Map 1.4 International Maritime Organisation's Arctic Polar Code area (*Source* PAME: Hjalti Hreinsson, Fishing vessels in the Arctic Polar Code area)

its reasoning in accepting or rejecting a claim, also leads to more claims and counterclaims.

The claims under Article 76 have significant economic and political potential as the states obtain legal rights of exploiting resources of the seabed and subsoil. Though the fishing rights remain confined to the EEZ, the nations can conduct research activities and also impose environmental restraints. Institutions formed under UNCLOS for global ocean governance and dispute resolution include the International Tribunal for the Law of the Sea (ITLOS) which is headquartered at Hamburg, International Seabed Authority (ISA) with its Headquarters at Kingston and the CLCS. The ISA organises and controls all mineral-related activities in the international seabed area falling outside national jurisdictions. The ITLOS is formed to adjudicate disputes arising out of the interpretation and application of the UNCLOS.

Several legal instruments have been signed by the members of the AC and are brought out in the following paragraphs Map 1.4:

(a) Agreement on Cooperation on Aeronautical and Maritime Search and Rescue (SAR) in the Arctic: Though the legal framework in governing the work of Arctic states was not available as AC was constituted without any treaty framework, yet after the 2008 Ilulissat declaration, a gradual process was started to formulate agreements with particular reference to the marine exploration and connected issues. The agreement on maritime SAR became the first legally binding instrument negotiated and adopted under the auspices of the Arctic Council. This agreement was adopted in 2011 and came in force in 2013.
(b) Polar Code: IMO's International Code for Ships Operating in Polar Waters was charted for special conditions prevailing in the Arctic. Thus specific parameters were charted like, only polar-class ships may operate in ice-covered waters with more than 10% ice, and ships will need to take ice- strengthening measures if operating in waters with less than 10 percent ice cover that is considered to pose a structural risk.[29] After it's coming into effect, the operation of the International Convention for the Safety of Life at Sea (SOLAS) and the International Convention for the Prevention of Pollution from Ships (MARPOL) are mandatory. The Polar Code covers the full range of design, construction, equipment, operational, training, search and rescue, and environmental protection matters relevant to ships operating in the inhospitable waters surrounding the two poles. The Polar Code entered into force on 1 January 2017.[30] There are several threats that ships operating in the Arctic have to face to include inclement weather, ice floes, narrow straits, and shallow waters, and so on. Since the prevailing conditions in Poles had peculiar geophysical characteristics, there were special parameters that were charted out to equip the ships travelling in these conditions to reduce the risk of any accidents, spills, and loss of life and property. Though there are calls to add a few issues which were left to be adequately addressed in the Code

---

[29] Turid Stemre, Background and status of the IMO Initiative to Develop a Mandatory Polar Code, presentation at IMO Workshop, Cambridge, 27–30 September 2011 https://www.kamikposten.dk/lokal/last/container/da/hvadermeningen/pdf/det_norske_sjoefartsdirektorat.pdf.

[30] International Maritime Organisation, IMO, 2019, accessed on 01 December 2019 from http://www.imo.org/en/MediaCentre/HotTopics/polar/Pages/default.aspx.

like the envisioned ban on the use of HFO (Heavy Fuel Oil), the extension of the code to fishing vessels, and so on. The Polar code geographical coverage on a map is shown as under.

(c) MAROL: The International Convention for the Prevention of Pollution from Ships (MARPOL) is the chief convention to address the issue of pollution by ships both through operational or accidental reasons. The International Convention for the Prevention of Pollution from Ships (MARPOL) is the main international convention covering prevention of pollution of the marine environment by ships from operational or accidental causes.[31] Since it encompasses both the clauses of pollution from accidental reasons or operational ones, it forms the base for the response, management, prevention of these accidents. The Convention currently comprises six technical annexes.

(d) Kirkenes Declaration/BEAC: In 1993, Denmark, Finland, Iceland, Norway, Sweden, Russia, and the European Commission signed the "Kirkenes Declaration" establishing the Barents Euro-Arctic Council. The Barents cooperation has fostered a new sense of unity and closer contact among the people of the region which is an excellent basis for further progress.[32] The BEAC comprises of the Nordic countries and Russia and EU and provides another forum with participation of Russia to diffuse any tensions between these nations. However, the Chair transition event from Sweden to Norway held in October 2019 was not attended by Russia and Finland.

(e) Northern Dimension: In 1999 the EU took the initiative to set up the Northern Dimension platform together with Russia, Norway, and Iceland, as a policy framework to promote dialogue on several issues, none of which touch on security or geopolitics.[33] The joint declaration of the Northern Dimension Parliamentary

---

[31] International Maritime Organisation, IMO, 2019, accessed on 01 December 2019 from http://www.imo.org/en/About/Conventions/ListOfConventions/Pages/International-Convention-for-the-Prevention-of-Pollution-from-Ships-(MARPOL).aspx.

[32] Barents Euro-Arctic Cooperation accessed on 12 December 2019 from https://www.barentscooperation.org/en/About.

[33] Dams Ties, Dr. Schaik Louise Van, Clingendael the Netherlands Institute of International Relations accessed on 01 December 2019 from https://www.clingendael.org/sites/default/files/2019-11/Poliy_Brief_The_Arctic_Elephant_November_2019.pdf.

Forum was concluded in November 2019 celebrating 20 years of partnership.[34]

(f) Agreement on Cooperation on Marine Oil Pollution Preparedness and Response in the Arctic: The AC had negotiated this agreement and was signed by all Arctic Council members in May 2013. There is no central authority, and disputes are to be settled directly between the parties.

(g) Agreement on Enhancing International Arctic Scientific Cooperation: The need to have an agreement among the Arctic states for greater scientific research cooperation was progressed between 2013 and concluded in 2017. The agreement in this regard was effective from 23 May 2018.

(h) 1990 International Convention on Oil Pollution Preparedness, Response and Cooperation (OPRC): All the Arctic 8 are party to this convention but it applies only to commercial shipping thereby excluding warships or any non-commercial ships. The framework is also very loose and does not have any dispute resolution procedure. There is no centralized enforcement authority and leaves assessment to the parties in the event of an accident.

(i) AC Arctic Offshore Oil and Gas Guidelines: These were taken out by PAME in 1997 and have been revised from time to time.

(j) There is Convention for the Protection of the Marine Environment of the North-East Atlantic (OSPAR) but it does not apply to the entire Arctic region and only 5 of the Arctic 8 have signed it. Another agreement between Denmark, Finland, Iceland, Norway, and Sweden Concerning Cooperation in Measures to Deal with Pollution of the Sea by Oil or Other Harmful Substances but like OSPAR this also does not apply to the entire Arctic region.

Other than the official and intergovernmental body of AC, few other informal groups/associations are functioning on the Arctic issues. Important among them include the Arctic Frontiers, Arctic Circle, etc. Since there is a large overlap between the Arctic nations with the NATO,

---

[34] Stortinget.no, accessed on 20 December 2019 from https://www.stortinget.no/contentassets/54e5750d20674a978dd60789eef15633/conference-statement-sixth-northern-dimension-parliamentary-forum.pdf.

EU and other European groups, there are a multitude of groups operational with varying memberships, some of these are depicted as under (Table 1.2).

The Arctic Frontiers is a group to link the government policy, business interests, and scientific pursuits by collaboration for growth and sustainable development of the Arctic region. The Arctic Frontiers partnership network consists of some of the world's leading actors in the Arctic. The competence and interdisciplinarity of the partner network are unique in both national and international contexts.[35] The clubbing of academicians with business leaders and government officials provides a broad framework for partnership and outreach activities which has both national and international ramifications.

The Arctic Frontiers conference is run every January, in Tromsø, Norway. The conference generally has a participation base of around 2000 participants, wherein the Non-Arctic States are out there to showcase themselves as Arctic actors and the Arctic states are promoting their trade and economic interests.

Another non-profit organisation having huge participation of diverse players like government, leaders, bureaucrats, organisations, corporations, etc., is the Arctic Circle. It is an open democratic platform with participation from governments, organisations, corporations, universities, think tanks, environmental associations, indigenous communities, concerned citizens, and others interested in the development of the Arctic and its consequences for the future of the globe. It is a non-profit and nonpartisan organisation.[36] The Arctic Circle Assembly meeting takes place in Reykjavik, Iceland, every October. Though there are political undercurrents in the meetings, economic agenda, climate change, sustainable development, etc., are more hyped. Rather the nature of these conferences of Arctic Circle as well as Arctic Frontiers is becoming hybridized, covering a plethora of subjects. Dr. Ólafur Ragnar Grímsson, former President of Iceland, is the founder of the Arctic Circle, which brings together different stakeholders for deliberation and discussion. Arctic Circle also organises smaller forums on specific issues, like the 2015 forum in Alaska and Singapore and the 2016 forum in Québec and Greenland.

---

[35] Arctic Frontiers, 2019, accessed on 01 December 2019 from https://www.Arcticfrontiers.com/about-the-conference/.

[36] Arctic Circle, 2019, accessed on 01 December 2019 from http://www.Arcticcircle.org/about/about/.

The 2019 assembly of the Arctic Circle saw speeches by John Kerry, Princess Victoria of Sweden, PM of Finland, Minister of Foreign Affairs of Iceland, Janet Mills, Henry Tillman, Japan's Ambassador in charge of Arctic affairs, Ambassadors of Singapore and Korea, China's Special Representative as well as researcher Yao Tandong and many other influential persons across the spectrum of politics-business-environmentalist-scientists, yet there was **no representation from India**.

The growing clout of Arctic Circle can be gauged by the fact and its partnership across the world as it will organise the Arctic Circle Japan Forum on 21–23 November 2020 at Tokyo in coordination with the Third Arctic Science Ministerial Meeting, which is co-hosted by the Icelandic Ministry of Education, Science and Culture, and the Japanese Ministry of Education, Culture, Sports, Science and Technology (MEXT). This will be followed by an Arctic Circle Forum in Abu Dhabi, which will be co-organised by the Ministry of Climate Change and Environment of the United Arab Emirates and Arctic Circle. The Forum will be devoted to the Third Pole—Himalaya and how lessons from the Arctic can inspire cooperation around the future of the Third Pole—Himalayan glaciers.

Sweden had hosted the first EU Arctic Forum in October 2019 towards greater synergy and cooperation between the two. The usage of the term Climate crisis during the forum highlighted the immense emphasis that's being laid on this menace.

As the name suggests, the Arctic Economic Council is primarily involved in economic and business-related progress and development by promoting partnerships and responsible business development. (We) work to facilitate responsible business and economic development of the Arctic and its communities. (Our) goal is to share and advocate for best practices, technological solutions, and standards. (We) support market accessibility and provide advice and a business perspective to the work of the Arctic Council. (Our) members represent a wide range of businesses operating in the Arctic—from mining and shipping companies to reindeer herding and indigenous economic development corporations.[37]

The membership types in the AEC are of following types:-

---

[37] Arctic Economic Council, 2019, accessed on 01 October 2019 from https://Arcticeconomiccouncil.com/about-us/.

(i) Legacy: AC member states and PPs.
(ii) Legacy (non-voting): Corporations, businesses, partnerships, and indigenous groups coming from both the Arctic and from the sub-Arctic region.
(iii) Permafrost: Small firms having their headquarters in any of the Arctic nations.

AEC came into existence in September 2014. A new development in 2019 was that the first joint meeting between the AC and AEC was held in Reykjavik, Iceland, on 09 October 19. The meeting brought together government officials of the eight Arctic States, business representatives, as well as PPs representatives, and also the WG representatives. A Memorandum of Understanding (MoU) was also signed between the AC and the AEC by which these have agreed to cooperate on many diverse areas like economic development, maritime safety, blue economy, education, and capacity building, and so on. A Memorandum of Understanding (MoU) was signed between the AC and the AEC in 2019[38] as per which these two bodies have agreed to cooperate on:-

- sustainable economic development;
- blue economy and maritime safety;
- improving telecommunications connectivity;
- education and capacity building;
- utilisation of best available information, including scientific research, best practices and, where relevant, traditional knowledge and local knowledge; and
- such other areas of cooperation as may be mutually acceptable.

The Arctic Coast Guard Forum (ACGF) is a forum between the coast guards to foster safe, secure, and environmentally responsible maritime activity in the Arctic. The members of the ACGF are the Arctic 8 countries. The strategic goals of the forum include strengthening of multilateral cooperation and coordination, seeking common solutions to maritime issues, sharing of information with the AC for sustainable development, having a transparent maritime environment, having sound

---

[38] Arctic Council, SAO Report to Ministers 2019, accessed on 22 November 2019 from https://oaarchive.Arctic-council.org/handle/11374/2354.

protocols for emergency response, preserve and protect the lives and culture of Arctic communities, having scientific research in support of its operations and incorporating best practices and technological solutions to address threats.

ACGF was officially launched in November 2015. The current chair of the AC also heads the ACGF and in 2019 before handing over the chair to Iceland, an Arctic super week, the Arctic Coast Guard Week, was held in April 2019. One Live Exercise Polaris 2019, a combined search and Rescue and Mass Rescue Operation Exercise, was conducted on 2 April 2019 in the Bay of Bothnia, in the sea area outside Uusikaupunki, Finland. The strategic goals of the forum are:-

- Strengthen multilateral cooperation and coordination within the Arctic maritime domain, and existing and future multilateral agreements,
- Seek common solutions to maritime issues related to the agencies fulfilling the functions of coast guards within the region,
- Collaborate with the Arctic Council through the sharing of information, Facilitate safe and secure maritime activity in the Arctic region, with sustainable development to be promoted as appropriate,
- Contribute to a stable, predictable, and transparent maritime environment,
- Build a common operational picture to ensure proper protocols for emergency response coordination, and safe navigation,
- Work collaboratively to advance the protection of the marine environment, Maximize the potential for Arctic maritime activities to positively impact the communities, lives, and culture of Arctic communities including indigenous peoples,
- Integrate scientific research in support of Coast Guard operations as appropriate,
- Support high standards of operations and sustainable activities in the Arctic through the sharing of information, including best practices and technological solutions to address threats and risks.[39]

---

[39] ACGF Arctic Coast Guard Forum, 2019, accessed on 11 November 2019 from https://www.Arcticcoastguardforum.com/about-acgf.

The founding document of the Arctic Council explicitly excludes military security matters from the Council's mandate and, to date; there are no other Arctic forums that deal explicitly with military security.[40] From the outset, security is one element that has been kept out of the purview of deliberations at the AC level. However, the Arctic Security Forces Roundtable is a semi-annual gathering usually attended by twelve nations focussed on improving communications and maritime domain awareness in the Arctic Circle. The twelve nations in the ASFR include Germany, France, Canada, Denmark, Finland, Iceland, the Netherlands, Norway, Russia, Sweden, the United Kingdom, and the United States.[41] However, Russia has not been invited since 2014 due to its Crimean annexation. Both the EU and China are also excluded from this select group. Other than the organisations mentioned above there are others like the Arctic Yearbook, Arctic Portal, Arctic Coastal Dynamics, Arctic NGO forum, Arctic Science Portal, Conference of Parliamentarians of the Arctic Region, the World Winter Cities Association for Mayors, and the Youth Arctic Coalition and several others which are working on diverse fields of common interest to the various stakeholders in the Arctic region. The "Arctic Yearbook seeks to be the preeminent repository of critical analysis on the Arctic region, with a mandate to inform observers about the state of Arctic politics, governance, and security. It is an international and interdisciplinary double-blind peer-reviewed publication, published online at [www.Arcticyearbook.com] to ensure wide distribution and accessibility to a variety of stakeholders and observers."[42]

INTRODUCTION

Chapter 2: Geopolitical and Economic Significance of the Arctic Region

This chapter gives an overview of the economic resource potential, shipping potential, and geopolitical fabric of the region along with the present progress on resource exploitation and disputes on resources. Due to the

---

[40] Arctic Institute, 2019 accessed on 25 October 2019 from https://www.theArcticinstitute.org/Arctic-security-forum-please-dont/?cn-reloaded=1.

[41] All Partners Access Network, 2019, accessed on 01 December 2019 from https://www.apan.org/(S(qdzq4igyfqecrqfaif5pbyip))/pages/case-study-asfr.

[42] Arctic yearbook, Arcticyearbook.com, 2019 accessed on 01 December 2019 from https://Arcticyearbook.com/about.

increase in economic growth in countries of the world, there is a rush to obtain and secure supplies of natural resources to fuel such growth. The Arctic, which was traditionally considered too remote and difficult, has emerged on the scene because it houses reserves of the considerable magnitude of petroleum, minerals, fish and forests, etc., as well as due to the impacts of climate change that has made the exploitation of natural resources much easier and swift.

The Arctic's geopolitical significance is due to its geographical location connecting the three continents of America, Europe, and Asia, and offering short trade routes. The interconnections and sea lanes offer better connectivity though there are vulnerabilities on the fragile environment and eco-systemic with the outside environment. Lately, the Arctic Region is drawing greater political interest from the diverse and increasing number of states which is also enhancing the geopolitical power play.

Chapter 3: India's Involvement and Engagement with the Arctic Region

Though geographically Arctic Region lies far from India, yet the factors on increasing geopolitical interests, impacts of climate change on Indian coastline and monsoons, and the need to secure energy supplies have brought the Arctic on India's radar. India's engagement with the Arctic though is at a nascent stage yet steps have been in areas of scientific advancement and studies, economic linkages, and corollary political and geopolitical levers. India has been looking at the Arctic mostly from a scientific prism yet there is a realisation that it has to view it from a strategic construct as well as climate change as well as strengthen the bilateral and multilateral cooperation with the Arctic states and the Arctic intergovernmental organisations.

This chapter gives an overview of India's engagement with the region in economic, commercial, political, geopolitical, and other spheres. A new concept of the 'Indo-Arctic' policy is the need of the hour which should be focussed on achieving the bilateral goals of the 'Indo' entity states encompassing Bangladesh and Myanmar in India's immediate east to Japan and South Korea in the Far East which are united in experiencing effects of climate change happening in the Arctic and impacting these, thus unifying their position.

Chapter 4: Unravelling Challenges in Arctic and India's Response Strategy

The Arctic is experiencing and facing the brunt of climate change and over the last century, the temperature rise in the Arctic has been two to three times greater than the global average. The volume of the Arctic Ocean is reported to have fallen by 75%, and it is predicted that in the coming decades the Arctic will be entirely ice-free during the summer months. Though the geophysical changes will open several economic opportunities yet there will be concurrent challenges namely the loss of pristine biodiversity, shipping-related pollution risks, and the irreversible impact on the Arctic indigenous population.

As far as the issue of sovereignty and jurisdiction goes, the five Arctic coastal states (the United States, Canada, Denmark, Norway, and Russia) are best equipped and on the front line in the face of the emerging challenges. However, there are growing calls and demands for ever greater international cooperation on these issues. India has been a stakeholder in the Arctic since the 1920 Spitsbergen Treaty and as an Observer for the last seven years. As a responsible power, India has called for the sustainable development of this unique and fragile environment and thus occupies a prominent position in the Arctic affairs. The bottlenecks, irritants, external interference, and influences are enumerated and a suggested Indian response is outlined in this chapter.

Conclusion and Recommendations

CHAPTER 2

Geopolitical and Economic Significance of the Arctic Region

"The Arctic is hot," Gustav Lind,[1] Chair, SAO, 2012.

"And, as you know, there are other people coming into the Arctic, and we don't like it. And we can't let it happen, and we won't let it happen."[2]
—Donald Trump, US President, 02 Oct 2019.

The statements made by the Chair of SAO and the US President over seven years though in entirely different contexts, however, are tied by one common element that of the growing limelight in which the Arctic is being viewed by the regional players and non-Arctic states in the region. China was not yet granted the status of an observer in 2012 and within 06 years of its entry into the region, the greatest and most powerful nations, USA is increasingly getting sceptic of its goals and objectives. In short, there is tremendous geopolitical and economic significance of the region which has been now been accepted and acknowledged. Both the continental and oceanic portions of the Arctic region is home to a

---

[1] Lind Gustav, Arctic Human Development Report: Regional Processes and Global Linkages, Norden, accessed 12 October 2019 from http://norden.diva-portal.org/smash/get/diva2:788965/FULLTEXT03.pdf.

[2] White House, Whitehouse. Gov, 2019, accessed on 12 November 2019 from https://www.whitehouse.gov/briefings-statements/remarks-president-trump-president-niinisto-republic-finland-joint-press-conference/.

© The Author(s), under exclusive license to Springer Nature Singapore Pte Ltd. 2024
N. Pareek, *India in the Arctic*,
https://doi.org/10.1007/978-981-97-3640-9_2

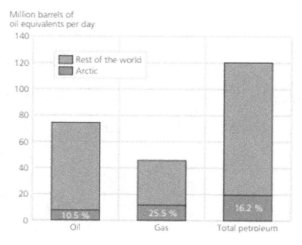

Fig. 2.1 Arctic share of global petroleum production (*Source* Lindholt. L, Arctic natural resources in a global perspective, The Economy of the North, p. 27, 2006)

plethora of natural resources, which has gained traction due to depleting resources elsewhere due to incessant exploitation of resources and hunt for unexplored areas. Among the many minerals, petroleum, fish, and forests and gold are the main ones that attract the interest of both developed and developing economies. As per some estimates, the northern expanse could be worth $17.2 trillion in crude oil and natural gas alone,[3] which is much bigger than the US economy. Arctic region is considered to be rich in oil, gas, gas condensates, rare earth minerals, and fisheries, yet the most prominent and promising resource remains the natural gas, which is believed to be in the region of one-third of the world's undiscovered reserves. The following two figures depict the Arctic's share in global petroleum production and proven petroleum reserves, which shows its significant share considering the modest size of the Arctic economies (Figs. 2.1 and 2.2).

---

[3] Vocativ, 2019, accessed on 12 September 2019 from https://www.vocativ.com/money/business/whats-the-north-pole-worth/#!bKmi1k.

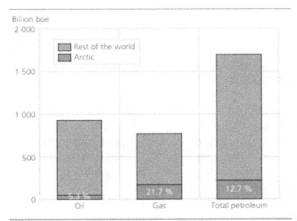

*Quantities indicated with reasonable certainty from geological and engineering information that that can be recovered in the future from known reservoirs under existing economic operating conditions.

Fig. 2.2 Arctic share of proven petroleum reserves (*Source* Lindholt. L, Arctic natural resources in a global perspective, The Economy of the North, p. 28, 2006)

However, the most valuable resources are gas reserves, which could amount to as much as 30% of the world's undiscovered reserves, as well as oil, which encompasses some 13% of the world's undiscovered stocks.[4]

Population/ Human Resource: The estimated population of the Arctic region is around 4 million (Mn), out of which the indigenous make for around 10%. It is abundantly clear that the population of the Arctic does not make it a significant stakeholder in global politics, yet the indigenous people of the Arctic have been making a living for several millennia by employing sustainable means of living. Many places like Greenland have the indigenous people in the majority, which in others they may be less. There are over 40 different ethnic groups living in the Arctic. These communities include Saami in circumpolar areas of Finland, Sweden, Norway, and Northwest Russia, Nenets, Khanty, Evenk, and Chukchi in

---

[4] S. Borgerson, C. Antrim, *an Arctic Circle of Friends*, (New York, 28 March 2009), http://www.nytimes.com/2009/03/28/opinion/28borgerson.html?_r=0 [accessed: 07/01/2018].

Russia, Aleut, Yupik and Inuit (Iñupiat) in Alaska, Inuit (Inuvialuit) in Canada and Inuit (Kalaallit) in Greenland.

As brought out in the foregoing paragraphs, the indigenous people organisations represented by the Permanent participants like the RAIPON, Saami Council, Aleutian, and others represent the different ethnic groups living in the Arctic. The ethnic groups include the Saami, Nenets, Khanty, Evenk, Chukchi, Aleut, Yupik, Inuit (Iñupiat), and several others. The Saami are among the largest groups and comprise more than 100,000 people. A UN report on indigenous people is available at https://www.un.org/en/events/indigenousday/pdf/Indigenous_Arctic_Eng.pdf on the theme 'INDIGENOUS PEOPLE INDIGENOUS VOICES.'

People Scientists have concluded that the native indigenous people have lived for around twenty thousand years in the Arctic and adopted the hunting, fishing, whaling, herding, and other means for sustainable living. As brought out earlier, the Inuits, Aleuts, Athabaskans, Yupik, and several others make up for the majority of the local people. They had devised means to sustain in the frigid environment by developing warm houses, and clothing to protect themselves from the frigid conditions. They pride themselves on ancient knowledge on predicting weather, languages, and don't follow the modern political divided between the communities. Many Arctic people now live much like their neighbours to the south, with modern homes and appliances. Nonetheless, there is an active movement among indigenous people in the Arctic to pass on traditional knowledge and skills, such as hunting, fishing, herding, and native languages, to the younger generation.[5]

As per studies, the Arctic populations are in a later stage in the demographic transition thus the rate of growth may be stable or even negative. The major factor which will have an impact on the rapid increase or decrease in populations in pockets will be the discovery of resources or depletions thereof. As per the Arctic Human Development Report," Urbanisation in the Arctic is accelerating, propelled both by local and global forces, and the Arctic is becoming more "marketable" and Arctic identities are seen increasingly as an asset."[6]

---

[5] National Snow and Ice Data Center, 2019, accessed on 10 December 2019 from https://nsidc.org/cryosphere/Arctic-meteorology/Arctic-people.html.

[6] Arctic Human Development Report, accessed on 12 October 2019 from http://norden.diva-portal.org/smash/get/diva2:788965/FULLTEXT03.pdf.

Hydrocarbons: As per records, the earliest oil production in Alaska was carried out in 1911; however, the discovery in Prudhoe Bay in 1967 commenced oil development in the Arctic. Likewise, Russia was also discovering oil and gas and in 1966, the Urengoy gas field was discovered which went into production in 1978. However, the recent surge was an aftermath of the US Geological Survey (USGS) findings of the potential reserves of hydrocarbons in the region. According to USGS, roughly twenty-two percent of the world's "undiscovered, technically recoverable" petroleum is located in the Arctic region, including thirteen percent of the world's undiscovered oil and thirty percent of its undiscovered natural gas. "About eighty-four percent of the estimated resources are expected to occur [in] offshore [areas]." Besides, 240 billion barrels of already-proven oil and natural gas reserves—about ten percent of the world's known petroleum—are located in onshore fields north of the Arctic Circle. As global reserves dwindle (leading to ongoing predictions of impending "peak oil"—the point at which oil demand eclipses global supplies), a new "Arctic Gold Rush" is underway to exploit these once frozen resource deposits."[7]

Among the Arctic 8, the maximum quantity of oil and gas resource is held by Russia, with around 40% of the oil and around 70% of the gas reserves. Resources in Arctic Region have been one of the primary reasons for the growing interest of the Arctic littorals as well as prominent non-Arctic states in recent times. This was also ignited due to the 2008 USGS report on the availability of resource base in the region as well as due to unprecedented thaw in ice caps and sea ice levels making exploitation much easier.

Gas hydrates are generally composed of methane and hence the term methane hydrates are also used to denote gas hydrates. These are formed under extremely cold conditions when the gas mixes with water and freezes into a solid form. Generally, gas hydrates are found below the permafrost and in some marine sediment. In the present times, the technology to extract these is still being developed and it will become an important resource in the future. Interestingly, the study (USGS) did not include gas hydrates which are likely more abundant in the Arctic.

---

[7] Rainwater Shiloh, International law and the "globalization" of the Arctic: assessing the rights of non-Arctic states in the high north, Emory International Law Review. 2015, vol. 30, issue 1, pp. 115–153, p.39.

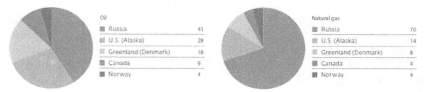

Fig. 2.3 Undiscovered hydrocarbon reserves among the Arctic coastal states (*Source* Russian strategies in the Arctic: Avoiding a new cold war, Heinenen, Sergunin, Yarovoy, September 2014, Valdai Club)

This could become an important energy resource in the future when technology facilitates its development.[8]

Another great favourable element in the favour of Arctic hydrocarbon resources is the high availability of natural gas and increasing transformation from oil to gas, due to growing environmental concerns. The distribution of oil and gas among the coastal states is depicted as under (Fig. 2.3).

After the 2008 USGS survey of hydrocarbon potential of Arctic, there has been a heightened scramble for the natural resources, which are becoming accessible due to the rapidly reducing ice cover. As per the USGS report, 'the total mean undiscovered conventional oil and gas resources of the Arctic are estimated to be approximately 90 Billion Barrels of oil, 1669 Trillion cubic feet of natural gas, and 44 Billion barrels of natural gas liquids.'[9] It is assessed that this buried oil and natural gas, could significantly alter the supply, prices, and distribution of energy around the world. Along with hydrocarbons, fishing, tourism, and exploitation of minerals will also assume greater significance. The depleting ice cover, growing worldwide demand for hydrocarbons, and domestic political policies of the Arctic nations will necessitate resource extraction of these non-renewable resources, sooner or later.

---

[8] Arctic_energy_resources_and_security, Pan European Institute, 2010, accessed on 11 November 2019 from www.utu.fi.

[9] USGS, United States Geological Service, 2019, accessed on 13 August 2019 from https://archive.usgs.gov/archive/sites/www.usgs.gov/newsroom/article.asp-ID=1980.html.

However till now, due to the prevailing slump in global crude prices and substantial exploration risks and lack of key technologies has deterred companies to suspend or abandon these projects. But the future global demand and supply equation, as well as substantial ice thinning, may change the situation. The irony of this frame for the Arctic is that Arctic renewable resources, which are the best basis for sustainable development, are already at risk due to the changing climate which is opening the access to the buried hydrocarbons. Exploiting oil and gas in the Arctic will magnify the climate risk while simultaneously introducing localised risks to those same renewable resources.[10]

Around 97% of total Arctic oil and gas production is located in Alaska and Northern Russia. Alaska contributes around 20% of total US production. The Russian Arctic Zone (RAZ) holds most of the Arctic's hydrocarbon reserves. This region of Russia is the most prolific producer of Russian gas (95%) and oil (about 70%). Russian geologists have discovered about 200 oil and gas deposits in the RAZ. There are 22 large shelf deposits in the Barents and Kara seas, which are expected to be developed shortly. The RAZ is also abundant in mineral resources. Its mining industries produce primary and placer diamond (99% of total Russian production), platinum-group elements (PGE) (98%), nickel and cobalt (over 80%), chromium and manganese (90%), copper (60%), antimony, tin, tungsten, and rare metals (from 50 to 90%), and gold about 40%) (Map 2.1).[11]

Novatek's largest discovery in 2018 was finding gas in North Obski-1 well in the South Kara Sea basin of Russia. There are estimates that the potential will be in the range of 11 Trillion Cubic Feet (TCF). The Circum-Arctic Resource Appraisal (CARA) report, the summary of which is placed under had arrived that the gas component is much higher in the Arctic than the conventional oil. Overall, the Arctic is estimated to contain between 44 and 157 billion barrels of recoverable oil. Billion barrel oil fields are possible at a 50% chance in seven assessment units. Undiscovered oil resources could be significant to the Arctic nations but are probably

---

[10] Kakabadse, y. (2015). Frontier Mentality Has No Place in the Arctic. *Harvard International Review*, vol. 36, issue 3, pp. 55–59. Retrieved from www.jstor.org/stable/43649294.

[11] Heinenen Lassi, Sergunin Alexander, Yarovoy Gleb, ussian strategies in the Arctic: avoiding a new cold war, Moscow, 2014, Valdai, Valdai Club, ISBN 978-5-906,757-05-0.

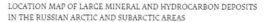
LOCATION MAP OF LARGE MINERAL AND HYDROCARBON DEPOSITS
IN THE RUSSIAN ARCTIC AND SUBARCTIC AREAS

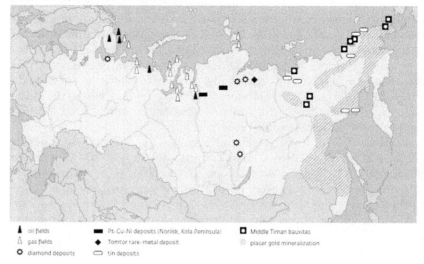

Map 2.1 Location Map of large mineral and hydrocarbon deposits in the Russian Arctic and sub-Arctic areas (*Source* Russian strategies in the Arctic: Avoiding a new cold war, Heinenen, Sergunin, Yarovoy, September 2014, Valdai Club)

not sufficient to shift the world oil balance away from the Middle East.[12] It also arrived at that the location of the finds was mostly in the Russian territory. The Circum Arctic Resource Appraisal report is placed Table 2.1 (Map 2.2).

A major problem in the exploitation of the resources is difficulties involved in dredging, a process of recovering minerals including hydrocarbons from the ocean floor. It is due to ice cover, permafrost, iceberg scour, and Arctic remoteness that dredging is a cumbersome and difficult

---

[12] Donald L. Gautier, Kenneth J. Bird, Ronald R. Charpentier, Arthur Grantz, David W. Houseknecht, Timothy R. Klett, Thomas E. Moore, Janet K. Pitman, Christopher J. Schenk, John H. Schuenemeyer, Kai Sørensen, Marilyn E. Tennyson, Zenon C. Valin, and Craig J. Wandrey, Oil and gas resource potential north of the Arctic Circle, Geological Society, London, Memoirs, vol. 35, pp. 151–161, 2011, https://doi.org/10.1144/M35.9.

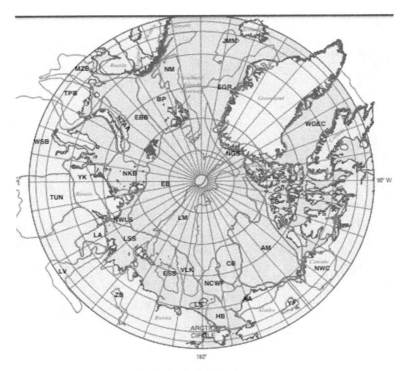

CARA Province Abbreviations

AA — Arctic Alaska (Chapter E)
AM — Amerasia Basin (Chapter BB)
BP — Barents Platform (Norwegian Petroleum Directorate, 2009)
CB — Chukchi Borderland (Chapter C)
EB — Eurasia Basin (Chapter DD)
EBB — East Barents Basin (Chapter O)
EGR — East Greenland Rift Basins (Chapter K)
ESS — East Siberian Sea Basin (Chapter Y)
FS — Franklinian Shelf (Chapter H)
HB — Hope Basin (Chapter D)
JMM — Jan Mayen Microcontinent (Chapter L)
LA — Lena-Anabar Basin (Chapter T)
LM — Lomonosov-Makarov (Chapter CC)
LS — Long Strait (Chapter AA)
LSS — Laptev Sea Shelf (Chapter W)
LV — Lena-Vilyui Basin (Chapter V)
MZB — Mezen' Basin (Chapter M)
NCWF — North Chukchi Wrangel Foreland Basin (assessed, not included in volume)
NGS — North Greenland Sheared Margin (Lincoln Sea — Sørensen and others, 2012; Wandel Sea — assessed, not included in volume)
NKB — North Kara Basins and Platforms (Chapter P)
NM — Norwegian Margin (Norwegian Petroleum Directorate, 2009)
NWC — Northwest Canada Interior Basins (Chapter G)
NWLS — Northwest Laptev Sea Shelf (Chapter S)
NZAA — Novaya Zemlya Basins and Admiralty Arch (Chapter Q)
SB — Sverdrup Basin (Chapter I)
TPB — Timan-Pechora Basin (Chapter N)
TUN — Tunguska Basin (Chapter U)
VLK — Vilkitski Basin (Chapter Z)
WGEC — West Greenland-East Canada (Chapter J)
WSB — West Siberian Basin (Chapter Q)
YF — Yukon Flats Basin (Chapter F)
YK — Yenisey-Khatanga Basin (Chapter R)
ZB — Zyryanka Basin (Chapter X)

Map 2.2 Circum Arctic Resource Appraisal (CARA) provinces abbreviations[13] (*Source* United States Geological Survey, Circum-Arctic Resource Appraisal: Estimates of Undiscovered Oil and Gas North of the Arctic Circle, 2008, accessed on 01 December 2019 from https://pubs.usgs.gov/fs/2008/3049/)

[13] United States Geological Survey, Circum-Arctic Resource Appraisal: Estimates of Undiscovered Oil and Gas North of the Arctic Circle, 2008, accessed on 01 December 2019 from https://pubs.usgs.gov/fs/2008/3049/).

Table 2.1 Province wise oil and gas reserves in the Arctic Region: Summary of results of the circum-arctic resource appraisal[14]

Province Code	Province	Oil (MMBO)	Total Gas (BCFG)	NGL (MMBNGL)	BOE (MMBOE)
WSB	West Siberian Basin	3,659.88	651,498.56	20,328.69	132,571.66
AA	Arctic Alaska	29,960.94	221,397.60	5,904.97	72,765.52
EBB	East Barents Basin	7,406.49	317,557.97	1,422.28	61,755.10
EGR	East Greenland Rift Basins	8,902.13	86,180.06	8,121.57	31,387.04
YK	Yenisey-Khatanga Basin	5,583.74	99,964.26	2,675.15	24,919.61
AM	Amerasia Basin	9,723.58	56,891.21	541.69	19,747.14
WGEC	West Greenland-East Canada	7,274.40	51,818.16	1,152.59	17,063.35
LSS	Laptev Sea Shelf	3,115.57	32,562.84	867.16	9,409.87
NM	Norwegian Margin	1,437.29	32,281.01	504.73	7,322.19
BP	Barents Platform	2,055.51	26,218.67	278.71	6,704.00
EB	Eurasia Basin	1,342.15	19,475.43	520.26	5,108.31
NKB	North Kara Basins and Platforms	1,807.26	14,973.58	390.22	4,693.07
TPB	Timan-Pechora Basin	1,667.21	9,062.59	202.80	3,380.44
NGS	North Greenland Sheared Margin	1,349.80	10,207.24	273.09	3,324.09
LM	Lomonosov-Makarov	1,106.78	7,156.25	191.55	2,491.04
SB	Sverdrup Basin	851.11	8,596.36	191.20	2,475.04
LA	Lena-Anabar Basin	1,912.89	2,106.75	56.41	2,320.43
NCWF	North Chukchi-Wrangel Foreland Basin	85.99	6,065.76	106.57	1,203.52
VLK	Vilkitskii Basin	98.03	5,741.97	101.63	1,156.63
NWLS	Northwest Laptev Sea Shelf	172.24	4,488.12	119.63	1,039.90
LV	Lena-Vilyui Basin	376.86	1,335.20	35.66	635.06
ZB	Zyryanka Basin	47.82	1,505.99	40.14	338.95
ESS	East Siberian Sea Basin	19.73	618.83	10.91	133.78
HB	Hope Basin	2.47	648.17	11.37	121.87
NWC	Northwest Canada Interior Basins	23.34	305.34	15.24	89.47
MZB	Mezen' Basin	NQA	NQA	NQA	NQA
NZAA	Novaya Zemlya Basins and Admiralty Arch	NQA	NQA	NQA	NQA
TUN	Tunguska Basin	NQA	NQA	NQA	NQA
CB	Chuckhi Borderland	NQA	NQA	NQA	NQA
YF	Yukon Flats (part of Central Alaska Province)	NQA	NQA	NQA	NQA
LS	Long Strait	NQA	NQA	NQA	NQA
JMM	Jan Mayen Microcontinent	NQA	NQA	NQA	NQA
FS	Franklinian Shelf	NQA	NQA	NQA	NQA
Total		89,983.21	1,668,657.84	44,064.24	412,157.09

process in the Arctic. Another set of problems includes the winter darkness, extremely cold climate, and permafrost. Thus, petroleum production

---

[14] Bird, Kenneth J., Charpentier, Ronald R., Gautier, Donald L., Houseknecht, David W., Klett, Timothy R., Pitman, Janet K., Moore, Thomas E., Schenk, Christopher J., Tennyson, Marilyn E., and Wandrey, Craig J., 2008, Circum-Arctic resource appraisal; estimates of undiscovered oil and gas north of the Arctic Circle: U.S. Geological Survey Fact Sheet 2008–3049, p. 4. [http://pubs.usgs.gov/fs/2008/3049/].

in the Arctic involves huge offshore investment and the requirement of skilled manpower and technological advancements.

Fishing: The Arctic waters are home to several species of fish and fishing has been one of the primitive practices of indigenous people. The Arctic supports 4 out of the world's 10 largest fisheries which are only going to increase. Fishing provides around 90% of export revenue to Greenland and around 33% to Iceland. Some estimates suggest that by the end of this century, the fisheries size could grow by around 37 times. Yet, there will be issues on the management of species, autonomous and self-sustaining ecosystems and the needs of the indigenous communities will have to be taken into account. Also because of the acidification of the ocean and an increase in the flow of freshwater and pollution and pollutants in the ocean, there will be threats to the fish stocks. As in the past, fisheries policies and their enforcement and effect on exploitation rates are important for the abundance of different fish populations. Fisheries policies will probably be more important for fish stock levels in the future, than the total effect of climate change.[15]

The important fish stocks include Alaska Pollock, Pacific cod, snow crab, Pacific salmon species, North-East Arctic cod, haddock, Norwegian spring-spawning, and many others. As per the table placed 2.2, the Arctic fish constituted around 10% of the world produce, which is quite high considering the small area of the Arctic Ocean. The Table 2.2 gives the availability of various fish types in the North-East Atlantic, Eastern Bering Sea, Western Bering Sea, Central North-Atlantic, and North-East Canada Seas along with differing varieties like crustaceans:-

The jurisdictional framework for international law on fisheries is provided under the provisions of the 1982 United Nations Convention on the Law of the Sea (UNCLOS). The international fisheries law applies to the marine Arctic and the (Central) Arctic Ocean. The definitions provided under UNCLOS of coastal states maritime zones, functional jurisdiction of coastal state under 200NM EEZ, and maritime zone beyond the EEZs. The changes in the climate are altering ocean currents thus the distribution and presence of commercial fish stocks are transforming. The changes in the ice levels and opening of economic and shipping pursuits, there will be a tremendous impact on fishing too. With

---

[15] L Lindholt, Arctic natural resources in a global perspective, The economy of the North, 2006 accessed on 01 December 2019 from https://pdfs.semanticscholar.org/0728/f33f18c5d382d1607a0b8da5005d2c387e3a.pdf.

Table 2.2 Marine fisheries in the Arctic (Million Tons)

Species	North-east Atlantic	Eastern Bering Sea	Western Bering Sea	Central North Atlantic (Iceland, Greenland and Faroe Islands)	North-eastern Canada (Newfoundland and Labrador Sea)	Total
Capelin	0.64			1.12	0.02	1.78
Herring	0.83		0.05	0.27	0.01	1.16
Cod fish						3.58
North-east Atlantic cod	0.49[1]			0.25		
Saithe north of 62°N	0.15					
Haddock, saithe				0.42[2]	0.01	
Pollack		1.50	0.40			
North-east Arctic haddock	0.08					
Blue whiting				0.28		
Greenland halibut	0.01			0.04	0.04	0.09
Pacific salmon		0.04	0.02			0.06
Other groundfish		0.20				0.20
Flatfish		0.06	0.01			0.07
Others	0.01	0.04	0.04	0.23		0.32
Total wild fish	**2.21**	**1.84**	**0.52**	**2.61**	**0.08**	**7.26**
Shrimps	0.06			0.13	0.10	0.29
Snow crab		0.01[3]		0.01	0.05	0.07
Total crustaceans	**0.06**	**0.01**		**0.14**	**0.15**	**0.36**
Aquaculture (salmon, trout)	0.09			0.01		0.10

[1] Includes coastal cod.
[2] See endnote 19.
[3] Includes king crab and Tanner crab.

Source Lindholt. L, Arctic natural resources in a global perspective, The Economy of the North, p. 33, 2006.

ice no longer impeding that it once was in this part of the world, mining and shipping companies are also moving in, using the same pathways that narwhals and belugas use to get to and from their winter and summering habitat. So is the military.[16]

Several Arctic fisheries agreements have been signed by various states and these include, International Pacific Halibut Commission, Pacific Salmon Commission, North Pacific Anadromous Fish Commission (NPAFC), and many others. However, the international agreement to prevent unregulated commercial fishing in the high seas of the Central Arctic Ocean (CAO) is a unique and novel agreement between the states that can be considered a landmark agreement to curb fishing till such time that scientific data is available for better management. This was signed between China, Japan, Russia, Iceland, Norway, South Korea, the European Union, the United States of America, Canada, and Denmark on 03 Oct 2018. The idea of this agreement had started with a consensus among the Arctic5 nations. As of now, this moratorium will be effective for 16 years or more, and a review will be made in due course of time.

---

[16] Struzik Edward, (Future Arctic _ Field Notes From a World on the Edge.pdf, n.d.).

Though as per the inception and governing guidelines of the Arctic Council, non-members including non-Arctic states have no right to make decisions, and even their contributions are also routed through the Working Groups, yet all 3 North-East Asian countries were signatories to the agreement to prevent unregulated fishing in the Central Arctic. This signing of the agreement by these 3 Asian nations is also an indicator of their hold and grasp over natural resources exploitation in the area as also a taciturn acknowledgment by the Arctic states of the need to engage to prevent reckless exploitation.

The CAOF Agreement is the first regional fisheries agreement adopted prior to the initiation of fishing in a specific area, and it has already been lauded as a science-based measure and a manifestation of the precautionary approach by representatives of States and Non-Governmental Organisations.[17] The Map placed below shows the geographical spread of the CAO boundary (Map 2.3).

Minerals: The Arctic contains rich sources of rare earth and other natural resources and minerals which are required for further research in scientific endeavours. The minerals include critical metals like copper, niobium, platinum-group elements, phosphorus, and so on. However the unique characteristics of the Arctic present economic problems and environmental problems of mineral exploration. The study of mineral exploration has to account for the geochemical and petrochemical features of their rocks and minerals. The Norilsk Nickel company which mines on the Taymyr Region in the north-central Siberia owns rights to about one-fifth of the entire World's.

Nickel deposits, while the Siberian Republic of Sakha (Yakutia) has an estimated one-quarter of the World's diamonds.[18]

The Arctic region also has huge mineral resources for example; Canada is the third-largest diamond producer in the world. Among the world economies, China, India, and Brazil have sustained demand for minerals and despite global slowdown as in 2008, the demand for minerals is not going to abate and mining will not only increase the shipping

---

[17] Valentin J. Schatz, Alexander Proelss, Nengye Liu: The 2018 Agreement to Prevent Unregulated High Seas Fisheries in the Central Arctic Ocean: A Critical Analysis, The International Journal of Marine and Coastal Law, https://doi.org/10/1163/15718085-23,342,015.

[18] Arctic Photo, 2019, accessed on 21 October 2019 from https://www.Arcticphoto.com/results.asp?gallery=gas+and+oil.

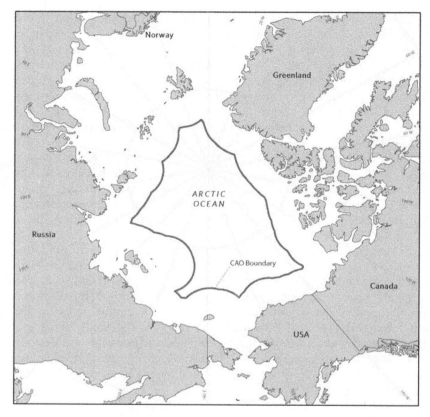

Map 2.3 Map showing Central Arctic Ocean (CAO) boundary[19] (*Source* https://www.sciencedirect.com/science/article/pii/S0308597X15002997)

traffic as well as require efforts like skilled manpower and equipment. A table showing estimated Arctic share of some raw materials in global production (in percent) is as under (Table 2.3).

Other than Hard coal, iron ore, Nickel, Cobalt, Chromites, Titanium, Tungsten, Bauxite, Zinc, Lead, Gold, Silver and Platinum, and many

---

[19] Pan Min, Huntington, Henry. P., A precautionary approach to fisheries in the Central Arctic Ocean: Policy, science, and China, Marine Policy, vol. 63, January 2016, pp. 153–157.

Table 2.3 Estimated Arctic share of global production of some raw materials

Iron and ferro-alloy minerals	
Iron ore	2.3
Nickel	10.6
Cobalt	11.0
Chromite	4.2
Titanium	0.3
Tungsten	9.2
Non-ferrous minerals	
Bauxite	1.9
Zinc	7.8
Lead	5.6
Copper	3.8
Palladium	40.0
Precious metal ores	
Gold	3.2
Silver	3.6
Platinum	15.0
Industrial minerals	
Diamonds - gem	26.8
Diamonds - industrial	23.3
Phosphate	3.7
Vermiculite	5.8
Fishery	
Wild marine fish	10.1
Crustaceans	5.3
Salmon and trout fish farming	7.7
Forestry	
Wood[2]	2.2

[1] Some Arctic shares are estimated and must be considered as approximate figures. Consequently, the findings in this table should be treated with caution.
[2] The Arctic share of global wood reserves is esimated to 8.2 per cent.

Source Lindholt. L, Arctic natural resources in a global perspective, The Economy of the North, p. 36, 2006.

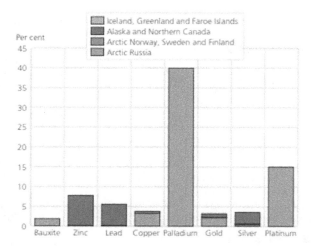

Fig. 2.4 Arctic share of global non-ferrous minerals and precious metals ore extraction (percent)[20] (*Source* Lindholt. L, Arctic natural resources in a global perspective, The Economy of the North, p. 30, 2006)

other metals including precious metals are mined in the Arctic region. The table below shows that Palladium and Platinum have the highest share at 40% and 15% in the global produce (Fig. 2.4).

Though mineral exploration has remained a challenge due to the harsh climatic conditions and vulnerability of the pristine ecosystems yet the climate change infused changes are opening up this frontier, even faster than expected. The various factors like remoteness of the Arctic region coupled with extremely cold conditions and continuous darkness and vulnerability of Arctic ecosystems also make the exploration difficult and cumbersome process.

Forestry: The boreal forests cover a large part of the terrestrial Arctic. The boreal forest has a limited variety of coniferous species (spruce, pine, and fir) and a few broad-leaved species, like birch and poplar. These are among the largest natural forests in the world but are uncultivated due to the harsh climate and lack of infrastructure. The resource potential of the

---

[20] Lindholt. L, Arctic natural resources in a global perspective, The Economy of the North, p 30, 2006 accessed on 01 December 2019 from https://pdfs.semanticscholar.org/0728/f33f18c5d382d1607a0b8da5005d2c387e3a.pdf.

Fig. 2.5 Arctic share of global wood volume of forests[21] (*Source* Lindholt. L, Arctic natural resources in a global perspective, The Economy of the North, p. 35, 2006)

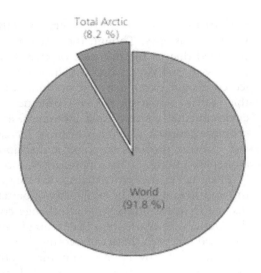

Arctic forestry is a minor 2.2% of total wood removal and has to catch up with the global norms. The share of Arctic wood in global wood, by volume, is 8.2% and the majority of the wood too lies in the Russian Arctic with some portion in Alaska and Northern Sweden and Northern Finland (Fig. 2.5).

Another worrying feature of recent times, however, is the raging wildfires which have both increased in intensity and duration, damaging boreal forests prominently around Alaska, Canada, Siberia and Scandinavia, and reducing their ability to be a carbon sink. It has also been noted that large beetle infestation is currently underway in south-central Alaska, killing trees over a vast area and causing large amounts of carbon losses.

Tourism: The Arctic region has been experiencing an increase in the number of tourist's arrivals, due to multiple reasons like increased awareness of the region, global activism on environment conservation and related issues, ease in transportation and communication in the region, interest and curiosity in Arctic indigenous communities, an extended tourist season, and so on. Globally, tourism is one of the most significant

---

[21] Lindholt. L, Arctic natural resources in a global perspective, The Economy of the North, p 30, 2006 accessed on 01 December 2019 from https://pdfs.semanticscholar.org/0728/f33f18c5d382d1607a0b8da5005d2c387e3a.pdf.

industrial sectors in countries/regions with exceptional biodiversity and natural landscapes. Though the actual number of tourists could not be compiled due to the presence of several sovereign states and including regions in sub-Arctic but the increase is phenomenal. The receding ice cover and easier maritime communication have also contributed to this increase. Tourism has also become a tool of education and raises environmental concerns and awareness, and thus the advanced nations promote tourism. There has been an increasing number of polar cruises too. Tourism provides economic and socio-economic growth and greater awareness among the local population, too.

There is a change from the Arctic being considered as niche tourism to the mainstream with the availability of better ships and luxury cruise ships making frequent forays. Climate change could cause a tourism boom in the Arctic, with cruise ships benefitting from melting ice caps giving them increased access to the area, according to a leaked UN report.[22] Though there has been growing interest in turning the Poles into a tourist destination, ship-based tourism is considerably better than commercial tankers in terms of environmental safety and pollution. However, there are concerns relating to the adequacy of environmental standards and ship safety.

Geothermal Energy: The potential of geothermal energy has been tapped with much success in the Arctic region. In terms of electrical production geothermal energy contributes 30% in Iceland. Nowhere else does geothermal energy play a greater role in a nation's energy supply and overall prosperity. Canada has also undertaken massive mapping exercise under the aegis of the Canadian national geothermal database and territory resource estimate in Nunavut, Yukon, Alberta, and British Columbia territories. India has also taken a cue from these developments and its first geothermal plant is likely to come up in Chhattisgarh. India's nationalised company, NTPC is likely to execute this project. A strange issue is that the possibility of geothermal energy is not yet explored in the Himalayas as they possess physical characteristics similar to the Arctic in many ways.

Submarine Cables: As per research, 99% of global communications are carried through optical fibre cables. This mode is not only cheaper and faster but also provides wider bandwidth as compared to satellite communication. There are more than 300 submarine cables connecting

---

[22] Daily Mail, UK, 2019, accessed on 11 November 2019 from https://www.dailymail.co.uk/travel/article-2591456/UN-climate-change-report-predicts-tourism-boom-Arctic-cruises.html.

continents and fulfilling the demands of globalisation of having instant communication.

The Arctic Ocean and the Southern Ocean are the only places that are not yet crisscrossed with fibre optic cables that carry the bulk of global communications. However, till now the Arctic Ocean due to prevailing ice cover and hostile weather and terrain configuration does not have submarine cabling, despite it providing the shortest distance between Europe and Asia. Shorter distance also results in shorter latency in communications, which can save millions of US Dollars (USD) every year. The plans to lay submarine cables have been in the pipeline for several years, including Russian project ROTACS (Russian Optical Trans-Arctic Submarine Cable System), Canadian project Arctic Fibre, Canadian Ivaluk Network, Emerald Express, and others. In June 2019, another MoU was signed between Cinia, a Finnish company, and Megafon, a Russian company to lay 10,000 Km of trans-Arctic cable. The Cinia alliance in this phase consists of Japanese and Nordic partners and Asian partners (China?) and an international investment bank. The cabling initiative and link will not only open huge data transfer, data hosting, and other economic opportunities in the region but also foster future growth and help sustain digitalisation. Recently, Finland PM Antti Rinne said in November 2019 that this project is the biggest priority for the Nordic countries. It is expected that direct traffic flow between Europe and Asia will grow more than 900% by 2024.

Arctic Freshwater Ecosystems: Freshwater ecosystems are an integral part of Arctic landscapes wherein around 121,000 lakes are found within the Arctic landmass. The lakes cover around 3.7% of the land area showing the diverse landscape. Lakes and river ecosystems are vital for the growth and ecological sustenance of the species found therein. The river deltas of Lena, Ob, and Yenisei are among the world's largest. The major lakes found in the region include the Great Bear Lake, Great Slave Lake, and Lake Taymyr.

Shipping Routes: The ice recession in the Arctic is extending the navigation window and also enhancing the geographic areas of possible transport passages which have remained ice-covered hitherto fore. The logical fallout of the receding ice cover was a prospect of the opening of new sea routes, namely, North East Passage (NEP), North West Passage (NWP), Trans Arctic Passage, and the Arctic Bridge route. Needless to mention, the Arctic region has become important due to the melting of the polar ice that has led to increasing economic opportunities, raw

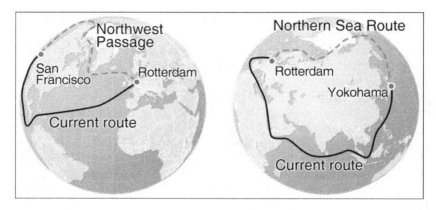

Map 2.4 North East Passage and North West Passage shipping routes

material, energy expansion, and use of the new maritime route.[23] Among these, the most promising and likely to be operationalised are the NWP and NEP/NSR. Among the Asian states, Japan and Korean policy documents convey conservative estimates and calling for detailed feasibility studies while China is relatively more ambitious in its approach. As far as the routes go, both Russia and Canada have cited Article 234 of UNCLOS which provides for protection and preservation of the ice-covered EEZ areas of the Arctic Ocean, resulting in laying exclusive rights over NWP and NEP/NSR, respectively (Map 2.4).

The map underneath depicts the North East Passage traversing Eastwards via the ice-free Norwegian and Barents seas around the Scandinavian Peninsula and across north-western Russia to the Kara Strait, which separates the Barents and Kara seas. From there it continues eastward through the Kara, Laptev, East Siberian, and Chukchi seas before turning southward to go through the Bering Strait between north-eastern Siberia and western Alaska, in the US The portion of the Northeast Passage between the Kara and Bering straits which remains ice-bound for most of the year is called the NSR. The NWP connects the Atlantic and Pacific Oceans through the Canadian Arctic Archipelago. The Arctic Bridge Route (ABR) is an underutilised seasonal maritime

---

[23] Singh, T. China and the Arctic: Evolving Geopolitics, ISASS, NIAS, National Institute of Advanced Studies, 2016.

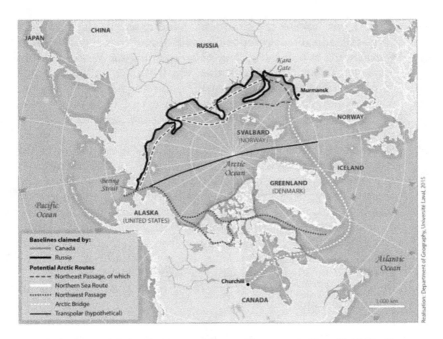

Map 2.5 Potential Arctic routes (*Source* Emmanuel Guy, Frédéric Lasserre, Commercial shipping in the Arctic: new perspectives, challenges, and regulations, Cambridge University Press, accessed on 01 December 2019 from https:// www.cambridge.org/core/journals/polar-record/article/commercial-shipping-in-the-Arctic-new-perspectives-challenges-and-regulations/24D92421C2024E9 3D8C48EF29FBAFCEA)

passage that runs between the Russian port of Murmansk and the Canadian port of Churchill, Manitoba (Map 2.5).[24]

Types of commercial shipping Traffic: The shipping traffic can be of these types:-

(a) Transit Traffic: The traffic is not associated with any regional dynamic and only navigates the waters of the Arctic only to obtain

---

[24] Global Risk Insights.com, accessed on 11 Sep 19 from https://globalriskinsights. com/2015/09/canada-and-russias-arctic-path-to-reconciliation/.

a short cut link to the Southern/Eastern sectors. Transit shipping is also in direct competition with the other routes like Suez Canal Route and also they may choose among the various options available. Transit shipping is that which utilises an Arctic route to connect the trading hubs of the Atlantic and Pacific Oceans, whereas destination shipping is the movement of bulk resources (such as oil, gas, LNG, or minerals) from the point of extraction to markets outside of the Arctic region.[25]

(b) Destination Traffic: Unlike the transit traffic, the destination traffic is bound to the region either by loading or unloading cargo in the region. There is no alternative for destination shipping and climate change will, therefore, impact the overall transportation cost by reducing the technical requirements for these ships. The most cargo shipping activity taking place in the Arctic in these times is to transport natural resources from the Arctic or to deliver general cargo and supplies Thus, cargo ship traffic in the Arctic presently is mostly regional, not trans-Arctic.

(c) Re-supply: This is another variant of the traffic and meant to supply to the local communities.

Distance Saved: The prominent reason for shipping companies to choose to transit through the NSR or the NWP is because of the economic advantage that accrues due to a reduction in both the distance as well as time. Table 2.4 gives out that there is substantial saving ranging between 10% to over 30% over certain routes. The table gives out the distance between major ports, using the NWP, NEP, Suez, and Panama, depending on the origin/destination is depicted as under:-

A corollary to the reduced distances is found in the reduction of costs for transportation as well as a considerable reduction in the emission, thus the cost–benefit analysis does portray a rosy picture if the other issues like navigation, search, and rescue, tough climatic conditions, etc., are put aside.

NEP/NSR: The Northern Sea Route (NSR) connecting Eastern Asia with Northern Europe is an emerging concept lately, which brings new

---

[25] The Arctic Institute, accessed on 16 Nov 19 from https://www.thearcticinstitute.org/complexities-arctic-maritime-traffic/.

Table 2.4 Distances between places by various passages

Origin-destination	Panama	Northwest Passage	Northeast Passage	Suez and Malacca
London - Yokohama	23 300	*14 080*	13 841	21 200
Marseilles - Yokohama	24 030	16 720	*17 954*	*17 800*
Marseilles - Singapore	29 484	21 600	23 672	12 420
Marseilles - Shanghai	26 038	19 160	19 718	16 460
Rotterdam - Singapore	28 994	19 900	19 641	15 950
Rotterdam - Shanghai	25 588	*16 100*	15 793	19 550
Rotterdam - Yokohama	23 470	*13 950*	13 360	21 170
Hamburg - Seattle	17 110	*13 410*	12 770	29 780
Rotterdam - Vancouver	16 350	*14 330*	13 200	28 400
Rotterdam – Los Angeles	14 490	*15 120*	*15 552*	29 750
Gioia Tauro (Italy) - Hongkong	25 934	20 230	21 570	14 093
Gioia Tauro - Singapore	29 460	21 700	23 180	11 430
Barcelona - Hongkong	25 044	18 950	20 380	14 693
New York - Shanghai	20 880	17 030	19 893	22 930
New York - Hongkong	21 260	18 140	20 985	21 570
New York – Singapore	23 580	*19 540*	23 121	19 320
New Orleans - Singapore	*22 410*	*21 950*	25 770	21 360
Maracaibo Oil Terminal (Venezuela) - Hongkong	18 329	*19 530*	23 380	22 790

Source Emmanuel Guy, Frédéric Lasserre, Commercial shipping in the Arctic: new perspectives, challenges, and regulations

trading opportunities for the upcoming decades. One of the biggest interests of Russia in the Arctic is the promotion of NSR as a stable and secure route of shipping connecting Europe to Asia. NSR offers one third distance reduction for full transit from Eastern Asia to Northern Europe. China has offered its assistance to Russia in the development of the NSR by providing advanced marine technologies and fleet modernisation.

Significantly, China is one of the emerging superpower economies in the world. It is estimated that China will acquire or operate 1/4 of the global commercial maritime fleet by 2030 (Global Marine 2015). Henceforth, increasing demand in coal, oil, and natural gas is expected, followed by fleet increasing capacity for bulk carriers, tankers, and LNG carriers.[26] The NSR transit points on a map are as under (Map 2.6).

[26] Pham Thi and Miltiadis Aravopoulos, Feasibility Study on Commercial Shipping in the Northern Sea Route, 2019, Chalmers University of Technology, Sweden.

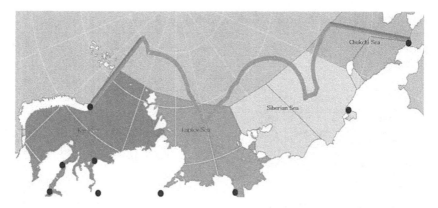

Map 2.6 Map showing NSR transit points (*Source* Pham Thi Bich Van, Miltiadis Aravopoulos, Feasibility Study on Commercial Shipping in the Northern Sea Route, p. 13)

The Northeast Passage is termed as Northern Sea Route by Russia and broadly follows the alignment along the Chukchi Sea, Siberian Sea, and Laptev Sea to the Kara Sea. The cost-efficiency potential of the NSR over the Suez Canal is 42%, enough to attract the industry players to make the required investments and Carbon Dioxide (CO_2) emission reduction up to 52%.[27] A peculiar feature of the NSR in the present times due to the thickness of the ice and shallow depths along the Russian coast opens up several permutations of navigation there is no fixed and static alignment of NSR. The various schemes of navigating the Russian coast by following various route are depicted in the map placed below. The Northeast Passage (NEP)—also called the Northern Sea Route (NSR) by Russia—follows the Siberian Arctic coast and crosses Russian Arctic straits between the mainland and Russian Arctic archipelagos: Novaya Zemlya, Severnaya Zemlya, the New Siberian Islands, and Wrangel Island.[28] As per the map below, there are at least eight key straits in the Russian Arctic and depending on the geophysical conditions a combination of routes can be

---

[27] Ibid.

[28] Lasserre, Arctic Shipping Routes from the Panama myth to reality, International Journal, vol. 66, issue 4, The Arctic is hot, part II (Autumn 2011), pp. 793–808, 2011 accessed from http://www.jstor.org/stable/23104393?seq=1&cid=pdf-reference#references_tab_contents.

adopted for shipping. The key straits in the route are depicted as under (Map 2.7).

In 2018, more than 18 million tons of goods were transported on NSR, an increase of almost 70% from 2017. As per estimates, the NSR will shorten the distance between North-East Asia to Europe by forty percent as compared to the Suez Canal route. A map depicting the NSR shipping traffic and vessels employed is as under (Map 2.8).

As a signatory to the UNCLOS, Russia is reaping the benefits of Article 234 of UNCLOS which permits it to monitor and control the movement of the vessels traversing the NSR as it lies in its EEZ. Presently, Russia levies icebreaker escort fees on vessel traversing the NSR and her control is unrestricted and absolute. In 2009, the fee was set to 40 USD per ton of container Cargo. This level of fees seems quite unrealistically high, and it is probably fair to conclude that fees are negotiable. However, in 2009, the Beluga ships paid only €60 000 in icebreaker fees, which clearly

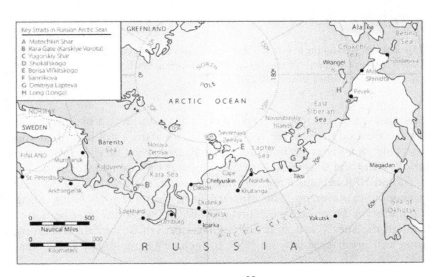

Map 2.7 Key straits in Russian Arctic Seas[29] (*Source* Gao Tianming & Vasilii Erokhin, Arctic yearbook 2019)

---

[29] Gao, T, & V. Erokhin, Arctic yearbook 2019, accessed on 23 Sep 19 from https://arcticyearbook.com/arctic-yearbook/2019.

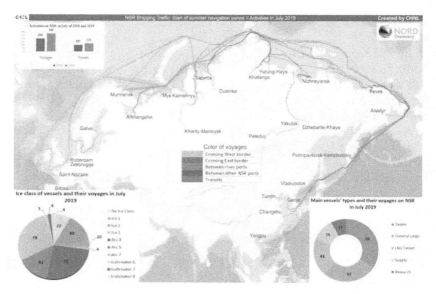

Map 2.8 NSR shipping traffic: Start of summer navigation/activities in July 2019[30] (*Source* https://Arctic-lio.com/nsr-shipping-traffic-start-of-summer-navigaton-period-activities-in-july-2019-2/)

show that icebreaker fees are negotiable.[31] Though there is opaqueness in Russian methodology of fee collection and the data is not published and accessible, yet there are indicators that Russia levies varying rates from various users and is open to lowering the rates on case to case basis.

Should NSR become a regular transit passage, there will be a great shift in geopolitical leverage. The itinerary from Rotterdam to Hong Kong is equidistant by either the Northern Sea Route or the Southern one through the Suez Canal, hence all regions north of Rotterdam and Hong Kong will profit greatly from NSR to include Japan, ROK, and China.

---

[30] Arctic Lio.com, accessed on 11 Oct 19 from https://Arctic-lio.com/nsr-shipping-traffic-start-of-summer-navigaton-period-activities-in-july-2019-2/.

[31] Arctis Knowledge Hub, Arctic Shipping Routes—Costs and Fees, 2019, accessed on 01 October 2019 from http://www.arctis-search.com/Arctic+Shipping+Routes+-+Costs+and+Fees.

Table 2.5 Number of transit voyages on NSR

Year	Number of transit voyages	Russian Flag	Others
2011	41	26	15
2012	48	18	28(7 states)
2013	71	46	25(11 states)
2014	31(crossed both boundaries) + 22 (crossed Western boundary)	25 + 22	6 + 0
2015	18	10	8
2016	19	7	12
2017	27	9	18
2018	27	8	19

Asia and Europe's most active and dynamic economies lie north of Hong Kong hence this becomes lucrative.

Though Russia and China stand to greatest advantage from the NSR shortcut, which roughly translates to saving of 5000 Km over the Suez route, yet the effect on East Asia, South East Asia as well as South Asia will be profound, too. China is not only eyeing the European markets for its exports but also hedging its risks by exploring options other than conventional southerly routes (notably, the Malaccan Straits) for energy transports. Also, because of potential traffic shifts, China's high-latitude shipping ports have an opportunity to become international shipping centres for East Asia.[32] Russia has claimed that the control of the movement of ships on its 200 NM EEZ in NSR is her responsibility. All vessels desirous of using NSR have to obtain permission from Russia before entering the area. Year-wise movement of ships on NSR for the year 2011 to 2018 as per data on NSR official website at https://Arctic-lio.com has been perused and is as under (Table 2.5).

The data on transit voyages for 2021 are as depicted below and show that there were 40 Eastward voyages and 31 Westward voyages (Map 2.9).

As per forecasts, the traffic of LPG will see the most growth on the NSR with time, and the traffic will quadruple within the next 15–20 years (Fig. 2.6).

A six-year international research programme, International Northern Sea Route Programme ran between June 1993 and March 1999 which

[32] Ibid.

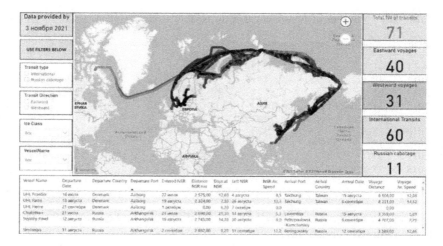

Map 2.9 Transit voyages on the NSR in 2021 (*Source* Arcticlio.com. Accessed at https://arctic-lio.com/transit-voyages-on-the-nsr-in-2021-the-results-as-of-the-current-date/)

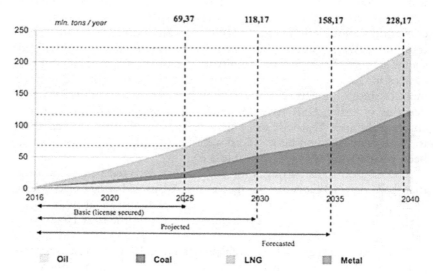

Fig. 2.6 Cargo forecast for NSR (*Source* Pham Thi Bich Van, Miltiadis Aravopoulos, Feasibility Study on Commercial Shipping in the Northern Sea Route, p. 15)

was designed to create a knowledge base about the ice-infested shipping lanes running along the coast of the Russian Arctic.[33] The partners for this project were Japan's Ship and Ocean Foundation and Russian Central Marine Research and Design Institute. The funding for the project was provided by Nippon Foundation/Ship & Ocean Foundation, Research Council of Norway, Norwegian Ministry of Foreign Affairs, Norwegian Regional Development Fund (SND), The Central and Eastern Europe Programme, The Norwegian Ministry of Industry and Trade, The Norwegian Ministry of the Environment, The Fridtjof Nansen Institute, Phillips Petroleum Company Norway, Norwegian Ship-owners Association, Norsk Hydro, Russian Federation, and Murmansk Shipping Company. The cooperation between Russia, Norway, and Japan is evident in this project.

North West Passage (NWP): The Northwest Passage is considered to be comprising of a variation of seven routes covering various straits between the Davis Strait/Lancaster Sound to the Bering Strait. Since most of these routes spanning between the Atlantic and Pacific oceans, on the Northern fringe all along the Canadian Arctic Archipelago, Canada also claims to exert territorial sovereignty over NWP. As compared to the NSR, NWP has greater geographical and ice induced limitations and remains severely restricted due to the ice conditions. Out of the seven possible routes, six of them start at Davis Strait and the seventh from Hudson Strait and the variations are as under[34] (Fig. 2.7).

The map depicting the variations and routes in the NWP is as under (Map 2.10).

Transpolar/Central Route: The trans-Arctic passage also called the transpolar route is not likely to be put into operation very soon due to thick ice cover. When put in operation, this route will entail a further reduction of around 20% on NSR and NWP. Since it is a future route that connects the Atlantic and Pacific oceans and it will traverse closest to the North Pole and centre of the Arctic Ocean. It is gauged at around 4000 Kms and is not a coastal route but a mid-ocean route. Since there

---

[33] Fridtjof Nansen Institute, INSROP accessed on 02 Jun 19 from https://www.fni.no/projects/international-northern-sea-route-programme-insrop.

[34] Scott Polar Research Institute, SPRI, 12 Dec 2019, accessed on 20 December 2019 from https://www.spri.cam.ac.uk/resources/infosheets/northwestpassage.pdf.

1: Davis Strait, Lancaster Sound, Barrow Strait, Viscount Melville Sound, McClure Strait, Beaufort Sea, Chukchi Sea, Bering Strait. *The shortest and deepest, but difficult and northernmost, way owing to the severe ice of McClure Strait. The route is preferred by submarines because of its depth.*

2: Davis Strait, Lancaster Sound, Barrow Strait, Viscount Melville Sound, Prince of Wales Strait, Amundsen Gulf, Beaufort Sea, Chukchi Sea, Bering Strait. *An easier variant of route 1 which may avoid severe ice in McClure Strait. It is suitable for deep draft vessels.*

3: Davis Strait, Lancaster Sound, Barrow Strait, Peel Sound, Franklin Strait, Victoria Strait, Coronation Gulf, Amundsen Gulf, Beaufort Sea, Chukchi Sea, Bering Strait. *The principal route; used by most larger vessels of draft less than 14 m.*

4: Davis Strait, Lancaster Sound, Barrow Strait, Peel Sound, Rae Strait, Simpson Strait, Coronation Gulf, Amundsen Gulf, Beaufort Sea, Chukchi Sea, Bering Strait. *A variant of route 3 for smaller vessels if ice from McClintock Channel has blocked Victoria Strait. Simpson Strait is only 6.4 m deep, it has shoals and complex currents.*

5: Davis Strait, Lancaster Sound, Prince Regent Inlet, Bellot Strait, Franklin Strait, Victoria Strait, Coronation Gulf, Amundsen Gulf, Beaufort Sea, Chukchi Sea, Bering Strait. *This route is dependent on ice in Bellot Strait which has complex currents. Mainly used by eastbound vessels.*

6: Davis Strait, Lancaster Sound, Prince Regent Inlet, Bellot Strait, Rae Strait, Simpson Strait, Coronation Gulf, Amundsen Gulf, Beaufort Sea, Chukchi Sea, Bering Strait. *A variant of route 5 for smaller vessels if ice from McClintock Channel has blocked Victoria Strait. Simpson Strait is only 6.4 m deep, complex currents run in it and in Bellot Strait.*

7: Hudson Strait, Foxe Basin, Fury and Hecla Strait, Bellot Strait, Franklin Strait, Victoria Strait, Coronation Gulf, Amundsen Gulf, Beaufort Sea, Chukchi Sea, Bering Strait. *A difficult route owing to severe ice usually at the west of Fury and Hecla Strait and the currents of Bellot Strait. Mainly used by eastbound vessels as an alternative is practicable.*

Fig. 2.7 Northwest passage transits (*Source* Scott Polar Research Institute, SPRI, 2019, https://www.spri.cam.ac.uk/resources/infosheets/northwest passage.pdf)

Map 2.10 North West Passage with its straits and variations[35] (*Source* Scott Polar Research Institute, SPRI, 2019, https://www.spri.cam.ac.uk/resources/infosheets/northwestpassage.pdf)

[35] Ibid.

are tremendous ice coverage and unpredictable weather conditions, navigation, emergency protocols, and SAR will entail greater costs and greater coordination for making it operational.

The greatest advantage the transpolar route offers over NSR and NWP is that lies and passes completely outside the territorial limits and EEZs of the coastal states and accordingly, it makes for a greater case of global commons for non-arctic and other countries. China had already crossed the route through its icebreaker in 2012.

Protection of Arctic Marine Environment (PAME)'s Arctic Ship Traffic Data (ASTD) project collects, maintains, and distributes accurate, reliable, and up-to-date information on shipping activities in the Arctic to arrive at true figures of shipping, pollution, and other effects of shipping and devise future strategy. The ASTD has been launched quite recently in February 2019. Since the framework of ASTD has been made under PAME, a permanent working group of the AC, there is implicit cooperation by the member states to share the data and its subsequent usage and dissemination. The Cooperative Agreement among the Arctic States Regarding Arctic Ship Traffic Data Sharing outlines access to ASTD and the use of its data.[36] There is also an ASTD Cooperative Agreement between the member nations about the sharing of data. As per SPRI data, there were 24 voyages made on NWP in the year 2019 till 12 Dec 2019. The data from PAME for the year 2018[37] is as under:-

(a) Total Number of ships in Arctic Polar Code area—1494
(b) Number of fishing vessels in Arctic Polar Code area—625
(c) Percentage of fishing vessels—42%
(d) Trend increase between 2013 and 2018—60%

PAME also takes out Arctic Marine Shipping Assessment (AMSA), Heavy Fuel Oil documents, and Arctic Ocean Review (AOR) and regional waste management documents to support its work for sustainable and environment-friendly shipping in the Arctic.

---

[36] PAME, Protection of Arctic marine environment, 2019, accessed on 11 November 2019 from https://pame.is/index.php/projects/Arctic-marine-shipping/astd.

[37] PAME, Hjalti Hreinsson, fishing vessels in the Arctic, 2019, accessed on 11 October from https://www.pame.is/index.php/document-library/shipping-documents/.

Maritime Boundaries and Agreements

The promulgation and acceptance of the UNCLOS and historical experience have demonstrated that maritime borders can be better solved by diplomacy and application of the principles and tenets of international law rather than by force or military action. History has confirmed that maritime borders have never been settled by the usage of force. Most notably, maritime boundaries have never been defined through force and conquest, but rather by the development and application of rules of international law that conceive of offshore rights as a derivative of rights on the land.[38] Unlike the Antarctic which is a landmass surrounded by Ocean, the Arctic Region has five coastal states, called the Arctic 5 which surround the Arctic Ocean. After the codification of customary international law, the UNCLOS (UN Convention on the Law of the Sea), and its ratification by all Arctic states less than the USA but having conveyed acceptance to the tenets of the same, the UNCLOS has become binding and enforceable. The UNCLOS has defined 3 key terms for exclusive exploitation by the members to include an area of 12 nautical miles from the coastline as the territorial sea. The members can also claim an area up to 200 Nautical Miles as EEZ Exclusive Economic Zone, wherein it exercises control over the water column as well as the sea bed. Another feature permitted the states to have inherent rights over resource exploitation on any adjoining continental shelf, a shallow area of ocean floor extending from the terrestrial landmass. Article 76 provides for cases where member states can claim areas exceeding 200 NM EEZ, based on evidence of extension of the natural landmass. The Russian claim on Lomonosov Ridge falls in this category. Numerous treaties on opposing or adjacent claims on Bay, straits, or common ocean areas have been finalised which are enumerated below. There have been some agreements between the Arctic states on the definition of boundaries, which are given below

(a) **1973 Canada–Denmark Boundary Treaty:** Based on the equidistance principle and has proved a sturdy base for a cooperative relationship. The only issue unsettled is that of Hans Island.

---

[38] ByersMichaelCam, Baker James, MaritimeBoundaries, InternationalLawAnd the Arctic, Cambridge University Press, 2013 accessed on 01 November 2019 at EBSCO Publishing: eBook Collection.

(b) **1990 Bering Sea Treaty:** The US had purchased Alaska from Russia on 30 Mar 1867 under a treaty for a sum of $ 7.2 Million. Since the end of World War II, there were differences between the USA and USSR in some areas lying between the nations. In 1990, a treaty for adjustment of 15,000 SQ NM was signed between the two nations. The agreement cedes to the United States jurisdiction over three areas previously claimed by the Soviets as under their control, while the Soviet Union gains jurisdiction over a smaller, previously unregulated area.[39] There were 'special areas' also designated to cite the accommodative nature of the treaty between the signatories (Map 2.11).

The Bering Strait, a narrow strip of 53-miles lies on a geo-strategically important portion of the Arctic Ocean and has repercussions on shipping along the Northern Sea Route or the Northwest Passage. Though after the conclusion of the treaty, the matter has not gained prominence but with increased shipping, its strategic value is going to rise.

(c) **Jan Mayen Treaties:** Geographically, though Jan Mayen is located closer to Greenland, yet there are claims of Norway and Iceland, too. In 2008, an agreement was reached between Iceland and Norway on continental shelf.[40] It is part of Norwegian territory and in Norway's nomenclature; both Svalbard and Jan Mayen are called 'SJ' territory. As per an agreement of 2008, Iceland and Norway have agreed on the aspect of the continental shelf which offers a fine example of reconciliation tactics between nations by successful dialogue. Another follow up agreement confirmed joint and cooperative hydrocarbon exploration, which can be taken as a model for the Canada-US dispute in the Beaufort Sea.

(d) **2006 Greenland–Svalbard Boundary Treaty:** This agreement settled the boundary between Greenland and Svalbard, Norway in 2006.

(e) **2010 Barents Sea Boundary Treaty:** The origin of the Barents dispute is in the year 1974 and had started with a dispute on three areas- Svalbard archipelago, Barents Sea, and Loophole. In 2010,

---

[39] UPI.com, accessed on 11 Sep 19 from https://www.upi.com/Archives/1990/06/02/Bering-Sea-boundary-agreement-signed/3221644299200/.

[40] Agla M Egilsdottir, 'Agreement between Iceland and Norway on the Continental Shelf Between Iceland and Jan Mayen', Reykjavik University, n.d., 82.

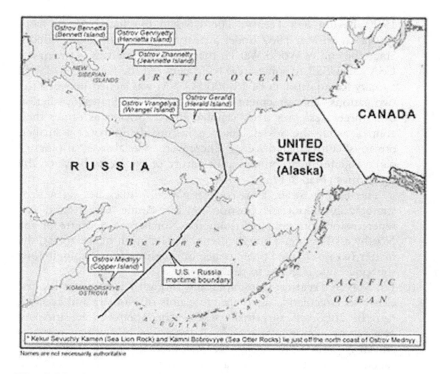

Map 2.11 Bering Sea and USA-Canada maritime boundary (*Source* https://en.wikipedia.org/wiki/USSR%E2%80%93USA_Maritime_Boundary_Agreement)

Russia and Norway have signed the Norwegian Russia Barents Sea Agreement in this regard. This area is a prime location for fishing, oil, and gas. The prominent hydrocarbon fields located in the vicinity of the Barents Sea include the Snøhvit gas field, (193 BCM), the Goliat oil field has estimated (174 Mn barrels) and Shtokman field which is rich in both natural gas and natural gas condensates. The Goliat oil field has estimated recoverable reserves of 174 million barrels. On the Russian side of the Barents Sea, the massive Shtokman gas field has an estimated 3.8 trillion cubic meters of natural gas and 37 million tons of natural gas condensates.[41]

It is a landmark treaty that took over four decades of negotiations and on the conclusion, has paved the way for greater understanding and diffusion of tensions. Another rewarding feature of the Barents treaty is that the continental shelves and EEZ and all ambiguities are removed.

Despite the members on differing tables of world order, they behaved with maturity and prevented escalation despite numerous differences. The grey zone agreement was abused by Iceland for excessive fishing and was later incorporated into loophole agreements. Finally, this agreement was signed in 2010 and is a landmark for others to emulate. The agreement also is trailblazing in that it was agreed bilaterally without the need for any dispute settlement bodies. The agreement signed in 2010 also re-emphasised that the Arctic coastal nations are adhering to international law and further reinforcing the contention of the Arctic coastal states of the 2008 Ilulissat Declaration that they have the shared responsibility on Arctic affairs.

(f) **Lincoln Sea:** The contention on the area of Lincoln Sea is between Canada and Denmark and was settled based on equidistance principal. There were two issues of contention between Canada and Denmark, and the issue of Lincoln Sea was resolved in 2012 leaving the issue of Hans Island as the pending issue.

(g) **The curious case of Svalbard:** Spitsbergen was the name, used for the 1920 treaty between various parties including India, then as a dominion for the UK. Its modern name is Svalbard with Spitsbergen being the largest island located there. In the nineteenth century, Svalbard was widely considered to be terra nullius and therefore open to all.[42] As per the 1920 treaty, accepted by 40 countries, including India, the Norwegian sovereignty was accepted. Svalbard offers a unique mechanism wherein the contracting parties reserve the right, to economic activity/ settlement on the island and that's how Russia has economic access and operates a coalmine at Barentsburg. Svalbard

---

[41] ByersMichael, Supra note 38.
[42] Ibid.

is also the preferred choice in the high-latitude research sites for better accessibility as well as climatic reasons. The 1920 Treaty has granted Norway conditional sovereignty over Spitsbergen/Svalbard's islands creating a curious case in political, scientific, and legal terms. The principle of freedom of scientific research and the principle of non-discrimination in conducting scientific pursuits apply to the signatories to the treaty. These principles have been fully respected by Arctic countries in furthering the domain of scientific knowledge within the realm of cooperation. Svalbard is one region that is demilitarised. There are currently 42 signatories to the Spitsbergen Treaty. Article 3 of the treaty prevents the exercise of sovereign powers and territorial claims over the archipelago, yet at least one Indian scholar has hinted that India may press for such rights![43] The research station of Ny-Ålesund is the northernmost settlement in the world and along with India's Himadri station; it has stations of Britain, Germany, France, Italy, China, Netherlands, Norway, South Korea, and others. Svalbard offers a unique example of shared sovereignty for emulating those principles to settle other terrestrial disputes. The Svalbard Treaty of 1920 had empowered Norway over territorial rights and extended "equal liberty of access and entry for any reason or object whatever" for nationals of all signatories. Due to this clause, China and India, as original signatories are maintaining permanent research stations at Svalbard since 2004 and 2008 respectively. A lingering question and reason for contention is that countries like Russia have been demanding that the terrestrial rights of equal treatment also applied to the coastal zones. This demand is made to obtain legal rights on the offshore oil and gas finds, to which Norway is contesting citing that the treaty covers only the land and no rights whatsoever accrue in the maritime zone.

---

[43] Prakash Arun (Adm), National Maritime Foundation, The Arctic Gold Rush: a poisoned chalice, accessed on 01 November 2019 from http://www.maritimeindia.org/View.aspx?id=1251.

Policy/ Policy Documents by Stakeholders

(a) **UK**: The UK is among the first of the observers' states to the AC and it was granted the status in 1998. It is among the first four original non-Arctic state Observers for the Arctic Council and was present during the Council's establishment. Though the UK is not an Arctic state, yet it's a geographic location in the Atlantic at the mouth of the GIUK gap which leads into the Arctic ocean as also its historical connections with Arctic fishing, exploration and friendly ties with NATO and other allies has prompted it to proactively publish two Arctic Policy Frameworks, outlining its plans to engage cooperatively with the Arctic states and other stakeholders in the region. UK's PRD (Polar Regions Department) represents the UK at the AC. The PRD conducts and organises diverse and cross-sectional discussions, incorporating the views of several departments to obtain a broad understanding. The UK also has been a hub of commercial hub including insurance, logistics, and financial services for consignments to the Arctic region. The UK continues to stress that "the change in the natural environment in the Arctic and High North is driving a change in the security environment and, as the region becomes more accessible, there has been an increase in military activity."[44]

Though the UK has been battling growing anxiety on its decision to exit the EU in 2016 and is concerned with the security dimension of the 'High North.' As per a 2018 UK's Department of Defence publication, the centrality of the UK's security is tied to the Arctic and the High North. The UK is dependent on Norway to supply it with natural gas to fulfil its demand. The issues missing or lacking in the UK's domain are merely SAR and infrastructural development and it is actively engaged in all other spheres. UK is dependent on Norway for most of its energy requirements and in wake of growing instances of USA's scepticism of Russia and Chinese ingress in the Arctic, and development of Arctic region by extensive mapping and advent of new knowledge and communications, the focus in the UK is on ensuring strengthened structures, in place. As an observer in the AC, UK has been stressing on adherence to international law including the UNCLOS, and recognises the sovereignty of the Arctic states. The first UK strategy was released in 2013.

---

[44] Duncan Depledge, Caroline Kennedy-Pipe, and James Rogers, 'The UK and the Arctic: Forward Defence', Arctic yearbook 2019, 2019, accessed on 01 December 2019 from https://Arcticyearbook.com/.

There are growing calls in Scotland with its expressions of Scottish 'Arctic-ness' since there are identity narratives that separate Scotland from the rest of the UK. UK's policy document is termed as 'Beyond the Ice' and was released, duly revised in April 2018.[45] The UK despite not being an Arctic state, has earmarked a Minister looking after the Polar Regions, too. The UK Arctic Research Station was established in 1991 in Ny-Ålesund, Spitsbergen, Svalbard, and the Kingdom of Norway. It sits as one of fourteen internationally operated stations that form part of this unique northernmost research community (Map 2.12).[46]

(b) USA: The USA has been an Arctic nation with important interests in the region since the purchase of Alaska from Russia in 1867. It was during the Clinton administration that the first Arctic Policy was released by the USA in 1994, however, an increased and rejuvenated focus was shown post the 09/11 attacks wherein the USA started to look for homeland security in a big way. As per its Arctic strategy of 2013, 'It wants to use an integrated Arctic natural resources management to balance economic development, environmental protection, and the cultural values of the indigenous population while increasing the understanding of the Arctic through increased scientific research and traditional knowledge.[47]

In the year 2019, the US has made pointed remarks citing its anxiety over an increasingly assertive China in the Arctic region. The US has in its Department of Defence June 2019 Arctic Strategy has warned that the predatory behaviour of the Chinese witnessed elsewhere will be demonstrated by her in the Arctic and there is a need to be wary of such strategies. In the year 2019, President Trump had made a tweet, reigniting the talk of purchase of Greenland which later drew criticism and rebuff by the Greenlandic Ministers. The USA also announced that it will re-open its diplomatic office in Greenland, which is logical fallout of the growing threats of emerging great power competition in the region. As a corollary to the US department of defence and government's Arctic strategy, the US Coast Guards (USCG) in its 2019 report' Arctic Strategic Outlook' had also listed the goals of the USCG to partner and with its allies and other stakeholders having Arctic interests to keep the Arctic as

---

[45] Arctic office, 2018, accessed on 12 November 2019 from https://www.Arctic.ac.uk/news/new-government-Arctic-policy-document-launched/.

[46] Ibid.

[47] US Department of Defence, "Arctic strategy 2013," http://www.defence.gov/Portals/1/documents/pubs/2013_Arctic_strategy.pdf. accessed on August 1, 2018, p. 2.

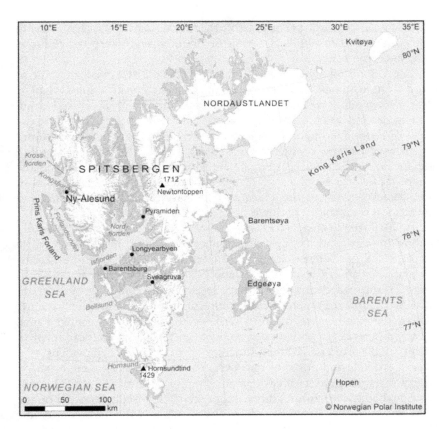

Map 2.12 Svalbard Islands and adjoining seas (*Source* Arctic office, www.arctic.ac.uk)

a conflict-free zone. The first US Arctic strategy came under the Clinton administration in 1994, but it was after September 11, 2001, that the real attention towards homeland security came on the table, including the Arctic region.[48] A new report from the US Coast Guard called "Arctic Strategic Outlook," which was released in April 2019, reveals that the

---

[48] Maria Ackrén, 'From Bilateral to Trilateral Agreement: The Case of Thule Air Base', 2019, Arctic yearbook 2019, accessed on 02 November 2019 from https://Arcticyearbook.com/.

US Coast Guard will partner with other Arctic nations, as well as with allies and other stakeholders having Arctic interests to keep the Arctic as a conflict-free zone.[49]

The US, becoming alive to the growing Chinese ventures had a role to play in the withdrawal of China Communication Construction Company Ltd from bidding from the construction of airports in Greenland citing visa issues and work permits problems. The USA is presenting alternatives of economic opportunities to the smaller Arctic states as a counter to growing Chinese economic clout. The recent US Arctic defence policy describes the region as a 'strategic corridor' connecting Europe and the Indo-Pacific region. Since both, the regions occupy a high pedestal in the defence policy of the USA, and accordingly, the Arctic's role and dimension is enhanced multiple times.

In 2019, the Pentagon had also commented on the Chinese expanding submarine fleet and its likely deployment destination in the Arctic. The department of Defence strategy had used the term for unveiling its strategy "in an era of strategic competition." In October 2019, President Trump had clearly stated that the increasing forays by outsiders in the Arctic are not wanted, clearly directing his focus on the Chinese. These statements were made in October 2019 and had named China clearly as a strategic great-power competitor. In 2018, American involvement in the exercise Trident Juncture witnessed the deployment of a carrier strike group north of the Arctic Circle for the first time in nearly thirty years which in itself conveys the shifting dynamics of NATO cooperation because of future threat scenarios. The Arctic Strategy of the US recognises the rights of indigenous people and emphasises scientific cooperation. The US is also alive to cooperation based on international institutions and international law.

The most recent Arctic defence policies by the US government along with its departments clearly characterise the Arctic as a 'strategic corridor' connecting Europe and the Indo- Pacific region. The renaming of the Asia Pacific to Indo Pacific was made by the USA to restrict and curb the Chinese influence and the Indo Pacific and Europe make for the pivotal points of US foreign policy. The US policies advocate that its policies have to Advance United States Security Interests, Pursue Responsible Arctic Region Stewardship and Strengthen International Cooperation in

---

[49] Ibid.

the affairs of the Arctic. US is more concerned about Russian claims of NSR being its internal waters and thus there is contention between the USA calling it an international waterway. On the issue of NWP, in the year 2019, US Secretary of state, Mike Pompeo had called Canada's claims on NWP as illegitimate, which was considered to be alarmist and militarist by certain quarters. Though there has been a 1988 Arctic Cooperation agreement between the two countries, the undercurrents do point to a simmering discontent. Though the USA claims that NWP is an international waterway yet Canada claims territorial sovereignty over it. The US has 3 polar icebreakers out of which one, Polar Sea is non-functional and the other two icebreakers—Polar Star and Polar Sea—have exceeded their intended 30-year service lives. The US Arctic Research and Policy Act (ARPA) of 1984 provides a comprehensive national policy dealing with national research needs and objectives in the Arctic. The most recent Arctic defence policy characterises the Arctic as a 'strategic corridor' connecting Europe and the Indo- Pacific region, the two main foreign defence foci of Washington, in which the growing power projection and influence by Russia and China must be balanced against to uphold the 'rules-based order' in conjunction with its Arctic allies, including within the confines of NATO.[50]

US is more concerned about Russian claims of NSR being its internal waters and thus there is contention between the USA calling it an international waterway. On the issue of NWP, it underlines that, under International law, a strait must meet a geographical and a functional requirement to be considered international. The geographical requirement is that it must be a water corridor between adjacent landmasses that links two bodies of the high seas or other waters. The functional requirement is that it be used as a route for international maritime traffic. "If a strait meets these two requirements and is thus international in the legal sense, foreign states have navigation rights, or right of transit, through the strait—which means that they do not have to request permission to navigate through it."[51]

---

[50] Jason S FN OSD OUSD policy (as) Hall, '2019-DOD-Arctic-Strategy', Office of the Under Secretary of Defence for Policy, June 2019, accessed on 21 October 2019 from https://media.defence.gov/2019/Jun/06/2002141657/-1/-1/1/2019-DOD-ARCTIC-STRATEGY.PDF.

[51] The Arctic: Canada's legal claims, (Ottawa, 24 October 2008), the Parliament of Canada, the Parliamentary Information And Research Service, Publication PRB 08-05E,

The major US Policy documents on the Arctic are January 2009 Arctic Policy Directive (NSPD 66/HSPD 25), May 2013 National Strategy for Arctic Region, January 2014 Implementation Plan for National Strategy for Arctic Region, January 2015 Executive Order for Enhancing Coordination of Arctic Efforts, December 2017 National Security Strategy Document, and US Special Representative for the Arctic (Vacant Since January 2017).

(c) **Germany:** The German Arctic strategy with the theme 'Assume responsibility, seize opportunity' and named *Leitlinien Deutscher Arktispolitik: Verantwortung übernehmen, Chancen Nutzen* (*Guidelines of the German Arctic policy*) was released in 2013. It published a revised and updated document in 2019. Germany was accorded observer status since 1998 and has placed its Arctic strategy at the centre of its foreign policy. Germany is an international actor in the High North and is committed to a high profile in polar research. Its icebreaker ship 'Polarstern is being used in ongoing MOSAiC expedition. Germany has remained vocal about having strong political engagement and economic connections with the Arctic. Germany is also a signatory of the 1920 Spitsbergen Treaty and has permanent observer status on the Arctic Council. As a major industrial and exporting nation, Germany looks at issues relating to shipping and energy and mineral to fuel her demand from the Arctic.

Broadly, Germany has voiced its stand on freedom of navigation through the Arctic and NWP and NEP/NSR to be considered as international straits. It has also emphasised that bilateral and multilateral mechanisms be utilised to address security in the region. Germany conducts scientific research under the umbrella of its Alfred-Wegener-Institute and maintains a joint research centre with France at Svalbard. Germany has been vocal in the Arctic issues, both as a major export source looking to leverage the shorter sea passages for transportation of its goods as also to understand the changing ocean currents which are impacting weather patterns in Northern Europe including Germany. The Arctic nations of Norway and Russia are also important for Germany as they supply the energy requirements thereof. Germany also aspires to fulfil its role as a technology supplier for hydrocarbon extraction, shipping, and offshore structures for frigid conditions. Germany possesses the world's third-largest merchant fleet and largest fleet of cargo ships and professes to

p. 3, http://www.parl.gc.ca/content/lop/researchpublications/prb0805-e.pdf. [accessed: 03 February 2014].

safe shipping and preservation of the environment. Germany in its 2013 policy had red-flagged that changing Arctic may bring about changes in security and politics, which turned out to be true with the 2017 Russian nationalisation of NSR. As a key NATO member, Germany views any potential security.

Germany is committed to scientific research, cooperation, and also bilateral agreements. Germany is striving for binding regulations for environmental protection and Arctic security. Germany offers its scientific expertise and outstanding experience in polar research to support peaceful and sustainable development.[52] The undefined and unelaborated German support on indigenous self-determination may be linked to the German opposition to Canada's NORDREG system, making it mandatory for ships passing through Canada's Arctic. In oblique terms, Germany has tried to question Canada's claim to sovereignty over NWP.

(d) EU Arctic Policy: The EU itself is a very complex governance entity and for it to devise a policy for the Arctic, a multinational heterogeneous organisation demands a well thought out policy. The European Commission is a full member of the Barents Euro-Arctic Council and also acts as an observer in the AC (without being a full observer) and its representatives are active in several of the Arctic Council's working groups, including the CAFF and PAME. Among the observers in the AC, the European Union (EU) is recognised as the de facto Observer of the Arctic Council.[53]

EU has close geographical vicinity to the European Arctic, making it the main destination for resources. The importance of Arctic is going to increase manifold in the future for the EU, considering the rapidly depleting ice cover and technological advances in sustainable exploitation. The flow of pollutants from the EU to the Arctic due to ocean currents and wind also makes a huge imprint on the latter. EU thus becomes one of the actors shaping the Arctic landscape and realities. Registration, Evaluation, Authorisation, and Restriction of Chemicals (REACH) and Persistent Organic Pollutants (POPS) regulation on the issue of pollution have been implemented by the EU. As for Arctic nations, Finland

---

[52] Vincent-Gregor Schulze, Arctic_Strategies roundup 2017, accessed on 10 November 2019 from http://www.Arctic-office.de/en/in-focus/Arctic-strategies-round-up/.

[53] Nord Douglas C, Leadership for the North, The Influence and Impact of Arctic Council Chairs, Springer Polar Sciences, p. 54, International Centre for Climate, University of Leeds, UK.

and Sweden are EU members, and Iceland and Norway are covered under EEA (European Economic Area). Given the emerging strategic and economic importance of the Arctic, an EU Arctic policy was first developed in 2008, calling for a united EU policy on the Arctic. The 2016 Joint Communication on the EU Arctic policy is built around three main policy objectives:

1. The promotion of the sustainable use of the resources;
2. The protection and preservation of the Arctic in unison with its population;
3. International cooperation.[54]

As a major and responsible consumer of energy, the EU is looking at all angles, i.e. environmental, political/governance, social, and economic to mitigate the adversarial consequences. Though EU is not yet an observer state given Canada's reservations on the grant of observer status to EU, following disconnect on seal hunting, and prompting the AC to bring out guidelines on the admission of Observers after the Kiruna Ministerial Meeting. The indigenous representatives were also opposed to giving observer status to the EU as they mainly want to assert their traditional rights to hunt seals, small whales, and polar bears and objected to the EU's ban on seal products. However, the Arctic Council receive[d] the application of the EU for Observer status affirmatively, but deferred a final decision and pending such decision, EU has been permitted to observe Council proceedings.

The EU has launched it's INTERACT (International Network for Terrestrial Research and Monitoring in the Arctic) project in the Arctic, with the UK's research facility as its partner. INTERACT is a network of 83 terrestrial field bases in northern Europe, Russia, the US, Canada, Iceland, Greenland, the Faroe Islands, and Scotland as well as stations in northern alpine areas. An analysis of the EU Arctic policy demonstrates that the foundation of the EU Arctic policy—the sustainable development of natural resources—remains important in the region and sits alongside the development, utilisation, and safety of the marine shipping capacity of

---

[54] Tina Hunter, 'Russian Arctic Policy, Petroleum Resources Development, and the EU: Cooperation or Coming Confrontation?', in *The European Union and the Arctic*, ed. Nengye Liu, Elizabeth A. Kirk, and Tore Henriksen (Brill | Nijhoff, 2017), https://doi.org/10.1163/9789004349179_008.

the region. The EU seeks to undertake such development and utilisation within a framework of international cooperation.[55]

(e) **Japan:** Japan became an Arctic observer in 2013 along with India, China, and other Asian countries. Its main interests like China is on the development of shipping since the opening of NSR will also lead to time and cost savings for her on energy imports. Its companies are investing in technological projects and carry out scientific cooperation. Japan also emphasises its efforts in the field of environmental protection and sustainable development. The government provides national funding to enhance Arctic research at universities and other institutions.[56]

Its policy was released in 2015. Japan is having a close partnership with Russia and the US. Japan vows to contribute to the international community through its action to Arctic issues like make full use of Japan's strength in science and technology from a global viewpoint, full consideration to the Arctic environment and ecosystem, ensure the rule of law, and promote international cooperation in a peaceful and orderly manner, and so on. Tonami and Watters described the Japanese Arctic policy as a "sum of many Parts."[57]

(f) **Russia:** Former USSR statesman, Mikhail Gorbachev is credited for his 1987 speech at Murmansk calling the Arctic as a 'zone of peace.' This had later led to the broadening and formulation of the concept of Arctic exceptionalism. This concept premised that the Arctic is insulated from the other international affairs and is thus not adversely impacted by the great power pressures due to existing cooperative structures in the Arctic.

The Russian Arctic contains major population centres unlike the other Arctic states, for example, Arkhangelsk has a population of 350,000. Russia has a sizeable portion of the Arctic coastline and considering its strategic dimension; Russian Northern Fleet is based near Murmansk, and contains a massive portion of Russia's nuclear submarine fleet. The Northern fleet, one of Russian four fleets, is the strongest one and possesses about two-thirds of Russia's total maritime strength. The Arctic Ocean provides a strategic gateway that allows its Navy to reach the

---

[55] Ibid.

[56] Vincent-Gregor Schulze, Arctic_Strategies roundup 2017, accessed on 10 November 2019 from http://www.Arctic-office.de/en/in-focus/Arctic-strategies-round-up/.

[57] A Tonami, Watters Japan's Arctic policy: a sum of many parts, accessed on 01 August 2019 from https://Arcticyearbook.com/images/yearbook/2012/Scholarly_Papers/4.Tonami_and_Watters.pdf.

northern Atlantic and deters the Western/ NATO misadventures. Russia owns the largest icebreaker fleet in the world. Russia had enunciated its policy vide 2001 Maritime Doctrine of the Russian Federation 2020. This document reasserts the sovereignty of the Russian Federation in its internal waters and claims rights over the EEZ and continental shelf. This policy also draws out the National Marine Policy (NMP) related to the development of petroleum resources. Russia had enunciated its policy vide 2001 Maritime Doctrine of the Russian Federation 2020. This document reasserts the sovereignty of the Russian Federation in its internal waters and claims rights over the EEZ and continental shelf. This policy also draws out the National Marine Policy (NMP) related to the development of petroleum resources. These include:

- The preservation of the sovereignty of inland waters, the Territorial Sea, and the airspace and subsoil of these areas,
- Protection of sovereign rights on EEZ and Continental Shelf (CS) for the development of natural resources, including the construction and operation of artificial islands, installations, and other structures, and.
- Protection of the Russian Federation with the marine areas, protection of national borders, including sea and air space.[58]

This 2001 policy was re-energised by the 2015 Russian Marine Doctrine which emphasises the issues of shipping, shipbuilding, and icebreakers. In 2016 Foreign Policy Concept was unveiled by Russia. In recent policy documents, Russia has emphasised the significance of the NSR both as a transit for Europe-Asia as well as its main transport route in the Arctic.

Russia has committed and pledged the respect of the international laws that govern the seas. The issue of NSR too figures in Russian plans since the 1930s and is not an aggressive and novel concept to impose hegemony. Certainly, there is a focus on military activity and increased personnel in the Arctic, especially around the Kola Peninsula and Murmansk, but Russia is re-vitalising its old structures in line with changing situations. Russia is endowed with the greatest resources in the

---

[58] Article 1: General Provisions, Vladimir Putin, 'Maritime Doctrine of Russian Federation.

2020' (2001) 1 http://www.oceanlaw.org/downloads/Arctic/Russian_Maritime_Policy_2020.pdf. accessed 30 Nov 2019.

Arctic and engagement with it will chart out future courses of cooperation and economic growth. The 2017 Russian doctrine emphasised the threats to its interests in the Arctic, showing scepticism of the western nations and its necessity to preserve its national interests. However Russia (then USSR) was maintaining large assets in the Arctic before its disintegration and even with the large scale militarisation, it is yet to reach scales of that era. Russia is seeking cooperation with other Arctic countries and the Arctic Council. With an eye on the development of NSR and the generation of revenue from it, Russia is investing in infrastructure, navigation, and state-of-the-art monitoring. Russia has also elaborated that the use of the Northern Sea route as a national integrated transportation system of the Russian Federation in the Arctic in many documents.

(g) Canada: In September 2019, Canada released the Arctic and Northern Policy Framework which provides overarching direction to the Government of Canada's priorities, activities, and investments in the Arctic to 2030 and beyond. Co-developed with Northerners, territorial and provincial governments, First Nations, Inuit, and Métis People, it replaces Canada's 2009 Northern Strategy and 2010 Statement on Canada's Arctic Foreign Policy.[59]

Canada had issued its 2009 Northern Strategy and 2010 Arctic Foreign Policy. These documents have been reinvigorated with its recent, September 2019, Arctic, and Northern Policy Framework.

The Canadian government has taken a broad view up to the next ten years or so, up to 2030, and has incorporated the views of its Northern populations and local and provincial governments in charting out its policy. Canada is committing itself to work under the framework of international law and work in a cooperative model with Arctic states. The exception to this is Hans Island, located between Canada and Greenland and Beaufort Sea between Canada and the USA. Canada is also claiming exclusive rights over NWP North West Passage since these are "internal waters" subject to its full jurisdiction and control. Canada supports AC diplomacy and cooperation between the Arctic8. Canada is looking at the socio-economic development of its local population and develops its military and SAR capabilities.

---

[59] Government of Canada, "Canada's Arctic Foreign Policy," http://international.gc.ca/world-monde/international_relations-relations_internationales/Arctic-arctique/Arctic_policycanada-politique_arctique.aspx?lang=eng, accessed on August 1, 2018).

Canada is striving for the development of its vibrant Northern communities and the Arctic is fundamental to its national identity. Canada has invested in berthing and refuelling facility in Nanisivik. The Canadian Rangers, who are drawn primarily from indigenous communities, are being expanded. Canada is also investing significantly in mapping the energy and mineral potential of the north.[60]

Canada has gained restraint and maturity vis-a-vis its PM Harper's statement of 29 August 2014 "an emboldened Russia is a threat to its neighbours in the Arctic, and Canada must be ready to respond to any Russian incursions in the region" and is focussing on the cooperative and collaborative mechanism, in line with the Arctic exceptionalism and understanding the merits of a cooperative mechanism over the competition.

(h) Denmark: Denmark's strategy was released in 2011 for the period 2011–2020 and it encompasses Denmark, Greenland, and the Faroe Islands. The Kingdom of Denmark has a peculiar case with independent nations, Greenland and the Faroe Islands.

The judicious and profitable use of resources is the priority. In the case of Greenland, it is the mining and oil-and-gas sector, for the Faroe Islands it is fishing. Denmark is also striving to promote the codification of Polar Law and supports the option of binding decision-making by the Arctic Council. However, Danish sovereignty is underlined by increasing military presence. The armed forces play an important role in the provision of a range of more civilian-related duties. For Greenland and the Faroe Islands, tourism, and the cruise industry, in particular, is of increasing importance. Renewable energies are perceived as an Arctic resource and their expansion is being pursued in all parts of the Danish Realm.[61]

The vision is to exploit the mineral resources in the Arctic under the best international practices and in continued close cooperation with the relevant authorities of the Danish realm and international partners.[62]

(i) Finland: Finland's strategy was released in 2013. Finland has handed over the AC Chairmanship in 2019 to Iceland. It has no direct

---

[60] Ibid.

[61] Vincent-Gregor Schulze, Arctic_Strategies roundup 2017, accessed on 10 November 2019 from http://www.Arctic-office.de/en/in-focus/Arctic-strategies-round-up/.

[62] Kingdom of Denmark, Greenland and the Faroe Islands: "Kingdom of Denmark Strategy for the Arctic 2011–2020," accessed on 01 November 2019 from http://library.Arcticportal.org/1890/1/DENMARK.pdf.

access to the Arctic Ocean but is seeking to cooperate with Japan and Russia on the technology front. The expertise in technology and digitalisation has ensured that some major data servers are already located in Finland. Being an EU member, it supports the EU candidature for an observer in AC and invests in forestry and renewable energies. Finland sees the European Union (EU) as a key factor in the Arctic region and supports efforts to consolidate the EU's Arctic policy.

Finland is also committed to issues of climate change mitigation and energy solutions, along with and digital services and functional data transfer. The 2019 agreement between MegaFon and Cinia is in this direction.

(j) **Iceland:** Iceland has assumed the chairmanship of AC in 2019. There have been implied overtures on the security architecture in the AC under Iceland's chair. It supports closer SAR cooperation and demilitarisation of the region. It had taken out a parliament resolution on Arctic affairs. As the smallest Arctic country, it is primarily focussed on fishing and tourism.

As the smallest Arctic country, Iceland pursues the agenda of security and economic development. Iceland's Parliament had adopted the resolution on Iceland's Arctic Policy in 2011 in which the strengthening of the multilateral intergovernmental forum of AC was stressed. It has also contributed to the preservation of the unique culture and way of life of indigenous peoples that have developed in the Arctic region.[63]

In September 2019 during the Arctic Circle meeting, Iceland's PM Katrin Jakobsdottir had raised the issue of discussing security issues under the ambit of the AC in her opening speech. She also left open for discussion whether AC is an appropriate forum for the same or is there a need to have a separate forum for the same. Though the statement was downplayed by the others in the AC, yet it conveys that geopolitical pressures are beginning to be felt and the indictors are already troubling the member states.

(k) **Norway:** Norway which had a strained border with Russia was sceptical of Russia, however, there has been some thaw lately. After the signing of the 2010 Barents Sea agreement with Russia, it released

---

[63] Ministry of foreign affairs of Iceland, "a Parliamentary resolution on Iceland's Arctic Policy (approved by althingi at the 139th legislative session March 28, 2011)," https://www.mfa.is/media/nordurlandaskrifstofa/a-Parliamentary-resolution-on-Ice-Arctic-Policy-approvedby-althingi.pdf. accessed on August 1, 2018.

its Arctic policy in 2014. For Norway, the hydrocarbon exploitation in the Barents Sea, and fishing and tourism are of great importance. It is promoting the development of innovative technologies and businesses and forging close cooperation with all including Russia. Norway exports its oil to Germany and the oil and gas industry is the largest contributor to its economy, and thus provides opportunities for increased employment and economic growth in northern Norway. It has also declared that the Arctic is the most important foreign policy objective.

Norway brings in US Marines on a rotational basis, to prepare for a potential skirmish with Russia, though there is a commitment to Russia not to station foreign troops on its territory unless faced with a threat. Norway had led the working group in the UN maritime organisation (IMO) on the work on Polar code. Norway draws guidance from its 2007 Soria Moria Declaration, to strengthen the Norwegian defence presence in the region.

(1) **Sweden:** Like Finland, Sweden also does not have direct access to the Arctic Ocean. It had released its Arctic strategy in 2011. To make up for the lack of a coastline bordering the Arctic Ocean, it is offering support services, scientific research, and public information to enhance its role in Arctic affairs. The development of research, academic innovations, mining, forestry, and tourism is being undertaken. It also focusses on Lapland development. Sweden views that the risks emanating from climate change will demand that preparations commensurate to the desired response is essential to protect humankind, economies, and human health and the future security risks will be considered in the light of climate change.

Thus like the common Arctic states' philosophy on climate change, Sweden has committed to promoting sustainable development in the entire Arctic region. Since security for Sweden is viewed from climate change prism, it is focussing on the economic and social development of its human capital for a better future. As a result of climate change, security may well become more a question of public crisis management in extreme weather situations; and adaptation to the changed climatic conditions to protect human life, health, and the economy.[64]

---

[64] Ministry of foreign affairs, the government of Sweden, "Sweden's strategy for the Arctic region," http://www.openaid.se/wp-content/uploads/2014/04/swedens-strategy-for-the-Arcticregion.pdf. accessed on August 1, 2018, p. 15.

(m) **Republic of Korea/ROK:** ROK was also granted observer status along with India in 2013 and it issued its Arctic policy in 2013 itself. The development of Arctic shipping and related industries is of paramount importance to the Republic of Korea and hence it had conducted the 7th Arctic shipping Seminar in Korea on 13 Dec 2018. Maersk also conducted its trial in 2018 which was discussed in that seminar.

Korea also conducted Arctic Partnership Week from 09 to 13 Dec 2019 at Busan BEXCO. One of these special sessions includes the Arctic Business Dialogue, co-organised by the Embassy of Denmark to Korea and the AEC. This event will gather an invited group of business representatives to discuss challenges and opportunities related to the Arctic business.[65] Korea invests in the development of marine technology, Arctic policy, science, technology, shipping, energy and resources, and other issues. Consequently, there are common policy interests of non-Arctic States, relating above all to freedom of navigation as well as the necessity of Polar research, but also peace and security in the region and the fight against global warming.[66]

(n) **Singapore:** Singapore has its observer status to the Arctic Council since 2013 and its place in the current maritime trade and commerce is very important. It has technical expertise in the areas of shipbuilding, port management, and SAR infrastructure and depends on global shipping through it. It has a keen interest in the effects of climate change in the Arctic and therefore supports climate research in the working groups of the Arctic Council.

(o) **Spain:** Spain has its observer status to the Arctic Council since 2006 and issued its strategy in 2016. It emphasises the position of opening sea routes which have an impact on its energy security, too. Its companies like the Chinese are also investing in Arctic ports to secure a long term plan and strategy for energy security. Spain has historical links to the Arctic, in the areas of seafaring, fishing, trade, and so on.

(p) **Switzerland:** Switzerland is the latest observer to the Arctic Council and was made an observer in 2017. Its policy document is titled Swiss Polar Research Pioneering Spirit, Passion, and Excellence issued in

---

[65] Arctic Economic Council, 2019, accessed on 01 November 2019 from https://Arcticeconomiccouncil.com/2018-Arctic-partnership-week-to-be-held-in-busan-korea/.

[66] Jessen H, Sustainable Shipping in a changing Arctic, p 154, World Maritime University, WMU Studies in maritime affairs, ISSN 2196–8772, https://doi.org/10.1007/978-3-319-78425-0.

2015. Due to similar climatological conditions, it is a leading nation in glacier and snow research. It has called for the peaceful and sustainable development of the Arctic.

(q) **Poland:** Though Poland is an observer to the Arctic Council since 1998, it has not issued any strategy paper on the Arctic and focusses on the EU stand on the Arctic.

(r) **NATO:** Only 5 Arctic states are members of the 29 members of NATO. Though NATO action has remained muted in the Arctic it is the major security alliance that can claim jurisdiction on the region. The Arctic is the gateway to the North Atlantic, and NATO is concerned with Russia trying to interdict access or interfering with sea lanes and undersea communication in the area.[67] NATO is though yet to devise an Arctic strategy. NATO though can never be an Arctic player and if any steps are taken in this direction it will point to a re-starting of the cold war, which will not suit anyone's interest. While NATO members do train and operate in the Arctic, this is limited and there are no large-scale NATO balancing missions there against Russia as opposed to other, more contested regions comprised of non-aligned states such as Eastern Europe.[68] Some European countries are linking their Arctic connection through NATO membership which follows a circumspect Russian viewpoint and does not align with the cooperative action framework prevalent on many issues.

(s) **China:** China which became an Arctic observer in 2013 has been actively pursuing its strategic and commercial interests in the region. As early as 2015, it had listed Polar Regions along with deep seabed and outer space as future frontiers which will witness great power competition. China also had traversed the transpolar route by employing its icebreaker before its admission to the AC as an observer. China has been actively carrying out trials on NSR by its government shipping company, COSCO extensively.

---

[67] Pezard Stephanie, The New Geopolitics of the Arctic, Russia's and China's Evolving Role in the Region, testimony presented before the Standing Committee on Foreign Affairs and International Development of the Canadian House of Commons on November 26, 2018.

[68] Adam P Macdonald, Precarious existence or staying the course? The foundations and future of Arctic stability, Arctic Year Book 2019, accessed on 10 December 2019 from https://Arcticyearbook.com/.

China has proactively engaged with the Arctic countries on a bilateral basis and has established its first overseas land satellite receiving station with Sweden. It has progressed with Finland on establishing a joint research centre for Arctic space observation. China has also built its indigenously manufactured icebreaker, *Xue Long II*, and it has been operationalised recently and there are impending plans to build a nuclear-powered icebreaker. China is cooperating with Greenland, based on economic investments in two mining projects. China's capital, technology, market, knowledge, and experience are expected to play a major role in expanding the network of shipping routes in the Arctic and facilitating the economic and social progress of the coastal States along the routes.[69] Special attention is paid to the development of Arctic shipping. With its commitment to the Arctic, China wants to strengthen its position as a global player in international politics.[70]

Though China calls herself a near-Arctic state it does not have any territory even in the region of sub-Arctic and does not have any Arctic territory. A nation with the inclination and wherewithal of a great power, which has been putting the USA on its toes, is aggressively enhancing its access in the region by building bilateral economic, scientific, and commercial ties. Its white paper issued in 2018 was a comprehensive one having ingredients like shipping, energy, AC, governance, climate change, and other issues. China claims to be a near-Arctic state and relies on its size, status, and nearness to the Arctic to claim its stakes in the region. China in its white paper has stressed the adherence to international law and respect for territorial sovereignty of Arctic states yet it demands that as a signatory to the Spitsbergen Treaty and UNCLOS, it has the rights to carry out Arctic research, fishing, navigation, and so on. The white paper carefully balances China's assertiveness with a balancing reassurance by credibly partnering with the Arctic states and gradually increases its role and influence. There is an inbuilt safeguard against the USA and Russia by partnering with the small Arctic nations which may act as a counterbalance if a need so arises.

Among the Arctic observers, China is championing and leading efforts by leveraging its technological prowess, infusion of capital, access to

---

[69] China's Arctic Policy, 2018. The State Council Information Office of the People's Republic of China, http://english.www.gov.cn/archive/white_paper/2018/01/26/content_281476026660336.htm. (accessed October 2019).

[70] Gregor Schulze, supra note 52.

markets, scientific knowledge, and experience for building a better future and progress of the Arctic region. It is particularly focussing on the shipping routes and all along development of coastal regions lying along the coastlines. Special attention is paid to the development of Arctic shipping.

China had elucidated its vision of extension of BRI (Belt and Road Initiative) with the cooperation of Arctic states to form the PSR (Polar Silk Road) in its 2018 white paper. This is also linked to the state-owned shipping company, COSCO which is fervently testing the Arctic shipping routes. Hence the NSR will be subsumed in the Chinese PSR and the PSR will encompass collaboration with Norway and Iceland, too. The (Chinese) willingness to develop Polar Silk Roads and extensive resources investments—with some estimates that China has invested over one trillion dollars into Arctic states' economies over the past decade (Rosen and Thuringer 2017)—signals rhetorical and practical steps towards incorporating the Arctic into its own BRI project.[71] A connected corollary to the PSR is to develop an alternate Arctic cooperative mechanism with Russian support to minimise the US diplomatic offensive. Yet China has correctly viewed that cooperative mechanism with small states and strengthening the AC will suit its long terms interests more favourably. In response to Mike Pompeo's statement, the response was calculated and measured as China had stressed its reliance and adherence to international law, making it abundantly clear that it harbours no ulterior ambitions to claim any rights outside the UNCLOS.

The Chinese also reasserted its commitment to scientific studies and environmental protection, themes that find coherent and consonant echoes among the Arctic states too.

Unlike closer neighbours of the Arctic region, China has demonstrated greater commitment and resolve and a clear vision for engagement with the Arctic region. The far-sighted goal of the Chinese to develop the Polar Silk Roads by way of massive capital infusion all along the routes/NSR by developing coastal infrastructure does convey that it is taking practical steps and not merely rhetoric to turn its goals into reality. China has partnered with Arctic research since long and its ice breaker', Xuelong's(Snow Dragon) showy expeditions. The willingness to develop Polar Silk Roads and extensive resources investments—with some estimates that

---

[71] Adam P Mcdonald, Precarious existence or staying the course? The foundations and future of Arctic stability, Arctic Year Book 2019, accessed on 10 December 2019 from https://Arcticyearbook.com/.

China has invested over one trillion dollars into Arctic states' economies over the past decade (Rosen and Thuringer 2017)—signals rhetorical and practical steps towards incorporating the Arctic into its own BRI project.[72] China has partnered with Arctic research since long and its ice breaker, Snow Dragon's, or "Xuelong's" showy expeditions. The 2009 statement by Chinese Rear Admiral Yin Zhuo stated, "The Arctic belongs to all the people around the world as no nation has sovereignty over it" and "China must play an indispensable role in Arctic exploration as we have one-fifth of the world's population"[73] which had created a furore in the Arctic 8.

There also has been considerable shift and maturity in the Chinese stand if the 2009 statement by Rear Admiral Yin Zhuo and the 2019 statement by the Chinese Ministry of Foreign affairs are considered and it is seen clearly that China has learnt from the observer status and is aligning its interests to fit in the overall gamut of AC. It has also refrained from making politically debatable statements and is sensitive to the demands of the Arctic states from a non-Arctic observer state.

China claims to be a frontrunner in Polar research by citing its historical connection to polar research and its serious efforts which have manifested in having a polar research institute and research icebreaker. The icebreaker was also obtained by China before it joined the AC as an observer. In terms of scientific pursuits, China claims its stakes as having the Tibetan plateau as the third pole and also due to the damaging impacts of climate change which will impact the production of cereals and other agricultural produce as also due to the fears of its coastal cities being threatened by rising sea levels. The Third pole programme is executed by the Institute of Tibetan Plateau Research under the aegis of the Chinese Academy of Sciences. China's production of maize, rice, and wheat may fall by more than 35% in the next 50 years because of Arctic climate change. Coastal flooding due to climate change will affect more than 20 million people in China during the next century.[74]

The most strategic advantage opening of NSR will offer to China will be diversifying its energy supply routes and reduce disputed chokepoints

---

[72] Adam P MacDonald, supra note 68.

[73] G G. Chang, *China's Arctic Play*, (Tokyo, 09 March 2010), The Diplomat, http://thediplomat.com/2010/03/chinas-Arctic-play/. [accessed: 08 February 2014].

[74] Andrew Chater (2016): Explaining Non-Arctic States in the Arctic Council, Strategic Analysis, https://doi.org/10.1080/09700161.2016.1165467.

like the straits of Malacca. Over and above this, there will be substantial cost and time saving as the distance and time between North-East Asia and Europe will be substantially narrowed. Quite like the Japanese and Koreans, the Chinese shipping and shipbuilding industry will also stand to gain with increasing traffic in the NSR.

The Chinese research station Yellow river station is operational since 2014 and it also has and a Polar research Institute in Shanghai. Polar Research Institute of China has been strengthened with the efforts of Norway and called a China-Nordic Arctic research centre (CNARC). As per her white paper of 2018, 'china hopes to work with all parties to build a 'Polar silk road' through developing the Arctic shipping routes. China will work with the Arctic states to strengthen clean energy cooperation, increase exchanges for technology, personnel, and experience in this field.[75]

(t) France: France was given the observer status in AC in the year 2000. As an active member of NATO and EU, France too dwells on the common principles like adherence to international law and a strong role for the EU in Arctic affairs. The areas of France's engagement include the environment, research, and mining. As a major cruise operator base, France is also eager in Arctic Cruise Tourism.

(u) Italy: Italy was granted observer status along with India and four other Asian countries in 2013. Italy has remained known for its exploration forays in the Arctic for long periods and still focusses on conservation of the environment along with scientific research.

(v) The Netherlands: The Netherlands has cited its vulnerability to climate change and rising sea levels as its threats. It has also called for the inclusion of the EU as an observer in the AC. It is seeking cooperation and engagement in economic sectors especially oil and gas, fisheries, and shipping.

The Arctic is clearly not terra nullius. There are sovereign countries with rich and long histories in the Arctic having the backing and support of international laws and rules as also the support of several neutral and global powers who have affirmed faith in their sovereignty and related rights. Hence the outgrowth of novel opportunities by changing climatological occurrences like global warming and the presence of rich buried

---

[75] China's Arctic Policy, 2018. The State Council Information Office of the People's Republic of China, http://english.www.gov.cn/archive/white_paper/2018/01/26/content_281476026660336.htm (accessed October 2019).

resources would not confer any rights on new stakeholders, either ethically, morally, or legally to ask for their respective shares. Over and above the sovereign states there are indigenous population groups like the Sami, Inuits, Gwich'in, and others who have traditional claims on these resources. The UNGA had also passed an important declaration on the rights of indigenous people in October 2006 affirming the rights of indigenous people. The Ottawa Declaration on the establishment of AC could be considered as a precursor and a farsighted step by the Arctic nations which had granted the indigenous people greater participation by making them permanent participants in the AC.

All three North-East Asian countries, i.e. Japan, China, and Korea are extensively cooperating at the level of engagement with the Arctic. They already have a mechanism of Trilateral High-Level Dialogue and have an annual meeting and are keen to establish a working group to further strengthen their efforts. All these countries possess and own icebreakers and also send expeditions each year to the Arctic, in the areas of shipping and shipping regulations, climate change, and science and technology. DSME (Daewoo Shipbuilding and Marine Engineering) of ROK has built more than 171 LNG vessels including many ice-class ones. The iconic *Christophe de Margerie*, the tanker that carried the first shipment of LNG from Russia's Yamal project was also from DSME. The shipbuilder from China and Korea are both employing the Arc7 Azipod system, which provides the propellers an ability to turn 360°, which is a key element for ice-class vessels. Korea had conducted an Arctic Conference in December 2018 and is actively pursuing the construction of its second research icebreaker to complement *Aaron, th*e first Korean research icebreaker which was launched as early as in 2009.

In innovative shipbuilding, Korea is working on ballast-free vessels, which will be key to safeguard the Arctic's marine ecosystem, when the traffic becomes large after prolonged periods of the opening of the sea routes, after colossal reduction in ice cover. Unlike China, which has bared its Arctic ambitions brazenly by coining the term near-Arctic state for itself and its repeated usage in various policy and other documents, Korea emphasises on multilateral and bilateral participation. Korea has been organising Arctic Partnership week as well as offering scholarships, preferably to members from the indigenous community to Korea Maritime Institute's Arctic Academy, every year.

The East Asian nations are watching the developments in the Arctic with keen penchant as they are among the chief energy consumers. Yet, in contrast to the Chinese, the Japanese and Korean policy documents show much greater responsibility to sustainable exploitation as well as sensitivity to the calls for compliance to rules based order. China is considered the leading maritime nation and Japan and Korea are pegged only one step below it. Though all three nations are endowed with remarkable shipbuilding and shipping industries and expertise, yet their policies on Arctic engagement are quite varied.

The increasing focus on oil and gas as major energy sources to fuel and fulfil world demand and the realisation that these resources are transient has pushed in a scramble to obtain rights over them. Concurrently, there has been increasing realisation that the carbon emissions are hastening the environmental damage which is making it easier and lucrative the exploration of natural resources in the Arctic region. The advancements in scientific studies and estimates, especially after the 2008 United States Geological Survey Report which covered with reasonable certainty the potential of the hydrocarbons in the Arctic has prompted the lucrative development of these. The quantum of undiscovered oil was pegged at 13% and undiscovered gas at 30% as per the USGS report, however, it did not include the gas hydrates which are likely to be more abundant than oil and gas. The Arctic finds also assume greater importance since the world's largest producers viz Qatar, Russia, Iran have nationalised companies, and the opportunity for international Western companies to increase their reserves ownership lies in the Arctic. The transition from oil to gas, which is more in abundance in the Arctic, will also lead to greater exploration and development in the region.

However, there are technical challenges and prohibitive costs involved due to the prevailing harsh environmental conditions and other challenges like shorter drilling season, the safety of the workmen, and risks to the facilities. The costs involved in setting up technologically advanced specialised equipment are manifold in comparison with other areas. The silver lining lies in the fact that the distances to potential consumers/ markets by the operationalisation of the shipping passages will be much shorter as compared to the traditional Southern routes however the construction of pipelines will require capital intensive outlays and the routes will be marred by seasonal climate disturbances.

Though some commentators had warned that conflicts might emerge over claims to resources based on disputed maritime boundaries but this eventuality is not likely to manifest as most of the resources lie in uncontested and undisputed continental shelves of the states. The estimates of oil lying in the Alaska region are pegged at around 30% and the estimates of gas lying in the Russian Kara Sea are pegged at around 40% and there are no disputes on the claims of the extended/continental shelf in sovereign territories. Moreover, the compliance to the UNCLOS and CLCS and associated venues for conflict resolution are adequate and sufficient. Thus the likelihood of conflicts in the Arctic region appears to be a farfetched eventuality.

CHAPTER 3

India's Involvement and Engagement with the Arctic Region

INDIA'S INVOLVEMENT AND ENGAGEMENT WITH THE ARCTIC REGION: I
(Scientific Engagement, Arctic Policy, and Geopolitical Goals)

> The leaders are determined to forge cooperation in geological exploration and joint development of oil and gas fields in Russia and India, including offshore fields. They will continue their work to develop the ways of delivering energy resources from Russia to India, including a long-term agreement for sourcing Russian crude oil, the possible use of the Northern Sea Route, and a pipeline system.[1]
> —India-Russia Joint Statement, 05 Sep 19
> We are extremely interested in the Arctic region and intend to play an active role in the Arctic Council too.[2]

India has had a long history and association with the Arctic region, right from the writings of Bal Gangadhar Tilak's 1903 piece, 'The Arctic Home

---

[1] India—Russia Joint Statement during the visit of Prime Minister to Vladivostok, 05 Sep 19, accessed on 11 November 19 from https://mea.gov.in/outoging-visit-detail.htm?31795/India++Russia+Joint+Statement+during+visit+of+Prime+Minister+to+Vladivostok.

[2] Syed Akbaruddin, official spokesperson for the Ministry of External Affairs, India (2012–2015), accessed 11 July 2019 from https://www.hindustantimes.com/delhi/india-to-play-active-role-in-Arctic-council/story-MRPA85wG4NsTAtV3okXFUL.html.

© The Author(s), under exclusive license to Springer Nature Singapore Pte Ltd. 2024
N. Pareek, *India in the Arctic*,
https://doi.org/10.1007/978-981-97-3640-9_3

in the Vedas' on which Prof (Dr) U K Sinha has commented that 'The contemporariness of India's relationship with the Arctic is unmistakable but there also exists racial, philosophical, anthropological, and linguistic dimensions, which remains much unexplored.'[3]

The 1903 book by Bal Gangadhar Tilak had preceded the colonial accession to Svalbard Treaty by India in 1920 and forms the basis for a historical-spiritual and cultural link to the Arctic. The above-mentioned joint statement by the Indian side conveys the changing and increasingly assertive nature of the policy towards the Arctic region and Russia. The above statement was made as a joint India-Russia statement after the visit of PM Narendra Modi to Vladivostok in September 2019 and is overly optimistic to have plans of a pipeline traversing such long distance to bring Russian energy resources to India. Though India has had a long history with the Arctic region yet it has not been adequately publicised in the Indian writings and literature except for some select works. The 1903 piece by Bal Gangadhar Tilak named 'The Arctic Home in the Vedas' dwells on India's philosophical, spiritual, and religious and racial connect with the Arctic. The first traces of India in the annals of Norwegian history go far back to the age of the Vikings, a thousand years ago. Around 400 years ago, when Mughal India was the world's second largest economy, Norway and Denmark founded the 'East India Company' to enable trade in textiles, spices, and dyes. As far as Indian Scientific engagement goes, late Prof. Mahendra Nath Bose had set his foot on the Arctic in 1962 to collect plant fossils and study paleo-climate of this region in collaboration with Norwegian scientists.

The Indian connection in the twentieth century was by way of colonial participation in the 1920 Spitsbergen Treaty, which came into force in 1925 and later admission as an Observer nation in 2013 in the AC. Indian Scientific pursuits with the Polar Regions were initiated in the Antarctic and then expanded and evolved in the Arctic. In continuation of its Antarctic expedition experience, India had launched its scientific expedition with a five-member scientific team to the Arctic Ocean in 2007 and later opened a research base named "Himadri" at the International Arctic Research Base at Ny-Alesund, Svalbard, Norway, in July 2008. The Indian research was directed to focus on atmospheric science, biological

---

[3] Sinha U., India in the Arctic: A Multidimensional Approach. Vestnik of Saint Petersburg University. International Relations, 2019, vol. 12, issue 1, pp. 113–126. https://doi.org/10.21638/11701/spbu06.2019.107.

science, cryosphere, glaciology, climate change-related biogeochemistry, Polar environment, and ecology.

As covered in the subsequent chapter, India's connection to the Arctic region draws parallels and inspiration from its Antarctic engagement. India had prominently raised the "Question of Antarctica" in the UN in the mid-fifties, just after her independence. Later when it established its research presence in Antarctica, which had a major bearing on both establishment of the Arctic research station and calls for inclusion as an observer in the Arctic Council. Indian participation and contribution in the Antarctic studies paved the way for its inclusion as an Observer in the AC. India had submitted its application in 2012, which was granted widespread support due to India's economic credentials, pluralistic and diverse society, and successful democratic model. The Observer status was granted in 2013 at the Eighth Biennial Ministerial Meeting of the Arctic Council in Kiruna, Norway, on 1 May 2013, along with 4 Asian countries and Italy. Though there have been some misses by senior ministers in the government including one letter to the SAGAA conference by the Minister of Earth Sciences and Science and Technology, Dr. Harsh Vardhan, in which it was stated that "Today, Indian scientists, in their unrelenting search for knowledge, have transcended both the poles and have successfully illustrated our presence in the Arctic Council since 2008"—which possibly was a reference to the Himadri station and not India's inclusion as an Observer in the AC in 2013.

As per the stated Indian position, declared by the Indian Ministry of External Affairs on its Arctic participation was India's interest in studying the climate change occurring in the High North. India initiated its Arctic Research Programme in 2007 with a thrust on climate change in the circumpolar north. The major objectives of the Indian Research in Arctic Region are as follows[4]:

- To study the hypothesised teleconnections between the Arctic climate and the Indian monsoon by analysing the sediment and ice-core records from the Arctic glaciers and the Arctic Ocean.
- To characterise sea ice in the Arctic using satellite data to estimate the effect of global warming in the northern Polar Region.

---

[4] Ministry of External Affairs, Government of India, *India and the Arctic* (2019), accessed on 01 November 2019 from https://mea.gov.in/in-focus-article.htm?21812/India+and+the+Arctic.

- To conduct research on the dynamics and mass budget of Arctic glaciers focussing on the effect of glaciers on sea-level change.
- To carry out a comprehensive assessment of the flora and fauna of the Arctic vis-à-vis their response to anthropogenic activities. Besides, it is proposed to undertake a comparative study of the life forms from both the Polar Regions.

The main points of India's research included study of correlation/teleconnections between Arctic climate and Indian monsoons by systemic study of ice cores and ocean sediments, employ India's satellites to study the extent of sea ice in the Arctic region, study of the loss of glaciers and the impact on raise in sea level, study the biotic and animate life forms at the Arctic and the fallout of human activities on them and to undertake a comparative study of life forms at both the Poles.

Indian Scientific Efforts

The Indian scientists visiting the Arctic in 2007 had carried the experience gained during India's similar endeavours at the Antarctic. Thereafter, the Himadri research station was operationalised in 2008 and has been conducting scientific experiments under the aegis of National Centre for Polar and Ocean Research, NCPOR (which was earlier called National Centre for Antarctic and Ocean Research, NCAOR) under the Ministry of Earth Sciences (MoES).

It is pertinent to mention that the International Polar Year was observed in 2007–2008 and India's commencement of research coincided with it. India became a member of the Ny-Ålesund Science Managers Committee (NySMAC) an organisation that is involved in enhancing cooperation and the coordination of scientific and research activities at Ny-Ålesund. The stated position of India's focus in Arctic research is[5]:

(1) "To study the hypothesised teleconnections between the Arctic climate and the Indian monsoon by analysing the sediment and ice-core records from the Arctic glaciers and the Arctic Ocean.
(2) To characterize sea ice in the Arctic using satellite data to estimate the effect of global warming in the northern Polar Region.

---

[5] Ibid.

(3) To conduct research on the dynamics and mass budget of Arctic glaciers focussing on the effect of glaciers on sea-level change.
(4) To carry out a comprehensive assessment of the flora and fauna of the Arctic vis-à-vis their response to anthropogenic activities."

In 2009, the country entered into a "Memorandum of Understanding" with the Norwegian Polar Institute "for collaborative research on such scientific themes such as shallow ice-core drilling, ice dynamics and monitoring of glaciers/ice cap margins in polar regions to understand the climate variability over both the high latitudes in the last millennia."[6]

As per the NySMAC website, Ny-Ålesund offers a wide range of shared scientific infrastructure to include Kings Bay Marine Laboratory, Zeppelin Observatory, Amundsen-Nobile Climate Change Tower, Gruvebadet Atmosphere Laboratory, and Light Sensitive Cabin.[7]

The heydays of seamless scientific participation by the observers in the initial days of AEPS were curbed successively and in the present times, observers shy away from the WGs meetings except for the participation at Ministerial and SAO meetings. The lacklustre scientific participation even at the WG level is due to the restricted domain of expertise, limited to the areas of the WGs. On the other hand, the Ministerial and SAO meetings don't afford an opportunity to proactively participate and are limited to merely attending those meetings. Since the Ministerial and SAO meetings are supposed to be attended by the diplomatic officers, India has been seen to be sending its scientists instead for even those as Observer States are constricted by lack of any participatory mechanism. There is also a variance between the pre-AC Observer States and the new ones like India with the former having their established scientists still entrenched in the WGs while the latter have no leverage in the WGs, too.

The present-day Ministry of Earth Sciences (MoES) was preceded by a Department of Ocean Development (DOD) which was formed in 1981 and tasked to organise, coordinate, and promote ocean development activity. In 1983, DOD spearheaded India's research activity in the

---

[6] Nadezhda Filimonova, Prospects for Russian–Indian Cooperation in the High North: Actors, Interests, Obstacles, Maritime Affairs: Journal of the National Maritime Foundation of India, 2015, vol. 11, issue 1, pp. 99–115, https://doi.org/10.1080/09733159.2015.1025537.

[7] Ny-Alesund Science Managers Committee accessed on 12 August 2019 from https://nyalesundresearch.no/nysmac/.

Antarctic, and in 1983, Dakshin Gangotri, India's permanent research station, was established in the Antarctic. The DOD was upgraded to a full-fledged Ministry in 2006 and designated as the Ministry of Ocean Development. In the same year, the other departments dealing with similar tasks like India Meteorological Department (IMD), Indian Institute of Tropical Meteorology (IITM), and National Centre for Medium-Range Weather Forecasting (NCMRWF) were merged in the Ministry and it was re-designated as MoES. The government also approved the setting up of the Earth Commission on the pattern of Space Commission and Atomic Energy Commission.[8] NCAOR was established in 1998 as an autonomous institute under the Department of Ocean Development and is responsible for the coordination and implementation of all of India's Antarctic and Arctic scientific research programmes.[9]

MoES has five autonomous bodies working under it to include National Centre for Polar and Ocean Research (NCOPR), National Institute of Ocean Technology (NIOT), Indian National Centre for Ocean Information Service (INCOIS), Indian Institute of Tropical Meteorology (IITM), and National Centre for Earth Science Studies (NCESS). These organisations have been spearheading the Indian Scientific research activity in the Arctic. This marked the trailblazing of India's Polar research programme.

Now, with Polar research stations at both Poles, India is striving to compare data, particularly glaciological data as it will be extrapolated to the third pole, Himalayas. Most of the Indian studies are in the direction to analyse the connection/co-relation between events at Arctic and Indian Monsoons, other than the global impact of rising sea levels due to ice thinning. In India, a developing country with a huge population still depending on agriculture, the availability of water for agriculture is a livelihood concern. The receding glaciers in Himalayas and ice loss are impacting the downstream availability of water, imperilling lives. Indian Scientific efforts are in this direction to understand the geology, climate, and hydrology of Arctic glaciers and the resultant changes due to ice shrinkages. As per the Annual Report of MoES for 2018–2018, 'The scientific studies in the Arctic hinge around Characterization of Polar

---

[8] Ministry of Earth Sciences, Government of India, 2019, accessed on 01 October 2019 from https://www.moes.gov.in/.

[9] Nadezhda Filimonova, supra note 6.

Aerosols, Hydrography of Kongsfjorden, and Cryospheric studies.' The Indian research station 'Himadri' was manned for over 120 days and a total of 32 researchers visited the station and another 2 have sailed in RV Lance under 19 different scientific projects.[10]

National Centre for Polar and Ocean Research, NCPOR (earlier NCAOR), was established in 1998 as an autonomous institute under the DOD and made responsible for coordination and implementation of India's entire Antarctic programme. Since its renaming, Arctic research has also been incorporated in its research focus. The NCPOR is tasked with carrying out geoscientific surveys in India's continental shelves and EEZs, exploring for resources like gas hydrates and multi-metal sulphides in mid-ocean ridges, coordinate and undertake effective research activities in Antarctica, the Arctic and the Southern Ocean, management of scientific and logistics activities in Indian Expeditions to the Antarctic, Arctic, and the Southern Ocean, management of Indian Antarctic Research Bases "Maitri" and "Bharati," and the Indian Arctic base "Himadri" and management of the MoES research vessel ORV Sagar Kanya and other vessels leased/hired/chartered by the Ministry. Several studies have affirmed that the Arctic Region is a 'driver' of the tropical climate in India and there is a link between the climatological, glaciological, and other developments on the intensity, coverage, and spread of Indian monsoon which has a consequent effect on the Indian agriculture sector and economy. The mandate of NCPOR is multi-dimensional:

- Leadership role in niche areas of scientific research in the domain of polar and ocean sciences.
- Lead role in the geoscientific surveys of the country's EEZ and its extended continental shelf beyond 200 M, deep-sea drilling in the Arabian Sea basin through the IODP, exploration for ocean non-living resources such as the gas hydrates and multi-metal sulphides in mid-ocean ridges.

---

[10] Government of India, Ministry of Earth Sciences Annual Report 2018–19, accessed on 01 January 2020 from https://moes.gov.in/writereaddata/files/Annual_Report_2018-19_English_0.pdf.

- Facilitatory role in the scientific research activities being undertaken by several national institutions and organisations in Antarctica, the Arctic, and the Indian Ocean sector of the Southern Ocean.
- Management role in implementing all scientific and logistics activities related to the Annual Indian Expeditions to the Antarctic, Arctic, and Southern Ocean.
- Management and upkeep of the Indian Antarctic Research Bases "Maitri" and "Bharati," and the Indian Arctic base "Himadri."
- Management of the Ministry's research vessel ORV Sagar Kanya as well as the other research vessels chartered by the Ministry.[11]

As per the NCPOR Annual Report 2018–2019, the allotment for Arctic programme in the year 2018–2019 was (Figs. 3.1 and 3.2).

The same, when compared with India's Antarctic programme, tells that there is substantial variation in fund allotment as well as preparation for setting up the third station in the South Pole.

The fund allotment by the MoES/Government of India to NCPOR and its further distribution in its programmes portrays a very appalling picture, wherein both the Antarctic programme and catering for the third proposed station in the South Pole are substantially large to the Arctic outlay. Another connected issue is that though the Rajya Sabha in its discussion has stated that funds for purchase/construction of Polar Research Vessel are lacking, the provisioning in depreciation of the Polar funds is phenomenal. Figure 3.3 displays the jarring difference in the allotment and expenditure of funds.

SCHEDULE 2 - RESERVES AND SURPLUS	31-03-2019	31-03-2018
6. Indian Arctic Programme		
As per last Account	45,302,852	49,175,482
Addition during the year	27,782,141	9,854,980
Less: Depreciation written off	17,883,603	13,727,610
Total	55,201,390	45,302,852
7. CLCS Programme		

Fig. 3.1 Indian Arctic programme (*Source* NCPOR Annual Report 2018–2019)

---

[11] National Centre for Ocean and Polar Research, NCPOR, 2019, accessed on 12 November 2019 from http://www.ncaor.gov.in/pages/view/260-welcome-to-ncaor.

SCHEDULE 2 - RESERVES AND SURPLUS		31-03-2019	31-03-2018
Capital Reserve:			
1. Antarctic Research			
As per last Account		480,003,948	509,835,700
Addition during the year		57,885,156	98,360,226
Less: Depreciation written off		137,390,768	128,191,978
	Total	400,498,336	480,003,948
2. Establishment of Third Station in Antarctica			
As per last Account		825,093,208	1,077,013,169
Addition during the year		-	-
Less: Depreciation written off		247,495,647	251,919,961
	Total	577,597,561	825,093,208

Fig. 3.2 Indian Antarctic programme[12] (*Source* NCPOR Annual Report 2018–2019)

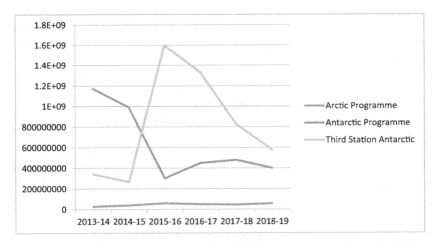

Fig. 3.3 Resource allotment for Polar programme (*Source* Annual Reports NCPOR, compiled by author)

HIMADRI 'the abode of snow' is India's first research station located at the International Arctic Research base, Ny-Ålesund, Svalbard, Norway. The research station was inaugurated on the 1st of July, 2008, by Shri

---

[12] NCPOR Annual Report, 2019, accessed on 22 September 19 from http://www.ncaor.gov.in/annualreports.

Kapil Sibal, the then Hon. Minister of Science and Technology and Earth Sciences. In the year 2018, the Indian station at Himadri was manned for over 120 days and a total of 32 researchers visited the station. Himadri provides extensive field and laboratory support required for pursuing research activities in the Arctic. NCAOR as a nodal agency makes sure the availability of the requisite facilities at the Himadri.[13]

To date over 200 researchers from several national institutes, universities, and colleges have accessed the facilities at Ny-Ålesund with base support from the *Himadri* station. For the last 3–4 years, *Himadri* has been manned from March to November on an average for over 175 days/year.[14] The station is run under the aegis and control of NCPOR and provides a secure base, equipped with modern scientific aids and instruments to direct Indian research efforts in the Arctic. Other than scientists from NCPOR, other researchers from several national institutes have accessed the facilities at Himadri and benefitted from the domain expertise offered by the Indian station at the High North. India's multi-sensor moored observatory 'IndARC' was deployed at Kongsfjorden, to collect sea truth data at close temporal scales even during the harsh Arctic winter. It was deployed on 23 July 2014 at 78° 56′ N and 12° E in the inner Kongsfjorden where the depth is ~180 m. It consists of several sensors which are located at 7 different depths to monitor the sea data (Fig. 3.4).

National Polar Data Centre (NPDC) is a depository of India's Polar research data. It also has the functionality of sharing and managing this data. It covers data from a broad spectrum of disciplines, including glaciology, resources and environmental science, oceanography, biology and ecology, atmospheric science, etc. Polar data sets received from different institutes of India have been migrated into the polar data portal. The Scientists/Scholars/Researchers could fill the online metadata form along with/without processed data by choosing the expedition(s) such as Antarctica, Arctic, and the Southern Ocean and save it. NPDC has

---

[13] National Centre for Ocean and Polar Research, NCPOR, 2019, accessed on 12 November 2019 from http://www.ncaor.gov.in/app/webroot/pages/view/340-himadri-station.

[14] EDOCS-4033-v1-2016–12–16_India_Observer_activity_report.pdf, n.d., EDOCS-4033-v1-2016–12–16 accessed on 12 July 2019 from https://oaarchive.Arctic-council.org/bitstream/handle/11374/1869/EDOCS-4033-v1-2016-12-16_India_Observer_activity_report.PDF?sequence=1&isAllowed=y.

Depth	Sensors
15m	Conductivity-Temperature-Depth (CTD), Flourometer, Dissolved Oxygen (DO), Nutrient, Photosynthetically Active Radiation (PAR)
25m	Single point current meter
30m	CTD, Flourometer, DO, Nutrient, PAR
50m	CTD
75m	CTD
100m	CTD, upward looking 300KHz ADCP
120m	CTD

Fig. 3.4 Various sensors on IndARC (*Source* ncaor.gov.in/pages/display/398 indarc)

become a nodal centre of "India's Data-sharing Network of Earth System Science."

The Indian Arctic research has been assisted and supported by the Norwegian government as Norway was one of the first countries to recognise India's independence in 1947. Soon thereafter in 1952, the Norwegian Parliament had established a fund called the 'India fund' for providing developmental aid to India. The scientific cooperation between the two governments has been profound and there have been instruments signed at the governmental level for a multilateral cooperation, which includes:

(a) Norwegian Polar Institute, NPI: A "Memorandum of Understanding" was signed between India's NCPOR and NPI considering that Norway and India have enjoyed strong bilateral ties for decades and Norway had been supporting India in many spheres including its Arctic inclusion. The specific areas of earmarked collaboration included shallow ice-core drilling, ice dynamics, and monitoring of glaciers/ice cap margins in Polar Regions.
(b) Research Council of Norway (RCN): Under the MoU with RCN, following a joint call in February 2015, 5 projects under Climate System in Polar Regions and 3 projects under the Geohazard theme have been supported in October 2015. These projects are in various stages of implementation. Major progress in the projects includes: (i) NCPOR-NPI team carried out geophysical surveys during the 2017–2018 field seasons in Antarctica and also drilled

a 153 m ice core at the summit of Leningradkollen ice rise in coastal Antarctica. The geophysical data and the ice cores are being processed and analysed. (ii) Arctic climate variability during the Mid-Pliocene Warm Period was studied using various proxies in the sediment samples collected from the various IODP Expeditions in the Arctic Ocean and Eastern Arabian Sea. (iii) Various CMIP5 models were used to study intra-seasonal variability of the Indian summer monsoon (ISM) and the teleconnection between ISM and the changing wind patterns. (iv) Diatoms in the marine sediment cores from two Arctic fjords were analysed to reconstruct the Sea Surface Temperature and Sea Ice during Holocene.[15]

Antarctic vs Arctic: Indian View

Though India had signed the Antarctic Treaty System (ATS) way back on 01 December 1959 yet its scientific exploration still is in a nascent stage. The accession to the ATS was delayed till 08 January 1982 when the first Indian expedition had reached the South Pole. Though during the third Indian expedition to Antarctica, its research station Dakshin Gangotri was commissioned, yet the scientific pursuits were limited in both the scale and fields. India's lack of resources, expertise, and knowledge warranted that it progresses its Polar pursuits drawing assistance and support from the leaders in the field, who have assumed pole positions in a global arena.

The geography, as well as political geography of both the Polar Regions, is quite apart as the Antarctic is governed by a treaty system and is primarily a no man's land while on the other, the Arctic is an ocean surrounded by the landmass of sovereign nations and the laws of UNCLOS and IMO govern the resource exploitation.

The lack of Indian roadmap for chartering its course in both the Poles, especially the North Pole, is compounding its problems and the focus remains divided between the scientific, environmental, commercial, and strategic with no laid out paths. Unlike the many Observer nations, which were quick to draw out their Arctic strategies/roadmaps to allay any fears of the member states and PPs, India is yet to issue its policy framework. Despite the low attention in both the public domain and the

---

[15] Government of India, Ministry of Earth Sciences, 2019, accessed on 01 October 2019 from https://www.moes.gov.in/.

policy circle, India does need to play an active role in the Arctic Council and craft its signals carefully rather than having sporadic Arctic briefings and communiqués.[16] Thus neither the challenges have been identified nor is there a clear Indian position on addressing those within the state policy parameters. Since there are huge physical distances involved, the Indian public discourse is detached from any interest in the Arctic affairs. There is a need to educate the children/public about the distinct and unique characteristics of the Arctic including its flora, fauna, natural wealth, indigenous communities, impacts of climate change as well as the politico-legal framework of the AC.

The discussion on climate change in India remains largely focussed on the conduct of conferences and debates and little tangible action. The research organisations have been seen to be utilising the primary data obtained from government installed and funded sensors into individual research contributions, which is a serious drawback and drain on exchequer's resources. A case in point is that the size of the Indian delegation to a conference named 'Polar-2018' was 18 in number, which was among the largest delegations and several papers presented there were multi-authored and based on government data. Since the conference was organised in Switzerland, the opportunity to participate also brings in the perks of tourism as well as expanding the scientific base, yet the country or the international research community has not benefited substantially and there have been no instances of recognition showered on Indian research endeavours.

The Antarctic Treaty has put aside territorial claims. The challenges in the Arctic have the potential to disrupt the stability in the region. India became an Arctic Observer during the Kiruna Ministerial Meeting in 2013 along with China, Japan, ROK, Singapore, and Italy. The grant of the status speaks about the international clout and recognition of India in the multilateral regional forum as a responsible partner and stakeholder. India had submitted its application to Sweden on 6 November 2012, for the spot of an Observer status in the Arctic Council. Thereafter, it was granted the Observer status in 2013 at the Kiruna Ministerial Meeting and India was re-elected as an Observer in the Arctic Council at the 11th Arctic Council Ministerial Meeting held at Rovaniemi, Finland, in May 2019.

---

[16] Sinha U.K., India in the Arctic: A Multidimensional Approach. Vestnik of Saint Petersburg University. International Relations, 2019, vol. 12, issue 1, pp. 113–126.

"Major theories of international relations, such as neorealism and liberalism, do not consider the relative importance of observers in alliances or international institutions."[17] The status of an Observer nation has to be confirmed every four years and maybe suspended, if in violation of the code of conduct. The Observer country has no authority to voice its opinions, no access to working documents and discussions, and the scope of its financing of the Council projects should also not exceed the amounts allocated by member states. The observers are free to work with the working groups of the Council, like PAME, ACAP, AMAP, and others.

Unlike China which is the most proactive Observer in the AC focussing on science, resources as well as routes, Indian efforts have remained mostly confined to the scientific domain. There has been no official Indian statement on the opening of shipping passages or the exploration of the Arctic natural wealth and resources. There is also a rift between the funding allotted by the national governments to the Polar pursuits. While China spends nearly 20% of its Polar expenditure on the Arctic, India is still allotting a minuscule fraction of its budgeted Polar outlay to the Arctic and is continually spending more and more sums of money on the Antarctic research.

As far as economic partnerships with the Arctic nations are concerned, China has invested in diverse projects in fields like mining in Greenland, terrestrial connections, and Information Technology in Finland, and other projects with Russia, Canada, and Norway. India has though been promising to partner with Nordic and Scandinavian nations on several fields yet the action on the same remains on a conceptual level with less tangible output. Though among the Asian nations, Japan was the first to partner in engaging with Arctic research yet its efforts have remained muted and sombre. With its neutral foreign policy, Japan has thus not raised any heckles among the Arctic States due to its pursuits unlike China and is watching closely the developments as it has its keen eye on opening of shipping routes and securing its energy supplies in the times to come through the Arctic routes. The Republic of Korea, Japan, China, and India all have active Arctic science programme and are running their Arctic research stations successively. China, Korea, and Japan each have icebreakers and research vessels to support their Arctic research pursuits.

---

[17] Andrew Chater, 2016, Explaining Non-Arctic States in the Arctic Council, Strategic Analysis, https://doi.org/10.1080/09700161.2016.1165467.

India's Arctic Policy: A Critical Appraisal

After much procrastination, the Indian government has released its much awaited and delayed Arctic Policy document on 17 March 22 with the theme being 'Building a Partnership for Sustainable Development.' It has been 15 years since India commenced its scientific research in the Arctic region and this policy document, charting out the direction that India aspires to assume, will be keenly examined by the diverse stakeholders of the region. The Arctic region connects three continents, which are the power centres of the global economy, trade, and military. Indian policy on global issues has gained much prominence with the gradual rise in its stature in fields of economy, diplomacy, commerce, and so on, and lately, India has been actively conveying and projecting its views on issues that concern her, with keen notice by world powers.

India is among the five Asian nations including China, Japan, Singapore, and Republic of Korea to be granted the Observer status in the Arctic Council (AC) during the Kiruna Ministerial Meeting in 2013. Then, many Indian experts called this foreign policy step an "Arctic victory" and a "major diplomatic achievement" for the Ministry of External Affairs of India.[18]

Among the Asian Arctic observers, both Korea (2013) and Japan (2015) had preceded China in issuing out their respective Arctic policies. China had released its white paper on the Arctic in January 2018. With the recent release of India's policy, Singapore remains the only Asian AC Observer state without a charted out Arctic Policy.

The policy document, in its concluding section, affirms that 'India's Arctic Policy is aimed to prepare the country for a future where the biggest challenges facing humankind, such as climate change, can be successfully addressed only through collective will and effort. India can, and is ready to play its part and contribute to the global good. Close partnerships with countries of the Arctic region and other international partners to ensure sustainable development, peace and stability in the Arctic region will also be essential for the realisation of India's national development plans and priorities. This approach is in accordance with

---

[18] Ramachandaran S., 2013. India's Arctic Victory: A Major Diplomatic Achievement. DNA. http://www.dnaindia.com/analysis/column-indias-Arctic-victory-a-major-diplomatic-achievement-1837329.

the Indian philosophy of *Vosudhoivo Kutumbokom* - the world is but one family.'[19]

The document also promises that 'India's Arctic Policy shall be implemented through an Action Plan and an effective governance and review mechanism consisting of an inter-ministerial Empowered Arctic Policy Group. Implementation will be based on timelines, prioritisation of activities and allocation of requisite resources. The implementation will involve all stakeholders including academia; the research community; and business and industry.'[20]

The policy comprehensively covers the various sectors in which India aspires to participate in the Arctic affairs yet falls short on tangible efforts like the other Observer States like China, Korea, and Japan, which have already instituted/commenced activities in diverse spheres. India's expertise in space technology with one of the most developed space programmes in the world can offer substantial benefits towards enhancing the digital connectivity footprint in the Arctic. India's Regional Navigation Satellite System (IRNSS), remote sensing facilities, and establishing ground stations to receive satellite data have been promised in the policy, though without concrete and measurable plans. Future plans on collaboration with Arctic States to strengthen partnerships in sustainable living and non-living resource exploration in the Arctic have been stated too, which is a beneficial takeaway for all parties.

In light of such profound and elaborate goals, it is imperative to critically analyse Indian efforts in balancing the delicate geopolitical and strategic goals that India aspires to pursue in this vital region. It is assessed that India's efforts in partnering and collaborating with the Arctic 8, especially in the domains of meaningful engagement with Permanent Participants, position on exploitation of Arctic resources and alignment of national policy with the climate change goals falls short of promises on certain parameters. The increasing economic, political, and geostrategic

---

[19] Ministry of Earth Sciences, accessed on 16 August 2022 at https://www.moes.gov.in/sites/default/files/2022-03/compressed-SINGLE-PAGE-ENGLISH.pdf.

[20] Ibid.

significance of the Arctic, which has witnessed tremendous transformation in recent times, calls for more robust and tangible assertions by stakeholders including India to fulfil its aspirations.[21]

STRATEGIC DIRECTION

The policy document was released by Union Minister of State (Independent Charge) Science & Technology; Minister of State (Independent Charge) Earth Sciences; MoS PMO, Personnel, Public Grievances, Pensions, Atomic Energy and Space, Dr Jitendra Singh on 17 Mar 22.

Despite being an AC Observer for nearly a decade, India continues to view the Arctic from a mere scientific prism and yet again missed on the opportunity to elucidate her geo-economic, geostrategic, economic, and geopolitical aspirations in the hugely vital region. The release of national policy by the Ministry of Earth Sciences (MoES) and not by the Ministry of External Affairs (MEA) reaffirms a stark deficit in national understanding of the complex and myriad framework that governs the Arctic and the increasing geopolitical and strategic relevance of the Arctic. India's reluctance to de-emphasise its scientific interest towards a more calibrated approach that takes into account the politico-strategic-economic dimensions in the Arctic reflects the tension between the exceptionalism and the realism of its Polar legacy.[22]

The MEA is responsible to chart out India's strategic goals and direction for policy formulation as well as strategic alliances, and the official stand of the government can be observed from its statements and issue briefs/statements as well as by official releases. At home, MEA is responsible for all aspects of external relations. Territorial divisions deal with bilateral political and economic work while functional divisions look after policy planning, multilateral organisations, regional groupings, legal matters, disarmament, protocol, and consular, Indian Diaspora, press and publicity, administration, and other aspects.[23]

---

[21] Pareek, N., Assessment on India's Involvement and Capacity-Building in Arctic Science, Advances in Polar Science, March 2021, vol. 32, issue 1, https://doi.org/10.13679/j.advps.2020.0027.

[22] Sinha U.K., India in the Arctic: A multidimensional approach. Vestnik of Saint Petersburg University. International Relations, 2019, vol. 12, issue 1, pp. 113–126.

[23] https://www.mea.gov.in/indian-foreign-service.htm.

There is no gainsaying that the Arctic research bases discreetly also act as pillars of geopolitical engagement and indirectly this scientific diplomacy ushers in peace and prevents conflict situations yet a holistic national policy enunciating a roadmap and vision for dealing in a region which has eight sovereign states (Arctic 8 namely, Finland, Denmark, the Russian Federation, the United States of America, Iceland, Canada, Sweden, and Norway), thirteen sovereign states as observers, various intergovernmental and inter-parliamentarian outfits, NGOs, and a complex governance structure was much awaited.

It has to be accepted that India's preoccupation with local and regional affairs as also with the vital geopolitical activities around the Indian Ocean, Indo-Pacific, and the Middle East takes away the bulk of Indian foreign policy emphasis and resultantly the Arctic affairs are left to the National Centre for Polar and Ocean Research (NCPOR) functioning under the Ministry of Earth Sciences (MoES) rather than the MEA. A connected strand to the changed focus of the Indian policy towards the Arctic has been aired by some who have aired fears that "India whose geostrategic position enables it to exert considerable control over the Indian Ocean Region (IOR) may suffer at the cost of the Arctic and the commercial viability of its polar routes"[24] (Saran, 2012). In the times when the Arctic has assumed a major position on the world stage in light of its climatic and geopolitical relevance, the above view appears to be myopic and misfounded and both the regions merit suitable and bespoke responses.

The Arctic region has witnessed the presence of all contenders of great power status and to carve out a strategy for India requires deliberate forethought. The realisation of the acute discrepancies in the Indian state capacity and mismatch between the stated objective as a major world power is being adroitly noticed by the world community and there seems to be a huge differential between the rhetoric and action. It is also established that mere soft power and scientific diplomacy are not enough to progress any claims for global/major power status and the Indian strategy needed to have a multi-pronged approach to carve out a niche role in the Arctic affairs.

---

[24] Shyam Saran, India's Stake in Arctic Cold War, The Hindu, 2012, accessed on 28 October 19 from https://www.thehindu.com/opinion/op-ed/Indias-stake-inArctic-cold-war/article13290404.ece.

India's Ministry of Environment, Forest and Climate Change (MoEFCC) is the nodal agency for coordination of efforts and commitment of national goals towards fighting climate change. The Ministry also serves as the nodal agency in the country for the United Nations Environment Programme (UNEP), South Asia Co-operative Environment Programme (SACEP), International Centre for Integrated Mountain Development (ICIMOD), and for the follow-up of the United Nations Conference on Environment and Development (UNCED). The Ministry is also entrusted with issues relating to multilateral bodies such as the Commission on Sustainable Development (CSD), Global Environment Facility (GEF), and of regional bodies like Economic and Social Council for Asia and Pacific (ESCAP) and South Asian Association for Regional Cooperation (SAARC) on matters pertaining to the environment.[25]

India's Department of Science and Technology functioning under the Ministry of Science and Technology (MoST) is also furthering individual collaboration in its domain areas with certain Arctic States. The International Cooperation Division of DST has the mandated responsibility of negotiating, concluding, and implementing Science, Technology and Innovation (STI) Agreements between India and other countries. Under the Agreement of Cooperation in Science and Technology concluded between the Government of India and the Government of Norway, the Department of Science and Technology (DST) of the Government of India and the Research Council of Norway (RCN) have started a programme for joint funding of Indo-Norwegian joint research projects in mutually agreed fields to achieve world-class scientific results.[26]

The Ministry of Tribal Affairs (MoTA) looks after the affairs of the indigenous people. Indigenous Peoples in India comprise an estimated population of 104 million or 8.6% of the national population. India voted in favour of the United Nations Declaration on the Rights of Indigenous Peoples (UNDRIP) on the condition that after independence all Indians are Indigenous. Therefore, it does not consider the concept of "Indigenous Peoples," and therefore the UNDRIP, applicable to India.[27]

---

[25] Ministry of Environment, Forest and Climate change, Introduction, accessed on 15 August 2022 at https://moef.gov.in/en/about-the-ministry/introduction-8/.

[26] Department of Science and Technology, Ministry of Science and Technology, accessed on 15 August 2022 at https://dst.gov.in/sites/default/files/Indo-NorwayJointC all-Nano-2018%20pdf.

[27] IWGIA, accessed on 16 August 2022 at https://www.iwgia.org/en/india.html.

This being the dichotomy, India though, provides special schemes for economic and social upliftment of these people, yet doesn't address these groups with their unique social structures like the Arctic States. As brought out in succeeding paragraphs, India's engagement with the Permanent Participants is acutely limited.

Other than these Ministries, as per the policy document 'The National Centre for Polar and Ocean Research (NCPOR),' Ministry of Earth Sciences, Government of India, is the nodal agency for India's Polar research programme, which includes Arctic studies. The Ministry of External Affairs provides the external interface to the Arctic Council. Several other Ministries and Institutes are also involved in Arctic activities and are poised to deepen their engagement in the future. These include the Ministry of Environment, Forests and Climate Change, Ministry of Science and Technology, Department of Space, Ministry of Petroleum and Natural Gas, Ministry of Ports, Shipping and Waterways, Ministry of Mines, Department of Telecommunications, Ministry of Commerce and Industry, Ministry of Agriculture and Farmers Welfare, Ministry of Fisheries, Animal Husbandry and Dairying, Ministry of New and Renewable Energy, Department of Biotechnology, and Council of Scientific and Industrial Research.[28]

India's MEA addresses the Arctic Region through three separate offices and there is no dedicated division looking into the finer nuances of the various levers that are at play in the region. The MEA's Americas Division looks after the USA and Canada while the Eurasia Division looks after Russia and the Central Europe Division is looking after the remaining five states, namely Iceland, Finland, Denmark, Sweden and Norway. The AC is in itself a very unique organisation and the disparate MEA's divisions are not able to do justice and thereby a void is experienced at the policy formation level. The most distinguishing feature of both the 'Arctic exceptionalism' and the interplay of politico-economic-geopolitical factors between the various member states in the AC has to be viewed holistically based on a common viewpoint rather than a disjointed platform. There is one Additional Secretary (Europe) who draws out the policy based on inputs provided by these three divisions and thus the finer issues of relations between the Arctic 8 as well as shifting discourse due to rotational AC chair as well as varying participation by the Arctic 8 in

---

[28] Ministry of Earth Sciences, accessed on 16 August 2022 at https://www.moes.gov.in/sites/default/files/2022-03/compressed-SINGLE-PAGE-ENGLISH.pdf.

international multilateral organisations tends to get missed. The existing disconnect between these three divisions does not provide a single point and seamless understanding of the complex Arctic issues and thus there are huge rifts in Indian position which could have afforded her with a robust strategic hedge as a safeguard for unforeseen situations. The diagram placed below succinctly places the context and role of the various government Ministries in this regard.

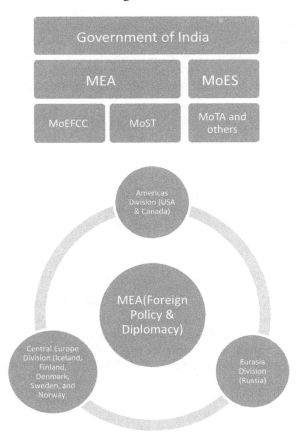

The process initiated after the end of the cold war by the liberalisation of the Indian economy brought her to the centre of the global economy owing to the size and geopolitical dimension. Resultantly, there were greater demands on diplomacy to mould and carve new policy engagements delving into the geo-economic and geostrategic realms. The changing attitude and perspective of erstwhile unconcerned states like the US and certain European countries also gave impetus to India's self-belief. Since then, India has been trying to associate herself globally by weaving bespoke narratives of engagement like neighbourhood first, Act East and so on. The ambition to be a great power, competing with a growing unilateralist and inwardly US, and ambitious and aggressive China are manifesting in greater power politics in international affairs. India's views on NSR and Arctic shipping as well as energy dependence and more importantly a more realist and practical approach, much more connected and synchronised with the changing geopolitical landscape in the Arctic, were keenly anticipated by the international players in the Arctic, yet the policy remains muted on several key issues enunciated in succeeding paragraphs.

Layout

The policy document covers the direction in six broad areas, namely Science and Research, Climate and Environmental protection, Economic and Human Development, Transportation and Connectivity, Governance and International Cooperation, and National Capacity Building in the Arctic region. Few major misses which have not been addressed in the Policy document include:

Permanent Participants (PPs)

The founding document of the AC had stressed the significance of the indigenous people of the Arctic and granted them a special voice at the high table. More specifically, the council states that "Decisions at all levels in the Arctic Council are the exclusive right and responsibility of the eight Arctic States with the involvement of the Permanent Participants."[29]

The AC is a wide and diverse platform bringing together Arctic 8, permanent participants, observers as well as international institutions, and it remains a decision-preparing rather than a decision-making institution. The 6 Permanent Participants are composed of various communities, with differing political-ethno-socio-cultural characteristics with each other

---

[29] Arctic Council, Observers, updated May 23, 2019, accessed on 30 July 2019, at https://Arctic-council.org/index.php/en/about-us/Arctic-council/observers.

belonging to a localised community. Though there is presence of Permanent Participants, Working Groups, Observers, etc., yet the decision-making authority rests entirely with the Arctic 8, as they discuss and chart out AC policy and direct the working groups. As per the Arctic Council Rules of Procedure, six Permanent Participants though are not granted voting privileges but they can participate in all meetings and can offer full consultation. Also, the UNGA had passed an important declaration on the rights of indigenous people in October 2006 affirming the rights of indigenous people. The Ottawa Declaration on the establishment of AC could be considered as a precursor and a farsighted step by the Arctic nations which had granted the indigenous people greater participation by making them permanent participants in the AC.

The Arctic is experiencing and facing the brunt of climate change and over the last century, the temperature rise in the Arctic has been two to three times greater than the global average. The volume of the Arctic Ocean is reported to have fallen by 75%, and it is predicted that in the coming decades the Arctic will be entirely ice-free during the summer months. Though the geophysical changes will open several economic opportunities yet there will be concurrent challenges, namely the loss of pristine biodiversity, shipping-related pollution risks and the irreversible impact on the Arctic indigenous population. The characteristics of loss of sea ice, shrinkages of ice cover, the spread of wildfires, etc., have a corresponding and disastrous impact on the Arctic ecosystems and are adversely impacting the habitats, mortality, and sustenance of indigenous people's livelihoods. There is also an impact on the marine food web and marine ecosystems, and there are concerns that the Caribou, Polar Bears, seals, etc., will not be able to cope up with the rapidly changing scenario. For indigenous people, the primitive practices of hunting, fishing, and gathering food is an important facet of their lives. Also, these practices require them to rely on a functioning cash economy. There will be issues relating to migration as well as a swell in Arctic tourism that can change the nature of the Arctic. Not only the Arctic flora, fauna, and aquatic lives but the human population also has to adapt to the changes and be resilient in their methodology.

The estimated population of the Arctic region is around 4 million (Mn), out of which the indigenous make for around 10%. It is abundantly clear that the population of the Arctic does not make it a significant stakeholder in global politics, yet the indigenous people of the Arctic have been making a living for several millennia by employing sustainable means of living. Many places like Greenland have the indigenous people in the majority, while in others they may be less. There are over 40 different ethnic groups living in the Arctic. These communities include Saami in circumpolar areas of Finland, Sweden, Norway, and Northwest Russia; Nenets, Khanty, Evenk, and Chukchi in Russia; Aleut, Yupik, and Inuit (Iñupiat) in Alaska; Inuit (Inuvialuit) in Canada; and Inuit (Kalaallit) in Greenland.

The indigenous people organisations are represented by the Permanent participants like the Russian Association of Indigenous Peoples of the North (RAIPON), Saami Council, Aleutian, and others representing the different ethnic groups living in the Arctic. The Saami are among the largest groups and comprise more than 100,000 people. A UN report on indigenous people is available at https://www.un.org/en/events/indigenousday/pdf/Indigenous_Arctic_Eng.pdf on the theme 'INDIGENOUS PEOPLE INDIGENOUS VOICES.'

People Scientists have concluded that the native indigenous people have lived for around twenty thousand years in the Arctic and adopted the hunting, fishing, whaling, herding, and other means for sustainable living. They had devised means to sustain in the frigid environment by developing warm houses and clothing to protect themselves from the frigid conditions. They pride themselves on ancient knowledge on predicting weather and languages, and don't follow the modern political divides between the communities. Many Arctic people now live much like their neighbours to the South, with modern homes and appliances. Nonetheless, there is an active movement among indigenous people in the Arctic to pass on traditional knowledge and skills, such as hunting, fishing, herding, and native languages, to the younger generation.[30]

As per studies, the Arctic populations are in a later stage in the demographic transition, and thus, the rate of growth may be stable or even negative. The major factor which will have an impact on the rapid increase or decrease in populations in pockets will be the discovery of resources or depletions thereof. As per the Arctic Human Development Report, "Urbanization in the Arctic is accelerating, propelled both by local and global forces, and The Arctic is becoming more "marketable" and Arctic identities are seen increasingly as an asset."[31]

---

[30] National Snow and Ice Data Center, 2019, accessed on 10 December 2019 from https://nsidc.org/cryosphere/Arctic-meteorology/Arctic-people.html.

[31] Arctic Human Development Report, accessed on 12 October 2019 from http://norden.diva-portal.org/smash/get/diva2:788965/FULLTEXT03.pdf.

Various scholars have enunciated that the exploration and climate change in the Arctic in itself present a paradox/dilemma or an antithesis. On the one hand, the nations' desire to uplift the economic status of their population by engaging in the commercial exploitation of their resources while simultaneously bowed down by the challenges to maintain the ecological balance and continue to the sustainable development of their indigenous people. These terms amply cover the predicament of fulfilling responsibility towards the environment or to progress the socio-economic upliftment of their populations. However, there are stark contrasts within the various states on issues like exploration and ecological preservation with varying parameters; hence the dilemma and paradox get further widened.

While Korea has been organising Arctic Partnership week as well as offering scholarships, preferably to members from the indigenous community to Korea Maritime Institute's Arctic Academy, every year India's engagement appears rhetorical and superficial.

India should take a cue from AC in governance issues, especially in rural backward areas so that there is strengthened networking between indigenous peoples' associations and a greater say in policies and schemes so that the fruits of economic development reach them. The representation and participation by India's indigenous groups in AC and especially PP's deliberations will strengthen India's standing in the AC and provide India reliable partner to stand by her side during trying times. However, other than mentioning that 'India has substantial expertise in meeting these challenges and is uniquely placed to make a positive contribution in collaborating with Arctic states to assist their indigenous communities to cope with similar challenges,' India has not entered into any joint programme with any of the PPs, so far. Neither has India initiated any programme with any of the Working/Expert Groups/Task Forces to study or improve the livelihoods of the indigenous people. 2019 Email response by PAME, Gwich'in Council, NAMMCO, EPPR, Saami Council, ACAP, OSPAR Commission, AMAP, CAFF, and Aleut International Association on India's engagement with these is placed at **Annexure V.** Other than these the other permanent participants like Arctic Athabaskan Council (AAC), RAIPON and Inuit Circumpolar Council (ICC) elicited no response and the data on India's engagement with these could not be ascertained.

Climate Change and India's Environmental Concerns

Lately, there are three prominent themes which have emerged threatening to disrupt the current structures in the Arctic region, namely a resurgent Russia which has perceptibly reignited the post-cold war geopolitics between the West and Russia, increasing focus on climate change amidst growing voices from increasingly militant young activists and general population and emergence of China as a global power with high aspirations.

Among these global agendas, climate change has assumed the zenith due to wide and cross-cultural and universal support demanding urgent government action. The impacts of global climate change are being experienced throughout diverse regions from Australia to Haiti, yet the most visible effects are being experienced in the Arctic region, with the region showing instantly recognisable signs of an increasingly warming planet. The alarming loss of ice cover, permafrost, and glaciers is pushing the world on an edge, forcing abrupt climate changes, denuding ice levels, inundating coastal areas, changing monsoons, and other sudden calamities leading to immense socio-economic suffering, migration, water stress, food shortages, and so on. The year 2007 saw a record low in the extent of summer sea ice and a similar situation was again encountered in 2012 and there are different predictions that the Arctic will be ice-free by 2044 or by 2067 based on various studies. "According to research published in the journal Nature Climate Change, the Arctic could be "functionally ice-free" by September 2044—and no later than 2067—assuming no changes to global carbon emissions." A rapidly receding sea ice is indicating that global climate change is taking its toll on the Arctic. The ice loss also causes greater coastal erosion due to the effects of warmer air and water leading to an increase in the storm, wave, and tidal activity.

The powers, even far away from the Arctic, both politically and geographically, have been making calls citing their stakes in the Arctic region for reasons of either their self-interests or for expressing concerns over the wider global implications of climate change. The focus of non-Arctic States scientific research in the Arctic is directly primarily to gain insights and devise methodologies to fight climate change.

India has been looking at the Arctic mostly from a scientific prism yet there is a realisation that it has to view it from a strategic construct as well as climate change as well as strengthen the bilateral and multilateral cooperation with the Arctic States and the Arctic intergovernmental organisations. **It is astounding to note that despite climate change being at the top of the AC agenda, the draft of India's Arctic Policy, released in January 21, had NO MENTION thereof.** As per the stated 2013 Indian position, declared by the Indian Ministry of External Affairs on its Arctic participation was India's interest in studying the climate change occurring in the High North. India initiated its Arctic Research Programme in 2007 with a thrust on climate change in the circumpolar north. Yet the absence of climate change from the draft policy document portrayed a myopic and disjointed view, which may have dismayed many who had high expectations from India.

The discussion on climate change in India remains largely focussed on the conduct of conferences and debates and little tangible action. The research organisations have been seen to be utilising the primary data obtained from government installed and funded sensors into individual research contributions, which is a serious drawback and drain on exchequer's resources. A case in point is that the size of the Indian delegation to a conference named 'Polar-2018' was 18 in number, which was among the largest delegations and several papers presented there were multi-authored and based on government data. Since the conference was organised in Switzerland, the opportunity to participate also brings in the perks of tourism as well as expanding the scientific base, yet the country or the international research community has not benefited substantially and there have been few instances of recognition showered on Indian research endeavours.

Given the increasingly assertive foreign policy and strategic direction by India, buoyed by the respected political leadership and international acclaim it is now the opportune time for India to assert its role and position in Arctic affairs. The Indian position is hugely influenced by the deep and strong bilateral relationship it enjoys with the USA, Russia, and other Scandinavian and Nordic States. India's active participation in scientific endeavours at multilevel bodies in the Arctic has been adequately acknowledged and appreciated yet there is further scope to enhance it manifold. There are other parameters to widen the engagement into areas of conservation of the pristine natural environment and limit the adverse effects of climate change globally.

India should follow the Chinese model of science diplomacy wherein China had announced its first overseas satellite data receiving station in the Swedish Arctic, cooperation with Iceland to establish the China-Iceland Aurora Observatory (CIAO) at Kárhóll, and plans to open a Polar Research Institute of China at Tuktoyaktuk, Canada, and so on. The efforts at continued scientific diplomacy should be promoted by way of joint research in climate change and changing the Arctic environment. The focus on geography, climatology (especially climate change), geology, glaciology, and oceanography must continue along with newer avenues like digitalisation efforts, laying of submarine cables, and so on.

The focus of most of the Arctic 8 has been to view human security and sustainable development from climate change prism, and thus, they are focussing on the economic and social development of their human capital. An explicit and defined Indian strategy to combat Climate Change would have endeared and strengthened its position both bilaterally and in the realm of international multilateral scientific diplomacy in the Arctic.

Though the entire South Asian region is grappling the serious threats of the grave and hazardous effects of climate change, yet India being the most populous is at the pivot of these changes. India after its liberalisation reforms initiated in the early 1990s experienced rapid economic growth. India witnesses GDP growth nearing 10% in some of these high growth years, yet it also manifested in unwelcome environmental problems affecting the infant mortality rate and life expectancy due to the high air and water pollution levels. World Health Organisation has also warned that India has been experiencing the ill effects of climate change. India also is rated as the second most-affected country in terms of casualties related to extreme weather. As per some reports, a change in average weather conditions also creates 'hotspots' and has negative impacts on both the living standards of the population and also GDP. Climate change will not only affect internal areas; in mountain areas, climate change will likely affect the frequency of natural disasters. This includes increasing the likelihood of events such as landslides, but also glacial retreat in the Himalayas. On the other hand, rising sea levels represent an existential threat to several coastal areas in south Asia: not only due to the increasing severity of tropical storms but because the large Bangladeshi share of the coast and most of the Maldives may disappear before the end of the twenty-first century.[32]

---

[32] D'Ambrogio E., 2019, India: Environmental Issues, https://www.europarl.europa.eu/RegData/etudes/BRIE/2019/637920/EPRS_BRI(2019)637920_EN.pdf.

The problem is compounded by the ineffectiveness of the regulatory mechanism due to poor institutional settings and lack of enforcement. Though the problems of environmental degradation are experienced across the world, India's problems get compounded due to its high population as also the high population density and growing urbanisation. Air quality in Indian cities is quickly deteriorating and it is today worse than the situation in China: in the 2018 World Health Organisation (WHO) global ambient air quality database, 11 of the 12 cities with the highest levels of small particulate – PM2.5 – are located in India.' The key problems faced by India include vehicular and industrial emissions, chemical and oil pollutions, lack of adequate sanitation, disposal and management of municipal waste, agricultural practices including logging and deforestation and stubble burning, and so on. The situation in November, December, and January becomes immensely critical due to the atmospheric conditions of low temperatures and human-induced post-monsoon biomass (stubble) burning by the farmer communities of Haryana, Punjab, and other countryside. These environmental problems lead to greater health and other social problems faced by the people which lead to a burden on human and economic costs. Chronic illnesses are also one of how the effects of environmental problems are encountered other than lower life expectancy and high infant mortality. The resultant cost due to these issues is lower productivity, poor quality of life, high level of misery, and other human rights issues.

The rural population still uses biomass extensively as fuel leading to health disorders as well as high infant mortality rates. The reliance on coal to power the thermal power plant leads to greater pollution and shows no signs of declining shortly. The forest cover has been worrisomely depleting too. The illegal cutting of trees, especially in the once forest-rich North-Eastern part of the country, is progressing with no checks. The depletion of underground water levels as also waste management is another area of concern. As per a report of National Institution for Transforming India (NITI) Aayog (Commission), India is placed at 120 in a list of 122 countries, on water quality index.

India with its huge coastline, fertile plains, and foothills, and several ranges of the Himalayan mountain ranges will experience the ill effects of climate change in varying forms and details. The impact on mountains will manifest in the form of natural disasters due to events like landslides and recession in glaciers. On the coastal zones, there will be calamities like inundation and submersion of several tracts by the rise in sea levels and the exaggerated impact of tropical storms/Tsunamis and so on.

The Kyoto Protocol (1997) which was signed by India had set the goal for the period from 2008 to 2012 to reduce GHG emissions to 5.2% of 1990 levels. Yet the targets were later adjudged too high for India. The Copenhagen Accord on climate change had left it to individual countries to devise the necessary regulations and thus granted greater autonomy to fix the responsibility to reduce greenhouse gas emissions. The problem of climate change agreements is juxtaposed with the problem of addressing the problem as a global one with localised inputs and individual contributions by each country to help in curbing the problem.

Given the foregoing, it is abundantly clear that a very difficult choice has to be made by the world community at large between economic development achieved by extraction and exploitation of the promise of huge natural resources hidden beneath and to preserve the last bastion of pristine and bountiful natural wonders. Most of the nations and people are divided into charting a middle path, of achieving some degree of balance between these scales by sustainable growth while maintaining the intricate ecological balance. Some governments, such as that of Russia, give greater weight to economic development during these uncertain global economic times, while others may be unable to afford costly infrastructure requirements or favour stronger conservation efforts.[33]

The world governments and the community, at large, have to deftly balance between the conflicting scales of exploiting the rare natural resources and maintaining the ecological systems, especially in the delicate Arctic ecosystem. The current Indian Policy is a story of dilemma and turmoil as India seeks to enhance its position in the global economy and for the same it needs continuous supplies of hydrocarbons, and simultaneously and contrarily, India proclaims to be standing for the reduction of carbon footprints and committed to climate change goals.

In the year, India, China, and several countries had participated in the GLACIER (Global Leadership in the Arctic: Cooperation, Innovation, Engagement, and Resilience) conference, however both countries

---

[33] Conley H, Pumphrey D, Toland T, et al., 2013, Arctic Economics in the 21st Century: The Benefits and Cost of Cold. Center for Strategic and International Studies, https://www.csis.org/analysis/Arctic-economics21st-century.

abstained from signing the joint declaration on conclusion of the conference, owing to the differences in sharing the climate change burden vis-à-vis the developed countries, citing their late entry in the industries led economic development.

There is a stark differential in the rhetoric and action by most of the countries on their adherence to mutually agreed climate change goals (Paris Climate Agreement) as the appetite for consumption of hydrocarbons is growing at an alarming rate while the promise for reduction in energy foot print is falling short on both expectations and commitments. India has also been found to be devoting much less on its association with international institutions to credibly reduce its carbon emissions.

Likewise in COP (Conference of Parties) 25, both India and China along with the USA and Brazil had also backtracked from climate change promises. The intransigence of big polluters—including China, the US, Brazil, and India—at the meeting led to the European Union, small island states, and members of the public expressing frustration.[34] The inherent dichotomy and contradiction in the objectives and aspirations among the developed and developing countries on the issue of fighting climate change in itself are leading to differing opinions and commitments to climate change goals. India, which has emerged as the world's fifth largest economy, is the third largest polluter of CO_2 emissions. However, with an entrenched belief to catch up, economically and industrially with the developed world, it seeks more time and concessions, which in turn leads to continuing indulgence in usage of hydrocarbons and thus receding in efforts to combat diminishing ice cover in the Arctic.

Nearly all the Arctic 8 countries as well as the working groups of the AC are committed and steadfast in adhering to the stated promises on the issue of fighting climate change. Despite simmering geopolitical tensions, all Arctic States and Indigenous Peoples' representatives acknowledged today the enormous threat of climate change to the region's nature and people.[35] Though the current Russia-Ukraine war has derailed some of

---

[34] Vaughan A., 2019, COP25 Climate Summit Ends in "Staggering Failure of Leadership". New Scientist (2019–12–16) [2019–12–17]. https://www.newscientist.com/article/2227541-cop25-climate-summit-ends-in-staggering-failure-of-leadership.

[35] WWF Arctic Programme, 2021, Arctic Council Unites on Climate Change Threat, Fails to Commit to a Net Zero Vision of the Arctic (2021–05–20) [2022–06–12]. https://www.arcticwwf.org/newsroom/news/arctic-councilunites-on-climate-change-threat-fails-to-commit-to-a-net-zero-visionof-the-arctic/.

the promises, yet Observer countries including India should demonstrate their resolute commitment to fight climate change.

INDIA AS AN OBSERVER

The observers occupy a unique position in the Council and exercise nominal influence in the AC as the power to moderate discussion and decisions rests with the member states alone. The AC members have a stake in admitting observers as they engage with them economically with promises of investments, infrastructural development, and socio-economic development of the communities. The observers, on the other hand, have varying incentives like economic exploration, scientific research, and diplomatic leverage, and so on. Council observers are less influential than states in the Council. Member states accept observers to make economic gains. non-Arctic states are interested in protecting the environment as well as making potential economic gains, in contrast to the more focussed motivations of member states.[36]

A normal tendency is to view India's status as an Arctic Observer vis-a-vis the responses of other Asian observers, namely China, Japan, and Korea. A common fabric among these three nations is that other than political and economic issues they have expanded their sphere in other domains like terrorism, SAR, and constructive business cooperation. Such an approach is missing in India's context as India has been repeatedly embarked on scientific pursuits alone. The North-East Asian nations are also hopeful that their coastline regions will further develop and have greater cooperative arrangements with other neighbouring countries in the times to come. China is also renting out two ports in North Korea to further fuel its exports to Europe and hydrocarbon imports from the Russian Far East. India though has remained aloof from the political participation in the AC meetings as well as by non-attendance of most of the meetings of the Working Groups as well as with Permanent Participants. This is indicative of an imbalance between India's physical scientific presences in the Arctic (e.g. Himadri station at Svalbard) and its participation in Arctic governance mechanisms.[37]

---

[36] Chater A., Explaining Non-Arctic States in the Arctic Council, Strategic Analysis, vol. 40, issue 3, pp. 173–184. https://doi.org/10.1080/09700161.2016.1165467.

[37] Chahal H., India in the Arctic. Regards Géopolitiques, 2016, vol. 2, issue 4, pp. 2–5. https://cqegheiulaval.com/india-in-the-arctic/.

The representation of India was done by the Secretary Ministry of Earth Sciences (MoES) Dr. M Rajeevan during the ceremony when India's Observer status was renewed in May 2019, thereby downplaying the importance for the region and affirming that India considers the region as a major scientific expedition threshold and not as a region with growing inter-regional and global geostrategic significance. Also, in view of the foregoing it emerges that Arctic figures for India as a field for mere scientific study rather than the tremendous geostrategic place it occupies which is not in line with the professed lofty goals that India has set for herself at international level.

Since Arctic Council Observer membership, as well as diplomatic relations with sovereign Arctic States, falls in the mandate of the MEA, yet India has been continuously viewing the Arctic through the scientific prism which impairs the geopolitical and geostrategic view, which is critical for India to enhance its position and credibility in the region.

The opening paragraph in the policy lists Russia (officially called the Russian Federation) among the eight countries as members of the Arctic Council. The usage of 'Russia' instead of the 'Russian Federation' smacks of lopsided diplomacy or error on part of the Indian government, especially in view of the ongoing Ukraine crisis, yet this issue is left for political scientists and analysts to comment.

As per para 1.2.2 of India's Policy, 'In 2016, India's northernmost atmospheric laboratory was established at Gruvebadet.' This statement gives the impression that India has established a Lab at Gruvebadet, yet Gruvebadet is an atmospheric laboratory and observatory located midway between Ny-Ålesund, the Zeppelin observatory and the Climate Change Tower. The building currently hosts instruments for among others aerosols sampling.[38] The main focus area of this Lab is atmospheric research. Today Gruvebadet has activities from CNR (Consiglio Nazionale delle Ricerche: Italy), NCPOR (India), NIPR (National Institute of Polar Research: Japan), KOPRI (Korea Polar Research Institute: South Korea), FMI (Finnish Meteorological Institute: Finland), and UiT (the Arctic University of Norway: Norway).

Since Svalbard, Norway has been welcoming international scientific research at various locations under the RiS (Research in Svalbard) programme with Gruvebadet having five rooms for instruments, where

---

[38] Ny-Ålesund Research Station, 2021, Gruvebadet Atmosphere Laboratory. https://nyalesundresearch.no/infrastructures/gruvebadet-atmosphere-laboratory/.

three rooms have inlets from the roof. The Indian presence at Gruvebadet is succinctly given out at NCPOR website at https://ncpor.res.in/arctics/display/395-gruvebadet-lab whereby the following instruments have been set up—Microwave Radiometer profiler, Micro Rain Radar, Ceilometer, Photo Acoustic Soot Spectrometer, Nephelometer, and Aethelometer.

As per the NySMAC website, Ny-Ålesund offers a wide range of shared scientific infrastructure to include Kings Bay Marine Laboratory, Zeppelin Observatory, Amundsen-Nobile Climate Change Tower, Gruvebadet Atmosphere Laboratory, and Light Sensitive Cabin.[39]

Arctic Resources

On the eve of Indian PM's visit to Vladivostok in September 2019, it was stated that cooperation in the search for Hydro-Carbon and LNG in the Far East and the Arctic have been agreed. This statement asserted that India was keenly watching and interested in the exploration of Arctic resources. This statement has relevance both in pragmatism in participating in unlocking resource potential of the Arctic as also progressing the Russian partnership in this field. An identical statement was also issued in October 2018 during the visit of Russian President to India, wherein it was stated that 'exploring opportunities for joint development of oil fields in the Russian territory, including in the Arctic shelf of Russia and joint development of projects on the shelf of the Pechora and Okhotsk Seas.'[40] These statements affirm Indian openness to having joint partnerships with Russia in the exploration of hydrocarbons in the Arctic region. Likewise, during the St Petersburg Declaration on 01 June 2017, it was stated that 'we are interested in launching joint projects on exploration and exploitation of hydrocarbons in the Arctic shelf of the Russian Federation.'

Speaking at a discussion at Valdai Discussion Club on 27 August 2019, the EAM had said that 'greater maritime opportunities would also arise

---

[39] Ny-Ålesund Science Managers Committee, 2019, Infrastructure and Shared Resources. https://nyalesundresearch.no/research-and-monitoring/infrastructure/.

[40] Ministry of External Affairs, 2018, India-Russia Joint Statement during visit of President of Russia to India (October 05, 2018) (2018-10-05) [2019-12-22]. https://mea.gov.in/bilateral-documents.htm?dtl/30469/IndiaRussia_Joint_Statement_during_visit_of_President_of_Russia_to_India_October_05_2018.

from what is happening in regarding the Arctic: 'the possibility of new maritime routes opening up'.[41] This was first acknowledgement by a senior government functionary on the impact of the opening of new routes which will have profound maritime opportunities. Though specifics like hydrocarbons transit, trade was not addressed yet it was the realisation of India accepting the tremendous geophysical and structural changes taking place which will have profound global impacts.

Should NSR become a regular transit passage, there will be a great shift in geopolitical leverage. The Indian policy document has briefly stated that 'Traffic, especially through the Northern Sea Route (NSR) is rising exponentially and is projected to rise to 80 million tons by 2024' and doesn't give out India's stand/reservations related to geopolitical levers accruing to China as well as the ecological and environmental costs with the operationalisation of NSR. Though the oil and gas from the Arctic region are lucrative, yet for optimally utilising the benefits of NSR, the areas best suited are those lying North of Hong Kong. The areas South of Hong Kong or beyond may have an equal or perhaps more benefit from the present Southern routes in terms of time, cost, seaborne threats, marine insurance, and so on. Thus given India's Geophysical location, it will not benefit directly from the Arctic shipping routes. Hence, India is in very unique position to chart out a carefully drawn out strategy to limit the Chinese influence as well as to stand shoulder to shoulder with its Arctic partners to limit the environmental degradation on this issue.

The Russian position on NSR may contain a potential for arguments/disagreements in the coming days. Since several countries including China have obliquely referred to the requirement of freedom of navigation in the Arctic, this issue has the potential for conflagration and needs careful handling. The Indian PM's speech had, in September 2019 in Russia, completely skirted the NSR and adopted a myopic and continental perspective on connection with Russia's Far East with the Indo-Pacific, instead of the assistance in developing the NSR to secure competitive payoffs later from the oil and gas riches located there.

Till now, the strategic rivalry between India and China was witnessed in areas of border disputes, sea power, and trade but the Arctic can

---

[41] Ministry of External Affairs, 2019a, External Affairs Minister's conversation with Valdai Discussion Club, Moscow on 27 August 2019 (2019–10–19) [2019–11–02]. https://www.mea.gov.in/SpeechesStatements.htm?dtl/31957/External_Affairs_Ministers_conversation_with_Valdai_Discussion_Club_Moscow_on_27_August_2019.

spiral this rivalry to newer dimensions of energy security and access to sea routes. For India, the headache is increased by the Chinese of not limiting its engagement only to NSR but the Polar Silk Road (PSR)'s goal and objective of deep economic integration with the Polar Region. Hence the transportation and communication realm of Russia's NSR will be expounded by political, institutional, and commercial instruments.

NSR offers one-third distance reduction for full transit from Eastern Asia to Northern Europe. China has offered its assistance to Russia in the development of the NSR by providing advanced marine technologies and fleet modernisation. As a signatory to the UNCLOS, Russia is reaping the benefits of Article 234 of UNCLOS which permits it to monitor and control the movement of the vessels traversing the NSR as it lies in its Exclusive Economic Zone (EEZ). Presently, Russia levies icebreaker escort fees on vessel traversing the NSR and her control is unrestricted and absolute. In 2009, the fee was set to 40 USD per ton of container Cargo. The countries most benefitting from the opening of NSR include Japan, South Korea, China, and Russia. China, which has been considered as a strategic rival by the USA will have the option of reducing its dependence on the Malacca Straits to route its hydrocarbons and other shipments through the NSR and thus diminishing the influence the USA and QUAD countries are levying by disrupting the Chinese rights on Malacca straits. Moreover, as brought out earlier, the NSR opening will also accrue substantial cost savings, due to shortened distances for the shipments vis-à-vis the Suez Canal route. A concurrent advantage will be experienced in these countries shipbuilding industries, due to increased demand for ships, especially ice-class ships.

Among the Asian States, Japan and Korean policy documents convey conservative estimates and call for detailed feasibility studies while China is relatively more ambitious in its approach. As far as the routes go, both Russia and Canada have cited Article 234 of UNCLOS which provides for protection and preservation of the ice-covered EEZ areas of the Arctic Ocean, resulting in laying exclusive rights over NWP and NEP/NSR, respectively.

India has to realise that its economic engagements in search of hydrocarbons are also contributing in one way or the other to the dismantling of existing structures in the Arctic region.

Disputation of Global Commons

While signing the AC admission norms as an Observer, each of the observer's states has acceded to abide by the governance structure, which offers the right to vote and voice on matters only to the circumpolar member states. There is another dilemma here wherein the adherence to United Nations Convention on the Law of the Sea (UNCLOS) claims specifically lowers the space for international scientific research as the area becomes sovereign territory with sovereign rights becoming applicable and the call for global commons is deflated.

Select Indian thoughts had called for declaring the Arctic as global commons, a view which has found less traction among the international fora as well as the Arctic States. Col PK Gautam has stretched the global commons domain and called on developing states to take a leadership position and not leave the matter to the developed countries alone.[42] In the years preceding India's inclusion as an Observer and even later, many Indian commentators hinted at the Arctic as a place for 'global commons,' a view which was emphatically demolished by the 2008 Ilulissat Declaration. This reasoning was specifically expressed by the notion of the Arctic as a "common heritage of mankind"—a vision that some Arctic rim states might have found both ill-conceived and misinformed.[43]

After inclusion as an Observer, India listed its interests in the Arctic region as scientific, environmental, commercial, as well as strategic.[44] In the same piece, India also called for the participation of all those actors who have a stake in the governance of global commons (ibid). It is apparent that the official stand of the Indian government centred on regarding Arctic as global commons, a view which has been reversed in consonance with the transformed geopolitical realm and steady realisation thereof affirmed in the current foreign policy.

External Affairs Minister (EAM) himself acknowledged during his speech on 14 November 2019 that 'The global commons is also more in disputation as multilateralism weakens. Even climate change is a factor,

---

[42] Gautam P K., 2011, Arctic as Global Common, IDSA. https://idsa.in/issuebrief/TheArcticasaGlobalCommon.

[43] Chaturvedi S., India's Arctic Engagement: Challenges and Opportunities. Asia Policy, 2014, vol. 18, issue 1, pp. 73–79. https://doi.org/10.1353/asp.2014.0037.

[44] Ministry of External Affairs, 2013, India and the Arctic. http://www.mea.gov.in/in-focus-article.htm?21812/India+and+the+Arctic/.

contributing to geopolitics amongst others by the opening of an Arctic passage'.[45] The moral high pedestal of an idealistic stand taken by Indian commentators (with some of the pieces even put up on MEA website) often drawing India's position in the Arctic as a place of global commons was also set aside by the EAM.

India by virtue of certain parameters like its size, democratic and inclusive society, vibrant multi-ethno-cultural-social fabric, and soft power makes it a candidate to aspire for great power status. Yet, there are several obstructions to this aspiration for assuming global leadership. In the current era of global politics, which is witnessing the third era of transformation since the 1987 Murmansk speech namely the period of the post-cold war peace, the era of a unipolar world under the USA and the current era of growing challenges to the world order by demanding global leadership by Russia and China.

The Arctic region which has already witnessed the presence of all contenders of great power status and carved out a strategy for India requires deliberate forethought. In light of the acute discrepancies in the Indian state capacity and the stated objective as a major power is being noticed by the world community and there seems to be a huge differential between the rhetoric and action. It is also established that mere soft power is not enough to any claims for global/major power and the Indian strategy has to have a multi-pronged approach to carve out a niche role in the Arctic affairs. In the recent past, India has been plagued by vocal internal strife, withdrawal from trade arrangements, and history of delayed implementation of projects. In light to effectively engage with the Arctic States bilaterally, India has to sort these matters urgently. Since the Arctic can be a playground to outsmart China, India will have to soft balance with others to develop and present a viable alternative to China.

India has maritime boundaries with Sri Lanka, Maldives, Myanmar, Indonesia, and Thailand, and two terrestrial nations, Pakistan and Bangladesh. Thus, India shares maritime boundaries with more states than it shares on the hinterland, and hence the importance of universal application and enforcement of UNCLOS has greater importance. India is a signatory to the UNCLOS and has settled its maritime border with

---

[45] Jaishankar, S., External Affairs Minister's speech at the 4th Ramnath Goenka Lecture, 2019, accessed on 12 December 19 from https://mea.gov.in/Speeches-Statements.htm?dtl/32038/External+Affairs+Ministers+speech+at+the+4th+Ramnath+Goenka+Lecture+2019.

Bangladesh based on the treaty parameters. Also in light of its stated stand on respect for international law and dispute settlement under the framework of such international law including UNCLOS does take away all claims on the Arctic as part of global commons as most of the area is claimed by respective countries under the UNCLOS framework on sovereign ownership. India has consistently favoured as per UNCLOS, the equidistant/median line as the line of maritime demarcation, and hence India's position on the disputed Hans Island and other disputes in the Arctic can be easily extrapolated. The India-Pakistan dispute in the Sir Creek area which remains disputed also lessens India's profile as it contains huge economic potential but the lack of political will and action to enforce sea Laws to strengthen its hold over marine resources and project itself as a firm state with necessary wherewithal or as a tool for conflict resolution has not been exercised. India's action in her neighbourhood on adherence to UNCLOS will echo on its position with respect to claims in the Arctic, too.

On the issue of climate change, India has been found to be dragging its feet in reiterating firm commitments. While India is within its right to specify its emissions pathway, it should not—at any forum—promise more than what it can deliver as this undermines the moral authority that India brings to future negotiations.[46] Since India occupies an important place in the future discourse on Arctic, in light of path breaking geopolitical developments, its policy will be keenly studied and provide strategic direction.

India enjoys considerable rapport and understanding with both Russia and the USA; despite their tensions, exacerbated with the Ukraine crisis, it calls for enhancing her stranglehold over the other members. Since smaller countries like Norway, Denmark, Sweden, and Iceland occupy a seat at the Arctic high table, and India enjoys friendly bilateral relations with them, this demands raising one's footing by adapting bilateral engagements to suit their demands and become an indispensable Observer state and gradually steer the course. The equation in the Arctic region is made more complex as there are several divergent states, non-state and international players, often with deviations in goals, objectives, and methodology which demands that India should chart out a policy discourse which

---

[46] The Hindu, accessed on 16 August 2022 at https://www.thehindu.com/opinion/editorial/sticking-to-commitments-the-hindu-editorial-on-indias-climate-change-goals/article65726909.ece.

is adapted and adopted by these diverse players which will further strengthen India's position.

India should also take a cue from its recent addition of a separate Division, NEST (New, Emerging and Strategic Technologies) in the MEA and set up either a separate Division or amalgamate the function of the existing Americas, Central Europe and Eurasia divisions to leverage and decipher the Arctic issues with precision. The existing disconnect between these three divisions does not provide a single point and seamless understanding of the complex Arctic issues and the creation of an umbrella subunit will offer better and precise inputs that will enlarge India's engagement. Also, the inputs and involvement of other Ministries like MoES, MoST, MoTA, and other think tanks should be leveraged into chartering fresh and incisive policy direction.

In the Arctic Circle assembly of 2019, India was the only exception that didn't depute any Ambassador/Special Representative like China, Japan, and Korea. It is vital to have a benign and responsible person, committed to climate change goals and with established and respected credentials to portray India's position. This Arctic ambassador will be the Indian voice of Arctic at unrepresented fora like SAARC, Bay of Bengal Initiative for Multi-Sectoral Technical and Economic Cooperation (BIMSTEC), India, Brazil, and South Africa (IBSA), etc., to garner the attention of these multinational fora and also emerge as a strong voice for Arctic affairs and thereby gain the trust of the Arctic nations.

The Arctic States and the AC along with its associated fora have been successful, especially in times where great power rivalry and inter-regional manoeuvrings were rampant in isolating and insulating the region from these dynamics. India, by its democratic heritage and collaborative lineage, fits the requirements of an external Observer state and must continue to build on its strengths for mutual betterment.

India's Geopolitical Goals

Geopolitics is derived from the combination of two words—Geography and Politics. The Geography includes both physical and human components and international politics includes the international relations between nations. There is variance in geopolitical goals, centred around an area depending on the interests of international actors and the presence of other interconnected issues like multilateral mechanisms and so on. The outlook and parameters for each nation have to be dwelled by an interplay of international relations and social, political, and historical phenomena. The term has been used to describe a broad spectrum of ideas, from "a synonym for international relations, social, political and historical phenomena" to various pseudo-scientific theories of historical and geographic determinism.[47]

In the years preceding India's inclusion as an Observer and even later, many Indian commentators hinted at the Arctic as a place for 'global commons,' a view which was emphatically demolished by the 2008 Ilulissat Declaration. After inclusion as an Observer, India listed its interests in the Arctic region as scientific, environmental, commercial, as well as strategic.[48] In the same piece, India also called for the participation of all those actors who have a stake in the governance of global commons.[49]

The Indian government has abstained from issuing a broad and comprehensive Arctic policy, and thus the Indian place in the Arctic remains unclear and nascent. Indian policy discourse has yet to produce a coherent or dominant opinion on the country's place in Arctic affairs.[50] The position of India is quite diverse as compared to the Arctic littorals, who claim rights to territorial seas, EEZs, and extended continental shelves, based on international law and other treaties, and India is trying to redefine its position by championing and assuming the cradle of a responsible emerging great power, based on friendly relations with the Arctic 8. Though the Arctic littorals are broadly viewing their territorial and economic claims under rights enshrined under international law and treaty obligations, India has claimed to be a stakeholder by understanding and analysis of the complex and fluid contexts in which the discourse and practices of Arctic governance are being debated and shaped at present.[51]

The dominant position among the Indian scholars hinge of viewing the Arctic from a global lens rather than a regional or local perspective is a broad view though magnanimous in outlook but is contrary to India's

---

[47] JSTOR, 2019, accessed on 11 October 2019 from https://www.jstor.org/topic/geopolitics/.

[48] India and the Arctic//Ministry of External Affairs. Government of India. 10 June 2013.
http://www.mea.gov.in/in-focus-article.htm?21812/India+and+the+Arctic/.

[49] Ibid.

[50] Lackenbauer Whitney P, India's Arctic Engagement: Emerging Perspectives, Arctic Yearbook 2013.

[51] Ibid.

views on Article 370 in J&K[52] and other domestic issues involving territorial delineation and rights. India can credit herself for raising questions on climate change and Western claims to sovereignty on Antarctica as early as in the 1950s. Despite being an early advocate, of a 'common heritage of mankind' India's call to UN on Antarctica went astray and the 1959 Antarctica Treaty was in a divergent direction.

Russia India Cooperation: Russia offers a lucrative alternate option to India to reduce its energy imports from the Middle East. In light of the strong partnership between India and the USSR in the era before the disintegration of the Soviet Union, the Russian Federation has been actively pursuing India to have its equity in Russian energy firms. Moscow has long sought Indian equity investment in Russian energy firms, especially in the expensive Arctic region, while India, whose energy needs are immense and growing, has substantially upgraded its quest for influence in the Arctic.[53] India, on the other hand, post its liberalisation of the economy in the early 1990s, has been relying on the Middle East to fulfil its energy needs. Though there has been some cooperation in this regard particularly after India has realised that it needs to secure its energy supplies from regional disruptions and geopolitical pulls and pressures, especially since the Middle East has a history of mutual suspicion and unresolved ethno-regional and economic disputes. In the mid-term, however, based on the states' interests and the existing long-standing partnership between the two countries, and involvement of Indian companies in the Russian energy projects in the Arctic region can be expected.[54] Despite growing economic cooperation with China, Russia is keen to hedge its stakes by involving its time tested partner India. The Russian quest will further establish its multipolar engagement, and for India, it credibly reaffirms its stature as a rising global power.

Though there has been some progress between Russian energy firms and their Indian counterparts in the past, the experience has been mixed. It is assessed that the deals which have been entered are more for fulfilling

[52] Ministry of External Affairs, Government of India, 2019, accessed on 01 December 2019 from https://www.mea.gov.in/articles-in-foreign-media.htm?dtl/31853/Changing_the_status_of_Jammu_and_Kashmir_will_benefit_all_of_India.

[53] The Maritime Executive, 2019, accessed on 01 December 2019 from https://www.maritime-executive.com/editorials/india-invests-in-russia-s-Arctic-offshore-oil-and-gas-industry.

[54] Nadezhda Filimonova, supra note 6.

the diplomatic and states' interests rather than for economic collaboration. The Indian experience in Licence 61, Imperial Energy, etc., has been sour, and within a short period, India is vying to dispose of its assets as there has been less than expected economic success.

It is with the strategy to diversify its supply of energy sources that as on 2019, India's ONGC Videsh Limited (OVL) has stakes in 39 oil and gas projects in 19 countries spread across Africa, Latin America, Eurasia, and Australasia. A concurrent theme is to reduce India's energy import dependence; however the geophysical and geographical demands still project that India's bulk of the demand will continue to be met by the Gulf region. While such measures will certainly help in getting assured supplies as well as giving some protection against high oil prices, they will have only a marginal impact on India's energy dependency on the Gulf.[55]

Oil and Natural Gas Commission (ONGC) is a Government of India company and has been conferred the status of Maharatna in 2010. It is engaged in E&P (exploration and production) and API (acquisition, processing, and interpretation) of seismic data and is an oil and gas conglomerate. It has its wholly-owned subsidiary and overseas arm, ONGC Videsh Limited (OVL), which is a Miniratna Central Public Sector Enterprise of the Government of India having current investments in the following three oilfields in Russia[56]:

(a) Sakhalin-1: The Sakhalin Island lies in the Russian Far East and closest to Japan and Sea of Okhotsk. There are many hydrocarbon fields in Sakhalin and OVL has stakes in the first discovery in Sakhalin, called the Sakhalin-1 field. Sakhalin-1 is spread over an area of approximately 1,140 Sq. Km., which includes three offshore fields, namely Chayvo (WD-15 metres), Odoptu (WD-25 metres), and ArkutunDagi (WD-35 metres). ONGC Videsh had acquired 20% Participating Interest (PI) in Sakhalin-I on 31.07.2001. Exxon Neftegas Limited (ENL) holds 30% PI and is the operator; SODECO holds 30% and the remaining 20% PI is held by Rosneft Subsidiaries. The map below depicts the physical

---

[55] Sikri Rajiv, The Geopolitics of Energy Security and Implications for South and Southeast Asia, ISAS, 2008, accessed on 12 November 2019 from www.isas.nus.edu.sg.

[56] ONGC videsh.com, 2019, accessed on 10 December 2019 from https://www.ongcvidesh.com/assets/cis-far-east/.

location of Sakhalin Island as well as the sites for various blocks earmarked therein for exploration (Map 3.1).

(b) Imperial Energy: Among the OVL's overseas purchases included Imperial Energy Corporation Plc., an independent upstream oil Exploration and Production Company has its main activities in the Tomsk region of Western Siberia, Russia. The Imperial Energy deal was finalised in 2009, and within the last 10 years, the Indian government has been rapped by CAG for wasteful expenditure as also the Indian government has realised that the project does not fulfil the claimed economic promise. Imperial's interests comprised of 10 E&P license blocks in the Tomsk region with a total licensed area of approximately 11,038 sq. km, which were granted to the Company from 2005 to 2017, have different validity dates, and will expire between the years 2027 and 2038. During FY'19, Imperial Energy's oil and oil equivalent gas production was about 0.242 MMtOE.[57]

(c) Vankor: The Indian stakes in Vankor oilfield were acquired in 2016 in two tranches in which 15% equity was taken in May 2016 and another 11% in October 2016 by OVL. The Vankor field is located in the north-eastern part of the West Siberian Basin in the Russian Federation. Vankor is Rosneft's and also Russia's one of the largest fields by production. During the PM's visit to Vladivostok in September 2019, there were plans to increase the Indian stakes to 49.9% by having the Indian consortium of OIL-IOC-BPRL with 23.9% PI and Rosneft with 50.1% PI is the Operator. ONGC Videsh Singapore Pte. Ltd was incorporated on 18.04.2016 in Singapore for the acquisition of shares in Vankorneft, Russia, through its subsidiary ONGC Videsh Vankorneft Pte Limited (OVVL). OVVL holds 26% shares in Vankorneft, Russia, and its share of production during FY'19 was 5.800 MMTOE[58] (3.2).

India has a dedicated Ministry, 'Ministry of Petroleum & Natural Gas,' to oversee the exploration, production, marketing, and entering into government-level contracts to fulfil the requirements of both oil and

---

[57] ONGC, Annual Report 2018–2019, accessed on 01 November 2019 from https://www.ongcindia.com/wps/wcm/connect/en/investors/annual-reports/annual-report-2018-19.

[58] Ibid.

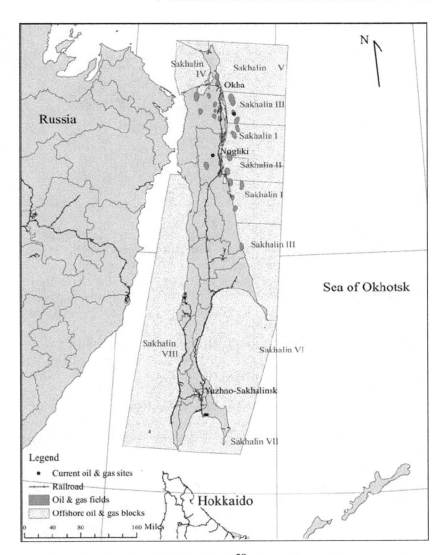

Map 3.1 Map showing Sakhalin Islands[59] (*Source* https://www.researchgate.net/figure/Map-of-Sakhalin-Island-showing-offshore-oil-and-gas-blocks-and-study-locations-Okha_fig1_248393621)

[59] Researchgate.net, accessed on 23 August 19 from https://www.researchgate.net/figure/Map-of-Sakhalin-Island-showing-offshore-oil-and-gas-blocks-and-study-locations-Okha_fig1_248393621.

Map 3.2 Map showing locations of Taas-Yuryakh and Vankor oilfields (*Source* https://www.telegraphindia.com/business/oil-trio-buy-stake-in-russia/cid/1462355)

natural gas for the country. It has various bodies and organisation to oversee the allied aspects of refining, distribution, import, export, and conservation of petroleum products. Oil and gas is the important import for (our) economy, many initiatives have been taken by the Ministry for increasing production and exploitation of all domestic petroleum resources to address the priorities like energy access, energy efficiency, energy sustainability, and energy security.[60]

Since India has been on a growth trajectory requiring huge amounts of energy resources for its transportation, infrastructure, mobility, and other sectors, it also takes out the roadmap for fulfilling its demand and addressing priorities on energy access and energy security. As per the Ministry, the sourcing of hydrocarbons for the country is covered under the 'International cooperation' available at http://petroleum.nic.in/about-us/international-co-opration. Map 3.3 depicting the current sourcing of hydrocarbons is.

The Ministry has also released its Hydrocarbon Vision 2025, which does give out the huge demand–supply gap in both oil and natural gas. Without divulging the regions, it does, however, chart out the need for equity participation in Russia, Iraq, Iran, and North African countries. As per the data from this report, the gap in demand and supply is as under (Table 3.1).

---

[60] Ministry of Petroleum and Natural Gas, 2019, accessed on 01 December 2019 from http://petroleum.nic.in/about-us/about-ministry.

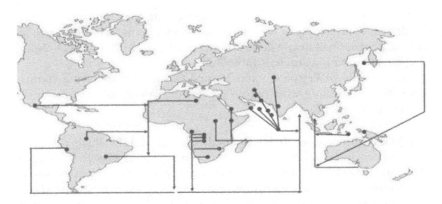

Map 3.3 Map showing sourcing of hydrocarbons by India[61] (*Source* http://petroleum.nic.in/sites/default/files/international_coopJul2019.pdf)

Table 3.1 Supply/demand of petroleum products (in MMT)

Supply/Demand-Petroleum Products (in MMT)

Year	Demand (without meeting gas deficit)	Demand (with meeting gas deficit)	Estimated refining capacity	Estimated crude requirement
1998-1999	91	103	69	69
2001-2002	111	138	129	122
2006-2007	148	179*	167	173
2011-2012	195	195**	184	190
2024-2025	368	368	358	364

* Assuming 15 MMTPA of LNG import by 2007.
** Assuming that by 2012, adequate gas is available through imports and domestic sources.

Source: Report of the Sub-Group on development of refining, marketing transportation and infrastructure requirements (1999).
As against this requirement the present domestic crude production is 33 MMT. The gap will have to be met through imports and increase in domestic production.

Source Hydrocarbon Vision 2025

[61] Ministry of Petroleum and Natural Gas, Government of India, accessed on 24 September 19 from http://petroleum.nic.in/sites/default/files/international_coopJul2019.pdf.

It is clear by a mere perusal of the above data that the cleft between the demand and supply is widening due to increasing economic activity and the demand will nearly double between 2011–2012 and 2024–2025. The gas situation is as under (Table 3.2).

The Ministry of Petroleum and Natural Gas has the following companies which are dealing with various aspects of hydrocarbon procurement and energy supply:

(a) Gas Authority of India Limited (GAIL): GAIL which functions under the Ministry of Petroleum and Natural Gas is the largest state-owned natural gas processing and distribution company in India. It also proudly claims that it is a Government of India undertaking as it was formed in the era of governmental control of strategic sectors and termed as "licence raj." Though later some licences were later issued to private companies like Reliance Industries and Shell Plc however GAIL maintains both the first-mover advantage and government support in its operations and has

Table 3.2 Supply/demand natural gas (MMSCMD)[62]

SUPPLY/DEMAND-NATURAL GAS
(in million standard cubic meters per day)

	(MMSCMD)
	DEMAND
1999-2000	110
2001-2002	151
2006-2007	231
2011-2012	313
2024-2025	391

Source: Report of the Sub-Group on development and utilisation of natural gas (1999).

As against this requirement, the present domestic gas supply is 65 MMSCMD. The gap will have to be met from imports, increase in domestic production and by switching to liquid fuels.

Source Hydrocarbon Vision 2025

---

[62] Ministry of Petroleum and Natural Gas, Government of India, accessed on 24 September 19 from http://petroleum.nic.in/sites/default/files/vision.pdf.

emerged with the most volumes of trade. The key items from the GAIL Annual Report 2018[63] are as under:

(i) Sourcing of Gas: With the established procedures of entering into long-term contracts for supplies of gas, GAIL had signed such agreements with Russia (2.5 MMTPA) and USA (5.8 MMTPA). The gas supplies from the USA have already commenced in 2018 from the Sabine Pass and Cove Point LNG projects in the USA. Also in 2018, the supplies from Russia's Gazprom started and thus GAIL is presently counted among the world's top 10 LNG portfolio holders (~14 mtpa).

(ii) LNG Shipping: GAIL had charter hired the vessel 'Meridian Spirit' for transportation of LNG sourced from the USA for 3 years from Total Inc., Norway.

(iii) LNG supply Agreements: GAIL and Gazprom had earlier agreed to purchase up to 2.5 million tons of LNG annually in 2012. However, in the intervening years, there could have no progress on the supply of the same. GAIL had signed an understanding with Gazprom Marketing and Trading Singapore (GMTS) for sourcing up to 2.85 MMTPA, LNG primarily from Yamal Liquefaction terminal with supplies commenced from 2018–2019.

(b) Oil India Limited (OIL): Like GAIL, OIL too is a Government of India undertaking which deals with exploration, production, and development of petroleum oil. As per the OIL India.com, Annual Report 2018–2019, it also holds stakes in foreign exploration areas. The report is available at (https://www.oil-india.com/Document/financial/Final-OIL-India-annual-report-2018-19-compressed.pdf). The stakes in foreign areas of OIL are:

(i) Vankorneft: OIL has a 23.90% stake in CJSC Vankorneft which has two licences, namely Vankor and North Vankor. As of present arrangements, the crude from its fields is being supplied to China and European countries and India does not

---

[63] Gas Authority of India Limited, GAIL, accessed on 12 November 19 from https://gailonline.com/pdf/InvestorsZone/AnnualReports/Annual%20Report%202018-19%20.pdf.

get the same. There are talks to expand the Indian share in Vankor to 49% by having 26% stakes with OVL ONGC Videsh Limited and the remaining 23% with the OIL, BPRL, and IOCL consortium. As on 31.03.2019, the 2P reserve position corresponding to OIL's Participating Interest in this asset has been estimated at 16.94 MMT of oil and 6.72 BCM of gas.[64]

(ii) Taas-Yuryakh: Indian Firms, Indian Oil Corporation Limited, and Bharat Petro Resources Limited, along with OIL have stakes in Taas-Yuryakh of 29.90% in Taas-Yuryakh Neftegazodobycha in Russia. In this arrangement, the OIL share is 33.5% among the Indian partners. After the disruption in oil supplies in 2019 due to a drone attack on Saudi Aramco facility, India had initiated talks with Russia to raise oil imports. As on 31 March 2019, the 2P reserve position corresponding to OIL's participating interest in this asset has been estimated at 12.15 MMT of oil. During 2018–2019, OIL's share of production in asset stood at 0.43 MMTOE.[65]

(iii) License 61: OIL had acquired a 50% stake along with another 50% by PetroNeft Resources Limited in 2014 in which the latter had offloaded its share of 50% to OIL. However, in 2019 the Minister of Petroleum and Natural Gas, Dharmendra Pradhan had said in the Parliament that the performance of the asset has not been as expected and OIL has initiated the process of the assets sale. During 2018–2019, OIL's share of production in the asset stood at 0.043 MMT. OIL's share of investment in this project is 619.47 crore (USD 93.72 million) as on 31 March 2019.[66]

(c) Petronet LNG Ltd (PLL): PLL is a Government of India undertaking in the LNG value chain to provide energy to the Indian market. It is promoted by a consortium of companies led by GAIL, ONGC, IOCL, and BPCL. PLL has set up the country's first LNG receiving and re-gasification terminal at Dahej, Gujarat, and

---

[64] OIL India.com, Annual Report 2018–2019, accessed on 12 December 2019 from https://www.oil-india.com/Document/financial/Final-OIL-India-annual-report-2018-19-compressed.pdf.

[65] Ibid.

[66] Ibid.

Table 3.3 Re-gasification terminals in India (MMTPA)[67]

Location	Owner and operator	Re-gas capacity (MMTPA)
Dahej (Gujarat)	PLL	17.5
Hazira (Gujarat)	Shell	5
Kochi (Kerala)	PLL	5
Mundra (Gujarat)	GSPC LNG Ltd	5
Ennore (Tamil Nadu)	Indian Oil	5
Kochi (Kerala)	GAIL	1.3
Total		38.8 MMTPA (140 MMSCMD)

another terminal at Kochi, Kerala. Its terminals account for around 40% gas supplies in the country and handle around 80% of LNG imports in India. At present, India is having six (6) operational LNG re-gasification terminals operational with a capacity of about 38.8 MMTPA (~140 MMSCMD). The re-gasification capacity is highest with PLL. The terminals for re-gasification in India are as under (Table 3.3).

The signing of an MoU between PLL and NOVATEK on cooperation concerning the joint development of downstream LNG Business and LNG supplies was signed during PM Modi's visit to Vladivostok in September 2019.

The Indian economy is a net importer of all energy requirements and is projected that with continuing growth in economic development, the energy requirements are going to further increase. To secure its energy basket, the Indian government is making concerted efforts to diversify the fuel basket by involving the newer forms of energy sources. The increased focus on LNG, CNG, Hydropower, Solar, and Nuclear energy is one of the diversification options with a view to both secure the supplies and concurrently reduce the carbon footprint. Both the Indian government and private sector companies are also venturing to acquire stakes in energy assets abroad. The Arctic region has immense potential to enhance India's energy security for which steps have to be taken with an eye to the future

---

[67] Ministry of Petroleum and Natural Gas, Government of India, accessed on 24 September 19 from http://petroleum.nic.in/natural-gas/about-natural-gas.

yet the deficiency of concrete Arctic roadmap is presenting an impediment that needs to be resolved earnestly.

India's import of liquefied natural gas has increased by 30.01% during 2018–2019 over the year 2017–2018. During April-September 2019, it decreased by 8.6% over April-September 2018. Import from Oman has registered a negative growth of 35.23% during the current period. The above top ten sources together have a contribution of about 96.04% in total import of the product and have high positive growth during the current period[68] (Table 3.4).

India's import of Petroleum oils and oils obtained from bituminous minerals crude has increased by 30.52% during 2018–2019 over the year 2017–2018. During April–September 2019, it registered a negative growth of 10.03% over April-September 2018. Import of the product

Table 3.4 Top Ten sources in respect of LNG Liquefied Natural Gas[69]

5. Top ten sources in respect of ITC-HS Code 27111100 (Liquified Natural Gas)

(Value in US$ Million)

S.No.	Destinations	2017-18	2018-19	% Change	Apr- Sep 2018	Apr-Sep 2019	% Change
1	Qatar	4,119.18	5,354.94	30.00	2,724.54	2,092.07	-23.21
2	Nigeria	1,101.63	1,186.68	7.72	813.42	583.55	-28.26
3	Angola	529.01	708.63	33.95	291.97	492.7	68.75
4	U Arab Emts	118.98	236.51	98.78	46.98	446.01	849.35
5	Australia	730.74	626.02	-14.33	372.23	322.8	-13.28
6	USA	164.03	527.14	221.37	251.51	311.61	23.9
7	Oman	205.57	613.11	198.25	199.75	129.39	-35.23
8	Equtl Guinea	369.36	398.00	7.75	181.94	119.06	-34.56
9	Cameroon	0.00	112.38	0.00	84.44	96.59	14.38
10	Malaysia	86.50	123.49	42.76	29.01	74.08	155.37
	Total of Above sources	7,425.00	9,886.90	33.16	4,995.79	4,667.86	-6.56
	% Share of above	91.43	93.64	--	93.94	96.04	--
	India's Total Import of 27111100	8,121.29	10,558.24	30.01	5,317.85	4,860.29	-8.6

Source DGFT/Monthly bulletin, Oct 2019

---

[68] Directorate General of Foreign Trade, Ministry of Commerce, 2019, Monthly Bulletin on FTS, DGFT, October 2019, DGCIS, Kolkata, p. 29 accessed on 01 December 2019 from https://dgft.gov.in/more/data-statistics.

[69] Directorate General of Foreign Trade, Government of India, Ministry of Commerce and Industry Department of Commerce, accessed on 12 November 19 from https://dgft.gov.in/sites/default/files/Monthly%20Bulletin%20on%20FTS%20October%202019.pdf.

from Russia registered a high positive growth of 95.24% during April–September 2019 over April–September 2018. Iraq is the most dominant source of import of the product[70] (Table 3.5).

India's import of Petroleum oils and oils obtained from bituminous minerals crude has increased by 30.52% during 2018–2019 over the year 2017–2018. During April-September 2019, it registered a negative growth of 10.03% over April-September 2018. Import of the product from Russia registered a high positive growth of 95.24% during April-September 2019 over April-September 2018. Iraq is the most dominant source of import of the product.[71]

As per the gas trade and indicators 2018 obtained from GAS 2018, Analysis and Forecasts to 2023, IEA (www.iea.org), the following facts emerge (Fig. 3.5):

Table 3.5 Top ten sources in respect of petroleum and bituminous crude oils

1. **Top ten sources in respect of ITC-HS Code 27090000 (Petroleum oils and oils obtained from bituminous minerals crude)**

(Value in US$ Million)

S.No.	Destinations	2017-18	2018-19	% Change	Apr-Sep 2018	Apr-Sep 2019	% Change
1	Iraq	17,544.24	22,265.04	26.91	10,820.02	11,264.37	4.11
2	Saudi Arab	15,262.60	21,381.04	40.09	10,441.12	10,229.60	-2.03
3	Nigeria	8,192.30	9,432.34	15.14	3,925.87	4,701.86	19.77
4	U Arab Emts	6,122.20	9,512.48	55.38	4,356.39	4,148.32	-4.78
5	Venezuela	5,859.30	7,247.67	23.70	3,871.90	2,758.87	-28.75
6	USA	609.47	3,588.91	488.86	1,755.69	2,668.96	52.02
7	Kuwait	5,283.96	5,430.90	2.78	2,372.65	2,241.30	-5.54
8	Angola	3,080.08	3,282.46	6.57	1,410.59	1,630.36	15.58
9	Mexico	2,751.73	4,260.78	54.84	1,660.73	1,560.36	-6.04
10	Russia	1,169.30	1,180.91	0.99	595.46	1,162.55	95.24
Total Of Above Sources		65,875.18	87,582.53	32.95	41,210.42	42,366.55	2.81
% Share Of Above		75.40	76.80	--	72.27	82.58	--
India's Total Import Of 27090000		87,372.27	1,14,042.12	30.52	57,024.65	51,302.52	-10.03

Source DGFT/Monthly bulletin, Oct 2019

---

[70] Ibid, p. 27.

[71] Directorate General of Foreign Trade, Ministry of Commerce, 2019, Monthly Bulletin on FTS, DGFT, October 2019, DGCIS, Kolkata, p. 29, accessed on 01 December 2019 from https://dgft.gov.in/more/data-statistics.

China has become the world's largest importer of natural gas driven by its commitment to reduce global emissions and fuel its economic growth. The USA is the world's top producer, of gas and accounts for almost 45% of the growth in global production and nearly three-quarters of LNG export growth. As the cleanest fossil fuel, natural gas should contribute to all of the energy-related Sustainable Development Goals, climate change mitigation, improved air quality, and universal energy access. A map depicting global gas consumption up to 2023 clearly shows that India is consuming only a fraction of gas vis-a-vis China.

2017 showed strong growth of 3% in global demand for natural gas and the global demand till 2023 is expected to cross 4 trillion cubic metre (tcm) and India contributes 7% to global growth. India's natural gas demand 2003–2023 is as under (Fig. 3.6).

India, being an agrarian economy, has numerous subsidies in fertilisers' usage and the demand for natural gas, as a feedstock for fertiliser production accounts for around 70% of its natural gas demand. India is the second largest consumer of fertilisers in the world with an annual consumption of more than 55 million metric tons. Among the various types of fertilisers used in India, urea is one of the highest consumed fertilisers in the country as a source of nitrogen. The consumption of urea in the country in 2019 was 29 million tons. DAP is the second major consumed fertiliser in the country. Looking forward the Indian Fertiliser

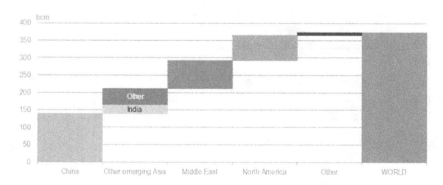

Fig. 3.5 Global Natural Gas Consumption growth 2017–2023 (*Source* GAS 2018, Analysis and Forecasts to 2023, IEA, pp. 12, www.iea.org)

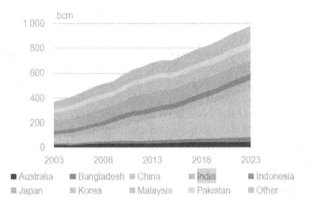

Fig. 3.6 India's Natural Gas Demand 2003–2023[72] (*Source* GAS 2018, Analysis and Forecasts to 2023, IEA, pp. 23, www.iea.org)

market is by 2024 growing at a CAGR of 12.3% during 2019–2024.[73] Likewise, the demand for natural gas is projected to grow at a rate of around 6% and the annual demand is likely to reach around 80 bcm/y by end 2023.F

ambition to double the share of natural gas in the country's energy mix over the medium term through reforms to encourage investment in domestic production and develop additional LNG import terminals. Transport is another source of demand increase to curb air pollution.[74]

The Arctic stands as a vanguard for tremendous socio-economic development and security interests for Russia. The Russian Arctic has immense natural gas and oil, the exploration of which will be its key to the socio-economic and infrastructure development in the region. It is estimated

---

[72] International Energy Agency, IEA, Gas 2018, accessed on 22 September 19 from https://www.iea.org/reports/gas-2018.

[73] Lok Sabha Secretariat, BACKGROUND NOTE ON "Tax Structure on Fertilizers Sector in Terms of GST and Import Duties Analysis of the Tax Structure of Raw Material and Final Products and Its Impact on Self-Sufficiency and Use of Fertilizers", November 2020, accessed on 02 August 2023, downloaded from https://loksabhadocs.nic.in/Refinput/Research_notes/English/30072021_153605_1021205101.pdf.

[74] International Energy Agency, 2019, GAS 2018 Analysis and Forecasts to 2023, IEA, accessed on 01 November 2019 from www.iea.org.

that Russia has 48 billion barrels of oil and 43 trillion cubic metres of gas respectively in its area.[75]

Unlike Russia which has issued numerous documents to deal with its military, maritime, navigation in NSR, the Indian side has been reticent in all spheres of engagement, except perhaps the scientific dimension. The Russian state links an increase in shipping through the NSR with national economic growth and the Northern territories' development by including the regions in a united economic and security space.[76]

After the Russian regime encountered Western sanctions post-Ukraine Crisis, it has been scouting for partners to fulfil the gap in investments. The sanctions had halted Rosneft's partnership with ExxonMobil and Statoil, leaving the Russians requiring investments, experts, and technology for offshore oil and gas projects. The Chinese have conveniently filled these gaps and Indian efforts have been rather lukewarm. The requirement of technological sound Western firms with domain knowledge and expertise of offshore exploitation will have to be co-opted by the Russians too. A brief on Russian companies is as follows:

(a) Novatek: Novatek is present in the Yamal LNG project located in Yamalo-Nenets Autonomous Okrug in North West Siberia with a 50.1% stake in the project. The annual production capacity of Yamal LNG is 16.5 million metric tons. A special LNG icebreaker tanker was designed and operationalised to transport LNG from Yamal without the need for an icebreaker. Yamal alone accounts for around 80% of Russia's natural gas production. Another field of Novatek's operation is the Utrenneye field, which is termed as Arctic LNG 2. The field is located in the Gydan Peninsula in YNAO approximately 70 km across the Ob Bay from Yamal LNG. Indian firm Petronet LNG Limited is partnering with Novatek to obtain delivery of supplies to India. These two firms are also planning to partner in establishing LNG retailing in India along with promoting LNG as a clean fuel and LNG-fuelled transport fleet. In September 2019, another MoU has been signed by NOVATEK with India's Petronet LNG Limited which envisages delivering

---

[75] Oil Price.com, accessed on 11 November 2019 from https://oilprice.com/Energy/Energy-General/Russias-Next-Oil-Boom-Is-Happening-In-The-Arctic.html#.

[76] Nadezhda Filimonova, supra note 6.

LNG supplies from NOVATEK's portfolio to the Indian market, including natural gas supplies for power generation, as well as investment by Petronet LNG in NOVATEK's future LNG projects and the joint marketing of LNG as motor fuel in India, including joint investment in developing a network of filling stations and a fleet of LNG-fuelled trucks.[77]

(b) Yamal: Yamal LNG is one of the world's largest LNG projects in the world which was launched in 2013. It gets its name from the Yamal Peninsula located in the Yamalo-Nenets Autonomous Okrug in North West Siberia. French company 'Total' is developing the enormous South Tambey gas and condensate field along with its partners Novatek, CNPC, and the Silk Road Fund. Yamal LNG has shipped the first LNG cargo containing 170 thousand cubic metres on 8 December 2017. Yamal LNG begins shipments from the second LNG train in August 2018. Yamal LNG commenced third LNG train production in November 2018.[78] The second LNG was shipped in August 2018 and production commenced on the third LNG train in November 2018. The Chinese stakes in the project stand at around 30% with CNPC and CNOOC holding stakes.

(c) Gazprom: Gazprom is a prominent gas player in Russia yet India does not figure in the list of its 27 foreign partners, available on http://www.gazpromexport.ru/en/partners/ accessed on 04 December 19.

(d) Rosneft: As stated above, Rosneft is the partner in Vankor and Sakhalin-1 oilfields. ONGC Videsh owns 26% stake in Russia's Vankor field and a 20% stake in Sakhalin-1 project. In 2009, it acquired Imperial Energy, an independent exploration and production company in Russia.[79] India has been in talks with Russia to have a stake in Vostok oilfields, one of the largest oil projects. In

---

[77] Novatek. Ru, 2019 accessed on 12 October 2019 from http://www.novatek.ru/en/press/releases/index.php?id_4=3401.

[78] Novatek, 2019, accessed on 01 October 2019 from http://www.novatek.ru/en/business/yamal-lng/.

[79] Times of India, ONGC evaluating stake buy in Russia's Vostok Oil project, 02 September 21, accessed on 02 August 2023, accessed from http://timesofindia.indiatimes.com/articleshow/85866314.cms?utm_source=contentofinterest&utm_medium=text&utm_campaign=cppst.

2020, Rosneft launched the Vostok Oil project, the largest in the global oil and gas industry.[80] The logistical advantage of the Vostok Oil project is the possibility to supply raw materials from the fields to all international markets, especially to the Asia–Pacific region.[81]

Rosneft believes that the project can be considered as the basis of the energy bridge between Russia and India, which will ensure the energy security of India in the face of increasing geopolitical risks. As part of the "Vostok Oil" project, it is planned to develop the Lodochnoye, Tagulskoye, and Vankorskoye deposits. The Payakhskoye field of Neftegazholding Company may also become part of it. Russian companies are planning to invest from 5 Tn to 8.5 Tn Roubles in this project.[82]

Commercial Ties

The commercial ties between and the Arctic 8 provide an unsatisfactory state, wherein the share of total exports of India to these countries stands at 19.35% of the total trade between April and October in 2019. Out of this 19.35%, the share of USA is 16.89%, meaning thereby that the remaining 7 states collectively have a share of a mere 2.46%. By this calculation, the total export to the Arctic 8 less USA stands at Rs 32,042.84 crores which is much less concerning the advocacy of strategic and bilateral ties. The trade figures for export to Arctic 8 come to Rs 255,010.051 (Table 3.6).

Other than the commercial and business relationship with the Arctic 8, the following tables depict the export and import destinations which show that barring the USA, which is a major trading partner of India, the other countries of the Arctic region don't figure in substantial bilateral trade (Table 3.7).

Import Data: The import data for Arctic 8 countries between April and September 19 is as under (Table 3.8).

---

[80] Rosneft.com, Rosneft at a Glance, accessed on 03 August 2023 from https://www.rosneft.com/about/Rosneft_today/.

[81] Ibid.

[82] CHNL IO, 2019, accessed on 01 August 2019 from https://Arctic-lio.com/news-review-of-the-events-on-the-nsr1-september-2019/.

Table 3.6 India's exports: export by region x countries

Department of Commerce: System on Foreign Trade Performance Analysis (FTPA) Version 3.0 Export by Region x Countries

Dated: 28/11/2019			Value in Rs. crores (P) Provisional	
Region/Countries	April–October 2018	April–October 2019 (P)	% Growth	% Share
(1) Europe	**254,545.18**	**252,569.90**	**−0.78**	**19.39**
1.1 EU Countries	**226,258.74**	**223,499.16**	**−1.22**	**17.16**
(1) NETHERLAND	33,267.66	37,195.16	11.81	2.86
(2) U K	37,466.81	35,717.21	−4.67	2.74
(3) GERMANY	36,126.32	34,404.77	−4.77	2.64
(4) BELGIUM	28,063.37	23,930.54	−14.73	1.84
(5) FRANCE	19,501.12	20,795.43	6.64	1.60
(6) ITALY	22,240.48	20,084.26	−9.70	1.54
(7) SPAIN	16,335.80	15,772.05	−3.45	1.21
(8) POLAND	6,197.01	6,287.91	1.47	0.48
(9) SWEDEN	3,224.04	3,066.34	−4.89	0.24
(10) PORTUGAL	2,863.42	2,996.92	4.66	0.23
(11) DENMARK	2,901.82	2,963.62	2.13	0.23
(12) CYPRUS	250.45	2,827.29	1,028.89	0.22
(13) IRELAND	2,128.22	2,254.36	5.93	0.17
(14) CZECH REPUBLIC	1,647.17	1,864.23	13.18	0.14
(15) AUSTRIA	1,896.89	1,806.65	−4.76	0.14
(16) HUNGARY	1,822.18	1,786.67	−1.95	0.14
(17) GREECE	2,077.91	1,670.56	−19.60	0.13
(18) ROMANIA	1,741.70	1,577.91	−9.40	0.12
(19) SLOVENIA	1,238.76	1,346.22	8.67	0.10
(20) FINLAND	1,060.40	1,097.43	3.49	0.08
(21) MALTA	748.38	948.15	26.69	0.07
(22) BULGARIA	984.78	690.46	−29.89	0.05
(23) SLOVAK REP	588.37	554.72	−5.72	0.04
(24) CROATIA	594.76	532.36	−10.49	0.04
(25) LATVIA	500.10	508.63	1.71	0.04
(26) LITHUANIA	498.27	474.01	−4.87	0.04
(27) ESTONIA	227.20	286.96	26.31	0.02
(28) LUXEMBOURG	65.34	58.32	−10.74	0.00
1.2 European Free Trade Association (EFTA)	**5,580.35**	**7,221.45**	**29.41**	**0.55**
(1) SWITZERLAND	4,328.82	5,192.02	19.94	0.40
(2) NORWAY	1,214.37	1,980.68	63.10	0.15
(3) ICELAND	22.11	30.08	36.05	0.00

(continued)

Table 3.6 (continued)

Department of Commerce: System on Foreign Trade Performance Analysis (FTPA)
Version 3.0 Export by Region x Countries

Dated: 28/11/2019

Value in Rs. crores
(P) Provisional

Region/Countries	April–October 2018	April–October 2019 (P)	% Growth	% Share
(4) LIECHTENSTEIN	15.06	18.68	24.07	0.00
1.3 Other European Countries	**22,706.09**	**21,849.29**	**−3.77**	**1.68**
(1) TURKEY	21,968.80	21,130.97	−3.81	1.62
(2) SERBIA	269.47	311.19	15.48	0.02
(3) ALBANIA	153.99	174.21	13.13	0.01
(4) MACEDONIA	73.35	94.58	28.93	0.01
(5) MONTENEGRO	168.46	74.71	−55.65	0.01
(6) BOSNIA-HRZGOVIN	72.02	63.63	−11.64	0.00
(7) UNION OF SERBIA & MONTE NEGRO		0.00		0.00
(2) Africa	**112,785.67**	**120,124.84**	**6.51**	**9.22**
2.1 Southern African Customs Union (SACU)	**18,553.62**	**18,547.53**	**−0.03**	**1.42**
(1) SOUTH AFRICA	17,476.49	17,378.51	−0.56	1.33
(2) BOTSWANA	672.31	715.82	6.47	0.05
(3) NAMIBIA	206.67	219.03	5.98	0.02
(4) LESOTHO	127.48	180.27	41.41	0.01
(5) SWAZILAND	70.67	53.91	−23.71	0.00
2.2 Other South African Countries	**6,148.37**	**11,931.86**	**94.07**	**0.92**
(1) MOZAMBIQUE	2,840.25	8,838.20	211.18	0.68
(2) ANGOLA	1,161.19	1,236.23	6.46	0.09
(3) ZAMBIA	1,240.70	1,051.18	−15.27	0.08
(4) ZIMBABWE	906.22	806.25	−11.03	0.06
2.3 West Africa	**28,031.45**	**33,030.33**	**17.83**	**2.54**
(1) NIGERIA	10,927.06	15,035.18	37.60	1.15
(2) TOGO	1,542.65	3,249.40	110.64	0.25
(3) GHANA	3,287.25	2,523.88	−23.22	0.19
(4) BENIN	1,444.17	1,848.11	27.97	0.14
(5) SENEGAL	2,600.46	1,828.97	−29.67	0.14
(6) COTE D' IVOIRE	1,660.29	1,697.78	2.26	0.13
(7) GUINEA	1,591.13	1,357.75	−14.67	0.10

(continued)

Table 3.6 (continued)

Department of Commerce: System on Foreign Trade Performance Analysis (FTPA) Version 3.0 Export by Region x Countries

Dated: 28/11/2019			Value in Rs. crores (P) Provisional	
Region/Countries	April–October 2018	April–October 2019 (P)	% Growth	% Share
(8) LIBERIA	610.81	1,080.37	76.88	0.08
(9) CAMEROON	664.25	800.30	20.48	0.06
(10) BURKINA FASO	696.67	617.04	−11.43	0.05
(11) MALI	478.63	551.84	15.30	0.04
(12) GAMBIA	535.42	539.35	0.73	0.04
(13) SIERRA LEONE	401.69	496.45	23.59	0.04
(14) CONGO P REP	503.26	432.57	−14.05	0.03
(15) NIGER	328.29	362.46	10.41	0.03
(16) MAURITANIA	457.53	320.01	−30.06	0.02
(17) GABON	219.85	201.89	−8.17	0.02
(18) EQUTL GUINEA	44.90	35.12	−21.78	0.00
(19) GUINEA BISSAU	27.69	32.75	18.29	0.00
(20) CAPE VERDE IS	4.79	10.27	114.31	0.00
(21) SAO TOME	4.58	6.58	43.72	0.00
(22) ST HELENA	0.11	2.27	1,902.03	0.00
2.4 Central Africa	**5,291.68**	**5,976.40**	**12.94**	**0.46**
(1) UGANDA	2,278.51	2,488.76	9.23	0.19
(2) CONGO D. REP	1,186.02	1,371.71	15.66	0.11
(3) MALAWI	865.87	836.39	−3.40	0.06
(4) RWANDA	613.68	539.11	−12.15	0.04
(5) C AFRI REP	31.78	327.05	929.12	0.03
(6) BURUNDI	204.11	226.41	10.93	0.02
(7) CHAD	111.71	186.96	67.36	0.01
2.5 East Africa	**32,083.20**	**27,959.28**	**−12.85**	**2.15**
(1) KENYA	9,330.68	8,101.72	−13.17	0.62
(2) TANZANIA REP	8,044.96	7,792.07	−3.14	0.60
(3) MAURITIUS	4,925.19	3,346.35	−32.06	0.26
(4) ETHIOPIA	3,042.54	3,301.49	8.51	0.25
(5) SOMALIA	1,767.95	2,369.98	34.05	0.18
(6) DJIBOUTI	3,536.07	1,385.00	−60.83	0.11
(7) MADAGASCAR	743.29	1,243.16	67.25	0.10
(8) SEYCHELLES	409.25	185.45	−54.69	0.01
(9) REUNION	205.26	163.40	−20.40	0.01

(continued)

Table 3.6 (continued)

Department of Commerce: System on Foreign Trade Performance Analysis (FTPA) Version 3.0 Export by Region x Countries

Dated: 28/11/2019			Value in Rs. crores (P) Provisional	
Region/Countries	April–October 2018	April–October 2019 (P)	% Growth	% Share
(10) COMOROS	78.03	70.67	−9.42	0.01
2.6 North Africa	**22,677.35**	**22,679.44**	**0.01**	**1.74**
(1) EGYPT A RP	11,788.90	10,709.21	−9.16	0.82
(2) SUDAN	3,332.85	3,823.32	14.72	0.29
(3) MOROCCO	1,897.78	3,635.64	91.57	0.28
(4) ALGERIA	3,981.38	2,774.21	−30.32	0.21
(5) TUNISIA	1,174.81	1,008.00	−14.20	0.08
(6) LIBYA	501.63	729.06	45.34	0.06
(3) America	**279,702.73**	**285,939.28**	**2.23**	**21.95**
3.1 North America	**240,217.38**	**246,483.58**	**2.61**	**18.92**
(1) U S A	212,760.37	219,981.18	3.39	16.89
(2) MEXICO	16,461.26	15,328.54	−6.88	1.18
(3) CANADA	10,995.75	11,173.86	1.62	0.86
3.2 Latin America	**39,485.36**	**39,455.70**	**−0.08**	**3.03**
(1) BRAZIL	15,113.03	16,054.28	6.23	1.23
(2) COLOMBIA	4,575.68	4,142.10	−9.48	0.32
(3) CHILE	3,981.57	3,559.46	−10.60	0.27
(4) PERU	3,075.54	3,206.60	4.26	0.25
(5) ARGENTINA	2,621.97	2,346.24	−10.52	0.18
(6) GUATEMALA	1,245.75	1,140.31	−8.46	0.09
(7) ECUADOR	1,331.70	1,014.01	−23.86	0.08
(8) DOMINIC REP	895.95	924.42	3.18	0.07
(9) PANAMA REPUBLIC	896.65	893.34	−0.37	0.07
(10) HONDURAS	659.57	764.22	15.87	0.06
(11) URUGUAY	841.45	736.02	−12.53	0.06
(12) VIRGIN IS US	15.04	542.88	3,509.89	0.04
(13) COSTA RICA	531.96	540.33	1.57	0.04
(14) PARAGUAY	675.83	513.51	−24.02	0.04
(15) BOLIVIA	367.52	466.75	27.00	0.04
(16) TRINIDAD	368.55	375.87	1.99	0.03
(17) VENEZUELA	350.94	369.39	5.26	0.03
(18) EL SALVADOR	314.45	309.26	−1.65	0.02
(19) HAITI	342.93	289.58	−15.56	0.02

(continued)

Table 3.6 (continued)

Department of Commerce: System on Foreign Trade Performance Analysis (FTPA) Version 3.0 Export by Region x Countries

Dated: 28/11/2019　　　　　　　　　　　　　　　Value in Rs. crores
　　　　　　　　　　　　　　　　　　　　　　　　(P) Provisional

Region/Countries	April–October 2018	April–October 2019 (P)	% Growth	% Share
(20) NICARAGUA	216.57	258.70	19.45	0.02
(21) JAMAICA	213.03	228.97	7.48	0.02
(22) CUBA	143.29	202.02	40.99	0.02
(23) NETHERLANDANTIL	123.07	133.37	8.37	0.01
(24) GUYANA	143.18	102.73	−28.25	0.01
(25) SURINAME	92.34	65.31	−29.26	0.01
(26) BELIZE	67.44	63.66	−5.61	0.00
(27) BARBADOS	45.00	42.15	−6.33	0.00
(28) BAHAMAS	19.68	31.22	58.66	0.00
(29) CAYMAN IS	19.93	22.89	14.85	0.00
(30) MARTINIQUE	15.55	18.34	17.94	0.00
(31) GUADELOUPE	16.42	18.08	10.13	0.00
(32) ST LUCIA	19.39	14.69	−24.22	0.00
(33) DOMINICA	5.44	12.09	122.15	0.00
(34) ST KITT N A	9.61	10.39	8.09	0.00
(35) BERMUDA	13.19	10.31	−21.86	0.00
(36) GRENADA	15.08	9.98	−33.80	0.00
(37) ANTIGUA	16.38	8.22	−49.83	0.00
(38) FR GUIANA	8.00	4.54	−43.26	0.00
(39) ST VINCENT	3.17	3.45	8.73	0.00
(40) TURKS C IS	1.17	3.32	183.34	0.00
(41) BR VIRGN IS	71.92	1.73	−97.60	0.00
(42) FALKLAND IS	0.01	0.56	5,757.29	0.00
(43) MONTSERRAT	0.39	0.40	2.75	0.00
(4) Asia	644,458.48	612,242.31	−5.00	47.00
4.1 East Asia (Oceania)	17,304.94	14,048.08	−18.82	1.08
(1) AUSTRALIA	15,251.70	11,874.78	−22.14	0.91
(2) NEW ZEALAND	1,540.29	1,597.87	3.74	0.12
(3) FIJI IS	267.94	259.61	−3.11	0.02
(4) PAPUA N GNA	198.18	244.36	23.30	0.02
(5) SAMOA	10.20	27.59	170.59	0.00
(6) TIMOR LESTE	14.95	19.74	32.01	0.00
(7) VANUATU REP	9.00	9.99	11.03	0.00

(continued)

Table 3.6 (continued)

Department of Commerce: System on Foreign Trade Performance Analysis (FTPA) Version 3.0 Export by Region x Countries

Dated: 28/11/2019   Value in Rs. crores (P) Provisional

Region/Countries	April–October 2018	April–October 2019 (P)	% Growth	% Share
(8) SOLOMON IS	7.09	8.75	23.49	0.00
(9) KIRIBATI REP	1.61	2.32	44.41	0.00
(10) TONGA	0.97	2.08	114.03	0.00
(11) NAURU RP	3.02	0.97	−67.82	0.00
(12) TUVALU		0.01		0.00
4.2 ASEAN	**147,364.99**	**133,519.73**	**−9.40**	**10.25**
(1) SINGAPORE	41,790.80	42,309.44	1.24	3.25
(2) MALAYSIA	26,775.78	25,230.93	−5.77	1.94
(3) VIETNAM SOC REP	27,740.77	21,433.48	−22.74	1.65
(4) THAILAND	18,442.99	18,121.58	−1.74	1.39
(5) INDONESIA	19,431.31	15,517.51	−20.14	1.19
(6) PHILIPPINES	6,861.00	6,131.71	−10.63	0.47
(7) MYANMAR	5,253.77	3,672.75	−30.09	0.28
(8) CAMBODIA	746.13	781.88	4.79	0.06
(9) BRUNEI	180.16	215.88	19.82	0.02
(10) LAO PD RP	142.28	104.58	−26.50	0.01
4.3 West Asia-GCC	**167,105.14**	**165,375.22**	**−1.04**	**12.70**
(1) U ARAB EMTS	122,206.57	121,635.65	−0.47	9.34
(2) SAUDI ARAB	20,949.55	23,323.48	11.33	1.79
(3) OMAN	9,321.06	7,906.41	−15.18	0.61
(4) KUWAIT	5,297.64	5,400.14	1.93	0.41
(5) QATAR	6,760.31	4,981.65	−26.31	0.38
(6) BAHARAIN IS	2,570.01	2,127.90	−17.20	0.16
4.4 Other West Asia	**40,350.32**	**46,240.48**	**14.60**	**3.55**
(1) ISRAEL	14,816.51	14,571.40	−1.65	1.12
(2) IRAN	12,153.43	14,423.71	18.68	1.11
(3) IRAQ	7,203.35	8,241.96	14.42	0.63
(4) JORDAN	1,724.52	4,654.88	169.92	0.36
(5) YEMEN REPUBLC	2,693.78	2,666.31	−1.02	0.20
(6) LEBANON	1,152.48	974.93	−15.41	0.07
(7) SYRIA	606.24	707.30	16.67	0.05
4.5 NE Asia	**171,546.85**	**164,773.38**	**−3.95**	**12.65**
(1) CHINA P RP	64,294.79	69,900.84	8.72	5.37

(continued)

Table 3.6 (continued)

Department of Commerce: System on Foreign Trade Performance Analysis (FTPA) Version 3.0 Export by Region x Countries

Dated: 28/11/2019   Value in Rs. crores (P) Provisional

Region/Countries	April–October 2018	April–October 2019 (P)	% Growth	% Share
(2) HONG KONG	53,774.11	49,826.03	−7.34	3.83
(3) JAPAN	18,771.89	19,276.37	2.69	1.48
(4) KOREA RP	20,612.22	19,135.46	−7.16	1.47
(5) TAIWAN	13,851.69	6,528.36	−52.87	0.50
(6) MONGOLIA	125.72	65.47	−47.93	0.01
(7) KOREA DP RP	111.70	38.38	−65.64	0.00
(8) MACAO	4.73	2.47	−47.79	0.00
4.6 South Asia	**100,786.24**	**88,285.41**	**−12.40**	**6.78**
(1) BANGLADESH PR	37,388.33	31,209.36	−16.53	2.40
(2) NEPAL	31,640.11	29,246.04	−7.57	2.25
(3) SRI LANKA DSR	17,297.63	15,806.32	−8.62	1.21
(4) PAKISTAN IR	8,132.05	4,637.22	−42.98	0.36
(5) AFGHANISTAN TIS	2,853.00	3,571.29	25.18	0.27
(6) BHUTAN	2,600.19	2,947.39	13.35	0.23
(7) MALDIVES	874.93	867.79	−0.82	0.07
(5) CIS & Baltics	**13,099.83**	**16,534.20**	**26.22**	**1.27**
5.1 CARs Countries	**1,653.42**	**1,919.29**	**16.08**	**0.15**
(1) KAZAKHSTAN	482.83	793.71	64.39	0.06
(2) UZBEKISTAN	788.29	791.19	0.37	0.06
(3) TURKMENISTAN	190.67	140.05	−26.55	0.01
(4) KYRGHYZSTAN	116.47	111.40	−4.35	0.01
(5) TAJIKISTAN	75.16	82.94	10.35	0.01
5.2 Other CIS Countries	**11,446.41**	**14,614.90**	**27.68**	**1.12**
(1) RUSSIA	9,138.08	11,723.99	28.30	0.90
(2) UKRAINE	1,394.77	1,846.27	32.37	0.14
(3) GEORGIA	368.05	321.87	−12.55	0.02
(4) AZERBAIJAN	170.80	243.90	42.80	0.02
(5) BELARUS	223.68	243.22	8.74	0.02
(6) ARMENIA	117.92	193.92	64.45	0.01
(7) MOLDOVA	33.11	41.73	26.03	0.00
(6) Unspecified Region	**13,289.50**	**15,144.24**	**13.96**	**1.16**
(1) UNSPECIFIED	11,490.00	10,590.81	−7.83	0.81
(2) GIBRALTAR	993.36	3,696.09	272.08	0.28

(continued)

Table 3.6 (continued)

Department of Commerce: System on Foreign Trade Performance Analysis (FTPA) Version 3.0 Export by Region x Countries

Dated: 28/11/2019

Value in Rs. crores
(P) Provisional

Region/Countries	April–October 2018	April–October 2019 (P)	% Growth	% Share
(3) PUERTO RICO	574.65	415.38	−27.72	0.03
(4) MARSHALL ISLAND	1.36	184.28	13,425.12	0.01
(5) SOUTH SUDAN	37.77	64.53	70.85	0.00
(6) NEW CALEDONIA	32.06	54.77	70.83	0.00
(7) ARUBA	37.88	36.35	−4.03	0.00
(8) ERITREA	46.94	31.35	−33.21	0.00
(9) FR POLYNESIA	26.67	22.69	−14.93	0.00
(10) MAYOTTE	9.44	13.27	40.63	0.00
(11) MONACO	10.90	6.34	−41.77	0.00
(12) STATE OF PALEST	6.27	6.02	−3.99	0.00
(13) FAROE IS	9.35	5.49	−41.32	0.00
(14) GUAM	2.50	3.72	48.95	0.00
(15) MICRONESIA	1.53	2.53	64.80	0.00
(16) US MINOR OUTLYING ISLANDS	3.68	2.36	−35.97	0.00
(17) COOK IS	1.27	2.07	62.91	0.00
(18) SAN MARINO	0.15	1.42	834.48	0.00
(19) NORFOLK IS	0.93	1.19	28.15	0.00
(20) AMERI SAMOA	0.13	0.85	569.84	0.00
(21) NIUE IS		0.58		0.00
(22) ANDORRA	1.25	0.52	−58.37	0.00
(23) N. MARIANA IS	0.24	0.34	43.30	0.00
(24) PALAU	0.27	0.27	2.93	0.00
(25) ANGUILLA	0.52	0.23	−55.75	0.00
(26) GREENLAND	0.00	0.19	187,400.00	0.00
(27) WALLIS F IS		0.16		0.00
28) ANTARTICA	0.02	0.15	534.19	0.00
(29) VATICAN CITY		0.14		0.00
(30) PITCAIRN IS	0.08	0.07	−12.82	0.00
(31) SINT MAARTEN (DUTCH PART)		0.05		0.00
(32) SAHARWI A.DM RP		0.01		0.00
(33) TOKELAU IS	0.01	0.01	−63.01	0.00

(continued)

Table 3.6 (continued)

Department of Commerce: System on Foreign Trade Performance Analysis (FTPA) Version 3.0 Export by Region x Countries

Dated: 28/11/2019			Value in Rs. crores (P) Provisional	
Region/Countries	April–October 2018	April–October 2019 (P)	% Growth	% Share
(34) ST PIERRE	0.07			
(35) PANAMA C Z				
(36) CURACAO				
(37) JERSEY				
(38) GUERNSEY				
(39) HEARD MACDONALD	0.19			
(40) INSTALLATIONS IN INTERNATIONAL WATERS				
Total	1,317,881.40	1,302,554.78	−1.16	100.00

Data Source DGCIS, Kolkata

Table 3.7 Total trade: top countries (2018–2019)[83]

Year: 2018-2019

Rank	Country / Region	Export	Import	Total Trade	Trade Balance
1.	USA	366,480.39	248,553.77	615,034.17	117,926.62
2.	CHINA P RP	117,289.11	492,079.28	609,368.39	-374,790.17
3.	U ARAB EMTS	210,210.93	208,550.77	418,761.70	1,660.17
4.	SAUDI ARAB	38,854.24	199,394.90	238,249.15	-160,540.66
5.	HONG KONG	91,117.42	125,971.91	217,089.33	-34,854.50
6.	SINGAPORE	80,942.25	113,918.75	194,861.00	-32,976.50
7.	IRAQ	12,506.50	156,600.99	169,107.49	-144,094.49
8.	GERMANY	62,200.63	106,130.52	168,331.15	-43,929.89
9.	KOREA RP	32,877.97	117,255.31	150,133.28	-84,377.34
10.	INDONESIA	36,871.06	111,148.53	148,019.59	-74,277.46
	Total of Top countries	1,049,350.51	1,879,604.75	2,928,955.25	-830,254.24
	India's Total	2,307,726.18	3,594,674.22	5,902,345.17	-1,286,948.04
	% Share of Top countries	45.47	52.29	49.62	64.51

[83] Ministry of Commerce and Industry, Department of Commerce, Export Import Data Bank, Total trade-top countries, 2018–2019 accessed from https://tradestat.commerce.gov.in/eidb/iecnttopn.asp.

Table 3.8 Import by India (April to September 2019) from Arctic Countries[84] (Rs in crores)

S. no.	Country	April to September 19	September 19
1	Canada	14,912.36	2068.21
2	Finland	2377.38	381.82
3	Denmark	2295.27	288.55
4	Iceland	18.35	5.10
5	Norway	1944.58	300.92
6	Sweden	4014.71	594.53
7	USA	134,438.58	19,771.85
8	Russia	24,343.44	2400.31
	Total	**184,344.67**	**25,811.29**

Source http://www.dgciskol.gov.in/Writereaddata/Summary_trade/IMSFT_2B_Sep%2019.pdf

The total trade figures of import from Arctic 8 come to Rs 184,344.67 for these 6 months as against a figure of Rs 255,010.051 for 9 months from April to October 2019(P) (Fig. 3.7).

Khanij Bidesh India Ltd (KABIL): The Indian government has also realised that the ensured supply of critical and strategic minerals is vital for a consistent supply of these to fulfil the requirements of the Indian domestic market. In this direction, a joint venture company, namely Khanij Bidesh India Ltd (KABIL), is planned to be established with the participation of three central public sector enterprises, National Aluminium Company Ltd (Nalco), Hindustan Copper Ltd (HCL), and Mineral Exploration Company Ltd (MECL).

KABIL would carry out identification, acquisition, exploration, development, mining, and processing of strategic minerals overseas for use by the country. During the 2019 Vladivostok declaration, a MoU was signed with Russian LLC Far East Mining Company. Minerals like Lithium form a major component of the drive to shift towards green mobility by way of electric vehicles and Cobalt will be sought by way of strategic tie-ups and partnerships. Because of the changing geopolitical landscape, the continued and assured supply of strategic minerals and superior technology will become increasingly important to sustain and modernise the domestic industry. A connected issue would be to stockpile these to insure against any disruptions.

[84] Ibid.

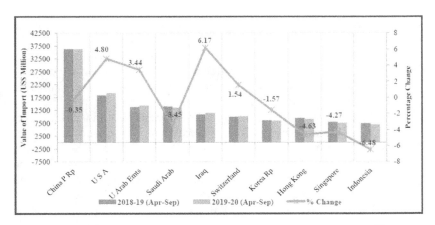

Fig. 3.7 Top 10 Sources of Import During April-September 2019[85] (*Source* Directorate General of Foreign Trade, Ministry of Commerce, 2019, Monthly Bulletin on FTS, DGFT, October 2019, DGCIS, Kolkata, pp. 29 accessed on 01 December 2019 from https://dgft.gov.in/more/data-statistics)

Other Issues

(a) **MOSAiC Expedition 2019:** The Multidisciplinary Drifting Observatory for the Study of Arctic Climate (MOSAiC) expedition was launched in September 2019 which will carry scientists on-board a research vessel over drifting sea ice for one year. Hundreds of researchers from 20 countries take part in this exceptional endeavour.[86] This Arctic science mission is the largest Polar mission in history, having the participation of 20 countries and hundreds of scientists. The mission will take the vessel close to the North Pole and the winter will be spent on-board the vessel. Various subject scientists would take samples and try to understand the Arctic in the crosshairs of global warming and to understand climate change better. The scientists are aboard the German icebreaker Polarstern and are supported by another ship on the expedition, the Russian research vessel Akademik Fedorov. The focus of the expedition in

---

[85] Ibid.

[86] MOSAiC, 2019, accessed on 20 October 2019 from https://www.mosaic-expedition.org/.

the scientific domain is—atmosphere, sea ice, ocean, ecosystem, and biogeochemistry. Conspicuously, there is no participation from India in this expedition. Another ship on the expedition is the Russian research vessel, Akademik Fedorov. The primary question the MOSAiC scientists are asking: what are the causes of diminishing Arctic ice? And what are the consequences?".[87]

The countries participating in the MOSAiC are: Finland, France, Russia, Japan, Korea, Spain, Germany, Netherlands, Sweden, Great Britain, Switzerland, Norway, Italy, Poland, USA, Austria, Belgium, Canada, China, and Denmark. A cursory look at the participant countries tells that all members less Iceland and all observers less India and Singapore are present in the expedition.

(b) **Polar Research Vessel (PRV)**: The Polar research and scientific diplomacy require some initiatives including the establishment of Arctic research facility/facilities, sending various scientific expeditions by chartering icebreaker/Polar research vessels and other engagements in science-related committees. Since India has established three research stations at the Poles, there is a need to access these all around the year, to obtain accurate scientific data. As per the plans, the implementation schedule/plan was as under:

(1) Finalisation of the design specifications including the on-board laboratory instrumentation and infrastructure.
(2) Floating of a Global Tender for the construction and identification of the Shipyard.
(3) Finalisation of the Agreement with the identified Yard.
(4) Initiation of construction of the Polar Research Vessel (2012–2013).
(5) Construction and sea trials (2013–2015).
(6) Commissioning of the vessel (2015–2016).[88]

---

[87] Npr.org, 2019, accessed 14 December 2019 from https://www.npr.org/2019/12/04/784691513/polar-bears-ice-cracks-and-isolation-scientists-drift-across-the-Arctic-ocean?utm_campaign=storyshare&utm_source=twitter.com&utm_medium=social.

[88] Ministry of Earth Sciences, 2019, accessed on 23 August 2019 from https://moes.gov.in/programmes/construction-polar-research-vessel.

Yet the Global Expression of Interest (EOI) for providing a competent experienced workforce in supporting was released by Goa Shipyard Limited on 30 April 2019.[89]

It is commonly understood that ships which are equipped with icebreaker capabilities are a must have for any nation, including India to be able to access the research station at Svalbard so as to fruitfully accomplish the scientific purpose for which research is being carried out in Arctic. As brought out earlier, the thawing of ice due to global warming and ill effects of climate change is opening new avenues and heightened economic activity in the Arctic region, which is both a boon for economic interests yet is exacerbating the ill effects of environmental degradation due to the aforesaid human activity.

However, a massive void in the Indian Scientific pursuits is that India does not possess a Polar Research Vessel or an icebreaker and has to rely on chartered vessels seriously limiting its research timeframe as well as the huge economic drain. This cleft in the professed research narrative despite having a physical presence for over 3 decades and the proposal for acquisition of a Polar Research Vessel approved in June 2010 but yet to materialise is impinging on the effort and also manifests in scanty Indian research with reputable standards.[90]

The approximately Rs 1000 crore project had roped in a Spanish shipbuilding company in 2015 but the contract fell through due to escalated costs. Later due to the focus of the Government on 'Make in India' there were certain other restrictions that had to be met and led to more delays.

The foregoing can be contrasted with Global Notice inviting Expression of Interest from shipyards for providing experienced workforce in construction of Polar Research Vessel (PRV) by Goa shipyards Limited on 15 April 2019. The Global Expression of Interest (EOI) for providing a competent experienced workforce to support the construction was released by Goa Shipyard Limited on 30 April 2019. The Indian inexperience in the construction of icebreakers and Polar research vessels, which can wade through 2 metres of ice but being attempted indigenously, may

---

[89] Gama, Goa shipyard limited, global notice inviting expression of interest from shipyards for providing experienced workforce in construction of Polar Research Vessel (PRV), accessed 21 January 20 from https://goashipyard.in/file/2019/05/Corrigendum-Global-EOI-for-experienced-workforce-Extended-28-May-2019.pdf.

[90] Nikhil Pareek, India in a Changing Arctic: An Appraisal, Ecocycles, vol. 6, isuue 1, pp. 1–9 (2020).

not meet the required standards. The requirement of a PRV also is important as India has plans to rebuild Maitri, its research station in Antarctica, and make it impervious to its harsh environment for at least 25 years.

As per the Rajya Sabha's Three hundred Fifteenth report of March 2018 on 'Demands for Grants (2018–19)' of the Ministry of Earth Sciences it had noted that acquisition of Polar Research Vessel under the PACER programme will be delayed due to paucity of funds.[91] Yet, from the foregoing, it is evident that over the last several years, India has been paying substantial sums of money to foreign-owned and operated polar research vessels. The availability and timeframe of operation of these vessels also have to be aligned with the chosen partner vessel companies and India does not have the flexibility and direction to venture at the chosen time and locations. Still, the problems like the MV Vasiliy Golovnin getting stuck in ice also arise frequently, leading to time and cost overruns and also leading to environmental damage by jettisoning cargo in seas. There are issues like sending of scientists to adjudge the suitability of polar research vessels, a job which can be suitably and effectively done by naval/coast guard crews, yet the fixation with bureaucratic red-tape is evident. Instead of incorporating hugely successful shipbuilding nations like Korea, China, or Nordic countries to progress its bilateral strategic engagement, India is progressing the design and fabrication of PRV in India, despite lack of experience and expertise. It is imperative for the policy advocates to assume control of this situation, earnestly.

Since India has been maintaining two research stations at the Antarctic and one in the Arctic, a proposal was initiated to obtain a PRV which was approved in June 2010 at an estimated cost of Rs.490 crore. The customary delays in the execution of projects by India are evidenced by the snail's pace in equipping a Polar Research Vessel, too. However, the current BJP government on assuming office in 2014 had also approved the PRV at a revised cost of Rs. 1051.13 crore on 29 October 2014 according to a sanction by the Cabinet Committee on Economic Affairs (CCEA). This gives out the following key aspects of Indian planning as:

(i) Research in Polar Regions is handicapped due to the unavailability of a PRV.

---

[91] Rajya Sabha, accessed on 02 June 2019 from https://rajyasabha.nic.in/rsnew/Committee_site/Committee_File/ReportFile/19/103/315_2019_1_14.pdf.

(ii) The incremental cost increase in the PRV from 490 crore to 1051.13 crore.
(iii) Delays in the procurement of a strategic and vital component of India's scientific research which leads to drain on the exchequer as huge sums of money are spent on hiring and chartering of vessels.
(iv) It projects the Indian efforts in implementing projects in a negative light with cost overruns and time delays.

Even as per the revised planning, the PRV was to be commissioned by 2015–2016 in its meeting held on approved the Revised Cost Estimates (RCE) for the acquisition of a Polar Research Vessel (PRV). As per the plans, a PRV was to be constructed and its sea trials to be undertaken between 2013 and 2015 and subsequent commissioning by 2015–2016, yet the Global Expression of Interest (EOI) for providing competent experienced workforce in supporting was released by Goa Shipyard Limited on 30 April 2019.[92] The joint participation in the construction of PRV from Norway, Finland, or Korea could have taken the bilateral cooperation further. Figure 3.8 shows the Polar expenditure of both Antarctic and Arctic.

On perusal of the above tables, it is clear the charter hiring expenses of ship and helicopter in respect of Arctic are neither included nor provided separately in the Annual Report 2018–2019. The NCPOR is

SCHEDULE-11-Antarctic Research	31-03-2019	31-03-2018
1. Charter Hire of Ship & Helicopter		
1. Charter Hire of Ship	83,916,179	396,698,610.00
2. Charter Hire of Helicopters	89,791,893	68,438,294.00
Total-1	173,708,072	465,136,904.00

Amount in ₹

SCHEDULE-13-Expedition to Arctic	31-03-2019	31-03-2018
1. Logistic Expenses	41,351,501	25,789,500.00
2. Operational Expenses	8,189,413	6,597,300.00
3. Station Expenses	4,557,926	10,437,626.00
4. Scientific Studies Support	5,732,288	11,119,583.00
Total	59,831,128	53,944,009.00

Fig. 3.8 Polar expenditure (*Source* NCPOR Annual Report 2018–2019)

---

[92] Goa Shipyard Limited, accessed on 04 October 19 from https://goashipyard.in/file/2019/04/EOI-29042019.pdf.

spending tremendous sums of money in chartering the vessels, and by its own admission that 'no significant marine scientific experiments could be launched' and (not undertaken) 'freedom of planning diverse scientific programmes' (Ministry of Earth Science, 2018).

For India to project an influential and active position in the Arctic scientific research, it is essential to have an all year round unbridled access to the region. To maintain some credibility in its research, there is a requirement to cover the deep Arctic and ice-covered waters of Antarctic. India should take a leaf from the USA, where its polar icebreakers are operated by the Coast Guards rather than being outsourced or chartered. The polar icebreaker research vessel is an essential feature of national policy in a rapidly changing Arctic region, which is evincing interest of a plethora of non-Arctic States and the consequent interplay of geopolitics and geo-economics. The share of scientist overnight stays at Ny-Ålesund, between 2005 and 2012 remained between 3.1% and 6.5%, which is quite less as compared to the stated objectives of scientific research.

(c) **PRV/Shipbuilding**: As part of India's Act East Policy the Indian PM Narendra Modi had visited the Republic of Korea from 18 to 19 May 2015 for deepening the economic cooperation between the two nations. It is reminded here that ROK was granted Arctic Observer status along with India in the 2013 Kiruna Ministerial Meeting. ROK is actively engaged with India in economic pursuits and its major companies like Hyundai, Samsung, LG, and several others are present in India in a big way. During this visit, Korean investments and manufacturing support in the areas of electronics, construction, railways, and defence equipment, sea-port, and shipbuilding sectors were discussed. It is also important to mention that the Koreans are among the world leaders in shipbuilding, and during the 2015 visit, a statement vowing to engage in the shipbuilding sector for the benefit of both the countries was made. Though the PM visited "Hyundai Heavy Industries (HHI)" shipyard and promises were made to collaborate on the manufacturing of LNG tankers required by India to fulfil its huge energy demand. There is a deal between India's GAIL to source LNG from the USA for the next 20 years up to the year 2037 and the tendering for the nine LNG ships for the same could not be finalised on India's insistence to build at least three such ships in India under her Make in India campaign. The LNG ships quite like the Icebreaker Research Vessels have to meet stringent standards and exceptional technology to build, which India does not possess and has no prior experience either.

The Koreans have three prominent shipbuilders, namely Daewoo Shipbuilding & Marine Engineering (DSME), Samsung Heavy Industry (SHI), and HHI, which had a successful order book, yet no deal was finalised with them. Later with diplomatic manoeuvring, some MoU were signed which offered benefit to both sides. However, such leverage was not employed by India to progress the building of PRV which has a major role to play if Indian Scientific pursuits have to attain some repute and renown.

The Korean experience in the consumer electronics sector with Samsung and consumer passenger vehicle segment with Hyundai are demonstrative that they have progressed with huge outlay on Research and Development and are operating as 100% privately owned businesses and not likely to dilute their stand in case of LNG ships too. The bottom line for India lies to eagerly devote more resources to her R&D so that the aspirations of indigenous development and production of such a vessel can be progressed within its own sphere.

India's Involvement and Engagement with the Arctic Region: II

(Political discourse, Academic pursuits, diaspora, and synergy with Arctic Council)

Political Discourse/Discussion

The country's legislature is mandated with the formulation, brainstorming, discussing, and arriving at positive outcomes in key policy courses and options. The consequent role of the legislature in charting out policymaking is a natural outcome of this process. In the context of Arctic, the 2014 Presidential visit by the then President Pranab Mukherjee to Norway and Finland was the first by any Indian leader crossing the

Arctic Circle. 'After 26 years, an Indian President will be visiting Finland. 'R Venkataraman had visited the country in 1988.'[93]

It is quite natural that high-level developmental cooperation and assigning priority to the region was given and reciprocated by the Arctic nations in light of the stress accorded by the Indian leadership. Within the Parliament, the decisions taken by the government are within the parameters of internal political dynamics and internal pressures and thus a consultative and broad-based view is taken before formulating key policy decisions. The government's action plan and approach on certain subjects can be ascertained by asking and reading the questions on matters of public importance. The questions are usually targeted concerning subjects dealt and covered by various Ministries/Departments. The relative importance of any subject can be gauged by reading the frequency, importance, and deliberations assigned to a particular subject.

The MoES deals with India's activities at Arctic region and the gist of questions on the Arctic in the various Lok Sabha and Rajya Sabha sessions (data as per MoES, accessed on 12 October 2019 from https://www.moes.gov.in/previous-sessions?field_category_value=All&title=Arctic&field_type_value=All) is as under (Table 3.9).

Select questions raised in both the Indian houses of Parliament on the issue of Arctic/AC membership are given in **Annexure II**. The data thereof has been accessed from MoES, accessed on 12 October 2019 from https://www.moes.gov.in/previous-sessions?field_category_value=All&title=Arctic&field_type_value=All. Based on the answers given by the Ministers, one key theme that emerges is that India was merely focussing on scientific endeavours and has been viewing the Arctic from an Antarctic lens.

Among the prominent themes that emerge from the Parliament debate on the issue of Polar research are the quantification of Indian Scientific efforts, the funding on research, the territorial claims, and India's position and the quest for India's Polar Research Vessel. Based on the answers given by the Ministers, one key theme that emerges is that India was merely focussing on scientific endeavours and has been viewing the Arctic from an Antarctic lens. The gist of these questions is as under (Table 3.10).

---

[93] Economic Times accessed on 12 October 19 from https://economictimes.indiatimes.com/news/politics-and-nation/president-pranab-mukherjee-to-visit-norway-finland-from-october-12/articleshow/44714708.cms.

Table 3.9 Questions on the Arctic in the Indian Parliament

Ser no.	Lok Sabha (LS) or Rajya Sabha (RS) session	Question number	Date	Remarks
1	17th session of 16 LS	Nil	Nil	Nil
2	247th session of RS	Nil	Nil	Nil
3	13th session of 16 LS	Nil	Nil	Nil
4	11th session of 16LS	Nil	Nil	Nil
5	4th session of 16 LS	1389	04/03/2015	
6	2nd session of 16 LS	4883	13/08/2014	
7	230th session of RS	Nil	Nil	Nil
8	229th session of RS	652	12/08/2013	
9	228th session of RS	1456	23/04/2014	
10	227th session of RS	Nil	Nil	Nil
11	226th session of RS	2372	03/09/2012	
12	226th session of RS	1618	27/08/2012	
13	10th session of 15 LS	6875	17/05/2012	
14	7th session of 15 LS	1365	03/03/2011	
15	6th session of 15 LS	Nil	Nil	Nil
16	4th session of 15 LS	Nil	Nil	Nil
17	218th session of RS	Nil	Nil	Nil
18	3rd session of 15 LS	3144	09/12/2009	
19	2nd session of 15 LS	Nil	Nil	Nil

Table 3.10 Discussion on Arctic Issues in Indian Parliament

Ser no.	Ques no	Date	LS/RS (assembly)	Nature of question
1	3991	06 August 14	LS	Arctic Council
2	2380	13 February 14	RS	Observers
3	2005	09 March 16	LS	Claims Territorial
4	4883	13 August 14	LS	Research Stations
5	988	02 March 16	LS	Polar Research
6	6595	06 May 15	LS	PRV
7	1495	04 March 15	LS	PRV
8	240	23 March 17	RS	Polar Research
9	1365	03 March 11	RS	Expedition Arctic
10	6875	17 May 12	LS	Arctic Steps, Funding

The MEA is responsible to chart out India's strategic goals and direction for policy formulation as well as strategic alliances, and the official stand of the government is observed from its statements and issue briefs/statements to press/official functions. The instances of engagement of Indian leaders and bureaucrats with Arctic countries from all data available on https//mea.gov.in are attached as **Annexure-III**. The gist of these is compiled as under (Table 3.11).

The data on various visits by the President, Vice President, PM, and External Affairs Minister (EAM) to various Arctic countries along with reciprocal visits by the heads of state/government of these countries is compiled as under. The details of various Memorandum of Understandings (MoU) signed are attached in **Annexure IV**, with details mentioned hereunder (Table 3.12).

UNSC candidature: The countries of the Arctic have also been voicing their views on India's inclusion in the UN Security Council, marking the level of trust and understanding between India and these nations. The same is visible by the Indian gratitude expressed during bilateral meetings (Table 3.13).

Quite like the outgoing visits, the incoming visits by leaders from the Arctic countries also affirm the mutual cooperation and focus on Arctic issues (Table 3.14).

A common feature of both the incoming and outgoing visits is that these are being represented by the highest level including the Royalty of certain nations. India has dwelled on the issue of enhancing scientific cooperation with Norway, USA, and Russia and expressed its gratitude to several nations for their role in extending the Observer status to India.

Study of Indian Research Contribution

A study was done by research personnel and it was found that the Observer States research contribution in the field of Arctic research is quite small in co-relation with the other research. India's research was even smaller vis-a-vis other AC Observers like Germany, People's Republic of China, and Japan as shown in Fig. 3.8. As expected, the Arctic Council Observers (France, Germany, the Netherlands, Poland, Spain, United Kingdom, People's Republic of China, Italian Republic, Japan, Republic of Korea, Republic of Singapore, Republic of India) have a lower proportion of Arctic Research compared with their total publication output, from 0.21 to 0.28% in different years, but the absolute number of Arctic

Table 3.11 Engagement of Indian Leaders/Bureaucrats with Arctic countries

S. no.	Date and occasion	Dignitary	Key point
1	27 August 19, Valdai Club	External Affairs Minister (EAM)	The possibility of new maritime routes opening-up
2	13 November 19, BRICS Summit	PM	Russian President invited India to invest in the region
3	14 November 19, RNG Lecture	EAM	Opening of an Arctic passage
4	10 September 19, Iceland Visit	President	India's desire to contribute meaningfully
5	07 September 19, Press Briefing	President	Very active in the work of the AC
6	05 September 19, Joint Statement	PM	Ready to play a significant role in the Arctic Council
7	04 September 19, Press Statement	PM	The search for Hydro-Carbon and LNG in the Far East and the Arctic has been agreed
8	13 June 19, SCO Summit, Press Briefing	Foreign Secretary (FS)	A new area of focus that was identified by both leaders is Arctic region oil and gas
9	07–14 December 18	Iceland Foreign Minister	Enhanced cooperation in the Arctic Council
10	05 October 18, Joint Statement	Russian President	Joint development of oil fields in the Russian territory, including in the Arctic shelf of Russia
11	23 February 18, Joint Statement	Canadian PM	Indian participation in Canadian Arctic research
12	23 January 18, WEF Summit	PM	The ice at the Arctic is melting
13	06 September 19, EEF	EAM	Rich natural resources of this region

(continued)

Table 3.11 (continued)

S. no.	Date and occasion	Dignitary	Key point
14	08 June 17	Minister of state for external affairs	Indian scientists today collaborate in research stations on the Arctic Ocean
15	01 June 17, Joint Declaration	St Petersburg Declaration	Projects on exploration and exploitation of hydrocarbons in the Arctic shelf
16	01 June 17, Press Briefing	PM	Joint exploration and exploitation of hydrocarbons in the Arctic area of the Russian Federation
17	30 August 16, India US S&CD	EAM	India will take part in the Arctic Science Ministerial
18	05 April 16, Joint Statement	Iceland Foreign Minister	Continued scientific cooperation
19	13 February 16, Joint Statement	PM Finland	Support for India becoming an Observer
20	24 December 15, Joint Statement	India-Russia Joint Statement	Joint scientific research in the Arctic region
21	02 November 15, Joint Commission	India Norway	Bilateral collaboration in education
22	01 June 15, Speech	President	Helped India achieve Observer status
23	01 June 15, Press Briefing	President	Sweden supported India's Observer application
24	09 May 15/Press Briefing	President	MoU with Rosneft for exploration on the Arctic Shelf is being progressed
25	11 December 14, Joint Statement	Russian President	Agreed to facilitate scientific cooperation
26	17 October 14, Media Interaction	President	India's Research is meant for the whole world

(continued)

Table 3.11 (continued)

S. no.	Date and occasion	Dignitary	Key point
27	16 October 14, Finnish Parliament	President	Deploy its significant Polar research capabilities and scientific understanding
28	13 October 14, Banquet	President	Norway helped India achieve Observer status
29	10 October 14, Media Briefing	President	Deep-sea probe up beyond towards the North Pole
30	21 October 13, Joint Statement	India-Russia Annual summit	Exploration for hydrocarbons in the Arctic region
31	21 October 13, Press briefing	PM	The pipeline will connect ultimately from Russia to India
32	18 October 13, Press Briefing	PM	Hydrocarbon in Arctic Shelf with companies such as Rosneft, Gazprom, and Novatech

publications grew up three times from 2001 to 2015.[94] The undermentioned graph clearly shows that India's scholarly output falls short of the other participants (Fig. 3.9).

A cursory reading of Indian authors' papers on the Arctic presents a view that mostly government-funded/sponsored think tanks and persons associated with these have been offered opportunities to participate in deliberations and events organised in the High North. Other than these, the officials from MEA and NCPOR on their official capacities have been travelling to attend the Ministerial/SAO/WGs meetings from time to time. There is a need to enhance the scope by incorporating diverse players like private companies, civil society organisations, NGOs, and scholars to garner novel views on Polar issues. This will not only offer to build a national consensus on the Indian policy framework but also

---

[94] Dag Aksnes, Igor Osipov, Olga Moskaleva, Lars Kullerud, Arctic Research Publication Trends: A Pilot Study, 2016, UArctic, FEFU, ISBN no: 978-0-323-47586-0.

Table 3.12 Outgoing visits to Arctic countries by Indian leaders[95]

S. no.	Year/month	Country	Dignitary	Remarks (on arctic, shipping, hydrocarbons)
1	December 2015	Russia	PM	
2	May 2015	Russia	President	MoU with Rosneft is being progressed
3	September 2015	USA	PM	
4	April 2015	Canada	PM	
5	June 2015	Sweden	President	
6	October 2014	Finland	President	
7	October 2014	Norway	President	
8	April 2013	Iceland	Icelandic President Ólafur Grimsson	
9	09 to 17 September 2019	Iceland	President	First presidential visit to NORDIC country
10	05 September 2019	Russia	PM	See Annexure II Para (f) for joint declaration
11	21 May 2018	Russia Informal Summit	PM	
12	16–20 April, 2018	Sweden and United Kingdom	PM	
13	April 2018	Denmark	Bilateral	
13a	April 2018	Norway	Bilateral	
13b	April 2018	Iceland	Bilateral	
13c	April 2018	Finland	Bilateral	
14	01 June 2017	Russia	PM	St Petersburg Declaration
15	09 July 2015	Russia	PM	
16	4–7 September 2013	Russia	PM	
17	20–22 October 2013	Russia	PM	Direct transportation of hydrocarbons from through the land route
18	21–27 September 2019	USA	PM	
19	25, 26 June 2017	USA	PM	

(continued)

[95] Ministry of External Affairs, Government of India, accessed on 22 December 19 from https://mea.gov.in/outgoing-visits.htm?2/outgoing_visits.

Table 3.12 (continued)

S. no.	Year/month	Country	Dignitary	Remarks (on arctic, shipping, hydrocarbons)
17	06–08 June 2016	USA	PM	Climate and Clean Energy MOU on Cooperation in Gas Hydrates
18	31 March 2016	USA	PM	
19	26–30 September 2014	USA	PM	
20	16 December 2011	Russia	PM	
21	6–9 October 2006	Finland	PM	
22	20 November 2009	USA	PM	

Table 3.13 Arctic countries on India's inclusion in UNSC

S. no.	Country	Occasion
1	Iceland	President visit, September 2019
2	Norway	President visit, October 2014
3	Finland	President visit, October 2014
4	Russia	PM visit, 01 June 2017
5	Russia	PM visit, 20–22 October 2013
6	Serbia	President visit, May 2015 (visit to Russia)
7	Sweden	President. 01 June 2015
8	USA	June 2017, PM visit
9	USA	September 2015, PM Visit

Source Compiled by author from Ministry of External Affairs, Government of India, accessed on 22 Dec 19 from https://mea.gov.in/incoming-visits.htm?1/incoming_visits and Ministry of External Affairs, Government of India, accessed on 22 Dec 19 from https://mea.gov.in/outgoing-visits.htm?2/outgoing_visits

assist in charting out policies on climate change, clean energy, and Polar geopolitics.

NCPOR under the administrative control of the Ministry of Earth Sciences (MoES) is the agency to coordinate and overall responsibility for the implementation of India's Polar research programme. The Indian

Table 3.14 Incoming visits to India by Heads of Arctic Countries[96]

Ser no.	Country and dates	Delegation	Remarks (Arctic specific)
1	Sweden, 02–06 December 2019	King Carl Gustaf XVI	
2	Finland, 04–07 November 2019	Foreign Minister	
3	USA, 26 June 2019	Secretary of state	
4	Norway, 07–09 January 19	PM	
5	Denmark, 17–18 December 18	Foreign Minister	
6	Iceland, 07–14 December 18	Foreign Minister	
7	Russia, 04–05 October 18	President	Greater expansion of India-Russia relations
8	USA, 05–06 September 18	Secretary of state	
9	Canada, 21–24 February 18	Foreign Minister	
10	Canada, 17–24 February 18	PM	To enhance geo-spatial collaboration and to consider Indian participation in Canadian Arctic research
11	Russia, 22 December 2017	Deputy PM	
12	Russia, 10–11 December 2017	Foreign Minister	
13	Denmark, 26–30 November 2017	Foreign Minister	
14	Finland, 22–25 November 2017	Foreign Minister	
15	USA, 24–26 October 2017	Secretary of state	
16	Russia, 09 May 17	Deputy PM	
17	USA, 29–31 August 2016	Secretary of state	Arctic Science Ministerial
18	Iceland, 03–10 April 2016	Foreign Minister	
19	Sweden, 12–14 February 2016	PM	
20	Finland, 12–14 February 2016	PM	

(continued)

[96] Ministry of External Affairs, Government of India, accessed on 22 December 19 from https://mea.gov.in/incoming-visits.htm?1/incoming_visits.

Table 3.14 (continued)

Ser no.	Country and dates	Delegation	Remarks (Arctic specific)
21	Norway, 02–04 November 2015	Foreign Minister	Bilateral collaboration in Arctic/Polar Research
22	Russia, 10–11 December 2014	President	
23	Russia, 18–19 June 2014	Deputy PM	
24	Russia, 24 February 2014	Deputy PM	
25	Canada, 22 February to 02 March 14	Governor General	
26	USA, 30 July–01 August 14	Secretary of State	
27	USA, 22 July 2014	Vice President	
28	USA, 23–25 June 2014	Secretary of state	
29	Iceland, 31 March–06 April 14	President	
30	Russia, 23 December 2012	President	
31	Canada, 04 November 2012	PM	
32	Russia, 13–15 October 2012	Deputy PM	
33	Canada, 12 September 12	Foreign Minister	
34	USA, 08 May 12	Secretary of State	
35	USA, 08 July 2011	Secretary of state	
36	Iceland, 03 May 11	Foreign Minister	
37	Russia, 19 December 2010	President	
38	Denmark, 14 December 2010	FM	
39	Russia, 28 November 2010	FM	

(continued)

Table 3.14 (continued)

Ser no.	Country and dates	Delegation	Remarks (Arctic specific)
40	USA, 04 November 2010	President	
41	USA, 24 May 2010	Under Secretary	
42	Russia, 09 March 2010	PM	
43	Norway, 01 March 2010	Foreign Minister	
44	Iceland, 15 January 2010	President	
45	USA, 08 June 2009	Under Secretary	
46	Russia, 12 February 2008	PM	
47	Denmark, 04–08 February 08	PM	
48	Canada, 10–12 January 08	Foreign Minister	
49	Russia, 25–26 January 07	President	
50	Norway, 14–16 December 06	Foreign Minister	
51	Russia, 16–17 November 06	Foreign Minister	
52	Norway, 29 October 06	Prince/Princess	
53	Russia, 16–17 March 06	PM	
54	Finland, 10–15 March 06	PM	
55	USA, 01–03 March 06	President	

Scientific endeavours in the Arctic remain rather modest with minimal international collaboration. As per a report, 63.1% of the publications had Indian authors only and one-fourth of the articles were published in Indian Journals only.[97] Collaboration across countries was not prevalent:

---

[97] Stensdal Iselin, Asian Arctic Research 2005–2012: Harder, Better, Faster, Stronger, Fridtjof Nansen Institute, May 2013.

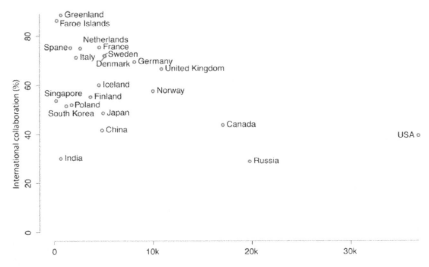

Fig. 3.9 Country-wise Scholarly Output on the Arctic (*Source* Dag Aksnes, Igor Osipov, Olga Moskaleva, Lars Kullerud, Arctic Research Publication Trends: A Pilot Study)

63.1% (65) of the articles had Indian author(s) only and almost one-fourth of the articles, 24.3% (25), were published in Indian periodicals. Figure 3.10 shows that the published research by India falls acutely short of the promise of stated Indian claims:

Diaspora: India has a sizeable Diaspora population, approximately 20 million nationals in various countries across the globe. The recognition of the potential of the Diaspora as a strategic asset is a recent development in Indian Foreign policy circles. As evidenced during the 'Howdy Modi' event in September 2019, the impact of Diaspora both on the host country and for their country of origin is large and impressive.

Table 3.15 has compiled information on Indian Diaspora in the Arctic region.

For better understanding and differentiation among the various categories, citizens are classified in resident Indians and NRIs (non-resident Indians), and Non-Citizens are classified into OCIs and PIOs.

Arctic research publications with Indian author(s), 2005–2012

Year	Number of publications
2005	6
2006	5
2007	4
2008	12
2009	17
2010	9
2011	29
2012	21
Total	103

Fig. 3.10 Arctic publications: Indian authors (*Source* Stensdal Iselin, Asian Arctic Research 2005–2012: Harder, Better, Faster, Stronger, Fridtjof Nansen Institute, May 2013)

Table 3.15 Population of Overseas Indians (compiled in December 2018)[98]

	Country	Non-Resident Indians (NRIs)	Persons of Indian Origin (PIOs)	Overseas Indians
156	Russian Federation	28,610	1,950	30,560
69	Finland	5,159	6,616	11,775
56	Denmark	8,100	3,100	11,200
88	Iceland	257	76	333
182	Sweden	15,349	10,370	25,719
35	Canada	184,320	831,865	1,016,185
142	Norway	7,718	12,300	20,018
200	USA	1,280,000	3,180,000	4,460,000

Source http://mea.gov.in/images/attach/NRIs-and-PIOs_1.pdf, Population of Overseas Indians, Ministry of External Affairs. (Serial Numbers as per MEA website

Diaspora has emerged as powerful entities in the case of Jews in the USA and Europe and there has been growing clout of Indians in Canada, the UK, and the USA in the political machinery and functioning.

[98] Ministry of External Affairs, Population of Overseas Indians accessed on 23 November 19 from http://mea.gov.in/images/attach/NRIs-and-PIOs_1.pdf.

Indian Diaspora has found its place of pride in the government's functioning as there are concerted efforts to connect with them and draw out mutually beneficial paths. The soft power potential of the Diaspora has been acknowledged due to India's growing economy and potential to provide skilled and dedicated, both white-collar workforce and blue-collar workforce across diverse regions. The economic liberalisation of India also coincided with the end of the cold war and fitted well in the West supported market-oriented economy and democratic credentials. The table below gives out that the size of Indians in the USA is phenomenal and is active in various fields like economic, social, and political. Another favourable factor was that Indians have occupied top managerial jobs in multinational corporations and were also active in political donations in the USA.

India's Contribution to Arctic/Arctic Council Since the Grant of Observer Status[99]

Ever since India's induction as an Observer to the Arctic Council, several projects were implemented in line with the objectives of various Arctic Council working groups. As per the four yearly reports submitted by India to the Arctic Council, her participation in the Arctic Contaminants Action Programme (ACAP) with special emphasis on Mercury Geochemistry in the Sediments of Kongsfjorden, Ny-Ålesund, and investigations of atmospheric aerosols and their characterisation over the Arctic during summer season were undertaken. In the field of Arctic Monitoring and Assessment Programme (AMAP), long-term monitoring of the Kongsfjorden system of the Arctic region for climate change studies and Monitoring of Arctic Precipitation was done. Likewise, in the field of Conservation of Arctic Flora and Fauna (CAFF), bacterial diversity in various niches around Ny-Ålesund, Svalbard, was undertaken. India also has bilateral collaboration with the Research Council of Norway.

As per the official document submitted by the Government of India to the Arctic Council,[100] Indian plans to:

---

[99] Arctic Council, 2019, accessed on 12 December 2019 from https://oaarchive.Arctic-council.org/bitstream/handle/11374/2256/INDIA_2018-05_Review-Report.pdf?sequence=1&isAllowed=y.

[100] Ibid.

(a) Extend ocean observations and modelling in the Arctic-North Atlantic region
(b) Deploy and service deep-sea moorings in the Arctic Ocean
(c) Set-up molecular and proteomics facilities in NCAOR
(d) Train and generate specialised manpower for more focussed research
(e) National collaborations among research and academic institutes for research in the Arctic
(f) International scientific collaborations to achieve the pan-Arctic mission.

India's Observer Report 2017–2019, submitted to the AC for renewal of India's Observer membership, is attached as **Annexure I.**

India's Engagement with Permanent Participants, Working Groups, NGOs of AC in the last five years

(a) **PAME**[101]

Since becoming an Observer in 2013, India's partnership with PAME is summarised as:

(i)	Proposals submitted, proposal accepted, outcomes:	None
(i)	Funding assistance:	None
(ii)	Papers submitted which were accepted and published by PAME:	None
(iv)	Any citation/reward/acknowledgement of prolific scientific work by India:	None
(v)	Any other information on India's endeavours:	None

India has participated in <u>one PAME Meeting</u> (held on **04–07 February 2019 at Malmo, Sweden**) since it became an Arctic Council Observer. This was the **first time a representative from India participated in a PAME working group meeting. And no presentation was given by the Indian representative.** The representative from Observer countries included China, the UK, Italy, Japan, Germany, Poland, Netherlands, ROK, and India. It also participated in a workshop 'Systematically

---

[101] Email dated 15 January 20, attached as Annexure-IV.

Engaging with Observers on PAME's Shipping-Related Work,' held on 04 June 2019 at London.

(b) Gwich'in Council[102]

(i)	Proposals submitted, the proposal accepted, outcomes:	None
(ii)	Funding assistance:	None
(iii)	Papers submitted which were accepted and published by PAME:	None
(iv)	Any citation/reward/acknowledgement of prolific scientific work by India:	None
(v)	Any other information on India's endeavours:	None

(c) NAMMCO[103]

(i)	Proposals submitted, proposal accepted, outcomes:	None
(ii)	Funding assistance:	None
(ii)	Papers submitted which were accepted and published by PAME:	None
(iv)	Any citation/reward/acknowledgement of prolific scientific work by India:	None
(v	Any other information on India's endeavours:	None

However, the email reply received from NAMMCO, giving out the observers from non-member parties at NAMMCO Council Meetings, is produced hereunder (Table 3.16).

(d) EPPR[104]

(i)	Proposals submitted, proposal accepted, outcomes:	None
(ii)	Funding assistance:	None
(ii)	Papers submitted which were accepted and published by PAME:	None
(iv)	Any citation/reward/acknowledgement of prolific scientific work by India:	None
(v)	Any other information on India's endeavours:	None

(e) Saami Council[105]

---

[102] Email dated 18 December 19, attached as Annexure-IV.
[103] Email dated 17 December 19, attached as Annexure-IV.
[104] Email dated 17 December 19, attached as Annexure-IV.
[105] Email dated 20 December 19, attached as Annexure-IV.

Table 3.16 Observers from Non-member Parties at NAMMCO Council Meetings

	Serial	Denmark	Canada	Japan	Russia	St. Lucia	Namibia	Nunavut
1992	1	1	2	1	1			
1993 Jan	2	1	2	1	1			
1993 Jul	3	1	2	2	2			
1994	4	1	2	2	1			
1995	5	1	1	3				
1996	6	1	3	4	6		1	
1997	7	1	4	2	1			
1998	8	1	1	3	1	1		
1999	9	1	1	2	3	1		
2000	10	1	1	2	4			
2001		No Council meeting in that year						
2002	11	1	1	1	1			
2003	12	1	2	2	1			
2004	13	2	1	2				
2005	14		2	1	3			
2006	15	1	2	1		1		
2007	16	1	2	1				
2008	17	1	1	2	1			
2009	18		1	2	1			
2010	19	1	2	2	2			
2011	20	1	1	2	2			
2012	21	1	1	2	3			
2013		No Council meeting in that year						
2014	22	1	1	3	3			
2015	23	1	1	2	3			
2016	24	1	1	2	1			
2017	25		1	2	0			3
2018	26	1	2	3	1			
2019	27	1	1	5	0			

Source NAMMCO, nammco-sec@nammco.org email dated 17 December 2019

(i)	Proposals submitted, proposal accepted, outcomes:	None
(ii)	Funding assistance:	None
(iii)	Papers submitted which were accepted and published by SC	None
(iv)	Any citation/reward/acknowledgement of prolific scientific work by India:	None
(v)	Any other information on India's endeavours:	None

(f) **ACAP**[106]

(i)	Proposals submitted, proposal accepted, outcomes:	None
(ii)	Funding assistance:	None
(iii)	Papers submitted which were accepted and published by SC	None
(iv)	Any citation/reward/acknowledgement of prolific scientific work by India:	None
(v)	Any other information on India's endeavours:	None

In November 2018, a representative of the Indian National Centre for Polar and Ocean Research (NCPOR) attended the ACAP Working Group meeting in Reykjavik, Iceland. India also submitted data to the AC expert group on Black Carbon and Methane in 2017. Though this is not connected to ACAP work and as per the report[107] 'Figure 3 presents black carbon emissions as submitted by participating Observer States, India also submitted black carbon emission data showing total black carbon emissions of 1,119 kilotons of black carbon per year in 2011, but without sectoral detail. Therefore, it could not be included here.'

(g) **OSPAR Commission** (not a working group of AC)[108]

Though OSPAR does not form part of strict AC or its bodies, yet 4 Arctic member states are part of OSPAR contracting parties. The area of OSPAR working in Arctic waters constitutes approximately 40% of the OSPAR maritime area. India is neither a contracting party nor an observer to OSPAR.

---

[106] Email dated 02 January 20, attached as Annexure-IV.

[107] Arctic Council, 2017, Expert Group on Black Carbon and Methane: Summary of progress and recommendations 2017. 49 pp.

[108] Email dated 06 January 20, attached as Annexure-IV.

(h) **AMAP**[109]

(i)	Proposals submitted, proposal accepted, outcomes:	None
(ii)	Funding assistance:	None
(iii)	Papers submitted which were accepted and published by AMAP:	None
(iv)	Any citation/reward/acknowledgement of prolific scientific work by India:	None
(v)	Any other information on India's endeavours:	None

(i) **CAFF**[110]

(i)	Proposals submitted, proposal accepted, outcomes:	None
(ii)	Funding assistance:	None
(iii)	Papers submitted which were accepted and published by AMAP:	None
(iv)	Any citation/reward/acknowledgement of prolific scientific work by India:	None
(v)	Any other information on India's endeavours:	None

In December 2018, a representative of the Bombay Natural History Society attended CAFF's Arctic Migratory Birds Institute (AMBI) technical workshop in Hainan, China, to help finalise <u>AMBI Work Plan 2019–2023</u>. In November 2019, the AMBI Chair and AMBI Global Coordinator attended the CWAMWAF conference in Lonavala at the invitation of the Bombay Natural History Society. AMBI staff gave two plenary addresses, participated in panels, and hosted a special session to further present and discuss AMBI implementation actions relevant to the Central Asian Flyway. Besides, AMBI staff was invited to Delhi to meet with relevant Ministerial staff to discuss further partnerships and AMBI implementation.

(j) **Aleut International Association**[111]

(i)	Proposals submitted, proposal accepted, outcomes:	None
(ii)	Funding assistance:	None
(iii)	Papers submitted which were accepted and published by AMAP:	None

---

[109] Email dated 15 January 20, attached as Annexure-IV.

[110] Email dated 15 January 20 and 16 January 20, attached as Annexure-IV.

[111] Email dated 17 January 20, attached as Annexure-IV.

(iv)	Any citation/reward/acknowledgement of prolific scientific work by India:	None
(v)	Any other information on India's endeavours:	None

Other than these, the other Working Group, SDWG, and permanent participants like AAC and RAIPON elicited no response and the data on India's engagement with these could not be ascertained.

The foregoing paragraphs show that India has been advancing its scientific, economic, hydrocarbon, and political cooperation and association with the Arctic States on a bilateral basis as well through the framework provided by the AC. Though on certain parameters it is gauged that India's efforts fall short of the promise like engagement with the AC's PPs and WGs yet, on the other hand, a definite advantage lies in India's politico-diplomatic engagement with the Arctic nations. The intermeshing of the economies is also restrained due to the huge geographic distances and lack of robust interconnectedness so far. These issues will be resolved with the inauguration of the INSTC in the coming days and other connectivity schemes in which Russia will act as an anchor.

India's Arctic engagement as viewed by her political, foreign policy, and scientific dimension does portray that India views herself as a natural stakeholder in the Arctic affairs and hence it aspires to obtain a special position to air its views on the Arctic affairs. There are a plethora of areas which mould India's Arctic discourse, namely energy requirements, resource exploitation and exploration, geostrategic concerns, and role in shaping Arctic governance. Though India has been comparatively mild and unassertive yet it possesses unique characteristics that provide her a special place, namely her democratic credentials, huge economy, and tremendous soft power capabilities. The scientific pursuits by India have immense potential to increase India's leverage in Arctic affairs and gain the trust of the Arctic States.

It has to be accepted that owing to India's preoccupation with local and regional affairs as also with the vital geopolitical activities around the Indian Ocean, Indo-Pacific, and the Middle East which take the bulk of Indian foreign policy emphasis and resultantly the Arctic affairs are left to the NCPOR rather than the MEA. A connected strand to the changed focus of the Indian policy towards the Arctic has been aired by some experts like Shyam Saran who have aired fears that "India whose geostrategic position enables it to exert considerable control over the IOR may suffer at the cost of the Arctic and the commercial viability of its polar routes."[112] In the times when the Arctic has assumed a major position on the world stage in light of its climatic and geopolitical relevance, the above view appears to be myopic and misfounded and both the regions will have to be charted suitable and bespoke responses.

The participation by India in AC meetings and with PPs/WGs has also been acutely deficient and thus few outcomes have been accomplished, so far. The earlier writings by Indian authors like PK Gautam, Kishore Kumar, Shyam Saran, and others were diametrically opposite to both the Indian position on adherence to UNCLOS and 2008 Ilulissat Declaration by the Arctic 5 and such discourses have the potential to derail the bilateral and multilateral bonhomie between India and the Arctic States. India's trade with the Arctic countries, except the USA, is also marginal and India needs to enhance the economic and commercial ties for further strengthening its Arctic connection.

From the time of India's independence under the stewardship of PM J L Nehru, India has been engaging with its Asian neighbours by deploying the soft power political strategy. With the centuries-old social, religious, cultural, civilisational, and other binding connections, the soft power leverage was used with aplomb to unite the Asian countries in India's fold with success. The utilisation of soft power as a foreign policy tool later gained much strength with India's economic rise in the last decade of the twentieth century and it emerged as a potent economic rival to the West as well as to an autocratic-hegemonic China. India had outbid China in the restoration of Angkor Wat temple in Cambodia and had eased the entry of Thai monks in India as pilgrims which were stellar examples of its soft power strategy. Under the present Indian BJP government under PM Narendra Modi, there are ongoing attempts to project the rich cultural–civilisational heritage of India and the declaration of International Yoga Day by the UN and the statements by world leaders to shift from handshake to Namaste during the COVID-19 outbreak were celebrated as victories for Indian soft power. Simultaneously, there are concerted attempts by the Indian Foreign Office, MEA to portray its

---

[112] Shyam Saran, "India's Stake in Arctic Cold War," The Hindu, 2012, accessed on 28 October 19 from https://www.thehindu.com/opinion/op-ed/Indias-stake-inArctic-cold-war/article13290404.ece.

historical legacy and engagement with the world to leverage the age-old connections between India and her partners. India in soft power is also projected through the hugely successful film industry, christened as 'Bollywood' which is a major draw among the Indian Diaspora and other countries. India is thus projecting itself as a repository of tradition blended with modernity to amalgamate and integrate the diverse cultures and peoples seamlessly. Major publicity campaigns including the 'Incredible India' to welcome tourists, 'Make in India' to attract foreign investment and businesses, and the domestic 'India Shining' campaign to woo voters have been initiated by India to demonstrate its foreign policy enmeshed in soft power apparatus. Indian Congress politician Shashi Tharoor had stated that to achieve the great power status aspiration, India possesses levers that are distinct from hard power, namely soft power by way of its rich culture, political values, and foreign policy which will provide India with a high seat at world polity.

Norway's Sovereign Wealth Fund is near the figure of 1000 billion USD and is indeed the world's largest. Notwithstanding the professed understanding and cooperation between Norway and India, a paltry 1%, around 10 billion USD is being invested in Indian portfolios. This ought to increase substantially to give a fillip to the Indian economic situation and strength to the bilateral relationship.

As per Dr. Shailesh Nayak, ex-Director of NCPOR-ESSO in his article 'Balancing Development and Environmental Concerns in the Arctic' published in Asia and the Arctic: Narratives, Perspectives and Policies (2016), it was stated that 'A polar remotely operable vehicle, indigenously built, will be deployed in the Arctic this year' yet there has neither been any development nor news on this development.

India's MEA addresses the Arctic Region through three separate offices and there is no dedicated division looking into the finer nuances of the various levers that are at play in the region. The MEA's Americas Division looks after the USA and Canada while the Eurasia Division looks after Russia and the Central Europe Division is looking after the remaining five states, namely Iceland, Finland, Denmark, Sweden, and Norway. The AC is in itself a very unique organisation and the disparate MEA's divisions are not able to do justice and thereby a void is experienced at the policy formation level. The most distinguishing feature of both the 'Arctic exceptionalism' and the interplay of politico-economic-geopolitical factors between the various member states in the AC has to be viewed holistically based on a common viewpoint rather than a disjointed platform. There is one Additional Secretary (Europe) who draws out the policy based on inputs provided by these three divisions, and thus the finer issues of relations between the Arctic 8 and shifting discourse due to rotational AC chair as well as varying participation by the Arctic 8 in international multilateral organisations tend to get missed.

CHAPTER 4

Unravelling Challenges in the Arctic and India's Response Strategy

> The Arctic] "has become a region for power and competition"
> "We are entering a new age of strategic engagement in the Arctic"[1]
> —Mike Pompeo, US Secretary of State

The above statement by the US' Secretary of State in May 2019 at AC Ministerial Meeting gives out that the view taken by the Trump administration on the Arctic is sceptical of re-emergence of great power rivalry and the Arctic becoming its playground. This speech was followed by the US Department of Defence taking out its Arctic strategy which also addressed the Arctic from the same prism of growing rivalry and challenges in the region.

The Arctic has been witnessing a reduction in ice cover, diminishing sea ice, and increased exploitation of resources in the region. This is coupled with an increase in human activities to include shipping and tourism, and thus, there is heightened interest as well as concerns about the negative impacts of climate change on this pristine region. The iconic Polar Bear was listed as threatened on 15 May 2008 and there is the tremendous

---

[1] Looking North: Sharpening America's Arctic Focus. Speech given by U.S. Secretary of State, Michael Pompeo in Rovaniemi, Finland, ahead of the 19th Arctic Council Ministerial Meeting, May 6, 2019. Available at: https://www.state.gov/looking-north-sharpeningamericas-Arctic-focus/.

impact of the human-induced changes on wildlife as well as the migration of fish stocks to new waters.

The AC working group of AMAP keenly observes and records the changes in the geophysical attributes of the Arctic and their finding forms the basis of the changing Arctic. As per various AMAP findings, the average warming in the Arctic is pegged at double the global rate and the rate of warming is on higher end in the winter months. The surface temperatures in the past five years, i.e. from 2014 onwards, have exceeded all historical data. The extent of maximum sea ice in winter months has thus been recorded at the lowest levels. The loss of winter sea ice in the last 40 years, from 1979 to present levels, has shrunk by 75% clearly showing the hastened losses due to climate change. The loss of glaciers prominently including the Greenland ice sheet is among the largest contributor to sea-level rise. The impact of these losses on Arctic flora and fauna as well as the marine ecosystem is also colossal. The shrubs are extending to tundra and declining tundra vegetation and many other associated variations. Marine environments are also affected: for example the loss of sea ice has triggered shifts in marine algal blooms, with potential impacts throughout the food web including krill, fish, birds, and mammals in marine ecosystems.[2]

The Arctic is also a region of strategic competition wherein five out of eight Arctic Council member states are NATO members, out of which Finland and Sweden, are active partners of NATO. Russia, a major Arctic state, considers NATO an existential threat to its security. The various emerging challenges across the domains of physical, strategic, and economic are as under:

(a) **Warming and Environmental Problems**

The Arctic Region is characterised by sea ice that has been growing over several millennia, until up to the twenty-first century. The multi-year sea ice used to melt between March and September and re-grow between September and March. However, the impacts of GHGs and climate change have transformed the region from that of the permanent

---

[2] Arctic Monitoring and Assessment Programme, Arctic Council, AMAP Climate Change Update 2019, An Update to Key Findings of Snow, Water, Ice and Permafrost in the Arctic (SWIPA) 2017, (2019) accessed on 1 November 2019 from https://www.amap.no/documents/download/3295/inline.

Fig. 4.1 Ice cover in the Arctic on 2 January 2019 (*Source* NOAA)

sea ice cap to the seasonal ice-free sea. The following two images downloaded from https://www.natice.noaa.gov/products/miz.html show the seasonal recession in ice cover between the same year (Figs. 4.1 and 4.2).

As per a study the ice cap in January 2014 was about 800,000 square kilometres lesser than the average recorded in the past 30 years. When the data of ice loss extrapolated and reported in the journal Nature Climate Change, it was assessed that the Arctic could be ice-free for all functional purposes as early by 2044 and latest by 2067. This assessment was made considering that all other parameters of global emissions remain on the projected path and there are no major changes. In mid-January (2014), the ice cap was about 800,000 square kilometres smaller than the average during the last 30 years.[3] As per a very recent news article according

---

[3] Y. Uutiset, Pohjoisnavalla vähän jäätä (A little ice at the North Pole), the Finnish News Agency Yle 1 Uutiset (Luonto 17 January 2014), accessed on 10 August 2017 from http://yle.fi/uutiset/pohjoisnavalla_vahan_jaata/7037199.

Fig. 4.2 Ice cover in the Arctic on 8 October 2019 (*Source* NOAA)

to research published in the journal Nature Climate Change, the Arctic could be "functionally ice-free" by September 2044—and no later than 2067—assuming no changes to global carbon emissions.[4]

The ice in the Arctic is multiyear making it thick and extending its coverage. The thickness, extent, and geographical coverage of this multiyear sea ice reflect the climate conditions that had prevailed in the past, leading to its formation and coverage. However, a rapidly receding sea ice is indicating that global climate change is taking its toll on the Arctic. The ice loss also causes greater coastal erosion due to the effects of warmer air and water leading to an increase in the storm, wave, and tidal activity. Because of these factors, the loss of multiyear ice and reduced coverage and extent of ice, the possibility of natural resources extraction and shipping is being fervently planned to lead to the unlocking of novel economic

---

[4] CBC accessed on 14 October 2019 from https://www.cbc.ca/news/canada/north/ice-free-Arctic-this-century-1.5370504.

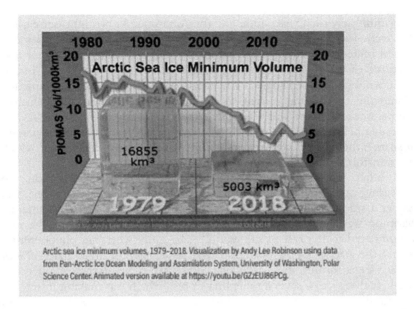

Fig. 4.3 Arctic Sea Ice minimum volumes 1979–2018 (*Source* AMAP, AMAP climate change update 2019, An Update to Key Findings of Snow, Water, Ice and Permafrost in the Arctic [SWIPA] 2017)

activities and increasing interest of both Arctic and non-Arctic states. Because sea ice acts as a barrier to marine transport and commercial activities such as shipping and the extraction of natural resources, the loss of sea ice is expected to open new economic activities[5] (Fig. 4.3).

Another worrying issue is the acidification of the ocean, due to increasing atmospheric carbon dioxide which is threatening marine life. As per a study conducted by ACIA (Arctic Climate Impact Assessment), it was revealed that warming in the Arctic is double the rate of warming in other parts of the world. The more worrying phenomenon is that the Arctic is now changing to a state wherein more than 50% of the sea ice

---

[5] Arctic Monitoring and Assessment Programme, Arctic Council, AMAP Climate Change Update 2019, An Update to Key Findings of Snow, Water, Ice and Permafrost in the Arctic (SWIPA) 2017, (2019) accessed on 1 November 2019 from https://www.amap.no/documents/download/3295/inline.

is forming new each year, quite like the Antarctic. As brought out earlier, the Arctic was a unique place as it had the system of storing the sea ice of several millennia. Since the receding sea ice is redrawing the extent and coverage of ice in the Arctic, the surface boundary of the Ocean is also transforming. These changes are bringing with it drastic and fundamental changes in the natural system with different dynamics from the historical parameters. More worrying is the fact that sea ice stored over several millennia being lost rapidly to climate change and the same is happening in years rather than decades or millennia, which shows the speed at which the transformations are happening in the Arctic.

Another worrying issue is the acidification of the ocean, due to increasing atmospheric carbon dioxide which is threatening marine life. As per a study conducted by ACIA (Arctic Climate Impact Assessment), warming was demonstrated by ACIA to be increasing at twice the rate as compared to the rest of the world.[6] The more worrying phenomenon is that the Arctic is now changing to a state wherein more than 50% of the sea ice is forming new each year, quite like the Antarctic. Earlier, the Arctic had sea ice of several millennia stored, which was making it unique. The fundamental change in the sea-surface boundary of the Arctic Ocean is creating a new natural system with different dynamics from anything previously experienced by humans in the region, and this environmental state change is happening on the time scale of years rather than decades.[7]

AMAP in its studies also concluded that the Arctic serves as a waste disposal place for persistent organic pollutants, produced in mid-latitudes.[8] The waning of ice cover is making the region both better accessible and lucrative for commercial exploitation of huge reserves of hydrocarbons, minerals, rare earth known to be trapped beneath the huge layers of permafrost. Because Arctic sea ice has a bright white surface, the vast majority of sunlight striking the ice is reflected into space. When the sea ice melts, more of the darker ocean surface is exposed to sunlight. Rather than reflecting sunlight into space, the darker ocean

---

[6] Annika E. Nilsson, "A Changing Arctic Climate: Science and Policy in the Arctic Climate Impact Assessment" (Ph.D. diss., Linkoping University, 2007).

[7] Berkman Paul, Geopolitics of Arctic Sea-Ice Minima, The Brown Journal of World Affairs, 2012, vol. 19, issue 1, Fall/Winter, pp. 145–153, Stable URL: https://www.jstor.org/stable/24590934.

[8] Koivurova, supra note 7 in Chapter 1.

surface absorbs the majority of that sunlight.[9] The waning of ice cover is making the region both better accessible and lucrative for commercial exploitation of huge reserves of hydrocarbons, minerals, rare earth known to be trapped beneath the huge layers of permafrost. Another ill effect of the loss of millennial old sea ice is the melting of ice which leads to exposure of the darker ocean surface to sunlight which has a tendency to absorb the sunlight and further accelerating more warming. On the other hand, the old sea ice has a bright white surface, which reflects the sunlight back into space rather than absorbing it, thus delaying the process of ice loss. With sea ice melting, glaciers receding, permafrost thawing, and Arctic storms picking up steam, dozens of low-lying coastal communities that are vulnerable to flooding and erosion, such as Shishmaref, Alaska, and Tuktoyaktuk, Northwest Territories, will have to be shored up or moved.[10] The effect on Inuits, Athabaskans, Sami, Aleuts, and several other indigenous groups will force them into social and economic adjustments and re-organisation. The effects on Polar Bears, Seals, Caribou, and around 20,000 cold-climate mammals, birds, invertebrates, plants, and fungi, and many other yet undiscovered microbes will be apocalyptic.

Figure 4.4 shows that ice cover in the Arctic is receding at a very fast pace.[11]

The scientific studies have established that the event of warming in the Arctic and the hastened ice loss is quite dissimilar to any such documented event in the past. The warming taking place in the Arctic is also accelerating faster than anything that has been documented over the past 2.6 million years.[12] The Mackenzie (largest undisturbed ecosystem in the world) and Peace-Athabasca deltas are demising due to the ill effects of climate change and the shrinking of glaciers. Another dimension of rising temperatures and disappearing sea ice also will precipitate storms earlier. The storm surges will extend their reach flooding communities, killing wetlands, and further increasing the rate of ice loss.

---

[9] Rebecca Bratspies, human rights, and arctic resources, 15 Sw. J. Int'l L. 251 2008–2009.

[10] Struzik Edward, supra note 16 in Chapter 2.

[11] Berkman Paul, Geopolitics of Arctic Sea-Ice Minima, The Brown Journal of World Affairs, 2012, vol. 19, issue 1, Fall/Winter, pp. 145–153, Stable URL: https://www.jstor.org/stable/24590934.

[12] Struzik Edward, supra note 16 in Chapter 2.

YEAR	SUMMER MINIMUM SEA-ICE EXTENT		
	million square kilometers	million square miles	Date
2007	4.17	1.61	September 18
2008	4.59	1.77	September 20
2009	5.13	1.98	September 13
2010	4.63	1.79	September 21
2011	4.33	1.67	September 11
2012	3.41	1.32	September 16
1979 to 2010 average	6.14	2.37	September 15

^{S} Satellite measurements of Arctic sea ice began in 1979 and the most extreme summer minima have all occurred in the past six years. Arctic Sea Ice News and Analysis from the National Snow and Ice Data Center (http://www.nsidc.org)

Fig. 4.4 Summer minimum sea ice extent

(b) **Terrestrial and Marine Environment**

The thawing of ice and drying grounds on terrestrial plains leads to doubling of Arctic fires at double the intensity. The characteristics of loss of sea ice, shrinkages of ice cover, the spread of wildfires, etc., have a corresponding and disastrous impact on the Arctic ecosystems and are adversely impacting the habitats, mortality, and sustenance of indigenous people's livelihoods. There is also an impact on the marine food web and marine ecosystems and there are concerns that the Caribou, Polar Bears, seals, etc., will not be able to cope up with the rapidly changing scenario. The release of methane and GHGs by the thawing of Arctic permafrost has also a substantial contribution to the warming. The changes like ice losses both on land and on sea, increasing thawing of permafrost, increase in onset of wildfires, changes in pattern and timing of seasons, and unseasonal storms have credibly conveyed that irreversible damage has already been caused to the Arctic environment and the impacts thereof will be felt in distant geographic regions too. The number of wildfires ignited by lightning has risen in Canada's Northwest Territories and in interior Alaska since 1975. Increases in temperature and precipitation correlate with increases in the number of lightning-caused wildfire ignitions.[13]

---

[13] AMAP, Arctic Monitoring and Assessment Programme, Arctic Council, AMAP Climate Change Update 2019, An Update to Key Findings of Snow, Water, Ice and Permafrost in the Arctic (SWIPA) 017, (2019) accessed on 1 November 2019 from https://www.amap.no/documents/download/3295/inline.

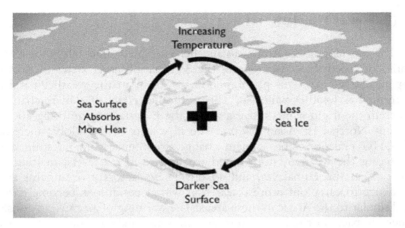

Fig. 4.5 Feedback loop (*Source* https://climatetippingpoints.info/2016/10/21/Arctic-sea-ice-and-positive-feedback-loops/)

(c) **Feedback Loops**

The term feedback loop depicts the situation where the output impacts the inputs. There are thus two kinds of feedback loops, positive and negative, in which either the process is amplified or inhibited, respectively. Climate change is imperilling the environment by juxtaposing change by "feedback loops" wherein an increase in temperatures changes the sea ice into the heat-absorbing ocean and exacerbating the problem into a spiralling frenzy. In September 2012, the area covered by Arctic sea ice dropped to 3.6 million square kilometres, almost 50% below the 1979 to 2000 average.[14]

As the ice melts, it exposes the darker land and/or ocean which absorbs the sunlight rather than reflecting it as sea ice does due to its shiny white surface. This absorption of heat further warms the atmosphere, which cyclically causes more ice and snow to melt (Fig. 4.5).

---

[14] US National Snow and Ice Data Center, "Arctic Sea Ice News and Analysis," available at http://nsidc.org/Arcticseaicenews/.

(d) **Winter Whiplash**

The warming of the Arctic has another associated effect felt in the territories of North-East Asia among the 3 Arctic observer states of Korea, Japan, and China. This phenomenon of a shift in the weather pattern is termed as weather whiplash. This is another effect of climate change, wherein the frigid winds moving across the Eurasian region bring cooler to this North-East Asian region. The ill effects of the global increase in GHG emissions and climate change are regularly manifesting and changing the weather, not limited to the rise in sea levels, melting of ice caps in the Himalayas, and so on. These factors give impetus and credence to carry out more research as winter conditions become harsh and similar to the Arctic in these areas. The warming of air causes a consequent impact on the air pressure and thus causing a pressure difference between North Atlantic and Arctic air systems which on interaction leads to severe winter weather conditions in North America and Europe.

(e) **Rising Sea Level**

One of the changes having an impact across continents will be the loss of ice sheets and glaciers which will have a corresponding effect on a rise in sea levels. As per an AMAP report, the Arctic had caused 30% of the total sea-level rise in the period between 1992 and 2017. The loss of glaciers due to human-induced activities will aggravate further in the coming decades, which may have a catastrophic impact on coastal countries like Maldives, India, and Bangladesh. The Arctic accounts for 48% (10 cm) of the total global sea-level rise that occurred from 1850 to 2000 and 30% of the total sea-level rise that occurred from 1992 to 2017.[15] As per the Fig. 4.6, it is also clarified that the coming decades will witness much faster and hastened ice losses and the impact thereof will necessarily lead to huge population displacement. Figure 4.6 depicts

---

[15] Arctic Monitoring and Assessment Programme, Arctic Council, AMAP Climate Change Update 2019, An Update to Key Findings of Snow, Water, Ice and Permafrost in the Arctic (SWIPA) 2017, (2019) accessed on 1 November 2019 from https://www.amap.no/documents/download/3295/inline.

the loss from local glaciers and ice caps over the projected time frame of next 10/60 years.

(f) Effect on Public health, Communities, and Economies

The Arctic indigenous people have been surviving on traditional methods and means for centuries and the changes in the ecosystem will endanger the traditional means of hunting, fishing, whaling, and so on. Climate change interacts with other environmental and health stressors (e.g. pollution, ocean acidification, erosion), along with a range of social, economic, and political factors (e.g. migration, resource extraction, local development, recreation, and tourism) that are fundamentally changing the nature of the Arctic. These changes challenge the ability of Arctic communities to adapt and maintain resilience.[16] For indigenous people, the primitive practices of hunting, fishing, and gathering food are an important facet of their lives. Also, these practices require them to rely on a functioning cash economy. There will be issues relating to migration as well as a swell in Arctic tourism that can change the nature of the Arctic. Not only the Arctic flora, fauna, and aquatic lives but the human population also has to adapt to the changes and be resilient in their methodology.

(g) Mapping of Arctic Ocean

The shape and depth of the ocean floor are termed as bathymetry and the Arctic Ocean's bathymetry is acutely insufficient because of the stiff weather conditions. The study of the ocean floor is vital to undertake ship safety as well as understanding the dynamics of the ocean and the formation of ocean currents and tides. Thus the knowledge which is crucial for seamless commercial activity, as well as SAR and other allied aspects, is incomplete. As per estimates, only 15% of the Arctic Ocean has been

---

[16] AMAP, Arctic Monitoring and Assessment Programme, Arctic Council, AMAP Climate Change Update 2019, An Update to Key Findings of Snow, Water, Ice and Permafrost in the Arctic (SWIPA) 2017, (2019) accessed on 1 November 2019 from https://www.amap.no/documents/download/3295/inline.

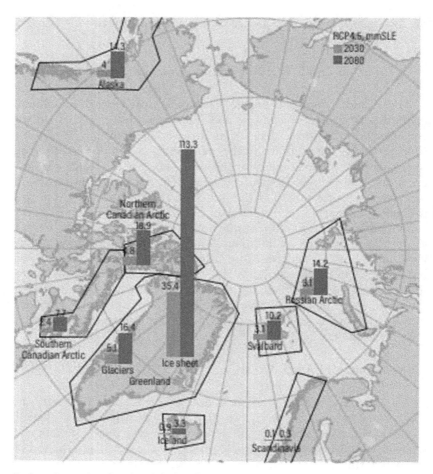

Projected mass loss from local glaciers, ice caps, and Greenland Ice Sheet for 2030 (pale bars) and 2080 (dark bars) (expressed in millimeters of sea level equivalence) under a moderate climate change scenario (RCP 4.5). Modified from SWIPA 2017.

Fig. 4.6 Projected ice loss till 2030 and 2080 (*Source* AMAP, AMAP climate change update 2019, An Update to Key Findings of Snow, Water, Ice and Permafrost in the Arctic [SWIPA] 2017)

mapped yet with the progress in usage of unmanned vehicles, space technology, and gravity studies; the bathymetry is likely to increase in the coming years.

Since the year around sea ice as well as extremely difficult research coupled with prohibitive costs has prevented and curbed the availability of bathymetry data, there is a consequent effect on the understanding of hydrological and other issues related to the ocean.

(h) **Positive Feedback**

The thawing of Arctic permafrost is an accepted reality and even if the highly ambitious Paris Agreement commitments are met, the permafrost is expected to shrink about 50% from today's levels. Increased thawing is expected to contribute significantly to carbon dioxide and methane emissions. The resulting warming will, in turn, lead to more thawing—an effect known as 'positive feedback.' This accelerated climate change could even throw the Paris Agreement's 2 °C goal off track.[17] The interrelation between the untrapping of the carbon in permafrost will also throw the climate change goals into a tipping point.

(i) **Short-Lived Climate Pollutants**

AMAP also found it in its studies that the Arctic also serves as a waste disposal place for POPs generated in mid-latitudes. The short-term climate pollutants, called so because unlike carbon dioxide which remains for long in the atmosphere these are more powerful and damaging to the environment. These include black carbon, methane, and troposphere ozone. Warming in the Arctic is also influenced by a cluster of pollutants known as "short-term climate pollutants," so-called because, unlike carbon dioxide which remains in the atmosphere for centuries, they remain for days or weeks and are more powerful short-term climate

---

[17] UN Environment Programme, UNEP, 2019, accessed on 1 September 2019 from https://www.unenvironment.org/news-and-stories/press-release/temperature-rise-locked-coming-decades-Arctic.

forcers than CO_2. They include black carbon, methane, and tropospheric ozone.[18]

(j) Atlantification and Pacification

The Arctic Ocean is also undergoing a rapid transformation by shedding its earlier distinctiveness to characteristics of the neighbouring regions. Though these terms are more aptly invoked in political and security dimensions yet the geophysical and environmental attributes are also witnessing the fallout.

(k) Permafrost Thawing

19 million square kilometres of land in the northern hemisphere (an area larger than the entire continent of South America) is "influenced" by permafrost. Most of this land is in Russia, Canada, Alaska, and Greenland.[19] The Arctic is assessed to be a carbon sink of 50% of the world's carbon trapped under the soil. The thawing of permafrost is starting to release the trapped carbon in the form of CO_2 and Methane and water which is also exacerbating the climate change situation.

(l) Polar Vortex

Due to the phenomenon of the polar vortex, the cold air from the region is being pushed southwards, which has the twin effects of intense weather events in the southern regions and it causes additional warmth in the Arctic air and thus aids warming and amplification of feedback loop.

---

[18] UNEP, What Future for the Arctic, a Background Paper for Arctic Side Event at the Governing Council, 2019, accessed on 6 October 2019 from http://www.un.org/esa/socdev/unpfii/documents/2013/agencies/2013_UNEP.pdf.

[19] Arctic WWF Org, accessed on 21 August 19 from https://arcticwwf.org/newsroom/the-circle/arctic-tipping-point/thawing-permafrost/.

Maritime Boundary Disputes in Arctic

(a) The Beaufort Sea

The only remaining maritime dispute in the Arctic region is that of the Beaufort Sea between the USA and Canada. Though some attempts were made in 2010 to resolve the issue, yet the same has not progressed, as desired. To present the Arctic as a region of cooperation, both these nations should expedite to relieve any misgivings on the prevalence of disputes. Currently, Canada and the United States share three maritime boundaries disputes in the area of the Beaufort Sea. The origin of the dispute can be traced to the US oil tanker SS Manhattan crossing the area without Canadian permission in 1969. These two countries had settled the issue of the Gulf of Maine by international mediation in 1984 and must follow suit to resolve this dispute. They can follow the Barents Sea resolution wherein a modified equidistance principle was adopted to settle the claims (Map 4.1).

(b) Hans Island

Hans Island, a barren island, having an area of half a square mile has been contested by Canada and Denmark. This boundary quarrel has been simmering between Canada and Denmark over the status of Hans Island, a 1.3 square kilometres barren feature that rests on the maritime border between Canada's Ellesmere Island and Greenland.[20] It is situated in the Kennedy Channel of the Nares Strait and can be considered as a large rock situated between Greenland and Nunavut. Traditionally being used by the Inuit as hunting grounds and also for navigation of explorers in ancient times, the dispute has been continuing since 1973 when Greenland and Canadian boundaries were being settled. Hans Island is the smallest among the three small islands, namely Franklin Island, Crozier Island, and the former. The only terrestrial dispute in the Arctic, it has not drawn much traction but only non-serious jokes about liquor in the Hans Island as a manner to assert sovereignty (Map 4.2).

---

[20] Standing Committee on Foreign Affairs and International Development of the Canadian House of Commons on November 26, 2018, Stephanie Pezard, The new geopolitics of the Arctic, Russia and China's evolving role in the region, accessed on 1 October 2019, from RAND corporation at https://www.rand.org/pubs/testimonies/CT500.html.

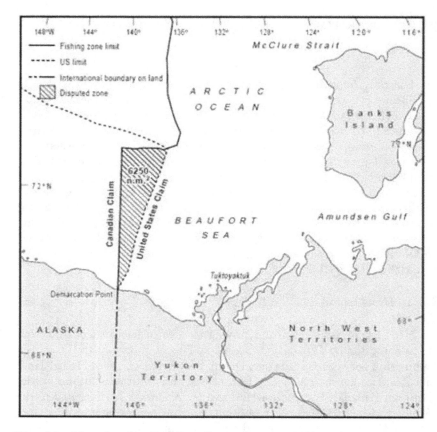

Map 4.1 Map showing Beaufort dispute between USA and Canada (*Source* Dovile Petkunaite, City University of New York)

(c) UN CLCS (UN Commission on the Limits of Continental Shelf) Claims

In 2007, a Russian submarine appeared to force that issue by planting a national flag, made of titanium, on the ocean floor beneath the North Pole, a gesture widely interpreted as symbolising Russian claims to the

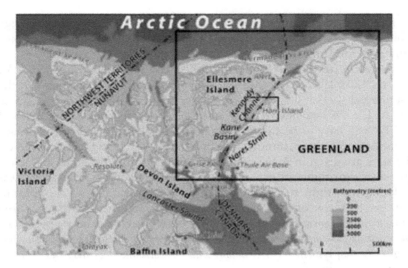

Map 4.2 Map showing the location of Hans Island (*Source* Nikoleta Maria Hornackova, Hans Island Case, A territorial dispute in the Arctic, accessed on 1 October 2019 from https://projekter.aau.dk/projekter/files/281245824/Master_Thesis_2018_Nikoleta_Maria_Hornackova.pdf)

Lomonosov area.[21] The mechanism of the UN CLCS has been used by the members to stake their territorial claims on the continental shelf. Five nations of the Arctic 8 have submitted their claims, which are produced in a table below with only Sweden, Finland, and the USA as the exceptions. Among these three, the USA is a non-signatory of the UNCLOS and cannot rightfully utilise the forum of UN CLCS, till such time it ratifies the UNCLOS. Among the Arctic 5, the process of claiming the extended continental shelf has been exercised by the four Arctic coastal states, except the USA which is a non-signatory to the UNCLOS, so far.

---

[21] Timo Koivurova, The Actions of the Arctic States Respecting the Continental Shelf: A Reflective Essay. Ocean Development & International Law, 2011, vol. 42, issue 3, pp. 211–226; Arvind Gupta, Geopolitical Implications of Arctic Meltdown, Strategic Analysis, March 2009, vol. 33, issue 2, p. 175; 'New Global Warming Report Deserves UN Push,' Korea Times, 7 October.

The most important among the claims are on the Lomonosov Ridge which has been claimed by Russia, Canada, and Denmark (Greenland) during various times.

The recourse to UNCLOS established CLCS is given out in Part VI of UNCLOS 1982. This gives out the mechanism of laying claims to the continental shelf and such provisions are given in Article 76 and Article 77. Article 76 lays out that for any claim over and above the 200NM of EEZ will have to be submitted by the coastal state along with relevant scientific findings for consideration by the CLCS. The rights conferred on the state are given in Article 77 which stipulates that the state shall exercise sovereign rights of exploration of natural resources over such areas including the right to exploit gas and oil deposits. The U.N. Convention on the Law of the Sea, for example, *"comprises 320 articles and nine annexes, governing all aspects of ocean space, such as delimitation, environmental control, marine scientific research, economic and commercial activities, transfer of technology and the settlement of disputes relating to ocean matters."*[22]

Part VI of UNCLOS covers the continental shelf, and Annex II to the treaty, which established the CLCS, is particularly pertinent. Article 76 and Article 77 are important as Article 76 states that "the coastal State shall establish the outer edge of the continental margin wherever the margin extends beyond 200 nautical miles," and that "Information on the limits of the continental shelf beyond 200 nautical miles... shall be submitted by the coastal State to the Commission on the Limits of the Continental Shelf set up under Annex II." And Article 77 states that "The coastal State exercises over the continental shelf sovereign rights for the purpose of exploring it and exploiting its natural resources, and that these natural resources include, among other things, mineral and other non-living resources of the seabed and subsoil, including oil and gas deposits."[23]

Russia was the first country to assert its claims under UN CLCS and submitted its claim on 20 December 2001 and Canada is the latest one to submit its claim on 23 May 2019. The Russian planting of a flag on the North Pole by using a submarine in 2007 had heightened the tensions

---

[22] Colonel (Retired) Risto Gabrielsson and Colonel (Retired) Zdzislaw Sliwa, Arctic the new Great Game or Peaceful Cooperation, Baltic Security and Defence Review, 2014.

[23] United Nations, un.org, accessed on 1 October 2019 from https://www.un.org/depts/los/convention_agreements/texts/unclos/unclos_e.pdf.

and scramble to stake claim to the resources in the Arctic. Like these two nations, Denmark has also formally submitted its claim on the Arctic seabed under UN CLCS in 2014. The consideration by CLCS may take several years and nations may not agree with its recommendations and may choose to submit another set of claims like the Russian revised claim of 2015. Once submissions have been evaluated by the CLCS, which may take several years, the three states will negotiate a delimitation agreement. Russia first made a scientific submission under UNCLOS in 2001, which it subsequently revised in 2015. Denmark completed its submission regarding the continental shelf around Greenland in 2014.[24]

The Danish claim, as well as the Canadian claim, overlaps with the Russian claim. The Arctic states have committed to resolve the delimitation of coastal state jurisdiction over the prolongation of seabed beyond EEZs in a peaceful manner. The political maturity shown by the Arctic states does convey that the resolution of these disputes will be employing negotiations and not any military threats/ muscle-flexing. A map depicting the Arctic territorial claims as well as national EEZs is as under (Map 4.3).

Norway is the only Arctic country to have been able to settle its jurisdiction on the extended continental shelf by and is fervently granting exploitation licences as the size of its extended shelf is around three-quarters of mainland Norway and thus providing it abundant potential of petroleum resources. Submissions, through the Secretary-General of the United Nations, to the Commission on the Limits of the Continental Shelf, under Article 76, paragraph 8, of the United Nations Convention on the Law of the Sea of 10 December 1982[25] are available on the given website. As Norway has been successful—the only Arctic country so far—in receiving jurisdiction over its extended continental shelf, it can now expand these activities over its 235,000 square kilometres large

---

[24] Durham University, 2019, accessed on 2 August 2019 from https://www.dur.ac.uk/ibru/news/boundary_news/?itemno=39095&rehref=%2Fibru%2Fnews%2F&resubj=Boundary+news+Headlines.

[25] United Nations, Oceans and Law of the Seas, accessed on 1 October 2019 from https://www.un.org/Depts/los/clcs_new/commission_submissions.htm.

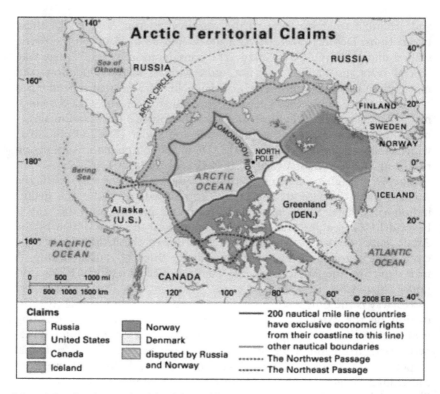

Map 4.3 Arctic territorial claims (*Source* https://www.researchgate.net/figure/Lomonosov-Ridge-donut-hole-and-national-exclusive-economic-zones_fig3_259694535)

continental shelves, equivalent to three-quarters the size of mainland Norway.[26]

The summary of submissions made by the various states to the UNCLCS for resolving the maritime claims is as under (Table 4.1).

---

[26] K. Keil, Spreading Oil, Spreading Conflict? Institutions Regulating Arctic Oil and Gas Activities. The International Spectator: Italian Journal of International Affairs, 2015, vol. 50, issue 1, pp. 85–110.

Table 4.1 Summary of submissions to CLCS

S No	State	Date of submission	Recommendations adopted on
1	Russian Federation	20 December 2001	27 June 2002
1a	Russian Federation	28 February 2013	11 March 2014
1b	Russian Federation	3 August 2015	
7	Norway	27 November 2006	27 March 2009
27	Iceland—in the Ægir Basin area and in the western and southern parts of Reykjanes Ridge	29 April 2009	10 March 2016
28	Denmark—in the area north of the Faroe Islands	29 April 2009	11 March 2014
30	Norway—in respect of Bouvetøya and Dronning Maud Land	4 May 2009	8 February 2019
54	Denmark—Faroe-Rockall Plateau Region	2 December 2010	
61	Denmark—in respect of the Southern Continental Shelf of Greenland	14 June 2012	
68	Denmark—in respect of the North-Eastern Continental Shelf of Greenland	26 November 2013	
70	Canada—in respect of the Atlantic Ocean	6 December 2013	
76	Denmark—in respect of the Northern Continental Shelf of Greenland	15 December 2014	
84	Canada—in respect of the Arctic Ocean	23 May 2019	

Note Serial numbers as per UN CLCS website

The unfolding of disputes in the Arctic is a new dimension, wherein legal claims are being backed up by verifiable scientific data. The course of dispute resolution would pave the way for managing resource disputes in the present era. The CLCS has no authority to enforce its decisions by only making recommendations, based on evidence. The resolution of the disputes on CLCS claims will have a perceptible shift in the economic balance and strategic power in the Arctic but it is assessed that the bilateral agreements will not only prove to be better but also the nations will take recourse to these as against any enlargement of conflict.

(d) The maritime border between Canada and Greenland is also pending and unsettled in the area of Lincoln Sea, as also there are overlapping continental shelf claims in the Labrador Sea between these two.

Till some time back it was held that the North Pole will not be subjected to territorial claims of the Arctic states, yet out of 5 littoral states, 3 have already submitted their respective rights on it, and the USA is likely to submit it on ratification of UNCLOS. Once confirmed these claims will then evict all cries by non-Arctic states to exploit Arctic natural resources, anywhere.

Arctic Security

Security, in an objective sense, measures the absence of threats to acquired values, in a subjective sense, the absence of fear that such values will be attacked.[27] Security can be understood as an absence of threats and the absence of any apprehension that the prevailing status quo will be disrupted. Before the closure of the cold war, classical security issues had occupied centre stage in Arctic affairs and therefore the region was heavily militarised. The Arctic region during the cold war was understood in military-security sense but a turning point was when it was labelled 'zone of peace' by Gorbachev in 1987. Thereafter it has been termed as a 'territory of dialogue,' 'high north, low tension' and broadly covered under the term of Arctic exceptionalism, meaning thereby that despite tensions elsewhere, they don't spiral and impact the Arctic and it remains an exception. Heininen's definition of comprehensive Arctic security is, "…military security is still very relevant, as is regional security due to impacts of climate change, energy security meaning both access to, and import and export of, oil and natural gas, and also environmental security due to oil transportation, nuclear accidents and impacts of climate change" and "to include the perspectives of human beings, societies, and regions, rather than just states."[28]

---

[27] A. Wolfers, National Security as an ambiguous symbol. Political Science Quarterly, December 1952, vol. 67, issue 4, pp. 481–502, https://doi.org/10.2307/2145138, https://www.jstor.org/stable/2145138.

[28] Hoogensen & Hodgson, "Arctic Exceptionalism" or "Comprehensive Security"? Understanding Security in the Arctic (Arctic Yearbook 2013.pdf, n.d.).

However, certain attributes are dynamic and have transformed substantially vis-a-vis the Arctic of the 1980s/1990s. Because of the complex geography encompassing several nation-states with differing political equations among each other as well as with stakeholders outside as also no binding geographical-political entity, the measure of comprehensive security is more apt in the case of Arctic. The Arctic assumes greater significance due to the geographical proximity of the two erstwhile superpowers USSR and America connected by the Arctic region. From the outset, security is one element that has been kept out of the purview of deliberations at the AC level."[29] The development of weapon systems that were leveraged with the shortest distance between these two adversaries for strikes against each other also heightened the pressure. During the cold war years, the Arctic had become the most militarised region of the world including the reconnaissance by long-range bombers, deployment of tactical nuclear missiles, and so on due to these mutual apprehensions and misgivings.

During various times, the Arctic has been called 'zone of peace,' 'territory of dialogue' and 'High North, Low tension,' and so on. The isolation and sequestering of the region from other geopolitical tensions elsewhere had led to being termed as 'exceptional.' From the outset, security is one element that has been kept out of the purview of deliberations at the AC level. Security in the Arctic has traditionally been discussed within non-military frameworks. The most pressing issue has been the region's susceptibility to climate change, including the erosion of polar ice and altered weather conditions, with the associated impact on local-level socio-economic affairs and indigenous persons.[30] The recent seven-hour visit of US Vice President Mike Pence to Iceland, in September 2019, was though politely snubbed by the locals and the meeting with Icelandic Prime Minister Katrin Jakobsdottir was also agreed to at the eleventh hour by the hostess yet it was a precursor to shifting security architecture in the region. Pence was the first US Vice President to visit Iceland since George H.W. Bush went to Reykjavik in 1983, similarly causing a stir with his "attendant paraphernalia of Air Force Two, bulletproof limousines and White House telecommunication equipment," the Washington Post

---

[29] Ilulissat Declaration, Ilulissat, Greenland, 28 May 2009, www.oceanlaw.org/downloads/Arctic/Ilulissat-Declaration.pdf.

[30] NATO, 2019, accessed on 24 September 2019 from https://www.nato.int/docu/review/articles/2019/06/28/the-changing-shape-of-Arctic-security/index.html.

reported at the time[31] as Iceland has remained peaceful and devoid of such security trappings accompanying the political leaders. Rather the AC and the general framework are complimented for its farsightedness and maturity in discussing and charting out the element of security in areas like environment, human security, inter-regional cooperation, and Indigenous self-determination among others. There has been a change in the overall security architecture in the Arctic with an increasingly overspill of great power rivalry between the USA and Russia. More importantly, the increasing interest and motivation of non-Arctic states like China, EU, UK, and Korea have also opened debate whether Arctic security is an international concern? The historical evidence suggests that security till now was considered in the prisms of climate change, environmental impacts of climate change, and the region's adaptability and the impacts of these on traditional livelihoods and socio-economic conditions.

The recent seven-hour visit of US Vice President Mike Pence to Iceland, in September 2019, was though politely snubbed by the locals and the meeting with Icelandic Prime Minister Katrin Jakobsdottir was also agreed to at the eleventh hour by the hostess yet it was a precursor to shifting security architecture in the region. There was the presence of US service members in Iceland till the Naval Air Station Keflavik was vacated on 30 September 2006. This partnership between the two NATO allies had lasted 65 years with a commitment that US service members will continue to work with, train with, and operate with their NATO ally, but troops will not be based in the island nation.[32] Pence was the first US Vice President to visit Iceland since George H.W. Bush went to Reykjavik in 1983, similarly causing a stir with his "attendant paraphernalia of Air Force Two, bulletproof limousines and White House telecommunication equipment," the Washington Post reported at the time[33] as Iceland has remained peaceful and devoid of such security trappings accompanying the political leaders. The timing of this visit to Iceland and the subsequent actions point out that the US wants to fully leverage Iceland as the current chair of the Arctic Council and possibly reinitiate the military

---

[31] Washington Post, 2019, accessed on 2 October 2019 from https://www.washingtonpost.com/world/2019/09/06/pences-security-detail-raises-eyebrows-peaceful-iceland/.

[32] US Navy, 2019, accessed on 19 September 2019 from https://www.navy.mil/submit/display.asp?story_id=25809.

[33] Washington Post, 2019, accessed on 2 October 2019 from https://www.washingtonpost.com/world/2019/09/06/pences-security-detail-raises-eyebrows-peaceful-iceland/.

Naval Base at Keflavik. "The United States looks forward to working with Iceland as the new chair of the Arctic Council to promote good stewardship of the environment and sustainable development in an Arctic region that remains stable and free from conflict."[34]

At one time, Iceland had more than 10,000 US service members based there. Then, the threats came from firstly Nazi Germany and then the Soviet Union. It was during World War II that the British followed by the US had vowed to defend Iceland against the Nazi threat. With a few short breaks, American service members have provided security for Iceland ever since. During World War II and the cold war, Iceland was critical to keeping the sea lines of communication open. The US maintained aircraft on Iceland to defend Iceland and the North Atlantic sea lanes against conventional military threats: submarines, ships, and aircraft. But those threats no longer exist.[35]

The Keflavik Naval Air Station in Iceland was manned by US service personnel till its vacation on 30 September 2006, as after the collapse of the USSR and a growing era of cooperative arrangement made it redundant. Since Iceland is a NATO ally country, the promise of joint training and operations between the US Navy and Iceland was though kept intact without being physically present there.

During World War II, the threat to the North Atlantic Sea was assessed from the Greenland-Iceland Gap (expanded to the GIUK Gap, Greenland-Iceland-United Kingdom) from Soviet Russia/Nazi Germany. The presence of US service personnel was felt essential to keep the SLOCs (Sea Lines of Communication) open. With the collapse of the USSR and the prevalence of Arctic exceptionalism, the old threats did also subside/collapse and no longer was the need felt to maintain the US base there. The threats though have manifested in newer forms like terrorism, drug trafficking, and importantly the shift in the global power structure in a multipolar world. With the alarming thinning of ice cover, economic and environmental security issues have surfaced with a scramble for accessing and exploiting the commercial potential.

---

[34] State Department, USA, 2019, accessed on 9 November 2019 from https://www.state.gov/iceland-national-day/.
[35] Ibid.

The recent developments like the visit of Pence and preceded by US Secretary of State Mike Pompeo in February 2019, followed by statements by Iceland's PM point out that plans are afoot to install new security architecture in the region, under US hegemony. The press statement by the USA on Iceland's National Day on 17 June also boasted of security and defence ties. The statement has components of support as well as overtures to brewing undercurrents. The USA thanked Iceland for its support to the USA in Afghanistan and to defeat ISIS.

The US is not only contesting claims of Russia on NSR and Canada on NWP and had called these as illegitimate. The USA is also critical of Beijing's expanding its Arctic interests, and a statement made by Secretary Pompeo had likened the Chinese attempts in the Arctic to the South China Sea (SCS), which was over the top considering that there is no common political or legal similarity of Arctic with the SCS. Secretary Pompeo in a statement said that China was seeking to develop strategies in the Arctic Ocean which were similar to those in place regarding the South China Sea, despite the two cases having dramatically different political and legal frameworks.[36]

In 2019, before the visit by US Vice President Pence to Iceland, there was a sortie of a B2 stealth bomber to Iceland. Not only this flight was popularised by the USA but also overtures on Naval Air Station Keflavik were incorporated as a forward base for preparations. The underlying message is that the security scenario is undergoing a rapid transformation and the security situation is becoming increasingly complex. A press release issued by the 'United States Air Forces in Europe – Air Forces Africa' on August 2019 stated: "The use of strategic bombers in Iceland helps exercise Naval Air Station Keflavik as a forward location for the B-2, ensuring that it is engaged, postured and ready with credible force to assure, deter and defend the US and its allies in an increasingly complex security environment."[37]

The timing of US statements and the location as Iceland becomes important as the current government is a coalition government formed after the parliamentary elections in 2017. Previously abandoned cold war-era military installations have been reopened and incursions by

---

[36] US Embassy, 2019, accessed on 9 October 2019 from https://ee.usembassy.gov/press-availability-at-nato-foreign-ministerial-2019/.

[37] Eurasia Review, 2019, accessed on 9 September 2019 from https://www.eurasiareview.com/16092019-concerns-about-military-build-up-in-iceland-oped/.

Russian aircraft and submarines into or close to other countries' Arctic spaces have become more frequent.[38] Among the coalition partner parties, the Left-Green Movement (LGM) is less forward-leaning towards the USA yet the coalition has two other parties, Independence Party and the Progressive Party, and despite the leanings of LGM known openly, there must be strong reasons for the USA to actively engage in such dealings, as the current PM herself has also voiced the security concerns. The USA is regretting its decision to hastily abandon the military bases in 2006. In a document produced in 2018, the US embassy in Reykjavik said that "(the) abrupt 2006 closure of Naval Air Station Keflavik changed the US-Iceland relationship fundamentally; the US remained treaty-bound to provide for Iceland's defence, but the physical manifestation of that commitment has disappeared."[39] The embassy noted that the political situation in Iceland since the financial crisis "strengthened pacifist political tendencies" and that "[while] the current government …is generally supportive of close ties with the United States, the Left-Green Movement (LGM) leadership is less forward-leaning toward US and NATO positions on security matters. We have to walk a fine line to maintain commitments in this area by being especially cognisant of the sensitivity of the issue within the government coalition."[40]

In the aftermath of the foregoing, the speech by the Iceland PM, Katrin Jakobsdottir, at Arctic council meeting in October stressing the need to include and incorporate security issues in the council points to rising geopolitical manoeuvring in the region, which should be a reason for alarm. At the very outset of her speech, she said that increased geopolitical tensions in the region are a deplorable development and highlighted that there is no specific Arctic forum to deal with hard security, territorial disputes, or the exploitation of natural resources. It is our collective responsibility to ensure peace and stability in the North Atlantic and

---

[38] NATO, 2019, accessed on 8 October 2019 from https://www.nato.int/docu/rev iew/articles/2019/06/28/the-changing-shape-of-Arctic-security/index.html.

[39] In-depth News, 2019, accessed on 1 October 2019 from https://www.indept hnews.net/index.php/armaments/nuclear-weapons/2972-concerns-about-military-build-up-in-iceland.

[40] Ibid.

the Arctic, preventing the area from falling prey to misguided geopolitical wrestling.[41] She found support in Finland's PM, Antti Rinne, who also argued that this kind of major issues should be discussed during times of peace, and wanted the EU on-board. Norway favours the most proactive Arctic defence policy of all NATO nations. Norway favours the most proactive Arctic defence policy of all NATO nations. They see the region as the alliance's unguarded flank and constantly prompt other member states to be well-informed and combat-ready.[42]

Unsurprisingly, Denmark had also voiced the need for a discussion on security policy in 2016. The country's Foreign and Security Policy had highlighted that there must be collective action and deliberations for discussion on having a structure or mechanism to discuss security given the increase in military activity and presence in the Arctic. This voice by 50% of the Arctic members to discuss and integrate security politics in the Arctic is an ample indicator of strengthening associations to check posturing by certain countries like Russia and China. The shift in discourse with Iceland at the helm draws on the radical change in the offing. The Iceland PM had further said, "Securing peace and stability in the North Atlantic and the Arctic and preventing the area to become a victim of a geopolitical power struggle is our responsibility."[43] Norway also conveyed its reservations and outgrowth from the opening of new sea routes to this region which will pave for fresh perspectives on security and politics.

Though the statements by political leaders have not been officially tabled formally by any of the governments yet a fresh beginning has been made. Are there attempts to revive NATO's opposition to Russia in the Arctic and veiled overtures to China on insecurity/reservations about its real motives? The Arctic Council, by now, has been successful in settling issues bilaterally among its members and is a central political forum for the region. Some scholars have rightly credited the AC as it provides coherent and regular communication between the two opposing power centres, which are yet again on a path of confrontation. The Arctic Council, by

[41] Government of Iceland accessed on 20 October 2019 from https://www.government.is/news/article/?newsid=629a6ec8-eb80-11e9-944e-005056bc530c.

[42] Maritime Executive.com, 2019, accessed on 9 September 2019 from https://www.maritime-executive.com/editorials/the-nato-alliance-s-role-in-Arctic-security.

[43] High North News, 2019, accessed on 1 October 2019 from https://www.highnorthnews.com/en/why-finland-and-iceland-want-security-politics-Arctic-council.

now, has been successful in settling issues bilaterally among its members and is a central political forum for the region. There is another feather in its cap, as it provides regular contact and communication between Russia and Western states and thus, by excluding security matters, the Arctic Council constitutes a beacon of hope in otherwise severely strained relations.[44]

The situation has though deteriorated with increased overtures by an increasingly assertive China, which has announced its grand plans to extend its Belt and Road Initiative in the Arctic region in the form of a Polar Silk Road. This Chinese plan is making the US wary of the reasons for China's forays and President Trump in 2019 had said clearly that 'we don't like the outsiders coming into the region.' Connected to the Chinese governmental diplomatic and strategic incursions is the economic and commercial expansion by Chinese corporations, eager to partake in the opportunities being presented by the Arctic ice melt.

The Chinese have also openly declared their intentions to seriously develop the resource capabilities for effective engagement with the Arctic and have been progressing the building of icebreakers, FNPP Floating Nuclear Power Plant, and aircraft carriers. The Chinese interest in exploiting Arctic fisheries, though in a regulated and sustainable manner, has already been asserted. The Chinese focus on icebreakers is also to reduce its dependence on the Russian icebreakers along the NSR. It is a matter of time that the Chinese will question the Russians on its escort regime along the NSR though in the present times the Chinese have chosen to play along on the Russian terms. The economic leverage of developing the ports and other infrastructure along the NSR can be leveraged on favourable terms at any later date, too. The role of nuclear icebreakers in the Arctic will be akin to that of aircraft carriers in oceans elsewhere and this strategy too is forward-looking by which China wants to fully circumvent its Malacca dilemma. China had released its white paper on her Arctic ambitions in 2018 and also announced its intention to develop a "Polar Silk Road" route through the region, constructing infrastructure and opening new shipping lanes through the warming waters. However, the US is continuously been wary and sceptical of Chinese plans and President Trump recently said that the region must be "free from external intrusion, interference, and coercion and we

---

[44] Arctic Institute, 2019, accessed on 1 October 2019 from https://www.theArcticinstitute.org/Arctic-security-forum-please-dont/?cn-reloaded=1.

believe that the affairs of the Arctic should be governed by the actual nations of the Arctic," and added. "And, as you know, there are other people coming into the Arctic, and we don't like it. And we can't let it happen, and we won't let it happen."[45] The much graver "threat" would be if Chinese corporations moved aggressively into the delicate region, looking to reap the rewards of the now rapid melt underway.[46]

With the expiry of the INF treaty in August 2019, it is an open issue that in a multipolar world, the growing clout, military prowess, and commercial deals of China are an eyesore and are viewed with suspicion by the US as well as some Arctic states. China has articulated that it is developing the nuclear-powered reactors for the purpose 'to develop natural resources in the Polar Regions.'[47]

The US, off late, has also been trying to bring on board the Arctic states into the folds of NATO to counter and check the Chinese and Russian influence in the region. The Secretary of State did not mince his words and openly named both Russia and China as threats, to be encountered with joint efforts of NATO countries. Secretary Pompeo had named both China and Russia as potential threats and called on the Arctic nations to support the USA in stalling the threats. The focus of the US is seen in the way it sees as Chinese attempts to have business transactions with underlying security components too. Others have similarly highlighted the geopolitical implications of pursuing FNPPs and nuclear icebreakers, as they would allow "China's blue-water fleet to open Arctic sea routes and circumvent the Malacca Strait." Or, to paraphrase another commentator, nuclear icebreakers are to the Arctic what aircraft carriers are to the Indo-Pacific.[48]

In light of the aforesaid developments, it is clear that the Arctic is seeing the dawn of a new 'triangular realpolitik' in which the two sides, i.e. Russia and China, have joined hands, at least for now. The third, USA is pitted against the differing ambitions of these two players which are being played out in several inter-lapping realms of sea passages, economic,

---

[45] Newsweek, 2019, accessed on 1 November 2019 from https://www.newsweek.com/donald-trump-us-block-china-expanding-Arctic-1462953.

[46] National Interest, 2019, accessed on 9 October 2019 from https://nationalinterest.org/feature/what-does-china-want-Arctic-78731.

[47] Ibid.

[48] The diplomat.com, 2019, accessed on 13 November 2019 from https://thediplomat.com/2019/09/checking-in-on-chinas-nuclear-icebreaker/.

strategic, freedom of navigation, and others. The recent statements and efforts of several statespersons are indicator enough of growing unease and plan to incorporate a new structure whose blueprint is yet to be drawn up. It will be prudent for the Arctic states to form lasting partnerships and utilise existing structures to prevent undue commercial exploitation without disrupting the prevailing peace. As expounded by certain quarters, the Arctic is a region that may see conflicts between nation-states due to its immense natural resource potential as well as control of Polar passages. Several fora need to act collaboratively and adopt clear-headed and visionary policy structures to prevent escalation threats. Despite lack of fervour control regime, the Arctic has largely remained trouble-free and given its strategic and environmental significance, stakeholders must take concerted action without unduly disturbing the dialogue through the Arctic Council and affiliated fora. The US, off late, has also been trying to bring on board the Arctic states into the folds of NATO to counter and check the Chinese and Russian influence in the region. The Secretary of State did not mince his words and openly named both Russia and China as threats, to be encountered with joint efforts of NATO countries. He said that it's our duty to adapt to challenges like radical Islamic terrorism, cyber-attacks, uncontrolled migration, Chinese strategic competition, and indeed, still, Russian aggression.[49] The focus of the US is clearly seen in the way it sees as Chinese attempts to have business transactions with underlying security components too. Mr. Pompeo said that it is a very different thing to engage in transactions that have a national security component to them. When a nation shows up and offers you goods that are well below market, one ought to ask what else is at play, why it was that that entity showed up with a deal that is literally too good to be true.[50]

Rather the Arctic 'exceptionalism' also stems from the progressive and wider definition of security being adopted in the region, beyond the domain of traditional security parameters. Though in 2019, there have been some provocative outbursts by the US officials including Secretary of State; Mike Pompeo called the region an arena of global competition. These developments show that the conceptions about security

---

[49] US Embassy, 2019, accessed on 9 October 2019 from https://uk.usembassy.gov/secretary-pompeos-press-availability-at-nato-foreign-ministerial-2019/
[50] Ibid.

are shifting from a cooperative framework towards a potential conflict scenario. The Arctic Year Book 2019 published by Arcticyearbook.com had also covered the theme 'Redefining Arctic security.' The Arctic is now facing a potential 'revenge of Realpolitik' with regard to regional security, as the strategic concerns of both major Arctic players, Russia and the United States, along with those of large non-Arctic states such as China, are starting to enter the region with much more regularity.[51]

However, the Arctic region has also been subjected to being a military front and a theatre of cold war rivalry and the arms race between the USSR and the USA, with the potent threat of nuclear war. The post-cold war period has seen greater commitment and resolve among the Arctic states in focussing on human security, environmental security, and a promise to maintain peace, stability, and constructive cooperation. Hence the security is understood by the Arctic 8 as less of military manoeuvres and tensions and more of political stability and with greater, mature, and alternative understanding. The recent developments and especially the posturing by the USA in 2019 though have initiated the discussion on having security structure/deliberations at some levels among the Arctic nations, though the same has not assumed the form of a state-sponsored agenda at AC, yet it provides the way things may unfold in the coming days. Rather the Arctic 'exceptionalism' also stems from the progressive and wider definition of security being adopted in the region, beyond the domain of traditional security parameters. Though in 2019, there have been some provocative outbursts by the US officials including Secretary of State, Mike Pompeo called the region "an arena of global power and competition" in May 19.[52] President Trump also added later that the region must be "free from external intrusion, interference, and coercion."[53] These developments show that the conceptions about security are shifting from a cooperative framework towards a potential

---

[51] NATO, 2019, accessed on 1 October 2019 from https://www.nato.int/docu/review/articles/2019/06/28/the-changing-shape-of-Arctic-security/index.html.

[52] Washington Post, 2019, accessed on 1 December 2019 from https://www.washingtonpost.com/world/national-security/pompeo-warns-of-dangers-of-russian-and-chinese-activities-in-the-Arctic/2019/05/06/e2e99690-7001-11e9-9eb4-0828f5389013_story.html.

[53] White House, 2019, accessed on 1 December 2019 from https://www.whitehouse.gov/briefings-statements/remarks-president-trump-president-niinisto-republic-finland-joint-press-conference/.

conflict scenario. The Arctic Year Book 2019 published by Arcticyearbook.com had also covered the theme 'Redefining Arctic security.' The post-cold war period has seen greater commitment and resolve among the Arctic states in focussing on human security, environmental security, and a promise to maintain peace, stability, and constructive cooperation. This has led to geopolitical stability despite or because of the heavy military (nuclear weapons) structures (global deterrence), impacts of climate change, better access to the exploitation of the region's resources (known as the 'Arctic paradox'), as well as the rise of human security as an important security concept.[54]

Resources: The application and ratification of UNCLOS by the Arctic states (and tacit approval by the USA) to follow its framework leave little scope for non-Arctic states to call for a stake in the region's natural resources. On the contrary, hoping and asking from any sovereign country to give up on its legal, irrefutable, and inalienable right on resources lying in its sovereign ownership is in itself a farfetched scenario. Since most of the resources lie in the sovereign territory of the respective states and the emphasis by everyone including non-Arctic states like China to comply with the rule-governed Arctic order based on international law leaves little scope for any conflict emerging out from ownership of resources.

Instead, the probability of geopolitical pressures from outside the region may spiral into the circumpolar region which may lead to a situation of conflict than overt competition within the Arctic itself. The signing of the International Agreement to Prevent Unregulated High Seas Fisheries in the Central Arctic Ocean (CAO) has also strengthened the base for cooperative governance in the Arctic. Such a precedent would be a valuable contribution to the effective governance of international waters in the Arctic and could provide a useful model for other regions as well.[55]

China's participation as a signatory to the fishing agreement also signals that it is working as a partner in areas of policy, science, resources, and international relations. The agreement on CAO has and will help to diffuse some misgivings on her quest for Arctic resources and offers another pathway for China. The increased economic manoeuvre by

---

[54] Arctic Yearbook, 2019, accessed on 1 December 2019 from https://Arcticyearbook.com/images/yearbook/2019/Introduction.pdf.

[55] Henry Huntington, A Precautionary Approach to Fisheries in the Central Arctic Ocean: Policy, Science, and China, Min Pan P, https://doi.org/10.1016/j.marpol.2015.10.015.

China, which has been an observer and has charted out its goals and vision, should also be a boon for small Arctic states to develop their infrastructural and resource potential.

The possible blackmail by China and Russia of attempts to downplay their aggressive stance by citing or emulating the Arctic model of cooperation and low tensions which could further legitimise those aggressive actions. This misuse of the regional structures and the region as a 'zone of peace' may have the potential by these to exploit the loose framework, presently devoid of any strict hard-nosed security structure.

Limitations of AC: The AC has been framed with peculiar yet robust characteristics of fostering intergovernmental cooperation between the member states albeit without any formalised structure or treaty obligations. Though the AC is over two decades old yet it does not have any stipulated budgetary allocations and all projects are sponsored by either of the states with tacit understanding and support of the other states. Since the security matters have been explicitly debarred from the discussions from the AC founding document, i.e. the Ottawa Declaration, the forum does not deliberate on any matters about security in its deliberations.

There is no legal entity of the AC as it is formed as an intergovernmental forum without any dedicated budget. There are no formal obligations on the states; thus the AC also lacks any authority to enforce its decisions. Rather it is a consensus-building approach wherein it offers its recommendations and assessment on most of the issues and invariably the members approve and ratify these by mutual agreement. The secretariat and projects are funded by voluntary funding by member states and by observer's funding with certain stipulations.

There have been discussions on having an Arctic Treaty and the role and responsibility of the international response to enforce a developed legal apparatus. However, to prevent any outside interference in Arctic affairs, the Arctic 8 had unequivocally rejected the idea of an Arctic treaty. "As an example, outside voices often advocated a comprehensive Arctic Treaty, which all eight AC members had rejected".[56]

The European Parliament in 2008 had made a controversial statement, calling for an international environmental treaty to be made applicable to the Arctic. This was the time that few scholars, NGOs, and environmental

---

[56] Piotr Graczyk and Timo Koivurova, "A New Era in the Arctic Council's External Relations? Broader Consequences of the Nuuk Observer rules for Arctic Governance." Polar Record, Cambridge University Press, 2013, pp. 1–12.

groups supported the same and made a voice for a firm legal framework. This call angered Arctic 5, who out rightly denied the same by making the 28 May 2008 Ilulissat Declaration by citing sovereign rights, sovereignty, and UNCLOS provisions on the Arctic Ocean, empowering them as stakeholders to guard the Arctic ecosystems. Thus a curtain was drawn on efforts of non-Arctic on governance in the Arctic by the 2008 Ilulissat Declaration by the Arctic 5, wherein adherence to rules of the law of the sea was quoted as sufficient for the resolution of Arctic international legal issues. Presently, while European Arctic powers try to keep the Arctic de-politicised, the US, China, and Russia know no such scruples, with far-reaching polar strategies that recognise the different logics of the geopolitics of the Arctic.[57]

The A5 had thus deftly employed the prevalent provisions of UNCLOS as well as their sovereign rights as applicable under its provisions to address and resolve both the opportunities and challenges that may arise in the Arctic Ocean. This declaration not only had the impact of fortifying the need by all to adhere to the provisions of the UNCLOS but also comply with the dispute settlement procedure outlined there under. The joint declaration at Ilulissat also listed the various issues like delineation of the outer limits of the continental shelf, freedom of navigation, marine scientific research, and other uses of the sea and so on given out in the UNCLOS as competent and adequate to address any issue if so may arise between the Arctic coastal states.

The Arctic 5 by the Ilulissat Declaration had affected the prevailing regional order in the Arctic and strengthened the position of Arctic coastal states in decision making. It also closed the governance gap and put an end to regional reform and asserted the influence of the coastal states. As per the declaration, the faith in the existing mechanism of AC is reaffirmed as adequate to address all issues of governance. However, a direct reference to the 1982 UN Convention on the Laws of the Seas (UNCLOS) was not made to presumably accommodate the USA, which is NOT a signatory thereof.

This declaration also debunked the myth of Arctic being a terra nullius and also the Arctic Ocean with its coastal countries forming the core of the Arctic. The exclusion of Iceland, Finland, and Sweden from the

---

[57] Dr Louise van Schaik, Ties Dams, The Arctic Elephant Policy Brief: Why Europe must address the geopolitics of the high north, November 2019, Netherlands Institute of International Relations.

treaty also unequivocally showed that the sovereign rights of the littorals will form the basis to resources. The action obviously had the impetus to re-territorise the region. The legal and institutional importance of the Ilulissat Declaration can also be gauged that in 2018, another Illulisat2 was held in Greenland to celebrate the 10th anniversary of its signing to reaffirm the political message.

The Realist school of international relations believes Great power competition between the USA, China, and Russia will define the future course of Arctic affairs as the growing scope of economic opportunities will expose the region to this contest to mould the region to their respective divergent advantages. The constructivists and institutionalist schools view that the presence of various interest groups, numerous organisations, and the activity of the global community will ensure that Arctic regional order prevails.

The Arctic region can pride in having multitudes of cooperative organisations having tiered membership as well as mandates. Adam P MacDonald has viewed that the Latent Balance of Power will let the present order prevail, despite opposing pulls. As per him the robust regional order will prevail based on the parameters like states' sovereignty, distribution of authority, and tiered and cooperative framework. This is so for the Arctic strategic landscape as it is premised on a Latent Balance of Power—defined by the region's geographic division of authority, strategic alignments, and state coherence—that has ensured territorial security, neutralised contests over hegemony, and facilitated the emergence of a decentralised but robust regional order.[58]

A common problem identified with the AC is that it is considered a soft law regime as it does not have any powers or tools of enforcement of its decisions and thus the function is more out of voluntary nature, bereft of any legally binding treaties. However, a problem with the Arctic Council is that it has always been a soft law regime, and there has never been any intention to create legally binding obligations for the Arctic states.[59] This is aggravated by the presence of the US, which acts as a father figure and imposes its dictates on the Arctic nations. This, however, does not take away the tested course of organised cooperation on common interests in

---

[58] Ibid.

[59] Erika Lennon, A Tale of Two Poles: A Comparative Look at the Legal Regimes in the Arctic and the Antarctic. Sustainable Development Law & Policy, 2008, vol. VIII, issue III, Spring, pp. 32, 33.

the Arctic region that will rather lessen the strategic rivalry of competing nations. Duncan Depledge and Klaus Dodds have described the governance arrangements as a "bazaar" in the piece,' Bazaar Governance: Situating the Arctic Circle. Governing Arctic Change: Global Perspectives'[60] implying that governance is interplay between various actors like governments, society, and businesses, and so on.

Status of Observers in the AC: As stated above, there are three categories of observers permitted in the AC, namely the non-Arctic states, intergovernmental/inter-parliamentary organisations, and non-governmental organisations. The foremost criteria of admitting the observers are stated and professed goals of these to further the Council's work in various fields. The initial foundations on admitting the observers were started even before the formal launch of the AC, with the participation of non-Arctic states like the Netherlands, Poland, the United Kingdom, and Germany in the framework of the 1991 Arctic Environmental Protection Strategy (AEPS). Thus soon after the 1996 Ottawa declaration which formally established the AC, these four non-Arctic states along with three intergovernmental/inter-parliamentary organisations (IGOs), namely Standing Committee of the Parliamentarians of the Arctic Region (SCPAR), United Nations Economic Commission for Europe (UN-ECE) and United Nations Environment Programme (UNEP) along with four non-governmental organisations, namely International Arctic Science Committee (IASC), International Union for Circumpolar Health (IUCH), World Wide Fund for Nature-Global Arctic Programme (WWF) and Northern Forum (NF) were admitted as observers in 1998 Iqaluit Meeting under the Canadian Chairmanship. With the elapse of time and streamlined rules of procedure, today there are a total of 39 observers in the AC. The protracted discussions about observer status in the Arctic Council (from China and the EU, among others) show that the institutional framework of the Arctic took time to find a stable and uncontroversial form.[61]

It is with gradual evolution that the role of observers has transformed substantially from being of full participation under the 1991 Rovaniemi

---

[60] D. Depledge and K. Dodds, Bazaar Governance: Situating the Arctic Circle. Governing Arctic Change: Global Perspectives. Eds. K. Kiel and S. Knecht. London, Palgrave Macmillan, 2017, pp. 141–160.

[61] Torbjørn Pedersen, Debates Over the Role of the Arctic Council. Ocean Development and International Law, 2012, vol. 43, pp. 146–56.

Meetings to curbed powers and limitations, later. The role of various AC chairs in this evolution also stands out with greater focus by the Scandinavian states to make the AC more participative and inclusive. The major onset of a collaborative and inclusionary mechanism in the Arctic, on scientific efforts to protect the fragile natural environment, could be attributed to the famous 1987 Murmansk Speech by USSR's leader Mikhail Gorbachev to make the Arctic region a 'zone of peace' and can be credited with drawing curtains on the Cold War and commencing a new era in Arctic affairs. Soon thereafter Finland advanced this concept by setting up the 1989 Rovaniemi Process which is considered to be the beginning of concrete steps towards the incorporation of the Arctic era. Finland had historically been successful in 1975 with the establishment of the Conference for Security and Cooperation in Europe (CSCE) which was regarded as a Finnish diplomatic masterstroke which had brought together opposing factions of Europe on a high table with the participation of leaders of West and the East for the first time. The non-Arctic states which attended the 1989 Rovaniemi Process included the United Kingdom, Poland, Germany, and the intergovernmental UNEP. The Rovaniemi Process paved the way for the 1991 AEPS, and from the outset, these four entities were accorded the observer status in AEPS.

The AEPS had formed four Working Groups (WGs), namely Arctic Monitoring and Assessment Programme (AMAP); Conservation of Arctic Flora and Fauna (CAFF); Emergency Preparedness, Protection and Response (EPPR); and Protection of Arctic Marine Environment (PAME) which were set up by AEPS to achieve its objectives to study, monitor, document, and protect the natural environment in the Arctic region. Other than the four observers, Japan and the Netherlands also committed to involve their experts working in the stated fields to support the efforts of the WGs and the focus was strictly on scientific studies and advancement. The cooperation of the observers was with the WGs in their respective areas of expertise and domain. The AEPS formed the backbone for 1996 Declaration on the Establishment of the Arctic Council at Ottawa, Canada, and the four non-Arctic states of United Kingdom, the Netherlands, Germany, and Poland were present at the inauguration signing ceremony in Ottawa and were granted official observer status in 1998 Iqaluit Meeting. The only non-Arctic state present at the ceremony was Japan, which had not applied for observer's status and thus remained outside the AC. The existing WGs of AEPS was merged into the framework of the AC on its formation. The status of various Observers in 1998 is as under (Table 4.2).

The number of Observers in 2006 had risen to 26 by 2006 which included six non-Arctic states, nine inter-parliamentary/ intergovernmental organisations, and eleven NGOs. The reason for this was that post the 2004 ACIA there was renewed and rekindled interest by the world community to gain a position at the AC to participate and express their views. 'From the perspective of the eight Arctic states, the key problem has been to reconcile the desire to elevate the international standing and legitimacy of the Arctic Council by keeping its door open to non-regional actors with a determination to maintain their own privileged position.'[62] There were sceptical views on the admission of new observers by the PPs who felt that their position would be weakened with the entry of observers, especially after the spat with

Table 4.2 Status of Arctic observers

Ser No	Entity	Description
1	World Wide Fund for Nature-Global Arctic Programme (WWF)	Non-Governmental Organisation Observer
2	International Arctic Science Committee (IASC)	-do-
3	International Union for Circumpolar Health (IUCH)	-do-
4	Northern Forum (NF)	-do-
5	United Nations Environment Programme (UNEP)	Intergovernmental and Inter-Parliamentary Organisation Observer
6	United Nations Economic Commission for Europe (UN-ECE)	-do-
7	Standing Committee of the Parliamentarians of the Arctic Region (SCPAR)	-do-
8	The Netherlands	Non-Arctic State Observer
9	Germany	-do-
10	United Kingdom	-do-
11	Poland	-do-

[62] V. Ingimundarson, Managing a Contested Region: The Arctic Council and the Politics of Arctic Governance. The Polar Journal, 2014, vol. 4, issue 1.

the European Union over ban on seal fur exports. The other observers had neither protested nor opposed the denial of observer status to the EU, which also revealed the divisions between the observers along many lines like political affiliations, regional structures, and so on. It is well understood that the denial arose from Permanent Participants' objections largely because of the EU ban on the import of seal fur. The restriction on EU was organised by the ICC which had mobilised other PPs and this was successful as the rules of engagement of the AC provide for a consensus decision and even one objection is adequate to veto any application. Likewise, the application of Greenpeace as an NGO observer was also not accepted due to its vociferous campaign against whaling and sealing, which had made the PPs as well as some member states apprehensive. The number of observers since then has risen and their details are as under (Table 4.3).

'The Arctic Council was able to move forward in its effort to rebuild its image and reinvigorate itself through the application of effective leadership during the second decade of its operation. It benefited from three successive Scandinavian Chairmanships (Norway 2006–2009, Denmark 2009–2011 and Sweden 2011–2013) that gave priority to making sure that the organization continued to produce first-rate scientific studies of the changing Arctic and saw to it that the necessary institutional reforms were undertaken'.[63] During the initial years after the institution of the AC, the leadership of the AC chair was devoted to streamlining the rules of engagement and involvement of the PPs in the decision-making process. However, the scientific work which had started under the Rovaniemi process continued steadfastly with shared resources and expertise of the WGs and the Observers like the IASC. The non-Arctic states also continued to support the WGs by polling in their respective domain specialists and expertise. Much before the 2008 USGS report on the resource potential of the Arctic, the AC had issued its 2004 Arctic Climate Impact Assessment (ACIA) which had jolted the world community to the perils of climate change on the Arctic along with the corollary unwinding of exploration of resources and opening of shipping passages.

The period thereafter witnessed the planting of a titanium flag by the Russian at the North Pole in 2007 and the 2008 Ilulissat Declaration by the five Arctic littoral countries. Around this time, it was being reported

[63] Ibid.

Table 4.3 Inclusion of Arctic observers[64]

Ser No	Entity	Description
1	World Wide Fund for Nature-Global Arctic Programme (WWF)	Non-Governmental Organisation Observer
2	International Arctic Science Committee (IASC)	-do-
3	International Union for Circumpolar Health (IUCH)	-do-
4	Northern Forum (NF)	-do-
5	Advisory Committee on Protection of the Sea (ACOPS)	-do-
6	Arctic Institute of North America (AINA)	-do-
7	Association of World Reindeer Herders (AWRH)	-do-
8	Circumpolar Conservation Union (CCU)	-do-
9	International Arctic Social Sciences Association (IASSA)	-do-
10	International Working Group for Indigenous Affairs (IWGIA)	-do-
11	National Geographic Society (NGS)	-do-
12	Oceania (O)	-do-
13	University of the Arctic (UArctic)	-do-
14	United Nations Development Programme (UNDP)	Intergovernmental and Inter-Parliamentary Organisation Observer
15	United Nations Environment Programme (UNEP)	-do-
16	United Nations Economic Commission for Europe (UN-ECE)	-do-
17	Standing Committee of the Parliamentarians of the Arctic Region (SCPAR)	-do-
18	OSPAR Commission (OSPAR)	-do-
19	North Atlantic Marine Mammal Commission (NAMMCO)	-do-
20	International Federation of Red Cross and Red Crescent Societies (IFRC)	-do-
21	Nordic Environment Finance Corporation (NEFCO)	-do-
22	Nordic Council of Ministers (NCM)	-do-
23	International Union for the Conservation of Nature (IUCN)	-do-
24	International Council for the Exploration of the Sea (ICES)	-do-

(continued)

[64] R. M. Hitchins Diddy, Non-Arctic State Observers of the Arctic Council: Perspectives and Views, Leadership for the North, The Influence and Impact of Arctic Council Chairs, University of Leeds, Leeds, West Yorkshire, UK.

Table 4.3 (continued)

Ser No	Entity	Description
25	The Netherlands	Non-Arctic State Observer
26	Germany	-do-
27	United Kingdom	-do-
28	Poland	-do-
29	France	-do-
30	Italy	-do-
31	India	-do-
32	Republic of Korea	-do-
33	Japan	-do-
34	People's Republic of China	-do-
35	Singapore	-do-
36	Spain	-do-
37	Switzerland	-do-

and felt in certain quarters that the AC had failed to discharge its obligations as it was bereft of any legal backing and jurisdiction to enforce its decisions. On the scientific front, though the WGs continued with their designated areas of work, yet the observers were relegated to a position of less authority and participation. In the formal structure of the AC, the Ministerial Meetings were hierarchically followed by the SAO meetings which were the avenues where major decisions were taken and the observers had no voting rights or say in such meetings. The participation by non-Arctic states and observers was thus confined to the WGs meetings which also were conducted in less formal structures, unlike the Ministerial and SAO meetings which had diplomatic settings.

OBSERVERS CRISIS AND JOINT STATEMENT

Admission of new non-Arctic actors as Observers and strengthening the role of the status might have broader consequences for the Council's design, functioning, and general direction in which international relations in the Arctic would unfold.[65] With the elapse of time, the original observers also began to feel the heat and were even relegated to secondary

---

[65] P. Graczyk, The Arctic Council Inclusive of Non-Arctic Perspectives: Seeking a New Balance, The Arctic University of Norway, 2012, https://hdl.handle.net/10037/6645

positions in scientific meetings of the WGs. On the other hand, the diplomatic representatives of the non-Arctic states who were deputed to attend the Ministerial and SAO meetings also felt shackled as they could express no recommendations but merely attend/observe the meetings. This resulted in a 2008 SAO meeting in which the observers expressed their desire to actively participate in decision-making processes in the Arctic over and above the scientific pursuits. The observers protesting the restricted roles included the IGOs, NGOs as well as non-Arctic states. The calls made by the observers were based on the deeper economic cooperation, peoples to peoples contact along with the scientific exploration, and technological integration which was stated to be the hallmark of the observers' participation, and hence they demanded to be accorded more rights in the AC. The observers were also more assertive in demanding a role in the Council. At the November 2008 Arctic Council meeting in Kautokeino, Norway, the Netherlands stated that 'observers wish to cooperate not only on science but also decision-making.'[66]

There were varying geopolitical and geo-economic considerations of the Arctic member states and this was further compounded by the reservations of the PPs who felt that with the entry of new observers their voices will be muzzled. Meanwhile, the growing interest of new entities wanting a seat at the AC also exerted pressure on the AC administration to deftly balance the situation to which a new scheme of admitting observers as 'ad hoc observers' was started in 2007. The period between 2006 onwards saw the AC chair being rotated among the Scandinavian countries, viz. Norway, Denmark, and Sweden. It was during the Swedish Chairmanship in 2013 that India along with five more was admitted as observer in Kiruna Ministerial Meeting. Before the Swedish Chairmanship, the Danes had charted a methodology of adjudging the observers based on a report submitted for the consideration by the AC on the efforts and a review of observer performance. The system instituted since has been in force even today and India had submitted its observer report in 2018 and was re-granted the observer status in May 2019. There was unstated punitive measure in the observer performance review and the status could be removed, at least theoretically on an observer not fulfilling the criteria.

The criteria and requirements for admission and renewal of the observer status had a strict focus to strengthen the status of the Arctic

---

[66] Andrew Chater, Explaining Non-Arctic States in the Arctic Council. Strategic Analysis, 2016, https://doi.org/10.1080/09700161.2016.1165467.

member states as well as PPs and express sovereignty of the Arctic 8 over the region. The entry parameters had not only the adherence to respecting the sovereignty of the Arctic Eight but also the role of the PPs in the AC deliberations and decisions. The signing of the entry requirements preserved and outlined the decision-making process as well as laid out the engagement by the observers at an appropriate forum, namely WGs so that events like 2008 SAO meeting observers' criticism be avoided. The previous observers had to also abide by the drawn-up rules of engagement and this acquiescence had set the stage for effective decision making in the Arctic region and Arctic affairs. This also demonstrated that AC had learnt from its history and made robust arrangements to prevent any disagreements in the future. Since the criteria were streamlined and clearly defined, it also made way for better communication among the observers and the AC members. The development led to the enunciation of Arctic Council Rules of Procedure, and Observer Manual for Subsidiary Bodies in 2013 with a clearly defined and structured procedure for admitting and engagement with the observers. This streamlining of the procedure with well-defined parameters also led to the softening of PPs stand as well as giving confidence to the entities desirous of an observer seat.

Divergence in Arctic Chairs

The AC chairs were wizened by the numerous challenges that were encountered like the opposition from PPs on granting observer status, observers' demands for greater integration and participation, streamlining of the rules of procedure, and so on. 'Since the Arctic Council is a consensus-based body, the endorsement of its actions by all Arctic states is essential to its continued functioning. On the one hand, the conditions of animosity may significantly reduce the scope of action for the chair and limit its potential to deliver. Yet on the other hand, they may potentially increase the importance of the Arctic Council chair in brokerage, identifying underlying areas of agreement and finding common ways to further cooperation.'[67] However with the granting of observer status to

---

[67] Malgorzata Smieszek and Paula Kankaanpää, Role of the Arctic Council Chairmanship. Arctic Year Book 2015, accessed on 2 June 19 from https://www.researchgate.net/profile/Melina_Kourantidou/publication/283045788_Towards_Arctic_Resource_Governance_of_Marine_Invasive_Species/links/56275f6908ae4d9e5c4f0940.pdf#page=247.

six nations at Kiruna in May 2013 and concrete steps laying out the steps and procedure for admission, withdrawal and renewal of observer status were undertaken. These measures ensured that the AC was working in a better and seamless fashion than before and with effective leadership and focus. During the second Canadian stint, the focus was on expanding the economic endeavours and provides greater opportunities to the indigenous population. Likewise the second chairmanship with the USA also showed credible efforts to incorporate the Arctic 8 and the PPs in collaborative decision making and prosperity with integration of the observers. The US had also organised a special observers session on the sidelines of the 2015 SAO meeting in Alaska.

The USA and the preceding Scandinavian Chairs were alive to the grouses of the Observers and conducted special observes' session in conjunction with the SAO meetings. The inputs provided by Germany, UK, and France were also incorporated in the Agreement on Science and Cooperation which was adopted in 2017 Ministerial Meeting. This can be contrasted with the Canadian chair whose focus was entirely on better economic opportunities for its indigenous population and meagre focus on observers' qualms.

The Arctic region can pride on the premise that the small nation-states wield much greater influence than regional and international organisations. The membership of several countries like France, Germany, UK, Sweden, and Finland as players in the Arctic but not as part of EU while Norway, Iceland, USA, and Canada play in the Arctic but not as part of NATO, thus the individual status of member states is much more important than the membership of global multilateral powerful organisations for the conduct of business. The first round of the rotational AC chairmanship concluded with Sweden in 2013 and the chair went back to Canada.

Geopolitical Implications of Ice Melting

The effects of melting ice will impact everyone but the impact and degree will vary. It is clear that several Arctic circumpolar nations stand to benefit from the opening of sea routes and easier exploitation of the resources, yet distant countries are likely to be adversely affected by rising sea levels, abject monsoons, and so on. Yet, there are non-Arctic states like China who are viewing to partake in the commercial exploits of resource extraction in the region and derive economic benefits. There are also multinational corporations eagerly watching the developments, intending to obtain rights to hydrocarbon exploitation, fishing, sea bed resources, and mining as well as shipping on newer routes to make commercial gains.

The small coastal nations lying in the Pacific Ocean and called Micronesia, Polynesia, and Melanesia are vulnerable to climate change and sea-level increase. Among these, the former is the most vulnerable. The Pacific Islands region, also called Oceania, is divided into three sub-regions: Polynesia, which includes Hawaii and New Zealand; Melanesia, including Vanuatu and Fiji; and Micronesia, which includes Kiribati, Nauru, and the Federated States of Micronesia. Because most landmasses are small islands and low-lying atolls, the Micronesian region is particularly vulnerable to sea-level rise and climate change.[68] There are associations formed by the small Pacific Island states, namely PIF (Pacific Islands Forum) and AOSIS (Alliance of Small Island States), PREP/SPREP (Pacific Regional Environmental Protection Programme), and a common call is related to environmental protection and mitigates climate change and formulates adaptation strategies. The US, UK, France, Australia, and New Zealand are also members of the SPREP. The UN has also garnered the participation of PSIDS (Pacific Small Island Developing States) as a partner in fulfilling the SDGs (Sustainable Development Goals).

Indian PM had extended a grant of $12 Mn (1 Mn each for each PSID) in September 2019 and also extended, a concessional Line of Credit of $ 150 million which can be availed by the PSIDS for undertaking solar, renewable energy, and climate-related projects based on each country's requirement was announced to strengthen the Act East Policy and commitment to assist the PSIDS in their development agenda.

There is a thought that has gained traction recently that the Arctic which had enjoyed a peaceful era, post-cold war period, is now transforming into a fragmented security scenario encompassing North America, Europe, and Eurasian sub-regions from the erstwhile integrated security region. The integrated security scenario was a fallout from the zone of peace speech by Mikhail Gorbachev which had led to the creation and management of institutions and pacifist views on dispute resolution. Following this landmark speech, the efforts were woven around the environmental challenges being faced by the region and led to the creation

---

[68] Ellise Akazawa, Vannarith Chheang, and Eleni Ekmektsioglou, Geopolitical Implications of an Ice-Free Arctic for the Asia–Pacific.

of BEAC, AEPS, and later the AC. Arctic boundaries had little effect on their core national interests, and states were unwilling to risk the global strategic balance or their diplomatic relations over trivial Arctic issues.[69] The Murmansk speech led to a post-Cold War Arctic with cooperative arrangements between the states and the indigenous people. These impetuses were the precursor to Arctic exceptionalism as a concept which lauded the Arctic as an apolitical space unaffected by the global power politics and becoming a role model in interstate cooperation and peaceful dispute resolution. The 2008 Ilulissat Declaration also cemented the concept of 'one Arctic' encompassing cooperation, common interests, and connections between the states of the circumpolar region.

Though the Arctic never formed its regional security complex as the linked security interdependence between the states was not elaborated but acted as an insulator between the RSC of European, North American, and Soviet RSCs. Even when the Arctic RSC emerged, it was more centred around environmental considerations rather than hard power and securitisation as security among the Arctic people is more linked to their natural environment.

This change is due to changing regional security dynamics given climate change and growing great power competition between Russia, China, and divided Western powers in the above named three sub-regions. The climate change and resultant interplay of geopolitics in interlinking Arctic security with the sub-regional politics and security narratives will dilute pan-Arctic governance. There will be fragmentation of the security and it will be customised to varying political, economic, social, and ecological conditions, thereby diluting the Arctic regional security complex.

The Arctic had a prominent strategic dimension during the period after the World War II and up to USSR disintegration as the prevailing thick ice was assuring a devastating second-strike capability to provide stability in the deterrence between the superpowers. During the various time in the superpower rivalry, the Arctic assumed the greater role and varied from being a military flank to a military theatre. Since during this period, the nations were divided between two opposing camps, this also prevented the formation of credible political institutions with the membership of the Arctic states. The structures of NATO and the Warsaw Pact were

---

[69] Greaves Wilfred, Arctic Break Up: Climate Change, Geopolitics, and the Fragmenting Arctic Security Region, Arctic Yearbook 2019, Arctic year book.com, 2019.

initiated during the hostile periods of the cold war. To assess whether the Arctic region is evolving into a region of cooperation or one of confrontation, a thorough understanding of the existing (and evolving) bilateral, regional, and international institutional frameworks with relevant regulations for the Arctic and their adequacy for solving possible controversies is paramount.[70]

After the breakup of the USSR, NATO had started to look southwards and the USA was busy dismantling terror/WMD in Afghanistan, Iraq, and so on. However, an increasingly Russia under President Putin and the Crimean/Ukraine experience changed the equation yet again. The swift and intrusive involvement of China as well as (now halted) EU also tilted the scales. The situation is skewed with five nations from the Arctic 8 being the members of NATO and Russia viewing NATO with scepticism and as an existential threat to its security, there is bound to be an increase in strategic competition.

The observers in the AC enjoy limited avenues as they don't have any say or voting rights. The most prominent reason for nations seeking to become observers is to contribute to governance issues especially related to environmental concerns in a rapidly transforming region, as the impacts thereof are experienced in distant regions. There is a latent desire among the observers to occupy a position to sway and hold discussions and moderate the subsequent resource exploration and participation in natural resources of the Arctic. Actors seek to contribute to the governance of environmental issues of global importance. Second, actors strive to gain as states develop the economic potential of the Arctic region. Existing literature overemphasises the importance of observers in the Council and their interest in Arctic economics to explain Council participation.[71]

The politics and interest of the world in the Arctic have substantially increased in the new millennium as earlier it was considered a mere buffer region between the superpowers during the cold war era. The 2007 planting of a flag by Russia and the 2008 Ilulissat Declaration, though were significant events, yet the turning point in the global interest was ignited on the report by USGS report on the hydrocarbon potential of

---

[70] K. Keil, Spreading Oil, Spreading Conflict? Institutions Regulating Arctic Oil and Gas Activities. The International Spectator: Italian Journal of International Affairs, 2015, vol. 50, issue 1, pp. 85–110.

[71] Andrew Chater, Explaining Non-Arctic States in the Arctic Council. Strategic Analysis, 2016, https://doi.org/10.1080/09700161.2016.1165467.

the Arctic. A point to ponder is the timing of the report in 2008, which had succeeded in the planting of a flag by the Russian at the North Pole and other developments happening at that time. A large majority of those fossil fuels 84% would be found offshore, most notably north of Siberia in Russia, in the waters north of Alaska, and also between Baffin Island in Nunavut, Canada, and Greenland.[72]

This possibility of huge reserves of energy supplies that too in a region, relatively free of political turmoil and instability was watched with eager anticipation, despite hurdles in extraction and transportation.

The SAO in May 2011 Ministerial Meeting had presented a detailed report on strengthening the Arctic Council institutionally.[73] The Arctic Council assumes the top place in matters of regional governance, but another view holds that Arctic governance should be viewed as a team effort with the participation of important fora like International Maritime Organisation (IMO), the UN Commission on the Limits of the Continental Shelf, the Arctic Coast Guard Forum, the University of the Arctic, IASC, COP, and other international environmental NGOs. However, an inherent flaw in its structure is the lack of its ability to deliver results. In certain quarters, a need is felt to restructure the working groups of the Council by inviting participation from indigenous communities and NGOs.

Arctic affairs are still nascent at the global affairs and some observers have called for the Arctic Council to strengthen the role and the capacity of Observers. This balancing between demands of non-Arctic states/observers and other non-state actors will require deft and mature handling, especially because the chairmanship is rotational, for two years each. The AC is a wide and diverse platform bringing together Arctic 8, permanent participants, observers as well as international institutions, yet it remains a decision-preparing rather than a decision-making institution. "The slow but steady growth of governance structures in the Arctic

---

[72] Lanteigne, supra note 18 in Chapter 1.

[73] The Arctic Council, Senior Arctic Officials (SAO) Report to Ministers, Annex 1, adopted by the Arctic Council at the First Council Meeting, Iqaluit, Canada, 17–18 September 1998, http://www.Arctic-council.org/index.php/en/document-archive/category/4-founding-documents.

Region is the result of processes in which initiatives to strengthen multilateral procedures are blended with – implicit and explicit – respect for Arctic states' national traditions and interests."[74]

The AC is a wide and diverse platform bringing together Arctic 8, permanent participants, observers as well as international institutions, yet it remains a decision-preparing rather than a decision-making institution. Since the AC is a soft law regime and dwells on mutual respect among the nations for other's national interests and traditions and gradually strengthen the multilateral arrangement but till now has proved itself to both adaptable to changes and sufficient to address the governance issues. A point to ponder is that the states/persons calling for reform in Arctic governance may have an ulterior agenda to disrupt the prevailing structures to obtain a greater voice, which is restricted in the present arrangement. It must be brought in mind that the current governance system is multi-tier having international, regional, sub-regional, national, and sub-national levels. Also, the impact of factors like globalisation, climate change, political polarisation, etc., has all impacts of Arctic governance.

MILITARY DEPLOYMENTS/SECURITISATION

The Arctic region had remained a potential flashpoint during the East–West rivalry during the cold war years, yet with the changing world order with the disintegration of the USSR, Afghan War, and changing face of Russo-US dynamic it slowly became a region of cooperation and shared vision among the Arctic states. The founding of the AC in 1996 was a major step in furthering these ideals of joint multilateralism and the region became an exception to the hard power rivalries and hence associated with Arctic exceptionalism.

The traditional strategic rivalries such as that between USA and Russia, India and China, USA and China and presence of all these actors in some way in the Arctic, coupled with a growing race for Arctic resources and desire to dominate its key geostrategic position joining three continents is pushing the Arctic onto the international prominence. The possibility of growing trade with the newly opening shipping routes is making the Arctic being viewed with a national security lens and hence a further

---

[74] Haftendorn, supra note 19 in Chapter 1.

emphasis on military instruments of power to protect and secure their national interests. For a variety of reasons, more aspects of Arctic politics and development have become 'securitised,' identified, and describes as an existential threat which requires a timely and specific set of responses.[75]

On 02 August 2019, one of the last arms control treaties of the cold war era, the INF treaty was recalled. Before that, both Russia and the USA have been strengthening their forces centred on the cold war analogy. The old equation has radically transformed with China emerging as a potent player in the international arena and has been testing missiles and hence INF treaty has lost most of its relevance. However, the revocation thereof is opening the arena for arms race yet again. The bipolar system has made a way of a trilateral one, though with varying degrees of competition and three-way balance of power in the Arctic region making it a dangerous move.

Russia

Russia has deployed massive forces along its Arctic coastline much to the chagrin of the other nations. Though Russia is only reconstructing its dilapidated assets of the USSR era, yet few view the same as an offensive gesture to pre-empt any NATO ally, especially Norway. However, the same has to be understood and viewed from the perspective of the adherence by Russia to the informal yet effective mechanism of AC for playing down any perceived threats. The likelihood of any disputes over perceptual differences over militarisation in the confines of any country's sovereign territory appears to be bleak and less. As per the 2008 Russian strategy effective till 2020 and having a far outlook had outlined the deployment of Russian forces to assert its claim on natural resources located therein. Russia's military capabilities in the Arctic have steadily increased over the past ten years. Russia has opened new airfields and refurbished old ones; created a dedicated northern command for the region; and set up two Arctic brigades. It also is planning to substantially increase its icebreaker fleet, which is already by far the largest in the world. Russia's new military base on Aleksandra Land is touted as the "largest building in the entire circumpolar high Arctic."[76]

---

[75] Lanteigne, supra note 18 in Chapter 1.

[76] P. Stephanie, supra note 67 in Chapter 2.

Russia has the largest area in the Arctic region and its population centres like Murmansk and Arkhangelsk are densely populated, in comparison with the North American Arctic. Russia is in an advantageous position due to its control over large finds of oil and gas, especially around Yamal. Russia is also a non-NATO Arctic coastal country and still maintains most of its submarine fleet near Murmansk/Kola Peninsula. Russia's annexation of Crimea and unrest in Ukraine has sent alarm signals to Norway, the USA, and other NATO Arctic members. In a nutshell, though, cooperation rather than confrontation has assumed the driver's seat in Russia's relations with Arctic nations.

All the Arctic coastal nations except Russia are part of the NATO and reinvigoration of the Arctic naval bases by Russia as outlined in its 2015 *Russian Marine Doctrine* was one of the reasons for growing scepticism. However, Russia has clarified that it wants to regain its status as a blue water force. There have been diverse views on the Russian designs but, understandably, Russia is reconstructing its dilapidated assets and its moves are not aggressive. This gains prominence because of the 2010 Barents Sea Agreement with Norway which hints at a more accommodative and cooperative strategy. In a nutshell, though, cooperation rather than confrontation has assumed the driver's seat in Russia's relations with Arctic nations. Cooperation at the working level remains high, as evidenced by the international and bilateral conventions negotiated with and signed by Russia since 2014, including most recently the 2017 Agreement on Enhancing International Arctic Scientific Cooperation and the US-Russian proposal (approved by the International Maritime Organisation) to create six two-way routes enabling safer shipping in the Bering Strait.[77]

The Russian military has for long employed its enhanced presence in the Kola Peninsula to provide depth to its defence and also centre on the vital GIUK gap and access to the Atlantic. The Kola Peninsula and its surrounding areas are considered of strategic importance for Russian national security. Perimeter defence around Kola and the extension of the 'Bastion' defence concept are designed to give Russia defence in depth.[78]

---

[77] Ibid.

[78] Boulègue Mathieu, Russia's Military Posture in the Arctic Managing Hard Power in a 'Low Tension' Environment. The Royal Institute of International Affairs, 2019, accessed on 1 November 2019 from https://www.chathamhouse.org/sites/default/files/2019-06-28-Russia-Military-Arctic_0.pdf.

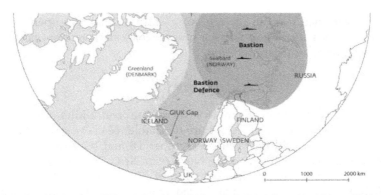

Strategic points of the Arctic region include the GIUK Gap and Svalbard archipelago. Shaded areas depict Russia's Bastion Strategy: darker shaded area: ambition of control, lighter shaded area: ambition of denial. Map: Kauko Kyöstiö. Source: House of Commons Defence Committee 2018.

Map 4.4 Map showing Bastion and extended Bastion (Map: Kauko Kyöstiö. *Source* House of Commons Defence Committee 2018)

The extended Bastion concept puts more pressure on North Atlantic SLOC as well as on the Baltic region. The Kola facility is developed as a Bastion defence and the perimeter of the peninsula is guarded in strength. As depicted by the Map 4.4 the strategic points around the Kola Peninsula are the GIUK gap and Svalbard archipelago and the Russian capability to exert influence on the mouth of North Atlantic and Baltic region.

Another Russian priority is to ensure the Northern Fleet's access to, and passage along, the Northern Sea Route (NSR) from the Atlantic Ocean to the Pacific Ocean. It is important to mention that some days before Exercise Trident Juncture in October 2018, Russia held its military exercise 'Vostok 2018' one of the largest Russian military exercises in last over two decades. Chinese artillery and aircraft, along with Brigade strength of Chinese troops, had participated in Vostok 2018 exercise showing their military cooperation.

Canada

Canada's *First Defence Strategy* (2008) and the *Northern Strategy* (2009) elucidate its defence plans for the Arctic and it regularly conducts military exercises and SAR (Search and Rescue) operations to hone its military skills. Then, Canadians had stated that "an emboldened Russia is a threat to its neighbours in the Arctic, and Canada must be ready to respond to any Russian incursions in the region."[79] Canada had also openly stated that Russia is a threat and Canada must prepare itself to respond to any Russian misadventure in the Arctic.

NATO

The claims and counterclaims for increasing and tilting the military balance by overtures in the Arctic are debatable. NATO exercise 'Trident Juncture 18 was held between 25 October 18 and 07 November 2018 around the area of Baltic and the Norwegian Sea. The exercise was large in scale as it witnessed the participation of 31 members including all 29 NATO members. NATO exercise called Trident Juncture 18 that was held from October 25 to November 7, 2018, in Norway and adjacent waters of the Baltic and the Norwegian Sea, with participation by all 29 NATO members plus Sweden and Finland, was described as NATO's largest exercise since the cold war and featured a strong Arctic element, including the first deployment of a US Navy aircraft carrier above the Arctic Circle since 1991.[80] The US deployed its Navy aircraft carrier above the Arctic Circle. The simulated enemy in the areas between Iceland and the Baltic Sea was to coincide with the limits of the Russian Bastion defence. These attempts for military exercise by NATO with its complement of Arctic states on the one side and Russia on the other lead to more suspicion and scepticism by Russia, which apes these in similar manoeuvres.

The NATO alliance and the transatlantic security community form the basis of some of the members who are also part of the AC like Norway. The purpose of an active Alliance policy is to reduce the risk of security policy crisis and armed conflict. An attack against a NATO member is an attack against the Alliance. NATO is a political and military alliance. The transatlantic security community is based on common values. The principle of collective defence is at the very heart of NATO's founding treaty. It remains a unique and enduring principle that binds its members together, committing them to protect each other and setting a spirit of solidarity within the Alliance. However, the Russians view NATO as well as its members with scepticism and in the arrangements of the AC,

[79] National Maritime Foundation, NMF, Arctic Perspectives2015.pdf, n.d.

[80] Congressional Research Service, Changes in the Arctic: Background and Issues for Congress, November 2019, accessed on 01 December 2019 from https://fas.org/sgp/crs/misc/R41153.pdf).

the actions by NATO have a dangerous proposition to tilt the delicate cooperative balance in the Arctic region.

THULE AIR BASE AND GREENLAND

The US had turned Greenland into its main surveillance and forward base owing to its strategic location as a transit between North America and Europe during the cold war era. The strategic location of Greenland, situated in the North Atlantic, will acquire greater significance with the melting of the ice and opening of new shipping routes. It also possesses considerable natural resources. Greenland was two times considered for purchase by the Pentagon leaders and the White House officials in the first decade of the cold war, however, this was never realised.[81] During the setting up of Thule Base, between 1951 and 1955, around 27 indigenous families had to be shifted. Greenland, which was a focal point for North America because of its strategic location as a midway /transit point between North America and Europe, has been recently in news due to US President ambiguous innuendoes for land purchase deal. It is on historical record that many Arctic nations including Russia, Canada, and Greenland had relocated several members of indigenous communities. In Greenland, the Danish government relocated several Inuit communities in the 1950s for various reasons. The entire village of Thule, for example, was moved 60 miles to the north in 1953 to make room for a US military base.[82]

Denmark keeps its hold in the Arctic region by maintaining sovereignty over Greenland. However, the equation has been changing with trilateral discussions between USA, Denmark, and Greenland and increased and emphatic voices on independence from Greenland. The recent tweet by US President in August 2019 hinting at plans to buy Greenland and later cancellation of his trip to Denmark due to the lack of interest by Denmark's PM Mette Frederiksen in negotiating a sale agreement over Greenland show that the US is seriously considering acquiring this territory. The Thule-base in Greenland has had an important role during the cold war as part of the US military sphere in the North. The role of the

---

[81] Ackrén Maria, From bilateral to trilateral agreement: The case of Thule Air Base, Arctic year book 2019.

[82] Struzik Edward, Supra note 16 in Chapter 2.

base has changed over time to become a radar station, but it is still part of the overall US defence system.[83]

In the past too, there were at least two attempts by the USA to acquire Greenland. Greenland may become a swing state as it negotiating for becoming independent from Denmark.

ARCTIC MILITARY CODE OF CONDUCT (AMCC)[84]

The short-lived fora like ASFR and Northern Chiefs of Defence Conference (NCDC) were set up in the Arctic region for enhancing military cooperation and gain mutual trust, though with limited and partial success. However post the Crimean crisis, this order has deteriorated and military competition has absorbed cooperation. There have been military exercises by both the camps, like Russia ("Sever," "Tsentr") and USA ("Cold Response," "ICEX," "Trident Juncture") and which has divided the camps, yet again. Unlike the SAR, MARPOL, UNCLOS, and other legal frameworks to safeguard the region, a framework around military security is missing. There is historical evidence of cooperation in this sphere which manifested in setting up ASFR and NCDC and hence this has to be progressively taken forward from here. Though India doesn't benefit directly from such an initiative yet such actions bolster her position as a Gandhian nation professing for peace on this region and reinforce her credentials among the Arctic states.

BREWING SINO-US COLD WAR

A new kind of rivalry is brewing between the USA and China, in another dimension of a cold war, though not involving any ideological battles like the battle between Socialism and Capitalism on opposing sides during the previous cold war. The new war has a changed dimension as both the USA and China are vying for global economic supremacy based on access to markets and resources in an increasingly globalised and connected global market.

---

[83] Ibid.

[84] Duncan Depledge, Mathieu Boulègue, Andrew Foxall, and Dmitriy Tulupov, Arcticyearbook.com, 2019, accessed on 1 December 2019 from https://Arcticyearbook.com/Arctic-yearbook/2019/2019-briefing-notes/328-why-we-need-to-talk-about-military-activity-in-the-Arctic-towards-an-Arctic-military-code-of-conduct.

The headache for the USA is compounded by having to face the twin threats, of an increasingly active China and simultaneous Russian military build-up in the Arctic. The USA is enhancing its Arctic military capabilities including the renovation of its icebreaker fleet and further developing North American Aerospace Defence Command (NORAD) with Canada. The emphasis on strengthening the US role in the European Arctic security, and direct military cooperation and exercises is also increasing. This can be viewed as fallout of the growing political and security cooperation between China and Russia.

The situation in the Arctic region due to the presence of both the actors of the previous cold war and the current cooperative regime between China and Russia as also the increasing role and activity of China may lead to disruption of the established pacifist structures. The hectic tussle to enlarge their respective spheres of influence and forcing other states to make difficult choices in joining either camp is likely to polarise the existing political structures and fora. The recent statements by several top US officials point to the increasingly sceptic USA which is being challenged by a growing and strong China in several dimensions like economic, commercial, and strategic. There is though a stark contrast to the times after the collapse of the USSR and post-cold war era which was marked by lower tensions and more emphasis on pacifist recourses. In the present times, it is felt in some quarters that the AC will be inadequate to address the more problematic and complex issues, relating to Arctic-related security issues. This may call for the incorporation of security issues or a security mechanism to deal with such issues. Alternatively, the rules of AC may have to be amended to include newer threats.

"China's vague and amorphous Community of Common Destiny concept, as well as the Western democratic model promoted by the United States, can hardly aspire to this role, given Beijing's undeniable propensity to bend the 'common destiny' to its own economic and political interests and Washington's overly pragmatic attitude to alliances with patently undemocratic regimes."[85] In a globalised and interconnected world, the Arctic politics, security, and discourse are being enmeshed with the US-China rivalry on issues like opposition to Huawei, recent and growing trade war, the legal issue on cyber espionage, 5G turf and

---

[85] Alexei Kupriyanov, Alexander Korolev, The Eurasian Chord and the Oceanic Ring: Russia and India as the Third Force in a New World Order, Valdai discussion club, September 2019.

trails including by other nations such as India and UK, which will have an impact on the regional dynamics too.

China was a net oil exporter till the 1990s and it is her spiked economic boom that has made it a current largest oil importer. Quite like China, even India's domestic crude supply has been overtaken manifold by their demand. Owing to the need of securing its energy supplies and possible disruption in supply routes like Malacca and Hormuz straits, China started looking at the immense potential of Arctic, quite early. In 2013, China paid Rosneft—Russia's state-owned oil company—$60 billion to develop oil fields in the Arctic Ocean.[86] China has for long been an advocate of a multipolar world and has employed both the economic and diplomatic instruments of power to win over allies/partners in the Arctic. Over the last decade, China has also cultivated strategic partners like Iceland, Greenland (Denmark), and Finland, to stand by it. The Chinese imports from the Arctic, once operationalised, will provide cost and time savings as they also supply diversification and security. To realise these benefits, China is already investing more heavily in Arctic shipping research than even the US.[87]

Other Factors

(a) Economics and Routes

Russia claims complete and unfettered control over the NSR. The nationalisation of the NSR, though detested by the USA not much hue and cry was raised as the USA can leverage shipping rights on NWP with Canada much more easily if required. Russia demands that any vessel wanting to traverse over the NSR should notify the authorities as per the stated procedure and also provide the transit fees to Russia. The fees charged will be towards providing safety, emergency response, and navigational guidance. Russia claims complete and unfettered control over

---

[86] Michael Byers, China Could be the Future of Arctic Oil, AL JAZEERA (22 August 2013, 2:09 PM), http://www.aljazeera.com/indepth/opinion/2013/08/2013821135829162420.html.

[87] Darryl D'monte, China Spending More on Arctic Sea Route Research Than US, BUS. STANDARD (14 March 2013), http://www.business-standard.com/article/economy-policy/china-spending-more-on-Arcticsea-route-research-than-us-113031400028_1.html.

the NSR. 'Hence, all vessels wishing to enter the Russian EEZ (Exclusive Economic Zone), within which the NSR lies, should notify the Russian competent authority beforehand. There are also heavy passage rights or fees, known as ice-breaker fees.'[88]

Recently, Russia has also approved an NSR Infrastructure Development Plan for the period up to 2035 which lays out that year-round navigation on the route will be operationalised by 2025. Russia has projected that 80 million cargo traffic on NSR will be a reality by 2024 and accordingly has also enhanced the service life of its available icebreakers. The Kremlin's assertion of legal, military, and commercial primacy over the NSR has been accompanied by robust rhetoric from the Russian Defence Ministry directed towards NATO as well as Sweden and Finland. Simulated attacks against military installations, bases, and exercise areas in the European High North have also been reported (Nilsen, 2019; Staalesen, 2019a).[89] Russia is also planning to build five new nuclear-powered ships and one Leader class icebreaker that should be sufficient as per its calculation to provide escort services over the NSR. Though Russia is not very optimistic about the transit shipments yet it is optimistic about destination shipping including LNG, coal, and other hydrocarbons.

The Russian position on NSR may contain a potential for arguments/disagreements in the coming days. Since several countries including China have obliquely referred to the requirement of freedom of navigation in the Arctic, this issue has the potential for conflagration and needs careful handling. Russia is thus eager to capitalise on the shorter access markets to its hydrocarbons as also monetary gains by imposing passage rights on vessels transiting through NSR.

When the curtains came down on the erstwhile USSR, not only was the threat of cold war extinguished but newer avenues of globalisation were initiated, opening doors to eager international trade, whereby the quantity, density, and dynamics of trade were transformed. It has been reported that around 80% of world merchandise trade by volume is being carried by ships and the sea trade is growing at a steady pace thereby the potential of shipping is enhanced. However since the Arctic shipping routes are yet to be commercially fully developed, there are restrictions

---

[88] Claes Lykke Ragner, 'Den Norra sjövägen,' In Barents – ett gränsland INorden, Ed. Torsten Hallberg, Stockholm, Arena Norden, 2008, pp. 114–127.

[89] Duncan Depledge, Caroline Kennedy-Pipe, and James Rogers, The UK and the Arctic Forward defence.pdf, n.d., Arctic Year Book 2019.

on both shipping and its insurance due to unpredictability. This also leads to more conservative estimates of the trade potential of NSR and NWP. As it was calculated, over 80% of world merchandise trade by volume and over 70% by value was carried by sea and world seaborne trade volumes were estimated to grow at a compound annual growth rate of 3.2% in 2017–2022.[90]

Both Canada and Russia are enforcing international legal regimes as applicable to NWP and NSR, respectively, being "internal waters" under international law, which grants that the sovereign control rests with them. As the Northern Sea Route falls primarily within Russian coastal waters there has been little dispute over Russia's capacity to substantially control navigation within these waters consistently with the law of the sea.[91] A variety of interconnected sea routes which pass between the islands that make up the Canadian Arctic Archipelago, the status of the Northwest Passage has been the subject of the ongoing dispute between Canada and the US. Though the friendly relations between the US and Canada have ensured that disputes arising from NWP have remained muted, but given the changing climate and opening of passages, this has the potential to erupt into a major dispute in the region. The competition in shipping and share in the production of icebreakers will be played out between Germany, China, ROK, and to a limited extent, Russia. Autonomy and claims to sovereignty also affect straits crossing through the Arctic that has seen an increasing amount of traffic. The problem lies in defining and demarcating international strait in concrete terms. The Russian drawing of straight borderlines around its large Siberian peninsulas is also debated but currently, others are complying with its dictates.

The European and Arctic states though are aware that 15 out of 20 of the world's largest cargo ports are located in East Asia, credibly affirming the economics of engagement and further benefits that will accrue with the considerable shortening of the routes with opening and operationalisation of NSR, NWP, etc.

---

[90] Didenko and Cherenkov—2018—Economic and Geopolitical Aspects of developing th.pdf, n.d.

[91] Rothwell Donald R., The Law of the Sea and Arctic Governance. Proceedings of the Annual Meeting. International Law in a Multipolar World, 2013, vol. 107, pp. 272–275.

(b) **China Threat**

China, as a rising political and economic power, has been subject to much scrutiny, especially from the West, about its emerging agenda in the Arctic region.[92] China has evinced interest in the Arctic even before becoming an observer in 2013. Its paramount interest is economic including the access to natural resources and energy security, followed by its safe transportation and logistics. It also espouses ecological and climatological research, and finally, it has geopolitical and military-strategic goals. The 2018 Chinese white paper on the Arctic is an ample indicator that the Arctic has become increasingly important to realise her great power ambitions. China has also identified the polar regions as "new strategic frontiers," which will witness rivalry and competition between the great powers.

The Chinese white paper highlights it as a near-Arctic state and claims rights due to non-Arctic states in the Arctic. The paper also stresses the need to conform to UNCLOS and other international and other global, regional, and multilateral mechanisms for joint efforts. The interconnectedness of shifting own climatic conditions due to global warming in the Arctic justifies the scientific pursuits and gives credence to these efforts. China then reasserts that resource development by opening maritime routes in the Arctic is related to the economic development and energy strategy of China and will be benefitted by China's capital, technology, experience, and market.

After the issue of the 2018 White Paper by China, it has been viewed with suspicion by the US and select Western countries due to its heavy economic heft in the region. China's behaviour in the South China Sea and the East China Sea is quoted as an example of China's aggressive designs citing fears of escalated and impending militarisation and competition for territorial claims. Steadily, China has been using its economic might to win over small Nordic countries like Iceland, Norway, and Finland to enhance its role and leverage in the region. Growingly the US has been a sceptic of these manoeuvres and has been making some noise as well as diplomatic approaches. China has clearly and unequivocally stated its economic objectives in the Arctic and promotes its technology,

---

[92] M. Lanteigne and S. Ping, China's Developing Arctic Policies: Myths and Misconceptions. Journal of China and International Relations, 2015, vol. 3, issue 1, https://doi.org/10.5278/ojs.jcir.v3i1.1144.

capital, and large markets for collaboration for the exploration of natural resources.

China has a broad view of the Arctic and it is showing wide and broad focus on energy supply, resource exploitation, shipping, and commercial partnerships over and above the scientific studies and climate change narrative. Concurrently the Russia and China alliance is posing challenges as the USA would lose its influence and trading partners with the onset of China. China had also attended the 2019 TSENTR along with military contingents from India, Kazakhstan, Kyrgyzstan, Tajikistan, Pakistan, and Uzbekistan in the mega event. Though Chinese participation is an eyesore owing to its threat of growing military cooperation with Russia, it had also participated in the VOSTOK 2018 exercise with Russia. "China is not a military threat to Europe right now, but if we are not careful about how we look at where and how they are investing, they become a very significant national security threat in the future that we may not be able to combat," a US European Command official said on condition of anonymity, ahead of the security talks in Greenland.[93]

Chinese range of interests in the Arctic has since widened and is becoming more focused on extractive, commercial, and shipping domains. In 2017, 11 of the 27 vessels that transited through the NSR originated from or were going to a Chinese port.[94] However, the promise of Chinese investments comes with a threat of its military presence. Earlier this year the Pentagon went further still, warning that China's expanding submarine fleet was moving closer to a deployment capability for the Arctic (Department of Defence, 2019). Meanwhile, speculation that the Chinese military would participate in Russia's Tsentr 2019 drills was confirmed in September (Buchanan & Boulégue, 2019). Although there is no open-source evidence that the Chinese military was directly involved in the Arctic component of Tsentr 2019, it is likely that it was monitoring the exercise carefully.[95]

China had named Polar Silk Road (PSR) in its white paper of 2018 and gradually China has become a preferred partner of Russia and other

---

[93] Stripes.com, 2019, accessed on 9 October 2019 from https://www.stripes.com/news/china-tops-agenda-as-military-leaders-from-11-nations-mull-Arctic-security-1.579881.

[94] Ibid.

[95] Depledge et al., supra note 44 in Chapter 2.

Nordic countries in matters of transportation, infrastructural development, and energy. The implementation of the PSR will require improvement of navigation and safety along the NSR. Both China and Russia have lofty plans for cooperation in fields of shipbuilding, icebreakers' assistance, and navigation, and other support services. The collaboration is working to the advantage of both the countries with convergence on economic, technological, and shipping fields. The Chinese white paper elaborates a vision of "Polar Silk Road (PSR)" against the background that China's Belt and Road Initiative (BRI) will bring opportunities to all parties concerned and facilitate connectivity and sustainable economic and social development of the Arctic.[96] For PSR to fructify will require the establishment of secure navigable maritime routes in the North. China has been gradually upping its stakes and involvement in the Arctic and its first icebreaker had undertaken the NSR journey in 2012 and this was followed in 2013 with a commercial ship M/V Yong Sheng. Russia was also quick to offer its partnership in 2017 during the meeting between President Xi and President Medvedev.

Towards its stated goal for greater polar connect, China has launched BNU-1 its polar observation satellite. With a spatial resolution of 75 metres, this satellite will reduce China's reliance on foreign satellites for polar observation data. It shall be instrumental in feeding polar data for promoting research as well as monitoring climate change.

(c) **Pollution and Accidents**

The exploration efforts in the Arctic were jolted at the initial stages in 1989 when the Exxon Valdez Oil spill took place on 24 March 1989 and this was shortly followed by Deepwater Horizon Methane explosion on 20 April 2010 in the Gulf of Mexico. These incidents were a precursor to the strengthening of exploration efforts in the Arctic region. While the former led to several legislations in the USA, the latter led to putting on hold the undersea semi-submersible rigging. The role of non-binding regulation, or soft law, is growing, with the Arctic Council

---

[96] State Council Information Office of the People's Republic of China, "China's Arctic Policy," January 26, 2018, http://english.gov.cn/archive/white paper/2018/01/26/content281476026660336.htm.

leading the way.[97] In the coming days, with an increase in discoveries and enhanced production, a corollary threat of accidents and large-scale oil spills in Arctic waters will also increase. The environment and conditions prevailing in the Arctic have an effect on the microbial populations and biodegradation in frigid waters is a relatively very slow process. The problem is also compounded by the fact that there are fewer waves in the Arctic and thus the dissipation and dispersal are also lessened. The lack of nutrients like Phosphorus and Nitrogen on which the microorganisms like algae feed on also detrimentally slows and restricts the breaking down process. Another threat to the sensitive ecological balance in the Arctic is the likelihood of an accident and pollution disrupting the fragile environment. The Table 4.4 shows that the number of ship casualties has seen a sharp increase in the recent years and this is going to multiply exponentially once large-scale exploitation of hydrocarbons and commercial shipping takes shape.

Table 4.4 Ship casualties in Arctic waters 2005–2014

	2005	2006	2007	2008	2009	2010	2011	2012	2013	2014	2015	2016	2017
Machinery damage/failure	2	3	5	13	14	16	12	13	20	27	46	32	46
Wrecked/stranded	1	4	10	11	14	9	9	8	10	14	6	11	9
Miscellaneous	0	0	5	1	4	4	2	6	5	5	6	4	6
Collision	0	0	0	1	4	10	4	4	2	0	3	2	4
Fire/explosion	0	0	3	1	2	6	6	1	4	2	4	1	3
Contact (e.g., harbor wall)	0	0	1	1	2	4	1	3	6	4	5	1	1
Hull damage	0	1	3	1	6	2	2	1	2	1	1	2	2
Foundered (i.e., sunk or submerged)	0	0	1	1	2	0	3	1	1	2	0	1	0
Labor dispute	0	0	0	0	0	0	0	0	0	0	0	1	0
Total	3	8	28	30	48	51	39	37	50	55	71	55	71

Sources: For 2005-2007: Allianz Global Corporate & Specialty, Safety and Shipping Review 2015, p. 28. (Table entitled "Arctic Circle Waters—All Casualties including Total Losses 2005–2014."). For 2008-2017: Allianz Global Corporate & Specialty, Safety and Shipping Review 2018, p. 29. (Table entitled "Arctic Circle Waters—Causes of Casualties (Shipping Incidents) 2008-2017.") The two tables include similar source notes; the one for the second source states: "Source: Lloyd's List Intelligence Casualty Statistics; Data Analysis & Graphic: Allianz Global Corporate & Specialty.")

Source Congressional Research Service, Changes in the Arctic: Background and Issues for Congress

---

[97] The Arctic Institute, 2019, accessed on 12 September 2019 from https://www.the Arcticinstitute.org/international-law-protect-Arctic-oil-spills/.

The main sources of marine pollution are—dumping of wastewater and garbage from ships, other direct discharge from ships, dumping of waste oil, indirect discharge from terrestrial activities, and oil spills, and so on. As per PAME's report on marine litter in the Arctic (2019) "Marine litter, including micro plastics, in the Arctic derive from human activities on both land and at sea.....most (50–100%) can be attributed to fishing activity, such as nets, floats, and other debris."[98] As per a PAME report, on fishing vessels in the Arctic, the accidents in IMO Arctic polar code area from 2005 to 2017 witnessed over 2000 accidents. The tabular representation is as under (Fig. 4.7).

The ecological catastrophes due to global warming and climate change could have a destructive and irreversible influence on ecology and also the indigenous population in the Arctic. The pollutants in the Arctic include Persistent Organic Pollutants (POPs), Heavy Metals, and Radioactivity among others. The ecological accidents in the Arctic can have long impacting consequences on the flora, fauna as well as the indigenous population. The number of 2000 accidents between the 12-year period from 2005 to 2017 shown above also shows that the fishing vessels pose the most serious threat as there is a lack of regulatory provisions as also

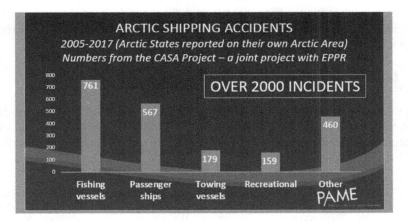

Fig. 4.7 Arctic shipping accidents, 2005 to 2017 (*Source* PAME: Hjalti Hreinsson, Fishing vessels in the Arctic polar code area)

[98] PAME: supra note 36 in Chapter 2.

varying degrees of standardisation among the Arctic states. Nonetheless, its (Arctic's) unique geographical, climatic, and biological characteristics mean that the Arctic is a 'sink' for certain pollutants transported into the region from distant sources, and pollutants from local sources with similar properties also tend to persist in the environment for long periods due to low temperatures and low biological activity.[99]

(d) Absence of Regulatory Exploration Framework

There is a lack of any regulatory mechanism in the Arctic towards resource exploitation. The exception to this lies in the Barents region, i.e. Norwegian part of Barents sea, which is covered by the OSPAR commission on protection of the marine environment of the North-East Atlantic from environmental damage. Since there has been a lack of Arctic-specific provisions and there should be greater consensus and agreement to draw out a framework considering that with the ever-increasing warming the exploration is also drawing closer with each passing day. All other geographical areas identified as crucial in the sense of ongoing or planned Arctic offshore oil and gas activities are covered by international, regional, and/or bilateral institutions that have partially or entirely unsuitable characteristics. Especially worrisome is the frequent lack of Arctic-specific provisions, lowering the value of precision for many institutions, and the generally weak values for delegation.[100]

(e) Freedom of Navigation

Shipping is the most used, most affordable, and most popular mode of transfer of goods and natural resources. Since it supports the bilk of international trade, the freedom of navigation and its curtailment has the

---

[99] Arctic Monitoring and Assessment Programme, Arctic Council, AMAP Arctic Pollution Issues 2015, Persistent Organic Pollutants; Radioactivity in the Arctic; Human Health in the Arctic (2019) accessed on 1 November 2019 from https://www.amap.no/documents/download/2222/inline.

[100] Ibid.

potential to initiate conflicts. The 2019 US-Iran Persian Gulf crisis was an example of restricting the shipping and Iran and the UK had both seized ships to exercise their might. There are stark differences with Russia's emphasis on NSR as its internal waters among the other nations like the USA and others.

The aspect of differences between the Russian regulation of NSR by stipulating a 45-day notice before traversing on NSR and other allied requirements of submitting ship data to it and the USA over the interpretation of freedom of seas is and remains a sore point between these two. This had led to the US' call for re-introduction of its FONOPS, Freedom of Navigation Operations there. Article 234 of the UNCLOS reads "to adopt and enforce non-discriminatory laws and regulations for the prevention, reduction, and control of marine pollution from vessels in ice-covered areas within the limits of the exclusive economic zone."[101]

With the ratification of UNCLOS by Arctic states, except the USA and coming in force of the Polar code, there is a complex interpretation of international laws that will gain prominence with greater instances of contentions of freedom of navigation in the Arctic seas. Many conditions have to be fulfilled to apply Article 234 UNCLOS but these conditions have overlap and are somewhat ambiguous, which is creating individual interpretations. Article 234 of UNCLOS provides the rights to the coastal states to enforce special regulatory and enforcement provisions to reduce and marine pollution within the limits of their exclusive economic zone (EEZ). Both Canada and Russia have enforced NORDREG Regulations and the NSR Rules, respectively, vide which certain requirements have to be fulfilled before obtaining requisite permissions.

(f) **Difficulties in Arctic Shipping**

Despite the huge cost and time savings and opening of shorter connections, the Arctic shipping suffers from certain difficulties which are as under:

---

[101] United Nations, 2019, accessed on 1 August 2019 from https://www.un.org/depts/los/convention_agreements/texts/unclos/part12.htm.

(i) Arctic Routes are not always shorter: In certain cases, the traditional routes may turn out to be shorter than Arctic routes depending on the destination and the originating station.
(ii) Reforming of Ice: The unpredictability of the ice levels leaves the forecasts skewed and unreliable and the possibility of formation of ice in winters prevents year-round shipping. Thus the seasonality of the ice recession and its re-formation prevents all-around shipping.
(iii) Prohibitive Cost: The prevailing stiff conditions in the Arctic have to be encountered by the construction of strengthened hulls to sail over frozen ice caps, strengthened ship construction with its high costs, much higher insurance premiums outgo as the conditions are unpredictable and uncertain as also higher fuel consumption while negotiating ice transits all lead to a rise in input costs. This also has an impact on the profitability of these ventures.
(iv) Accurately predicting a freeze-up extent and breakup will remain very difficult.
(v) The possibility of drifting ice moving with currents and winds and will possibly clog specific straits, especially in the Canadian Arctic.
(vi) Growlers and small icebergs will force ships to greatly reduce their speed, as the possibility of encountering such blocks of ice increases.
(vii) The transit passage requires that the ships have an ice-strengthened hull, powerful night ice spotting radars, to navigate. The requirement of having a trained and experienced crew and special equipment to cope with icing will be required.
(viii) Mapping is still inadequate in these waters.
(ix) Shallow and narrow straits limit the options for the ship size and the same has to be reduced. It is also pertinent to mention that the average depth of the Arctic Ocean is much less as compared to the other oceans, which makes sailing of large ships difficult. The average depth of the ocean is about 1050 metres, with the deepest sounding around 5150 metres. Bathymetrically, the Arctic marine area is relatively shallow with broad continental shelves. The shelf extends 100 to 200 kilometres from the United

States and Canada, and more than 1,000 kilometres in places extending north from the Russian Federation[102].

(x) Along Arctic routes, there is no intermediate market (stopovers).

The foregoing presents both opportunities and challenges, which have to be managed within a multilateral cooperative framework and robust governance (Fig. 4.8).

With the joint efforts of Organisation for Economic Cooperation and Development (OECD) and the institution of MARPOL and Polar code in the Arctic, detailed and mandatory compliance to stiff environmental guidelines must be ensured. These will include the prohibition on the carriage of Heavy Fuel Oil (HFO) as well as ballast discharge in the Arctic waters. The use and carriage of HFO are already banned in Antarctic waters. This gains importance due to increased shipping activity in NSR, NEP as well as calls to adhere to climate change goals.

	Size (million km²)	Percentage of Earth's Total Surface	Greatest Depth (m)	Average Depth (m)
Pacific	155.557	30.5	10,911	4,300
Atlantic	76.762	20.8	8,605	3,300
Indian	65.556	14.4	7,258	3,900
Southern	20.327	4.0	7,235	4,000-5,000
Arctic	14.056	2.8	5,160	1,050

Table 2.1 Arctic Ocean compared to other oceans. *Source: AMSA*

Fig. 4.8 Comparison of oceans depths[103] (*Source* AMSA, Arctic Marine Shipping Assessment report 2009)

---

[102] AMSA, Arctic Marine Shipping Assessment report 2009, accessed on 27 September 2019 from https://www.pmel.noaa.gov/arctic-zone/detect/documents/AMSA_2009_Report_2nd_print.pdf.

[103] Ibid.

(g) Hydrocarbon Exploitation

The scientific exploration estimates have indicated that the large parts of the Arctic oil reserves are largely offshore, and will require technical expertise and sophisticated technology for its extraction. As per estimates, of the total resources, 84% are expected to be offshore and the competition from extraction from shale, oil sand, and other resources also poses issues on the cost of extraction, making it a difficult choice. To further compound the matters, there are uncertainties on the projected potential resources, lack of credible survey data, high cost due to the stiff conditions and inclement weather, and offshore projects' economic feasibility. It may be recounted that Royal Dutch Shell's exploration and drilling efforts in the Chukchi Sea were short of expectations. Also, Cairn Energy's huge investments in Greenland's coast were short on discovery. Between the nations too, there are variables like Canada which is focussed on environmental constraints of exploitation while Russia looks it as an economic opportunity. The Russians also have an advantage in partnering with China with its huge demand for energy making it a potential and prospective long-term collaborative partner.

In the case of Arctic, there are twin problems, firstly of concretely identifying the quantity and location of undersea resources due to inadequate bathymetry and secondly of multiple problems associated with deep-sea exploration. The location of these hydrocarbons is also in deeper depths, unlike the more shallow portions of the Arctic Ocean and thus the problems get compounded by the requirement of drilling at low temperatures, high pressure in the range of 300 bar, and through solid rock to reach the reserves. In water 3000 metres deep, the ocean temperature is as low as 0–3 °C (32–38 °F), while the pressure is 300 bar (4388 psi). Here, we drill through a further 6000 metres of rock to reach the reservoir. How is it possible to produce oil and gas under such conditions?[104]

As of now, not much progress has been made in offshore oil development in the Arctic and varying approaches are being adopted by nations wherein some have abstained from exploitation while others are pressing ahead eagerly. However, despite the odds mentioned above, the insatiable demand for energy worldwide even though requiring capital

---

[104] Equinor.com, 2019, accessed on 11 September 2019 from https://www.equinor.com/en/magazine/the-final-frontier.html.

intensive equipment and risky exploitation will still have energy companies investing in Arctic oil and gas endeavours. To summarise, the major challenges in exploration in the Arctic include limited exiting infrastructure, harsh climate, competition from other areas and types, long lead times, lack of common law, the magnified impact of pollution/accident, and financial viability. Thus there are twin issues of lack of certainty on estimates of recoverable oil and gas and the exploration thereof will be a relatively costly affair.

(h) **Status of Arctic Ocean**

Though the first claims to divide the Arctic Ocean were made by Canadian senator P Poirier in early parts of twentieth century yet it is quite a modern phenomenon that the UNCLOS was adopted, signed, and ratified by Norway in 1996, Russia in 1997, Canada in 2003, and Denmark in 2004. As mentioned earlier, the USA has not signed the UNCLOS. As of now, the individual claims on EEZ and extension of the EEZ to 350 Nautical Miles made by various states are under consideration by UN CLCS. The Russian claim on the Lomonosov Ridge in 2001 and another differing claim in 2006 by Canada and Demark have kept the debate alive and open. However, a collaborative stand taken in the Ilulissat Declaration in 2008 put to rest any outside involvement, and the parties consider themselves competent to resolve the issues within themselves.

The interesting feature in the race for hydrocarbon exploitation has shown that the possibility of finding hydrocarbons in the central part of the Arctic is zilch. This is the area that may fall short of UNCLOS extended EEZs of respective countries when settled. Yet the central part of the Arctic Ocean will become, perhaps, an expanse with no clearly defined territorial or political delineation. Since its status is ambiguous under UNCLOS, Russia followed by Canada and others have dashed, reminiscent of the imperial era. The first claims to possession of the Arctic Ocean were made more than 100 years ago. In a 1907 speech to the Canadian Senate, P. Poirier suggested dividing the Arctic into sectors (McRae, 1994), and in 1925, Canada officially claimed the sector between 60° and 141° W.[105] As is visible from the Map 4.5, the presence

---

[105] Wojciech Janicki, why Do They Need the Arctic? The First Partition of the Sea, Arctic, March 2012, vol. 65, issue. 1, pp. 87–97, accessed on 1 July 2019 from http://www.jstor.org/stable/23187227.

of hydrocarbons and valuable resources is one of the main reasons for the claims made by nations.

The Map 4.5 reaffirms that most of the Arctic's petroleum and natural gas reserves lie in areas that already form part of one or more exclusive economic zones; hence the quest/claims for wider areas raise a deliberative question whether the Arctic states are scrambling for the unmeasured and acutely difficult and unprofitable exploitation mechanism for the undersea resources or it for a great call to exercise/enforce political will.

(i) Common Heritage of Mankind

The UNCLOS Article 136 and Article 137 layout that areas lying outside of EEZ of sovereign countries form part of the common heritage of mankind. The seabed beyond the extended continental shelf has been termed as "the Area." Under Article 136, the mineral resources beyond national jurisdiction (i.e. "the Area") are the "Common Heritage of Mankind (CHM)."[106] Since UNCLOS has been accepted by over 168 countries and most of the major global powers abide by the provisions thereof, there is little scope for any deviation from the provisions of UNCLOS. No State shall claim or exercise sovereignty or sovereign rights over any part of the Area or its resources, nor shall any State or natural or juridical person appropriate any part thereof. No such claim or exercise of sovereignty or sovereign rights nor such appropriation shall be recognised.[107] It is amply clear in the provisions of UNCLOS that no nation shall claim or stake claim to the common heritage of mankind and in case it does, such claim shall have no legal sanctity.

The Indian position becomes starkly clear as it ratified UNCLOS in 1995, and therefore it is bound by the provisions of the convention. The claims by Russia and other Arctic nations for extension of their respective EEZs also have been undertaken under the clauses of UNCLOS and logically, India by inference has acceded/conceded to the claims. The UNCLOS convention declares the area and high seas to constitute the common heritage of mankind, but is there any space left for exercising

---

[106] National Maritime Foundation, Arctic Perspectives 2015, Edited by Vijay Sakhuja and Gurpreet S. Khurana, p. 88.

[107] United Nations,un.org, United Nations Convention on the Law of the Sea, accessed on 10 July 2019 from https://www.un.org/depts/los/convention_agreements/texts/unclos/unclos_e.pdf.

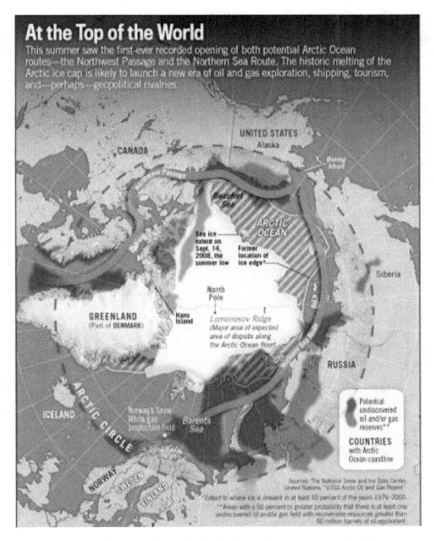

Map 4.5 Map showing the North Pole and Lomonosov Ridge (*Source* Congressional Research Service, Changes in the Arctic: Background and Issues for Congress)

this in the Arctic after taking into account the submission made by the nations to the CLCS?

(j) **Institutional Checks**

The hydrocarbon exploitation activity has considerable transboundary consequences on the neighbouring political entities as well as on the fragile marine and coastal environment in which such activity will be implemented. Because of the extremely cold climate, the extracted product also degrades very slowly in the Arctic environment and appropriate clean-up capabilities currently do not exist in the Arctic. Arcticwwf.org and its 2019 Arctic Council Conservation Scorecard which is placed below examine the action plan by the Arctic 8 on several parameters to fulfil their responsibilities as the primary stewards of the region. The 2019 findings in the scorecard show "Arctic states are **not fulfilling** their roles as the prime stewards of the region. They must do more at the national level to follow up on their international commitments and coordinate more effectively with each other to provide a united Arctic position at relevant international fora and negotiations."[108] The graphical depiction thereof is as under (Fig. 4.9).

However, a surprising finding given by the wwfarctic is that the Arctic states are not doing adequate to support the stated objectives of conserving the pristine Arctic environment. Another feature of the report is that Finland, Norway, and Sweden are the only countries that have not been graded 'D' in any of the parameters while bigger countries like the USA and Russia have been given two and one such gradings, respectively. Finally, the fact that environmental risks connected to Arctic oil and gas development, especially offshore, are potentially transboundary makes national regulations for Arctic oil and gas activities even more inadequate.[109]

Neoliberal scholars have pointed out that states design international institutions to further their goals and this makes an institutional check on exploration and exploitation a difficult proposition. The UNCLOS does

---

[108] Arcticwwf.org, 2019, accessed on 2 December 2019 from https://Arcticwwf.org/work/governance/acscorecard19/#download.

[109] K. Keil, Spreading Oil, Spreading Conflict? Institutions Regulating Arctic Oil and Gas Activities. The International Spectator: Italian Journal of International Affairs, 2015, vol. 50, issue 1, pp. 85–110.

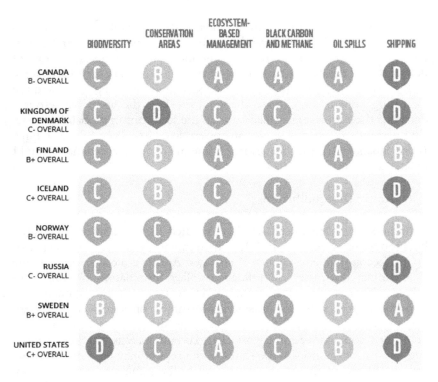

Fig. 4.9 Arctic countries scorecard on environmental conservation (*Source* WWFARCTIC.ORG, 2019, Arctic council scorecard 2019)

not have special provisions to deal with the peculiar characteristics of the Arctic and though there are many regional, international and bilateral arrangements to curb a potential conflict situation arising from exploration/exploitation activity yet they are found to be less than adequate as the geographical coverage, participation, and enforcement parameters are lacking and not enforceable, at least in the present set-up.

(k) **Maritime vs Terrestrial**

The growing interest in the Arctic is linked to resource exploitation and shipping routes, which are primarily maritime and in turn attention from the indigenous population's livelihoods, and sustainable development is put on the back burner. This also gains prominence as the Arctic 5 in comparison with Arctic 8 are powerful and influential states, capable of deflecting the deliberative attention of the AC, in forum and discussions.

Because of the foregoing, the presence of major global powers, and the increasing impetus on climate change, as well as the insatiable resource demands the Arctic region has assumed the forefront in global discourse. The presence of all major global powers like the USA, Russia, China, India, Japan, etc., either as permanent members or observers has brought greater attention and focus on the region.

(l) **Arctic Disequilibrium**

Some social sciences scholars have studied the disequilibrium created between humans, animals, and the environment given the changing socio-political-economic-environmental changes. Academics can strongly hinge the national discourse and influence policy formulation on respective subjects. There is also a stark contrast view with which the commentators view the region; with the outsiders/non-Arctic ones anxious and sceptical of growing conflict scenarios while the Arctic ones seeing the silver lining in a cooperative framework. In a certain analysis, the involvement and interest of the non-Arctic states in the region may have caused some apprehensions on the role and necessarily the same was viewed within economic and strategic considerations though India would not have any massive economic takeaways from the region.

INDIA'S RESPONSE STRATEGY

The broad framework for the Arctic region will be to work around the interplay and interaction between strategic geography and power politics. The study of geopolitics is within the realm of realism in international relations. 'The climate induced changes in the Arctic are likely to dominate the discourse, but political and strategic developments in the Arctic cannot be at the margins of India's mental map'.[110] As a region of high-risk climate vulnerability and high-reward economic development, the

---

[110] V. Sakhuja, India and the Arctic: Beyond Kiruna, ICWA Indian Council for World Affairs, 2014, www.icwa.in.

Arctic has emerged as a critical arena in the twenty-first-century geopolitics, scientific, research, and commerce. The future pattern of climate change and ice melting will undoubtedly open areas for cooperation but also potential competition and contestation.[111]

The survival of the nation is the most important facet of this approach and thus the concept of security is ingrained in it. The geopolitics in the Arctic context is apt as there are multitudes of communication connections emanating from there and importantly, in an era of shrinking oil/gas and natural resources, this region has tremendous amounts of unexplored and virgin assets.

Iftikhar Gilani warned recently in the same newspaper, if India does not develop an Arctic policy that restrains China, it is "heading for near diplomatic disaster."[112] Thus, there are sceptical and myopic views focussed on regional dynamics that fail to grasp the full magnitude and scale of the geostrategic position unravelling in the Arctic, and India should be taking a broad view of the situation.

The Arctic region has presented itself as an ideal model of international cooperation, whereby the states in the AC have been magnanimous to tide over the interstate competition to progress the common strategy. The AC is one of the few intergovernmental bodies, functioning effectively and efficiently by wilful compliance to the institutional framework. The cooperative mechanism adopted by the AC has been instrumental in ensuring that despite differences between the nations, the escalation has been successively curbed and mitigated.

The alarmist view on the Arctic which had pitted that the scramble to rush for the natural resources will pit nations against each other and there will be contests based on territorial claims, freedom of navigation, claims on continental shelves, etc., yet till now, the AC structures have proved to be resilient to such pressures. The climate risk at the Arctic is attributed to the non-reaching of consensus among the big polluters including India under the framework of the UNFCC COP mechanism and is a global phenomenon. However, it is a different matter that the effect is more pronounced and more acutely experienced in the Arctic owing to its unique geophysical features. The exploration and exploitation

---

[111] Sinha U. K., India in the Arctic: A multidimensional approach. Vestnik of Saint Petersburg University. International Relations, 2019, vol. 12, issue 1, pp. 113–126.

[112] Strategic Study India Blogspot, 2019, accessed on 22 November 2019 from https://strategicstudyindia.blogspot.com/2014/04/enter-asia-Arctic-heats-up.html?m=0.

of resources are thoroughly regulated both internationally and nationally, and most resources fall within clear national jurisdiction.

Michael Byers (supported by Dr. Njord Regge elsewhere) in his pieces has elaborated that the Arctic governance model offers an example of complex interdependence wherein despite the annexation of Crimea by Russia in 2014, regional cooperation continued in several spheres among the Arctic nations. This speaks a lot about the efficacy of loose and tiered governance mechanisms of the AC. The concept of complex interdependence has been acknowledged to have brought cooperative mechanisms to tide over crisis events. Complex interdependence was developed in opposition to core realist assumptions, which are described by Keohane and Nye as 'security is the dominant goal; states are the only significant actors, and force is the dominant instrument.'[113]

This concept was in contrast to the realist theories which rely on security as a dominant objective. Some examples, which stand out in the case of Arctic, include the 2003ACIA Arctic Climate Impact Assessment, 2008 AMSA Arctic Marine Shipping Assessment which was successfully adopted despite differences in global issues between major powers. Despite the souring of military and economic relations, the issues on SAR, fishing, navigation, discussion on continental shelves went unabated. This was a case study on successful handling on the separation of issue areas and the effectiveness of trans-governmental and transnational issues in settling disputes. In short, the structure established by AC stood firmly due to the pre-existence of complex interdependence which helped preserve cooperation in some issue areas and thus prevented conflict escalation and also reduced the impact of a crisis.

The USA, which is not a signatory to the UNCLOS, has also reaffirmed that it will abide by the framework of UNCLOS for compliance. It has reassured that (it) "remains committed to this legal framework and to the orderly settlement of any possible overlapping claims."[114] One of the major grounds of US objections to UNCLOS was the concerns on 'commons heritage' and its subsequent exploitation. Though presently the USA has not signed the mechanism yet it had confirmed vide 2008

---

[113] Byers, supra note 38 in Chapter 2.

[114] The Ilulissat Declaration, Arctic Ocean Conference, Ilulissat, Greenland, 27–29 May 2008.

Ilulissat Declaration and at other avenues that it supports the settlement of any conflicting claims by utilising the tenets of the UNCLOS.

Though the Polar region does not have a history of cooperation, on the contrary, there have neither been any serious disagreements, too. The only major nation with inclination, wherewithal, and technological expertise to exploit fisheries, navigation, and other natural resources is China. With increased resource exploitation, there is the potential for enhanced risk of environmental impact but also demands greater foreign access by States which may not traditionally have had an interest in the region.[115]

It is abundantly clear that due to the presence and interests of Great Powers competing for influence, resources, and win over allies the Arctic landscape will witness rivalry and competition with its associated pulls and pressures. However, the time tested procedures and established bodies and multilateral multi-tiered organisations have the expertise to absorb these pitfalls. The intrinsic rights of Arctic 8 including Russia are inalienable and undeniable. Any moves to try to oust or block may prove to be counterproductive and may backfire.

INDIA'S EQUITY IN HYDROCARBONS

(A) Imperial Energy: The Comptroller and Auditor General (CAG) in its report of 2011 had reported that the ONGC Videsh Limited (OVL) had incurred a loss of Rs 1182.14 Crore between January 2009 and March 2010 due to its inability to achieve the estimated production of 35,000 barrels of oil per day (BPD) in the Imperial Energy Corporation project[116] CAG also criticised OVL's approach in Sudan, Myanmar, Libya, Turkmenistan, Qatar, Congo, Colombia, and Nigeria.[117] In 2019, OVL was still trying to transfer its stake in Imperial Energy Corp to a Russian firm to reduce potential losses from the $2.1 billion acquisition.[118]

---

[115] Rothwell, supra note 24 in Chapter 1.

[116] Live mint, 2019, accessed on 2 October 2019 from https://www.livemint.com/Politics/SMfGRXnMMpmV9fLYiCZrcL/CAG-criticizes-OVL-for-expensive-acquisition-of-Imperial-Ene.html.

[117] Ibid.

[118] Livemint, 2019, accessed on 11 October 2019 from https://www.livemint.com/companies/news/ongc-videsh-looks-to-pare-stake-in-one-of-its-costliest-acquisitions-1549309182513.html.

(B) Sakhalin-1: OVL and its partners in Russia's Sakhalin-1 project had paid Russian giant Rosneft $230 million to settle an oil production dispute out-of-court in 2018. Rosneft had dragged the Sakhalin-1 consortium to court alleging "unjust enrichment and interest gained by using other people's money" and claimed $1.4 billion in damages. OVL being a 20% partner had shelled out $46 million in this deal. OVL, the overseas arm of state-owned Oil and Natural Gas Corp (ONGC), had bought a 20% stake in 2001 for $1.7 billion. The project started production in 2005. Since that time, the consortium faithfully executed its obligations under the Production Sharing Agreement (PSA) and the Russian government in 2017 extended the pact by a further 30 years, until 2051.[119]

Till now, India has been cautious in its approach in decisions concerning participation in Russian oil and gas projects in the Arctic region. The factor on the actual quantum of the resources and the challenges in exploitation may have made the Indian participation modest. It is pertinent to mention that India had left the negotiations on the Yamal LNG deal, too.

Russia-India hydrocarbon cooperation can lead to diversification of its hydrocarbon imports, widen its interests in the Arctic region, and perhaps act as leverage to supplies to other countries based on its equity holding. However, other than the loss-making IEC project, the majority stake and control in the Russian energy projects remain with Russia and hence India's options are negligible. This cooperation has the potential to counterbalance the Russia-China cooperation, but India has been outpaced, at least till now by an aggressive China.

The investments by OVL in foreign oil and gas projects are 25 MMTOE. India's oil and gas companies have established their presence in 26 countries adding nearly 25 MMTOE of equity oil and gas to the existing production.[120] If this compared with the annual consumption of energy at 2016 levels of 724 MTOE, it is seen that these are quite insignificant at less than 3.5%. India's GDP increased at a CAGR of 7%

---

[119] Livemint, 2019, accessed on 02 October 2019 from https://www.livemint.com/Companies/a0cTDrfhET3sq7kFHPS8cK/OVL-partners-to-pay-230-million-in-out-of-court-settlement.html.

[120] Ministry of Petroleum and Natural Gas, 2019, accessed on 12 August 2019 from http://petroleum.nic.in/about-us/international-co-opration.

and India's primary energy consumption increased at a CAGR of 6.7%, from 394 million tons of oil equivalent (MTOE) to 724 MTOE.[121] This gap is likely to widen in the coming days as India's demand for energy will increase due to economic progress and government impetus on infrastructure development.

India's Gas Price

Most LNG-related prices around the world followed an upward trend in 2018, influenced by rising oil prices and strong LNG demand in Asia. Northeast Asian spot price averaged $9.78/MMBtu in 2018. India had to pay dearly for having entered into long-term contracts at high rates.[122] The Indian firms had to pay a higher price than the spot and hub prices causing losses to the exchequer (Fig. 4.10).

Thus, it is seen from ONGC's data and reports that India's contract process is higher than other spot and hub prices. Thus the Indian experience in obtaining stakes in hydrocarbon aboard does not seem to be a

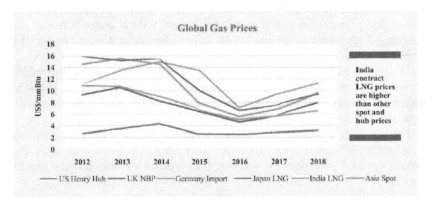

Fig. 4.10 Global gas prices, 2012 to 2018 (*Source* Annual Report, ONGC, 2018–19, p. 148)

---

[121] Ibid.

[122] Oil and Natural Gas Corporation, Annual Report-2018–2019.pdf, accessed on 22 December 2019 from https://www.ongcindia.com/wps/wcm/connect/en/investors/annual-reports/annual-report-2018-19.

profitable venture. Rather the advantage it has is because of mammoth size in the energy import pie, for which the OPEC/IEA and others are vying for a share in the Indian market.

India has abjectly failed to utilise its non-partisan and democratic character and also as an observer state and thus is not competing for the exploitation of economic gains as well as other issues related to the exploitation of new routes that provide 40-percent shorter distances between Europe and East Asia. Generally, India is seen to have taken the lead among Asian Observer states placing more weight on environmental and scientific rather than the economic potential of the region.[123] This focus on utopian ideals to emerge as a World Guru too is not bearing any tangible fruits for either India's diplomacy or stature in the world.

The Indian PM's speech had in September 2019 in Russia completely skirted the NSR and adopted a myopic and continental perspective on connection with Russia's Far East with the Indo-Pacific, instead of the assistance in developing the NSR to secure competitive payoffs later from the oil and gas riches located there. Despite a promise of $1 Bn L of C, India did not figure in the countries investing in the Far East as per the statement of Yury Petrovich Trutnev, deputy prime minister of Russia and presidential envoy to the far eastern federal district. As per the speech, 17 different countries invest in the Far East: China, Japan, the Republic of Korea, Australia, New Zealand, Vietnam, to name a few. Since 2014, nearly 32% of all direct foreign investment came to our region.[124] However, President Vladimir Putin had pointed out, "we see its [NSR's] future as an international transport artery capable of competing with traditional sea routes in cost of services, safety, and quality."[125]

Hence there is a mismatch in the views with which India and Russia view not only Russia's Far East but also prospects associated with the unlocking of hydrocarbons and shipping routes in the Russian Arctic region.

---

[123] Uttam Kumar Sinha and Arvind Gupta, The Arctic and India: Strategic Awareness and Scientific Engagement. Strategic Analysis, November 2014, vol. 38, issue 6, p. 883.

[124] Forum Vostok, 2019, accessed on 14 September 2019 from https://forumvostok.ru/en/about-the-forum/.

[125] The official site of the Prime Minister of the Russian Federation, "Vladimir Putin's Speech at the Forum," Presented at the second International Arctic Forum "The Arctic Territory of Dialogue," Arkhangelsk, September 22, 2011, http://archive.premier.gov.ru/eng/events/news/16536/print/.

Russia-India: Reaching New Heights of Cooperation Through Trust and Partnership, 2019

2019 has been a remarkable year for invigorating and giving a concrete dimension to the Russia-India energy partnership. India also was jolted like the world with the Saudi Aramco attack in September 2019 which highlighted the threats to global supplies by political and non-political players.

Both countries are adopting a road map to establish a "Far Eastern Energy Corridor" that would boost Russian oil, gas, and coal exports and trade to India. A Memorandum of Intent was signed between the Ministry of Shipping of the Republic of India and the Ministry of Transport of the Russian Federation on the Development of Maritime Communications between the Port of Chennai, Republic of India, and the Port of Vladivostok, Russian Federation. Going by the declaration at Vladivostok, the Eastern corridor is being set up for the mutual benefit of both the countries as Russia gets to diversify its energy customer base from present Europe and China, and India also reduces its dependence on her traditional suppliers. Given ongoing friendly partnership between India and Russia and also the fact that both countries enjoy political and economic framework, which is aided by the fact that India does not harbour any geopolitical ambitions, this issue will offer tremendous opportunities to both the countries.

In the present times, Russia is the largest oil supplier to China, and in December 2019 the gas supply to China via the 'Power of Siberia' was also commenced. To secure a pie in the Russian LNG, a Memorandum of Understanding between the Joint Stock Company NOVATEK and PETRONET LNG Limited on cooperation concerning the joint development of downstream LNG Business and LNG supplies was also signed. India's H-Energy Global Ltd and Russia's Novatek on Wednesday signed an agreement to provide long-term liquefied natural gas supplies to India and other markets, the Russian media reported.[126] Indian petroleum firm, IOCL is also exploring options for increasing stakes in Rosneft for oil purchases and expanding investments to secure supplies. Indian firms

---

[126] Economic Times, 2019, accessed on 22 December 19 from https://economictimes.indiatimes.com/industry/energy/oil-gas/h-energy-russias-novatek-to-set-up-jv-to-sell-lng-in-india/articleshow/70974320.cms?from=mdr.

have expressed interest in investments in multibillion-dollar Russian Arctic LNG-2 and Arctic LNG-3 projects. Likewise, the options for a share in Rosneft's $157 billion Vostok Oil project are also being discussed.

The distance, time as well as associated risks and costs involved in transporting hydrocarbons from Russia to India, has to be compared with similar ventures from the Middle East and Australia. The Russian option is costlier compared to Qatar and the Middle East as well as few others elsewhere. Likewise, India and Russia don't have a contiguous border and laying of pipelines traversing long distances and difficult terrain, thus taking away the profitability. In the beginning, a Memorandum of Understanding was signed between Coal India Limited and Far East Investment and Export Agency to cooperate in coking coal mining projects implementation in the Russian Far East.

The Vladivostok-Chennai maritime journey will entail around 24 days compared to 40 days from the other European route. The prospects and viability and likely benefits will only be clarified with the progress of the circuit. There are no disruptions like piracy in this route, though Chinese interference at a later stage can't be deciphered with certainty in the present timeframe.

The progress on expanding hydrocarbons trade between the tested partners though appears to be delayed but is a step in the right direction. The signatory corporations and entities must develop the agreements to a lucrative and profitable venture as the foundational basis has been provided at the governmental level. In the present global order, both India and Russia are growing and aspirational powers which on joining hands will be propelled in pursuits thereof. Since their cooperation in other fields like defence, cultural, and technical has already proved fruitful and backed by firm political backing, there should be minimal barriers in fulfilling these economic and energy goals. This also demands that a commercial basis for smooth execution of agreements like avoiding double taxation, bilateral trade agreements, and a legal and bureaucratic framework is also geared up to fulfil these objectives. The extension of one Billion Line of credit by India demonstrates that the economic foundation of mutual partnership is being strengthened.

Analysis of Transforming Indian Policy

The statements made by Ministers in Parliament, Answers to questions by MPs and press interactions on policy issues, other than those by the MEA don't present a clear position of the Indian strategic stand. Indian Foreign Policy has undergone swift transformation and realignment, which is overtly visible and being projected after the decisive BJP victories in general elections in 2014 and 2019. The process initiated after the end of the cold war by the liberalisation of the Indian economy brought her to the centre of the global economy owing to the size and geopolitical dimension. Resultantly, there were greater demands on diplomacy to mould and carve new policy engagements delving into the geo-economics and geostrategic realms. The changing attitude and perspective of erstwhile unconcerned states like the US and certain European countries also gave impetus to India's self-belief. Since then, India has been trying to associate herself globally by weaving bespoke narratives of engagement like neighbourhood first, Act East, and so on. The ambition to be a great power, competing with a growing unilateralist and inwardly US, and ambitious and aggressive China is manifesting in greater power politics in international affairs. India's views on NSR and Arctic shipping as well as energy dependence and more importantly a more realist and practical approach, much more connected and synchronised with the changing geopolitical landscape in the Arctic were viewed in the statement of 05 September 19 on India-Russia partnership. The Indian diplomacy and MEA appears alive to the situation and there is a perceptible change on many issues and India's assertive is visible in following these themes:

(a) **Greater Maritime Opportunities**

Speaking at a discussion at Valdai Discussion Club on 27 August 2019, the EAM had said that 'greater maritime opportunities would also arise from what is happening in regarding the Arctic: 'the possibility of new maritime routes opening up'.[127] This was first acknowledgement by a senior government functionary on the impact of the opening of new

---

[127] Jaishankar, S, External Affairs Minister's Conversation with Valdai Discussion Club, Moscow on 27 August 2019, accessed on 2 November 2019 from https://www.mea.gov.in/Speeches-Statements.htm?dtl/31957/External_Affairs_Ministers_conversation_with_Valdai_Discussion_Club_Moscow_on_27_August_2019.

routes which will have profound maritime opportunities. Though specifics like hydrocarbons transit, trade was not addressed yet it was the realisation of India accepting the tremendous geophysical and structural changes taking place which will have profound global impacts.

(b) **Disputation of Global Commons**

External Affairs Minister (EAM) himself acknowledged during his speech on 14 November 2019 that 'The global commons is also more in disputation as multilateralism weakens. Even climate change is a factor, contributing to geopolitics amongst others by the opening of an Arctic passage'.[128] The moral high pedestal of an idealistic stand taken by Indian commentators (with some of the pieces even put up on MEA website) often drawing India's position in the Arctic as a place of global commons was also set aside by the EAM. In any case, most of the territory in the Arctic region is claimed by the sovereign states under binding UNCLOS regulations. India is also a party to UNCLOS and the calls of global commons are contrary to both international legal norms and the observer's code, wilfully accepted by all observer nations, including India at the time of admission.

An assertive China has made the debate on the Arctic as global commons an issue that calls for a concerted action plan by the Arctic 8 with the incorporation of China. It is also a natural extension that if China is accorded additional rights, countries like India, Netherlands, ROK, etc., will also call for their inclusion which will compound the mechanism. What is yet to be defined is that the demand for rights also has a corollary in responsibilities and there is no multilateral binding framework, in the Arctic to demand and enforce the same. Countries like Germany and the Netherlands also have claimed at various times, that areas in the Arctic which lie outside the jurisdiction of states under parameters of UNCLOS should be considered global commons. They desire to undertake scientific pursuits in such areas for the public good to protect the interests of future generations. Both Arctic 5 and Arctic 8, will oppose any move by non-Arctic states to levy such arrangements in the region and the official

---

[128] Jaishankar, S, External Affairs Minister's Speech at the 4th Ramnath Goenka Lecture, 2019, accessed on 12 December 19 from https://mea.gov.in/Speeches-Statements.htm?dtl/32038/External+Affairs+Ministers+speech+at+the+4th+Ramnath+Goenka+Lecture+2019.

governing light of the region will remain the broad framework of the AC and the adherence to international law and regulatory framework.

It has been stated by the EAM himself that global commons are in disputation and hence the terming of Arctic as a common heritage of mankind may only cause strain and stress with India's relations with the Arctic states and hinder India's aspirations for a greater role in the Arctic region. Also, the AC framework and the adherence to the international law regimes like UNCLOS leave little scope for any global commons in the Arctic and the AC mechanism has only grown and progressed with the changing times by incorporating new challenges in its fold.

In the coming days, China will become more assertive and emboldened with the deep economic linkages with the Arctic countries to seek greater participation in Arctic affairs including calls for governance. Meanwhile, as China moves away from its traditional energy suppliers towards Russia, it is strategically freeing itself from the insecurities from shipping in waters of the Indian Ocean. There are no potential choke points on the NSR, except perhaps Bering Strait, within the influence of the USA. The geographical proximity coupled with the strategic partnership with Russia will also benefit China.

(c) **Arctic Resources**

On the eve of PM's visit to Vladivostok in September 2019, it was stated that cooperation in the search for Hydro-Carbon and LNG in the Far East and the Arctic has been agreed. This statement asserted that India was keenly watching and interested in the exploration of Arctic resources. This statement has relevance in both pragmatism in participating in unlocking resource potential of the Arctic and progressing the Russian partnership in this field. An identical statement was also issued in October 2018 during the visit of Russian President to India, wherein it was stated that 'and exploring opportunities for joint development of oil fields in the Russian territory, including in the Arctic shelf of Russia and joint development of projects on the shelf of the Pechora and Okhotsk

Seas.'[129] These statements affirm Indian openness to having joint partnerships with Russia in the exploration of hydrocarbons in the Arctic region. Likewise, during the St Petersburg Declaration on 01 June 2017, it was stated that 'we are interested in launching joint projects on exploration and exploitation of hydrocarbons in the Arctic shelf of the Russian Federation.' This assertive and focussed stance of the Indian Government, which had been emphasising only the scientific aspects of India's Arctic presence, is a clear indicator that India is attaching great significance to the Arctic affairs and has realised the potential of cooperation in partaking in the resources, too.

(d) Cooperation in the Arctic

In June 2019, before the SCO summit, another statement hinting at growing focus on the Arctic was asserted 'A new area of focus that was identified by both leaders is Arctic region oil & gas...... new dimension of cooperation in the Russian Far East and the Arctic.' It is amply clear that after the assumption of the Modi 2.0 government, the realisation of the importance of Arctic for India is firmly established and is being pursued with relentless vigour and focus.

(e) The Adherence to UNCLOS

India has maritime boundaries with Sri Lanka, Maldives, Myanmar, Indonesia, Thailand, and two terrestrial nations, Pakistan and Bangladesh. Thus India shares maritime boundaries with more States than it shares on the hinterland and hence the importance of universal application and enforcement of UNCLOS has greater importance. India is a signatory to the UNCLOS and has settled its maritime border with Bangladesh based on the treaty parameters. Also in light of its stated stand on respect for international law and dispute settlement under the framework of such international law including UNCLOS does take away all claims on the Arctic as part of global commons as most of the area is claimed by

---

[129] India-Russia Joint Statement During Visit of President of Russia to India (5 October 2018), accessed on 22 December 2019 from https://mea.gov.in/bilateral-documents.htm?dtl/30469/IndiaRussia_Joint_Statement_during_visit_of_President_of_Russia_to_India_October_05_2018.

respective countries under the UNCLOS framework on sovereign ownership. India has consistently favoured as per UNCLOS, the equidistant/ median line as the line of maritime demarcation, and hence India's position on the disputed Hans Island and other disputes in the Arctic can be easily extrapolated. The India-Pakistan dispute in the Sir Creek area which remains disputed also lessens India's profile as it contains huge economic potential but the lack of political will and action to enforce sea Laws to strengthen its hold over marine resources and project itself as a firm state with necessary wherewithal or as a tool for conflict resolution has not been exercised.

(f) **India's Environmental Concerns**

Though the entire South Asian region is grappling the serious threats of the grave and hazardous effects of climate change, yet India being the most populous is at the pivot of these changes. India after its liberalisation reforms initiated in the early 90s experienced rapid economic growth. India witnesses GDP growth nearing 10% in some of these high growth years, yet it also manifested in unwelcome environmental problems affecting the infant mortality rate and life expectancy due to the high air and water pollution levels. The situation of Indian cities is among the world's worst as 11 of the 12 cities with the highest levels of PM2.5 (Particulate Matter 2.5) are located in India. Regularly measured at over 100—the US considers a safe limit to be 35—the level of PM2.5 sometimes is measured as being in the hundreds.[130] World Health Organisation has also warned that India has been experiencing the ill effects of climate change. India also is rated as the second most-affected country in terms of casualties related to extreme weather. As per some reports, a change in average weather conditions also creates 'hotspots' and has negative impacts on both the living standards of the population and also GDP. Climate change will not only affect internal areas; in mountain areas, climate change will likely affect the frequency of natural disasters. This includes increasing the likelihood of events such as landslides, but also glacial retreat in the Himalayas. On the other hand, rising sea levels represent an existential threat to several coastal areas in south Asia: not

---

[130] The Interpreter, accesses on 11 July 19 from https://www.lowyinstitute.org/the-interpreter/choking-point-india-environment-crisis.

only due to the increasing severity of tropical storms but because the large Bangladeshi share of the coast and most of the Maldives may disappear before the end of the twenty-first century.[131]

The problem is compounded by the ineffectiveness of the regulatory mechanism due to poor institutional settings and lack of enforcement. Though the problems of environmental degradation are experienced across the world, India's problems get compounded due to its high population as also the high population density and growing urbanisation. Air quality in Indian cities is quickly deteriorating and it is today worse than the situation in China: in the 2018 World Health Organisation (WHO) global ambient air quality database, 11 of the 12 cities with the highest levels of small particulate—PM2.5—are located in India.'[132] The key problems faced by India include vehicular and industrial emissions, chemical and oil pollutions, lack of adequate sanitation, disposal and management of municipal waste, agricultural practices including logging and deforestation and stubble burning, and so on. The situation in November, December, and January becomes immensely critical due to the atmospheric conditions of low temperatures and human-induced post-monsoon biomass (stubble) burning by the farmer communities of Haryana, Punjab, and other countryside. These environmental problems lead to greater health and other social problems faced by the people which lead to a burden on human and economic costs. Chronic illnesses are also one of how the effects of environmental problems are encountered other than lower life expectancy and high infant mortality. The resultant cost due to these issues is lower productivity, poor quality of life, high level of misery, and other human rights issues.

The rural population still uses biomass extensively as fuel leading to health disorders as well as high infant mortality rates. The reliance on coal to power the thermal power plant leads to greater pollution and shows no signs of declining shortly. The forest cover has been worrisomely depleting too. The illegal cutting of trees, especially in the once forest-rich North-Eastern part of the country, is progressing with no checks. The depletion of underground water levels s also waste management is

---

[131] Enrico D'Ambrogio, India: Environmental Issues, EPRS, European Parliamentary Research Service, PE 637.920, April 2019.

[132] Ibid.

areas of concern. As per a report of NITI Aayog, India is placed at 120 in a list of 122 countries, on water quality index.

Though several programmes have been launched by the Government of India like Ujjawala Yojana (clean cooking scheme), Ujala Yojana (focus on energy-saving lighting), Swachh Bharat (Clean India), Namimi Gange (Clean Ganga), Smart Cities Mission and many others, yet there has been no let-up in the prevailing pollution levels or improvement in the environment.

The Indian Government has launched a National Clean Air Programme (NCAP) as a national-level strategy to tackle the air pollution problem in the country. As per the plan, there is a target to reduce air pollution by 20% to 30% over a graded and gradual manner with the index year taken as 2017. There is a Graded Response Action Plan (GRAP) to measure and report the AQI (Air Quality Index) and its categorisation has been made as Moderate to Poor, Very Poor, Severe, and Severe + or Emergency. The central government has also launched an application, called 'SAMEER' for providing air quality information to the public. This app also has a feature to lodge complaints on air pollution to the controller.

India also launched the International Solar Alliance (ISA) and is eagerly seeking membership of the world community to this alliance to switch over from conventional energy reliance to greater emphasis on renewable means. Though the most benefits of solar power can be harnessed between the Tropics of Cancer and Tropic of Capricorn, India is openly welcoming other states also to increase the coverage of the alliance. ISA has been conceived as an action-oriented, member-driven, collaborative platform for increased deployment of solar energy technologies to enhance energy security and sustainable development, and to improve access to energy in developing member countries.[133]

India with its huge coastline, fertile plains, and foothills, and several ranges of the Himalayan mountain ranges will experience the ill effects of climate change in varying forms and details. The impact on mountains will manifest in the form of natural disasters due to events like landslides and recession in glaciers. On the coastal zones, there will be calamities like inundation and submersion of several tracts by the rise in sea levels and the exaggerated impact of tropical storms/Tsunamis and so on.

---

[133] International Solar Alliance, accessed on 12 July 19 from https://isolaralliance.org/about_us_history.php.

(g) Promise on Climate Change Agreements

The Kyoto Protocol (1997) which was signed by India had set the goal for the period from 2008 to 2012 to reduce GHGs emissions to 5.2% of 1990 levels. Yet the targets were later adjudged too high for India. The Copenhagen Accord on climate change had left it to individual countries to devise the necessary regulations and thus granted greater autonomy to fix the responsibility to reduce greenhouse gas emissions. The problem of climate change agreements is juxtaposed with the problem of addressing the problem as a global one with localised inputs and individual contributions by each country to help in curbing the problem.

India has assured a long-term commitment that its per capita emissions will never exceed that of the developed world. However, considering the lackadaisical pace of progress even on key projects there needs to be greater emphasis as well as a projection by India of its strategies, efforts, and commitment to obtain the support of Arctic countries.

(h) India's Contribution to the Cost of Cold Development

Given the foregoing, it is abundantly clear that a very difficult choice has to be made by the world community at large between economic development achieved by extraction and exploitation of the promise of huge natural resources hidden beneath and to preserve the last bastion of pristine and bountiful natural wonders. Most of the nations and people are divided into charting a middle path, of achieving some degree of balance between these scales by sustainable growth while maintaining the intricate ecological balance. Some governments, such as that of Russia, give greater weight to economic development during these uncertain global economic times, while others may be unable to afford costly infrastructure requirements or favour stronger conservation efforts.[134] Even among the Arctic nations, Russia and Norway are actively engaged in drawing out the economic development, while others have remained cautious due to the environmental concerns and/or due to the requirement of immense

---

[134] Conley Heather, Toland Terence, and Mihaela David, Arctic Economics in the 21st Century: The Benefits and Cost of Cold, Center for Strategic and International Studies, 2013, CSIS Europe Program, accessed on 1 June 2018 from https://www.csis.org/analysis/Arctic-economics-21st-century.

capital to explore the resources. The infrastructural requirements include deep-water ports, icebreakers, support vessels, satellites, helicopters and aircraft, airstrips, roads and pipelines, and so on. The entire infrastructural framework can be jolted by one oil spill that can disrupt the fragile environment with immeasurable catastrophe. India has to realise that its economic engagements in search of hydrocarbons are also contributing in one way or the other to the dismantling of existing structures in the Arctic region.

A well-thought-out and deliberate balance has also to be struck between the seeking of securing energy supplies and profits from hydrocarbons and on mitigating the environmental deterioration, exacerbated due to the former actions. It appears that current India's Arctic policy is caught between the two opposing and divergent poles of India being a responsible member of the international community with a focus on parity and proportionate burden-sharing in climate change and contrarily on being a developing country with immense demand for energy resources by involvement in emerging opportunities in the Arctic.

In August 2015, India and China along representatives from several countries including the Arctic had attended GLACIER conference. India and China, however, didn't sign the joint declaration at the end of the conference, hence raising questions on their commitment to slow the pace of global warming, with effects in the Arctic. Likewise in December 2019 at the COP 25 conference on climate change, India and USA were among the prominent countries not agreeing to a reduction in GHGs and curb emission, which sends a wrong signal about its seriousness and intent in controlling climate change.

The dilemma in the professing to the climate change goals on the one hand but simultaneously continuing with the exploration and resource exploitation activity which is leading to further greater emissions is unmistakeable. Another human-induced corollary to the rising global warming and climate change is far greater requirement which is now being felt for fuels for cooling and warming purposes.

The US has been found to be dragging its feet in meeting the climate change goals promised by it earlier and likewise has been procrastinating on imposing restrictions on its domestic polluters. Likewise in COP25, both India and China along with the USA and Brazil have also backtracked from climate change promises. The intransigence of big polluters—including China, the US, Brazil, and India—at the meeting led to the European Union, small island states, and members of the public expressing frustration.[135] The chief polluters of today including the USA, China, and India have thus been backtracking from their promises and the consequent ill effects experienced in the Arctic have to be addressed by a concerted plan by the world community. The CO_2 emissions by India stand at number 3 in the world after China and the US and this lays tremendous responsibility as India vows to accede to climate change goals, which is a difficult path as the country is still on the path of economic growth. The analysis shows that India can achieve its NDC target with currently implemented policies. (We) project the share of non-fossil power generation capacity will reach 60–65% in 2030, corresponding to a 40–43% share of electricity generation. India's emissions intensity in 2030 will be ~50% below 2005 levels. Thus, under current policies, India is likely to achieve both its 40% non-fossil target and its emissions intensity target.[136]

The analysis by the climate action tracker placed below shows that India can achieve its NDC target with currently implemented policies. However, the analysis is showing a better performance because of India possessing a massive population base, which in turn reduces the per capita carbon emissions as also since the country is battling extreme poverty in select regions, which also has an impact on per capita fossil fuel consumption. It is only a matter of time that the base parameters for measuring these indices are revised and on a holistic and broad base, India is not expected to fare better (Fig. 4.11).

(i) **India as an Observer**

The observers occupy a unique position in the Council and exercise nominal influence in the AC as the power to moderate discussion and decisions rests with the member states alone. The AC members have a stake in admitting observers as they engage with them economically with promises of investments, infrastructural development, and socio-economic development of the communities. The observers, on the other hand, have varying incentives like economic exploration, scientific

---

[135] New scientist, 2019, accessed on 17 December 2019 from https://www.newscientist.com/article/2227541-cop25-climate-summit-ends-in-staggering-failure-of-leadership/.

[136] Climate action tracker, CAT, 2019, accessed on 12 November 2019 from https://climateactiontracker.org/countries/india/.

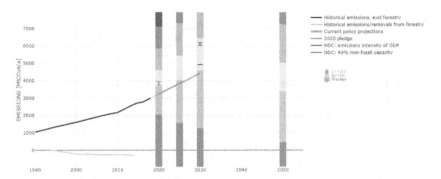

Fig. 4.11 Emissions by India, projection up to 2050 (*Source* https://climateactiontracker.org/countries/india/)

research, and diplomatic leverage, and so on. Council observers are less influential than states in the Council. Member states accept observers to make economic gains. Non-Arctic states are interested in protecting the environment as well as making potential economic gains, in contrast to the more focused motivations of member states.[137]

A normal tendency is to view India's status as an Arctic observer vis-a-vis the responses of other Asian observers, namely China, Japan, and Korea. A common fabric among these three nations is that other than political and economic issues they have expanded their sphere in other domains like terrorism, SAR, and constructive business cooperation. Such an approach is missing in India's context as India has been repeatedly embarked on scientific pursuits alone. China had purchased its ice breaker Xuelong (Snow Dragon) in 1993 from Ukraine and has been undertaking polar research since 1994. China also set up its Arctic research base in Svalbard in 2004 under the aegis of the Polar Research Institute of China. In 2013, the year in which China was accorded the Observer status, its icebreaker also undertook a journey across the NSR to Bering Strait, and while returning even skirted the NSR and followed the alignment of the transpolar route. The North-East Asian nations are also hopeful that their coastline regions will further develop and have greater cooperative arrangements with other neighbouring countries in the times to

---

[137] Andrew Chater, The Explaining Non-Arctic States in the Arctic Council. Strategic Analysis, 2016, https://doi.org/10.1080/09700161.2016.1165467.

come. China is also renting out two ports in North Korea to further fuel its exports to Europe and hydrocarbon imports from the Russian Far East. India though has remained aloof from the political participation in the AC meetings as well as by non-attendance of most of the meetings of the Working Groups as well as with Permanent Participants. This is indicative of an imbalance between India's physical scientific presences in the Arctic (e.g. Himadri station at Svalbard) and its participation in Arctic governance mechanisms.[138]

While signing the AC admission norms as an observer, each of the observer's states has acceded to abide by the governance structure, which offers the right to vote and voice on matters only to the circumpolar member states. There is another dilemma here wherein the adherence to UNCLOS claims specifically lowers the space for international scientific research as the area becomes sovereign territory with sovereign rights becoming applicable and the call for global commons is deflated.

The representation of India was done by the Secretary Ministry of Earth Sciences (MoES) Dr. M Rajeevan during the ceremony when India's observer status was renewed in May 2019, thereby downplaying the importance for the region and affirming that India considers the region as a major scientific expedition threshold and not as a region with growing inter-regional and global geostrategic significance. Also, India has though renamed NCAOR to NCPOR but has been continuously using the old acronym in the document, submitted at the international level thereby underlining that Arctic figures for India as a field for mere scientific study rather than the tremendous geostrategic place it occupies which is not in line with the professed lofty goals that India has set for herself at international level.

India's reluctance to de-emphasise its scientific interest towards a more calibrated approach that takes into account the politico-strategic-economic dimensions in the Arctic reflects the tension between the exceptionalism and the realism of its polar legacy.[139] Since Arctic Council Observer membership, as well as diplomatic relations with sovereign Arctic states, falls in the mandate of the MEA, yet India has been continuously viewing the Arctic through the scientific prism which impairs the

---

[138] Chahal Husanjot, CQEG, accessed on 22 November 19 from https://cqegheiulaval.com/india-in-the-arctic/.

[139] Sinha U.K., India in the Arctic: A Multidimensional Approach. Vestnik of Saint Petersburg University. International Relations, 2019, vol. 12, issue 1, pp. 113–126.

geopolitical and geostrategic view, which is critical for India to enhance its position and credibility in the region.

(j) **Investments**

It is assessed that India's lukewarm response to Russia's calls for investments in its Arctic oil and gas projects will further tilt the geopolitics of energy in favour of China and other European countries. In any case, the European market has been a priority for Russia, since it brings Russia both economic and geopolitical benefits as well as its relative geographical proximity. Russia views its energy resources as a key strategic asset. India was allowed to invest in the Sakhalin-1 project on very favourable terms because of political considerations. As compared to oil, gas offers less flexibility as its transportation requires huge investments in laying pipelines and trains. This also entails securing and establishing long-term and strategic partnerships for its success as the gestation is longer. India must get involved in Eurasian oil and gas projects, not only for its energy security but for political and strategic considerations since Eurasia is likely to remain an important centre of global geopolitics. As a long-time trusted friend and strategic partner of Russia, India could expect Russia to be positively inclined towards its quest for access to Eurasian energy.[140]

Demand for oil will increase because of increasing urbanisation and development of the transport sector, whereas the demand for gas will be driven primarily by the power and fertiliser sectors (80%) and some from the transport and household sectors. Unfortunately, India's indigenous oil and gas production has reached a plateau.[141]

India's bilateral ties with some of the Arctic countries are marred with political manoeuvring. India-Sweden defence cooperation has been jinxed since the early days. New Delhi had not favoured Viggen fighters over Jaguars in the 1970s and even the Gripen lost the race for India MMRCA to Rafale. The Bofors scandal had soured the relations not too long ago. India and Norway had sourness over the latter's support for LTTE in Sri Lanka. There have been other prominent grouses by India on lack of

---

[140] Rajiv Sikri, The Geopolitics of Energy Security and Implications for South and Southeast Asia, ISAS, 2008, accessed on 12 November 2019 from www.isas.nus.edu.sg

[141] Ibid.

adequate investment by sovereign funds in India and so on. However, the maturity between the nations is on a high note and issues of prominence like climate change, human security, terrorism, etc., are holding the mantle showing both the maturity and rounded development of bilateral ties.

(k) Lack of Strategic Vision

The conservatism in Indian Policy is marked with a myopic view wherein the Indian Policymakers are yet to take a long-term view of the exceptionally grave challenges that are unravelling in the Arctic. Thus, India's policy on the Arctic has been one of conservatism and caution till now and the long-term goals have not been enunciated.

The Indian Foreign Policy, which is often a highly individualistic affair and shifts with the focus and orientation of the top Indian Foreign Service officers and also carries the idealistic and ideological framework of the Nehruvian era.[142] Miller (2013) explained India's lack of strategic vision in foreign policymaking is attributed to the fact that New Delhi's foreign policy decisions are often highly individualistic. Although foreign policy decisions are entrusted with the Prime Minister's office, the National Security Council, and the Ministry of External Affairs, Indian Foreign Service officers fill all three offices and their top positions. Indian Foreign officers are given a high level of autonomy and allowed to make individualistic decisions, which result in bottom-up foreign policy that lacks a long-term view and strategic vision.[143] The stark contrast between the feats among the Asian countries granted observers' status in 2013, especially among China and India, is apparent by the economic, strategic, and geopolitical leaps by the former while India has been found to be constricted by the lack of a clear strategic direction.

Resultantly, policy decisions are strongly influenced by personalities, political elites, and the bureaucracy.[144] Since there is no streamlined and

---

[142] Nikhil Pareek, India in a Changing Arctic: An Appraisal, Ecocycles, 2020, vol. 6, issue. 1, pp. 1-9.

[143] Aki Tonami, Asian Foreign Policy in a Changing Arctic, The Diplomacy of Economy and Science at New Frontiers, Palgrave Pivot, 2016, ISBN 978-1-137-53746-1 (eBook), https://doi.org/10.1057/978-1-137-53746-1.

[144] U. Sinha, India in the Arctic: A Multidimensional Approach. Vestnik of Saint Petersburg University. International Relations, 2019, vol. 12, issue 1, pp. 113-126.

defined policy outcome and objectives, there is a serious departure with the change in personalities and political dispensation which has a negative consequence on the stability, direction, and approach to key issues.

(l) **Difference in Polar Funding**

The research bases in both the Poles also act as a common interface for scientific and quasi-diplomatic engagement between the nations. The research presence of several Asian states as observer states in the Arctic leads to the establishment and strengthening of inter- and intraregional connections. Collaboration and data sharing concerning Arctic research stations are key instruments for integrating rising Asia in the Arctic in a peaceful way.[145] The research bases discreetly also act as pillars of geopolitical engagement and indirectly this scientific diplomacy ushers in peace and prevent conflict situations. Though, India like most other observers has been focussing more on the Antarctic than the Arctic. As per data available on NCPOR Annual Report 2018–19, there is a huge difference in the funds allotted and allocated in the funding between the Antarctic and Arctic. The same is seen clearly in Fig. 4.12.

The figures for grant in aid from the Ministry of Earth Sciences received for Antarctic Research in the year ending 31 March 2018 were Rs 1,169,933,123 against Rs 67,671,619 for the Arctic Programme. In terms of percent, the figure stands at 5.78%, while in the year 2019, the figures were Rs 899,071,401 and Rs 77,714,731, respectively, and the percentage at 8.64%. Other than these figures for grant in aid, the expenditure by NCPOR for the Antarctic for the year ending 2018 and 2019 was 1,041,741,145 and Rs 761,680,634, respectively.[146] The corresponding figures for Arctic research were Rs 53,944,009 and Rs 59,831,128 in 2018 and 2019. The percentage for the Arctic to Antarctic

---

[145] Michael Evan Goodsite, Rasmus Gjedssø Bertelsen, Sandra Cassotta Pertoldi-Bianchi & Jingzheng Ren Lize-Marie van der Watt & Halldor Johannsson, The Role of Science Diplomacy: A Historical Development and International Legal Framework of Arctic Research Stations Under Conditions of Climate Change, Post-Cold War Geopolitics and Globalization/Power Transition. J Environ Stud Sci, 2016, vol. 6, pp. 645–661, https://doi.org/10.1007/s13412-015-0329-6.

[146] NCPOR Annual Report 2018 and Annual Report 2019, accessed on 23 November 19 from http://www.ncaor.gov.in/annualreports.

SCHEDULES FORMING PART OF INCOME & EXPENDITURE ACCOUNT
FOR THE YEAR ENDED 31-03-2019

Amount in ₹

SCHEDULE-7 Grant-in-aid	31-03-2019	31-03-2018
1. From Central Government-MoES, New Delhi		
1. Antarctic Research	899,071,401	1,169,933,123.00
2. Establishment of Third Station in Antarctica	247,495,647	251,919,961.00
3. Southern Oceanographic Studies	41,875,899	209,643,199.00
4. NCPOR	218,520,623	187,201,782.00
5. In-House R&D	1,320,133	2,052,830.00
6. Indian Arctic Programme	77,714,731	67,671,619.00
7. Ice Class Research Vessel	2,166,118	2,124,523.00
8. CLCS Programme	4,169,363	5,242,731.00
9. Integrated Ocean Drilling Programme (IODP)	4,492,158	5,825,189.00

Fig. 4.12 NCPOR, income, and expenditure account (*Source* NCPOR Annual Report, 2018–2019)

research on a year-to-year basis for 2018 and 2019 is thus 5.17% and 7.85%.

The Indian Arctic programme is relatively new as compared to the Antarctic programme and can offer various diplomatic and strategic levers for expanding India's stature and influence in the North. The Chinese example of economic engagement with the Arctic countries has led to its mercurial rise in the Arctic affairs, so much so that even the USA is getting sceptical of its bilateral ties. Unlike the Antarctic which is governed by treaty obligations, the loose intergovernmental structure provides a multitude of opportunities to the observers to participate and enhance the discourse, yet Indian efforts are more focussed on the South, thereby the geostrategic significance of the High North is being disregarded which needs to be remedied urgently.

The availability of hydrocarbon resources in the Arctic is established but a key uncertainty remains that of the timeframe and possibility of resource extraction by the respective Arctic states, which hold rights over the exploitation of resources lying in their Exclusive Economic Zones (EEZ). The staking of claims over the EEZ, some of them with overlapping boundaries, has prompted certain states to see their national security and sovereignty at risk and this realm poses the potential of a possible conflict.

Surprisingly, the major Arctic powers, i.e. the USA, Russia, and Canada, are articulating their risks by enunciating the threats and justifying their positions. They are concurrently gearing up their hard power and military manoeuvres which pose the threat of escalation and actual conflict. The increase in hard security by militarisation, installing of radars and EW devices, and beefing up of military bases by nations has a corollary in mirroring of these by the perceived adversary. The big three of the Arctic are the leaders in risk representation and escalatory confrontational actions.

The dynamics of conflict in the Arctic can be viewed from the prisms of expansion of national coastal limits by staking claims to extended continental shelves, growing geopolitical power games, exploration and energy policies of states with divergent and conflicting of interests, and the nationalisation of sea passages like the Northern Sea Route (NSR) by Russia. The geopolitical play and impact of external events like the 2014 Ukraine crisis, with Russia annexing Crimea, can jeopardise the relations in the AC and the Arctic region. The structures to deal with security and military issues in the AC like the Northern Chiefs of Defence Forum and the Arctic Security Forces Roundtable have thus been found to be jammed/rendered standstill. The impact of non-Arctic states like China which has also become increasingly active in the region poses the threat to circumvent the Arctic legal order.

Among the Arctic states, Canada had expressed reservations over Russia's sole control over NSR, notwithstanding similar quagmire over the NWP. Canada's extension of the NORAD (North American Aerospace Defence Command) with the USA asserts the linkages between Canada's sovereignty, security, and defence along its Northern borders. The USA has been growingly becoming assertive and vocal on the Arctic becoming the geopolitical and geo-economic playground impacting American security. With the disputation on the NSR with Russia, the USA has cited that Bering Strait can turn into a strategic chokepoint. Likewise Russia with its 7000 km coastline and several rivers draining connect it with the mainland. The spatial control over NSR will afford to increase its sphere of influence in the Arctic. Russia has modernised its military capabilities and conducts military exercises. The risk representations by these states point to a growing threat of a potential conflict situation in the Arctic region in the coming times. The entry of China in the Arctic discourse has enlivened the issues of dealing with the global commons, the effects and impact of climate change outside the region, and the interests and stakes of other non-Arctic states in the region.

The Arctic region and the AC have remained the hallmark of cooperative and collaborative mechanism but certain challenges which can adversely impact include the heightened tensions between USA-Russia, undefined chartering by non-Arctic states like China, challenges from a rapidly warming environment, handling of sea passages and sovereignty and maritime borders to name a few. The existing deficiencies in lack of any structured security apparatus, weakness of the UNCLOS in dealing with conflicting claims, and so on further complicate the Arctic geostrategic realm.

CHAPTER 5

Conclusion and Recommendations

Conclusion

India occupies a prominent and unique position in the world today being bestowed with certain characteristics and credentials which include being the world's largest democracy with a rapidly growing emerging economy slated to touch USD 5 trillion very soon. The physical geography and the geopolitical role coupled with the world's second-largest population base and exceptional physical characteristics including a long coastline, deserts, and mountainous belt make it which is distinctive and hard to find in other countries. The booming economy and trade partnerships also make India an increasingly influential global player which is sustained by a mature and centrist central political leadership. India's impetus affects regional as well as global political discourse and the position adopted by India is viewed with serious anticipation the world over. Among the AC observers, India's position is also very unique as it is considered a mature, centrist, and modern democratic nation that will have a significant impact on the outcomes of fulfilling the Sustainable Development Goals as well as the global climate targets.

Since the liberalisation ushered in the early 1990s by India, the gross domestic product (GDP) has nearly tripled and India stands as the third-largest contributor to global growth, after the US and China. With its unique and diverse socio-economic conditions, the intraregional growth between the various states and union territories is also having stark contrasts. Simultaneously the demand for resources such as food, energy, and minerals with growing urbanisation and economic growth will cause increasing dependence on hydrocarbons, marine resources, and imports. The pitfalls from rapid industrialisation and economic progress will have a concurrent voluminous increase in greenhouse gas emissions from coal-fired power plants, transport sector, and spiralling energy consumption. Owing to the grave ecological situation, it is anticipated that India will experience increasingly frequent extreme weather events and disasters. India's role as a security provider in the Indian Ocean Region and as a major power in Asia in terms of security and defence policy will lead to posturing to safeguard its strategic autonomy and attach importance to the rules-based order. The peninsular strategic location and a professional and world-class defence services make India a major power in Asia in the field of security and defence.

With these characteristics comes the onerous responsibility to ensure regional peace and stability, free from external and debilitating influences. It is in India's interests that international and regional relations are conducted as per prevailing international law to avoid conflict situations and ensure the maintenance of the international legal order and strengthen multilateral governance. The problem is compounded by the fact that the Asian region is experiencing turmoil and changing balance of power and thus the responsibility becomes acute and demands a more active and influential role in global and regional forums. Though other Arctic observers like China and UK have tried to justify and fit in their respective stakes by situating 'near-Arctic' and 'sub-Arctic' in their policy statements, India has yet to define its nearness and links with the Arctic, in terms of parameters like economics, people to people contacts, common vision on climate change and environmental conservation, etc., as the other variables like geography, language, culture, and history don't afford nearness in the Indian context. India has not established any sound basis for her engagement, other than the pursuit of scientific studies and research.

With the continuously changing situation at the North Pole, witnessing record lows of the polar ice sheet melts, the avenues to exploit the vast untapped hydrocarbon deposits and shipping shortcuts are opening up to commercial and lucrative development. As a result, the Arctic is rapidly becoming globalised garnering attention of the global comity of nations including India, who are vying for a say and place in Arctic affairs.

In the present scheme of things, Arctic governance is dominated by only the regional actors, as non-Arctic states are denied an equal footing, voting rights, and proper place. This calls for raising one's footing by raising bilateral engagements to an indispensable state and letting the members speak on their behalf. In a globalised and connected world, Arctic no longer remains an insulated region, and both regional players and non-Arctic members will have to endeavour tide over the inhibiting factors. In the backdrop of these developments, the role of the Arctic region in world affairs and India's position in charting its course assumes a central position that will not only impact her internal policies but also be a trailblazing initiative for the multilateral and intergovernmental set-up in the AC. The Arctic, which has grabbed the limelight in recent years, is a central region that demands greater attention due to its role in shaping the planet's climate and weather patterns. It is also creditworthy that the region is home to exotic marine, freshwater, and terrestrial life forms the preservation of which is a common responsibility of mankind. The unique structure of the AC has also facilitated cooperation and deliberations between the scientific community, national governments, and NGOs so that effective policies are drawn. The tiered fora in spheres like business, indigenous organisations, and scientific bodies have also led to the formation of many inter- and intraregional partnerships.

India's direction in the Arctic has been focussed primarily to understand Arctic's role in affecting and causing changes in the Indian monsoons and climate. However, there has been a marked shift in the recent years where India is gradually becoming more assertive with a view towards the strategic and geopolitical significance of the region and the consequent Indian role in modulating the course. The geophysical impacts of a warming Arctic and loss of ice sheets are assessed to cause an unprecedented rise in sea levels and disruption in seasonal climatic conditions. Since the changes in the Arctic will have an impact across geographically distant regions such as India, thus it is attracting keen interest and action by stakeholders.

Governance in the Arctic region remains with the Arctic 8 with passive participation by the Observers including India which leaves the observers with limited say and role. However, the silver lining in this arrangement lies in the fact that Arctic governance is positively bound by the adherence to international law and multinational bodies and thus it is vital for India to partner with the other Asian observers and international organisations like the UNCLOS, CLCS, UNEP, UNDP, and others. Since India enjoys a friendly and positive bilateral relationship with all the Asian observers including China on international issues like terrorism, climate change, etc., it is prudent to build a mutually beneficial collaborative roadmap for engagement in the Arctic. The equation in the Arctic region is made more complex as there are several divergent states, non-state and international players, often with deviations in goals, objectives, and methodology which demands that India should chart out a policy discourse which is adapted and adopted by these diverse players which will further strengthen India's position.

Though India's scientific skills and progress in the Polar Regions have stood the test of time, yet the North still lags far behind as compared to India's Antarctic pursuits. Under the then PM Mrs. Indira Gandhi, India had embarked on the journey of scientific progress and commenced its Antarctic research earnestly. The Arctic journey had commenced in 2007 when a team of five scientists had visited the International Arctic Research facilities at Ny-Ålesund and started studies in the fields of atmospheric science, microbiology, and earth science and glaciology. On the other hand, the strategic direction of Indian efforts remains blurry and undefined in the absence of a policy framework.

The progress by India in the past six years as an observer has not evinced commensurate and regular participation in the Working Group meetings and engagement with the Permanent Participants as evinced by the responses received from nine of these and brought out in Chapter 2. The seriousness and commitment of observers are usually judged on the parameters of such involvement which still requires more active and deeper association. With the position that India occupies and the aspirations to be a global power, it is expected that India will engage in more productive and deliberate participation. Since there are several drivers of India's Arctic engagement, it is imperative that other than scientific exchanges, India also contributes to AC and its associate bodies by positive, robust, and visible participation.

The lack of a policy document outlining India's vision appears to be the first major hurdle that needs to be addressed. India's stand on global issues though has been outlined with much praise in international organisations like the UN; the urgent need of the hour is to have a deliberate strategy with key components on international scientific collaboration on climate change, sustainable development, preservation of natural refuge at the Arctic, and the Arctic as a "global knowledge commons."

Owing to certain gaps in the Indian approach enumerated in Chapter 3, it appears that India is yet to harness its full potential in the Arctic region, considering its historical, cultural, diplomatic, and scientific skills and there is scope for much-needed impetus. The areas for enhancing the scientific research potential strengthened economic linkages and developing deeper bilateral relations are the prominent ones calling for renewed focus. India's core strengths lie in her commitment to institutional and broad-based cooperative arrangements and it is high time to garner strategic direction by the renewed focus on climate change, scientific research, and strengthening the AC structure which will result in enhanced international acclaim and clout.

With a time tested partnership with Russia, India needs to strengthen its friendship to reap rich benefits for both the countries as both are large powers having stakes in the future balance of power. China which is rapidly emerging as a global power has its neighbours in both Russia and India and both exercise considerable influence concerning the Arctic waters and for the Indian Ocean region, respectively. The promise that India-Russia friendship holds will have a telling impact on the course of the future on the Arctic as well as the brewing second cold war and importantly for their future as well. India, by its strategic hold and position, is among the dominant state in the Indo-Pacific region while Russia is becoming the main player in the Arctic-Pacific circuit. Since the trade, as well as hydrocarbon routes, has to rely on these routes, the position of India and Russia is complementary to each other and will help in boosting trade.

After India's admission to the AC as an observer in 2013, there was a high profile visit to the Scandinavian countries by the President in 2014 which laid a foundation for strengthening the political and economic partnerships with the Arctic states. The Scandinavian countries have an edge in maintaining world peace as well as leadership in clean energy, communications, and defence. Norway has been assisting India with both its capital and technical expertise in developmental aid as well as for scientific research as an observer. A connected corollary to India's observer status is the entry of China, which had raised heckles on these two observers bringing their rivalry in the Arctic and disrupting the Arctic governance structures. However, both countries have acted maturely and there is greater promise in a cooperative and collaborative arrangement. The great power competition has not been extended to the Arctic by India and it stands by her commitment to environmental protection, sustainable development, and responsible economic development and such actions have earned accolades.

India has not expressed any inclination to participate in military exercise/engagement in the Arctic and low-level participation in marine rescue exercises/ SAR will assist in establishing some military contacts. India's legacy and historical ties lay testimony to the stated objectives of promoting economic development and environmental preservation by adherence to multilateral policies and existing structures for a greater good and India's position is slated to increase in the coming days.

Among the various non-Arctic Observer States' interests revolve around the resource supply as well as sectoral challenges. The gravest challenge which finds a common thread is the global concern manifesting in the disruptions caused due to climate change. One major disadvantage/hindrance though which has been observed is that there is no mechanism for interaction and political coordination among the diverse Arctic observers. Neither has been any political outfit constituted even though on many issues the observers speak in one voice and such a mechanism could have not only strengthened the observers but also assisted in the governance regime of the AC.

Among the five Asian Observers, the three North-Eastern states, viz. China, Japan, and ROK/Korea, also figure prominently as the world's leading maritime nations. The maritime dimension of these states differentiates these from India substantially as they ascribe the elements of maritime business, shipbuilding, and shipping and the financial muscle to equip themselves for the challenges opening with the operationalisation of new shipping routes in the Arctic. The narrative from Korea and Japan in viewing the NSR as a potential route for shorter energy supplies is more modest as compared to China. Thus even among the North-East Asian states, there is caution as well as restraint concerning both the financial/economic sense for investments in the Arctic and the political and economic risks emerging there from. India as an observer stands quite distant from these Asian states as it lacks the experience in shipping and shipbuilding as also the immediate benefits of a shorter destination shipping don't affect her as much as the former. Hence the Indian approach has to be more focussed on the political and geostrategic dimension emerging in the Arctic which rather makes the Indian position more advantageous if India plays her position deftly.

The granting of observer status to five Asian countries (and Italy) in 2013 was an acknowledgement of the growing economic and political significance of these countries, yet in the last six years the progress among these five nations has varied substantially. While China has made progress by leaps and bounds there are mixed results for the others. With the mercurial progress in science, the rapidly transforming Arctic has caught hold of the world community with talks afoot on the impact such transformation will have on the opening of shipping passages, resource extraction, growth of transit, and destination shipping trade which will offer a mixed bag of both disputes and prospects.

In this situation, the most demanding responsibility falls on developing and advancing nations like India which has considerable clout in the international sphere and enjoys support from multiple nations in the Arctic region. India also has long-standing strategic competition with China and many powers view India as a countervailing force to China. India has deftly and maturely managed its strategic autonomy without engaging in outgrown commitments. India has handled both China and the US, key players in the Arctic without any substantial interruptions, as both are its top trade partners and hold key to India's growth into a prominent regional power. India prides itself on its historical link to the Arctic by the 1920 Spitsbergen Treaty and the huge physical divide between her and Arctic does not provide an obstacle to further her scientific and strategic interests. India also stakes claim to the Arctic table by having a huge mass of ice sheets in its backyard, the Himalayas, the largest repository of ice outside of the Polar Regions. The adverse impact of ice melting in Poles is impacting the weather conditions, seasonal monsoon rainfall, and sea-level rise around India and thus forms the backbone of India's justification for its interest in the Arctic. As a major democratic power, India promises to work on the principles of multilateral cooperation and cooperative inclusion in the AC, values which are universally acknowledged and accepted, owing to India's promise and commitments.

The non-Arctic nations are interested and look to the Arctic in light of future considerations as the region will witness amplified opportunities that will emerge due to resource extraction, shipping, tourism, and so on. However, a concurrent corollary to this may be presented with the unravelling of external influences in the region which may have a detrimental effect on prevailing cooperation. India, since its admission in the AC, has been focussing on scientific engagement, without precisely articulating its strategic interests. It is in 2019 that after S. Jaishankar has donned the mantle of EAM, a perceptible change is noticed in Indian policy with a clear assertion on resources, routes, and national strategy. There are fears that great power rivalries, often by matters outside the Arctic, may manifest in Arctic affairs, unduly skewing the environment. The India–China relations will also have to stand this test.

The concept of Arctic isolationism appears to be a pipe dream because of the globalisation and integration of the world nations and though certain quarters had preferred that segregation of Arctic from outside influence yet it is difficult to achieve. China and India have emerged as rapidly progressing global economies, with a tremendous appetite for energy requirements and vibrant interconnected economies. A minor slowdown in these economies has the potential to slow down global growth too. India's interests in the Arctic can be summarised concerning fulfilling its energy security, the opening of new routes, impact on natural resources due to climate change, and growing international competition. Till 2019, more than 6 years after becoming an observer and 12 years after installing its research station, India yet remains a new and young player in the region. There is a divergence in India's gains with the changing geo-economic stature of the Arctic as India's edge in enforcing its military doctrine on China is getting eroded with the opening of NSR as also the operationalisation of 'Power of Siberia' and other Sino-Russo economic and energy ventures. However, India possesses an inherent advantage as a counterbalance to China, which is being viewed increasingly with suspicion and scepticism in the region, and India has to deftly employ means so that her stakes are not diluted with a growing China.

Till now, the strategic rivalry between India and China was witnessed in areas of border disputes, sea power, and trade but the Arctic can spiral this rivalry to newer dimensions of energy security and access to sea routes. For India, the headache is increased by the Chinese of not limiting its engagement only to NSR but the PSR's goal and objective of deep economic integration with the Polar region. Hence the transportation and communication realm of Russia's NSR will be expounded by political, institutional, and commercial instruments. The Chinese core expertise of massive and rapid industrialisation, urbanisation, and infrastructural prowess will fit the bill of the small Arctic nations' aspirations. Since the Arctic region can also provide abundant raw materials and minerals to sustain Chinese industries on an assured basis, the supply chains, inventories, and the markets if attuned to the Chinese promise will leave the Indians on economic isolation. The Chinese terrestrial connection with the Arctic region will see further impetus when soon to be commissioned rail connection between Narvik and Xian crossing through Russia; Kazakhstan is made operational. The Yiwu-London rail link has already been running. Hence, the NSR connectivity has inbuilt redundancy already in place with other connectivity plans.

India has enjoyed the upper hand in areas of soft power and information services. And despite grabbing a mammoth size of the Indian market, the Chinese view India as a potent challenge not only to its expansion but also the democratic ideals, pluralistic society, and so on. Indian challenge also becomes bigger when viewed in terms of its association with Quad, Indo-Pacific, and potency of IN. The manner in which India can exert on maritime choke points like Strait of Malacca, Sunda, Lombok, Hormuz, and the Persian Gulf makes China anxious. The aggressive posturing by China in the South China Sea is being quoted by the USA to whip up the sentiment in Arctic discourse as is evidenced by the events of 2019. These actions of China are also viewed with suspicion by the neighbouring littoral countries, some of them with whom India enjoys strategic partnerships too, which causes sullenness in China. Though India's trade deficit with China is a whopping $51 billion yet the two economies have become so entwined that any knee-jerk reactions will be counterproductive.

In the short term, India though can draw solace from the fact that countries sceptical of China will put their bets on India. The first among these players is the USA and China has to deal with India as a counterbalance. Because of this, when engagement in the Arctic is at nascent stage and battle lines yet to be drawn, it will be prudent for India to broaden its engagements both bilaterally with Arctic nations and through the mechanism of AC. Eurasia is likely to remain an important centre of global geopolitics. If India remains committed to an overarching India-United States strategic relationship, which has already had a negative fallout on India's relations with Russia, there is not much hope for a meaningful India-Russia energy relationship. Thus India has to balance its strategy, association, and dialogue with Russia and the USA in a way so that the other partner is not antagonised and a strategic balance is maintained.

Since GHGs and climate change impact the world community at large and at diverse locations as witnessed in the recent floods in Venice, bush fires and flash floods in Australia, and so on the geophysical changes in the Arctic are having and will continue to have impacts over the globe. This phenomenon has a unifying impact as it joined the economic, security agendas of the Arctic and other regions together. This is changing the architecture and strategic boundaries, allies, and networks, and India has to view the same in light of its national strategic interests.

Various scholars have enunciated that the exploration and climate change in the Arctic in itself present a paradox/dilemma or an antithesis. On the one hand, the nations' desire to uplift the economic status of their population by engaging in the commercial exploitation of their resources while simultaneously bowed down by the challenges to maintain the ecological balance and continue to the sustainable development of their indigenous people. These terms amply cover the predicament of fulfilling responsibility towards the environment or to progress the socio-economic upliftment of their populations. However, there are stark contrasts within the various states on issues like exploration and ecological preservation with varying parameters; hence the dilemma and paradox get further widened.

India is occupying a position different from the USA and China and can assume the leadership position by showing its tangible commitments to the world and Arctic nations in particular. All stakeholders are engaging the Arctic region, multilaterally and bilaterally through dialogue, treaties, regulations, and incentives, to ensure that the impacts of climate change and environmental degradation are curbed and the region develops sustainably.[1] Democratic countries have been conducting debates on the Arctic region as well as on goals and commitments at COP (Conference of the Parties) under the UN FCCC. India, due to its geostrategic location should view the Arctic from a different perspective as the conditions favouring China do not apply to her. The economics of shorter routes and savings of time, in the case of India, are not so different from the existing southern routes than the Arctic ones. Hence its considerations have to be abreast of the reality that unlike gains that accrue to North-East Asia, her situation doesn't merit greater windfalls.[2]

Since India does not possess the financial muscle to match the Chinese investments, a strategy to question the Chinese attempts in Greenland and Iceland, as happened in Hambantota, Sri Lanka, of turning the small counties into strategic vassals through debt-trap diplomacy will have to be addressed at both bilateral and multilateral fora.[3]

---

[1] Nikhil Pareek, supra note 142 in Chapter 4.

[2] Nikhil Pareek, supra note 142 in Chapter 4.

[3] Ibid.

Given the increasingly assertive foreign policy and strategic direction by India, buoyed by the respected political leadership and international acclaim it is now the opportune time for India to assert its role and position in Arctic affairs. The Indian position is hugely influenced by the deep and strong bilateral relationship it enjoys with the USA, Russia, and other Scandinavian and Nordic states. India's active participation in scientific endeavours at multilevel bodies in the Arctic has been adequately acknowledged and appreciated yet there is further scope to enhance it manifold. There are other parameters to widen the engagement into areas of conservation of the pristine natural environment and limit the adverse effects of climate change globally. The suggested roadmap for greater and effective participation by India in Arctic affairs is given in the following recommendations.

Recommendations

Given the foregoing, it emerges that though India has been involved in the Arctic yet there is much greater potential for deeper involvement and broader engagement considering, there are immense geostrategic and geopolitical opportunities waiting to unravel. Among the various parameters of participation with the Arctic states and the AC, it emerges that though India has progressed its scientific pursuits with aplomb the same cannot be said of the wide politico-economic-strategic dimension at tiered levels within the framework of the AC. A prominent silver lining is seen with the signing of the recent India-Russia strategic partnership as well as assertions by the current External Affairs Minister underlining the geostrategic significance of the region.

It is also learned reliably that the National Security Council Secretariat (NSCS) had also convened a multi-organisation meeting with the participation of officials of the MEA, MoES, and NCPOR, to formulate a broad-based and holistic policy on India's engagement with the Arctic region. The donning of policy mantle by the MEA to chart out the foreign policy position as well as tiered engagement at various levels will provide the much-needed policy discourse and impetus to India's position. The highlighting of the clear government position on the exploitation of resources, energy supplies, governance, and adherence to a rules-based order, etc., will not only enunciate clarity on Indian position but also integrate the multiple agencies and bodies in a seamless arrangement for tangible and noticeable gains. The following are the chief recommendations for strengthening and revitalising India's engagement with the Arctic:

Formulate Official Policy (Framework)

India is not accustomed to an institutionalised doctrinal approach commonly referred to as official/white papers. Channels of inputs into policymaking from non-partisan experts remain unstructured and impromptu. This lethargy and non-committal approach is in stark contrast to the advocacy of India as an inclusive, pluralistic democracy and ambitions of a world Guru. The dominant narrative in India's Arctic policy remains focussed on science and scientific research which is conservative in its outlook.

Both Korea and Japan had preceded China in issuing out a comprehensive Arctic policy. Nations like Germany who have no territorial connection with the Arctic have also issued the policy on the region, considering its tremendous impact on international economics, trade, climate change as well as research and technology. There are interconnected issues like freedom of navigation, control of straits, adherence to UNCLOS, dispute resolution, etc., involving countries with which India has traditional and historic friendship; hence the view adopted by India will have considerable merit. The changing geopolitical landscape in Arctic though demands that sustainable resource development, as well as looming dangers of environmental degradation, **is** spelt out clearly by stakeholders like India. It is high time that this is transformed into a firm assertion with clearly defined goals and outcomes.

In terms of semantics, India has to be careful in drawing out a policy framework/white paper rather than a strategy as some of the sovereign states of the AC may feel embittered if a strategy is put across by a non-member over territories under their jurisdiction.[4] This policy (framework) document should bring out the priorities, key focus areas, and commitments of the Indian government for a mutually beneficial lasting partnership. This document will have to focus on coordinated action based on best practices and hope for a better and sustainable future for humankind. This will also entail regular revisions, in line with changing geopolitical environment and modifications by the Indian government,

---

[4] Ibid.

to suit her requirements.[5] This is critical, as there is no domestic control over international events and the environment, which is ever-changing.[6] A suggested index of India's policy framework for the Arctic Region may include defining the following parameters:

(a) Vision
(b) Vectors
(c) Policy
(d) Execution
(e) Results and Analysis and
(f) Participation in Working Groups.

Considering the global ambitions that India nurtures requires that it states its vision to be declared and effectively communicated to all concerned. Though the Arctic states have preferred to keep non-Arctic states at an arm's length but with greater globalisation and integration, it is imperative to formulate lasting partnerships by transparent and open communication. The rights of indigenous people maintaining security in a growing alarmist environment also demand a concrete policy approach.

Though the economic and commercial benefits of the shortened transit passage of NSR do not impact India as much as to North-East Asian states due to its geographical location, yet there are more pressing issues like GHG emissions, climate change, ice cover recession, etc., impacting the Arctic, on which India's policy is keenly awaited and sought by the AC states and others. On several transactional issues like business, diplomacy, and science to get a comprehensive and integral view on long-term strategic interests will require a streamlined and precise policy framework as also cooperation and participation within the established structures.

Emphasise Scientific Diplomacy

Science can play a larger role in shaping foreign policy and mould interstate relations and thus is an invisible organ of the state power to extend its reach. Science diplomacy stood its ground, even during heightened tensions between Russia and the Western nations during the Crimean

[5] Ibid.
[6] Ibid.

and Ukraine crises and thus it served as a valuable link between the states in near political conflict situations. Scientific endeavours and its enlargement into avenues like opening new research stations and participation in multi-institution research projects like MOSAiC also can cement the legitimacy of one's national claims. Other than conducting valuable research to understand and share the climatological, environmental, and other scientific disciplines, this tool also establishes one's credibility as a responsible stakeholder while asserting the sovereign claims of Arctic states.

It is due to scientific cooperation that rising Asian powers including India have been peacefully included in the Arctic region. A very pertinent example of flawless cooperation in science diplomacy is that despite China and Norway having extremely strained diplomatic and political relations because of the grant of Nobel Peace Prize to dissident Liu Xiaobo in 2010, it did not impact the Chinese Yellow River research station in Svalbard and Sino-Norwegian Arctic science collaboration continues. In effect, states and institutions are applying science as a tool of diplomacy to demonstrate a presence in the Arctic Ocean and to foster cooperation independent of political, economic, or cultural dynamics.[7] India should follow the Chinese model of science diplomacy wherein China had announced its first overseas satellite data receiving station in the Swedish Arctic, cooperation with Iceland to establish the China-Iceland Aurora Observatory (CIAO) at Kárhóll, and plans to open a Polar Research Institute of China at Tuktoyaktuk, Canada, and so on. The efforts at continued scientific diplomacy should be promoted by way of joint research in climate change and changing the Arctic environment. The focus on geography, climatology (especially climate change), geology, glaciology, and oceanography must continue along with newer avenues like digitalisation efforts, laying of submarine cables, and so on.

57 scientists from 18 national institutions, organisations, and universities have participated in the Indian Arctic Programme. The organisations include Geological Survey of India (GSI), Centre for Cellular and Molecular Biology, Space Applications Centre, Bhabha Atomic Research Centre and National Geophysical Research Institute among others. Other than scientific disciplines, arts, cultures, films, newer media, and knowledge

---

[7] Donald L. Gautier et al., Assessment of Undiscovered Oil and Gas in the Arctic. Science, 2009, vol. 234, 1175–1179.

domains should be progressed so that there is greater understanding and response between India and Arctic 8.

India is in an advantageous position as it harbours no militaristic ambitions in the Arctic and it may derive benefit and also gain the trust of Arctic 8 by suggesting that the terms on scientific research being 'limited to peaceful purposes' as stated in UNCLOS be amplified. In light of divergent geopolitical interests of various nations, the need for greater transparency in scientific activity may assuage the genuine misgivings about certain assertive countries. An enunciated policy with the explicit interconnection between science and law and clarifying the role of research stations will ensure that research stations are used effectively for peaceful purposes. A leadership role can be taken by India in this direction to update and strengthen the legal framework and to ensure that research interests are managed effectively. The view of the Arctic to a non-scientist with knowledge of defence studies, security architecture and policy formulation, strategic and tactical insights, and military infrastructure will be quite in contrast to the above. India must formulate greater involvement of diverse scientific pursuit to obtain a comprehensive and broad view of the situation and recommended options. India should enhance its financial, scientific, and political resources for Arctic research and formulate long-term policies for its Arctic engagement.

South Korea launched the Asian Forum for Polar Sciences (AFoPS) in 2004 with China and Japan as founding members and in 2006, India and Malaysia joined the Forum. India must leverage this powerful coterie on scientific cooperation and later extend its mandate to cover governance and legal regime in the Arctic. It will be beneficial to the group when their joint and collaborative voices are considered favourably in the AC, for better economic dividends. The utilisation of the existing AFoPS can be turned into a collaborative scientific discussion forum between the Asian Arctic observers, for which India should take the lead.

Policies on Indigenous Population

The AC has extended extensive participation to the indigenous population groups in all activities of the Council. India should take a cue from this in governance issues, especially in rural backward areas so that there is strengthened networking between indigenous peoples' associations and a greater say in policies and schemes so that the fruits of economic development reach them. The representation and participation by India's indigenous groups in AC and especially PP's deliberations will strengthen India's standing in the AC and provide India reliable partners to stand by her side during trying times. India's indigenous groups should partner with international NGOs or form a grouping and seek membership as an NGO observer for heightened interaction and cooperation with the PPs for greater and long-term rewards.

Among the non-Arctic Asian Observers, only China and India have resident indigenous population groups. India has tried to sustain and maintain these populations in the natural habitats with minimal interference preserving their centuries-old rituals, livelihoods, and way of life. The indigenous people in AC are accorded very high status as PPs at the top level with the member states. Given the special status accorded to these persons at Arctic/AC and also because China with its authoritarian and stifling opposition to diverse ethnic groups like the Uighurs, Tibetans will not allow the participation of such indigenous persons with outside world and AC, India must utilise this lever to effectively engage with the PPs. This will not only endear India to the PPs and assist in furthering India's developmental agenda with the nation-states having PP populations but also garner support and mutual identification for greater benefits.

India's Stakes

India prides itself on certain unique parameters like a wondrous largest successful democratic model, a phenomenally large economy, and an even larger population and being a role model for growing economies and developing countries. It also harbours an aspiration to play an increasingly central role on the world stage, for which India is striving to obtain a United Nations Security Council seat. India has also carefully balanced its growing energy requirements with deftness and it has to evolve a determined, coordinated, and sustained long-term strategy to ensure its energy security because of the changing dynamics of the opening of Arctic shipping lanes and access to Arctic resources. India should involve subject experts, academicians, and scientists over and above the diplomats to obtain a tiered and multilevel understanding of the issues and participation.

Fighting Climate Change

The warming Arctic will have disastrous, unyielding, and unprecedented effects on sea-level rise, droughts, floods, and changes in crop yields all across the globe. India derives its stakes in the Arctic from the ill effects of climate change on corresponding and meteoric fall in agriculture production and other effects on agricultural issues coupled with threats of inundation of coastal centres due to rising sea levels. The reverberations will be experienced in far off Maldives, India, and others which will experience drastic volatilities in weather patterns impacting the socio-economic conditions.

Climate change had a role in converting the Arctic from a flourishing habitat of woolly mammoths and other now-extinct animals to a barren desolate place. Climate change, though has an uncanny and immeasurable occurrence, waiting to again transform the Arctic and the onus and responsibility lies on not only the Arctic states, and other members of the AC but the world community as a whole to see that the future of the Arctic, which is inextricably tied to other areas of human habitation, does not spiral out uncontrollably to cause unexpected misery and suffering. The policies and decisions are taken now may steer the course for our generations to repent or marvel at the natural wonder that is the Arctic. Rather climate change gives a unique geosyncretic opportunity to India to not only exert its influence on global environmental politics but also blunt some geostrategic advantages of its adversaries by calling for global participation to cease endless exploitation in the Arctic. This dimension of soft power diplomacy by disassociating itself from a military-security perspective but propagating the environmental concerns, it may still be able to not only attain parity with other aspiring global powers and also establish itself as a responsible power, harbouring no expansionist ambitions.

There is a need to fight climate change at all levels. There must be strong measures at the international level, supplemented at the regional level, under the framework of UNFCCC to weed out industrial pollutants that will go a long way in addressing some issues. There is a need to adhere to Timelines, Targets, and Milestones by all the stakeholders committing to implement and monitor the goals laid down under the framework of the Convention on Biological Diversity, Regional Seas Programme of UNEP (United Nations Environment Programme). Time to do something, of course, is running out. Rapidly unfolding events in the Arctic will soon overwhelm the ability of decision-makers to do anything meaningful about rising sea levels, coastal erosion, and powerful storms that are extending their reach farther and farther inland. India can no longer expect to rely on mere promises to curb environmental pollution, reduce GHGs, and so on. Neither the passive presence in polar research stations like Himadri alone is going to make up for concrete actions that it must make to establish its credentials as a responsible power committed to a green earth.

Third Pole Vision and Asian Partnership

India can derive parallels between its Antarctic expedition's scientific expertise and legacy as also the state having the Third Pole, the Himalayas in its backyard to boast its credentials. India can put forward the Arctic governance example to build trust and foster intergovernmental cooperation to bring together India, China, Nepal, Pakistan, Bhutan, Afghanistan, and also Myanmar and Bangladesh among nations that are impacted by the developments in the Himalayan-Third Pole region. It is prudent that India's neighbours be co-opted in a broad strategy so that not only India's position is strengthened but the resources are not monopolised by certain countries alone. It will pay handsome dividends to assume support of Asian partners and assume a lead position in sustained deliberations to obtain a lucrative and mutually beneficial arrangement.[8]

Among the Asian nations, India and China have been enriched by the observer status in the AC and can bring forth the insight and experience for the region's benefit. However, the dimension of the Third Pole remains conceptual and India has not been able to integrate this into the broad Arctic discourse.[9]

The definition of the Third Pole as encompassing the Himalayas was coined by the Icelanders. Meanwhile, China which has established the research centre named the 'Third Pole Environment' refers to the same as analogous to the Tibetan Plateau. 'The Third Pole refers to the unique high-mountain region centered on the Tibetan Plateau. It stretches west to the Pamir-Hindu Kush region, east to the Hengduan Mountains, north to the Kunlun and Qilian mountains, and south to the Himalayas, encompassing over 5 million square kilometers with an average elevation of over

---

[8] Nikhil Pareek, supra note 142 in Chapter 4.
[9] Ibid.

4,000 meters above sea level.'[10] The geopolitics of the coinage and usage of this term is varied as it is visible by the statement at the conclusion of Arctic Circle's Abu Dhabi forum, 'The inspiring history of international scientific cooperation in the Arctic, including on glaciological research, is of great significance to the future study of the Third Pole / Himalayan glaciers.'[11] Meanwhile India has off late been distancing itself from the same as it evident from the speech by Secretary, West of the MEA, 'Clearly, the regional dynamics and the profiles of the countries of the Arctic region and the Himalayan region are totally different. Our preference is to refer to the Himalayas as "Himalayas" and not as the "Third Pole".'[12]

Define Energy Needs/Security

In the era of liberal globalisation, the relationship between nations hinges on the ability to fulfil the energy demands and India being a growing consumer has to diversify its energy matrix. India currently imports more than 80% of its energy requirements and predominantly it is sourced from the Middle East including Saudi Arabia, Iran, Iraq, and others. A safe bet to insure against future geopolitical risks and to ensure regular and assigned national energy requirements lies in tapping and exploring the Arctic as a major future source.[13]

One of the reasons for lacklustre Indian participation in equity participation in Arctic hydrocarbon resources can be attributed to the uncertainties associated with the exploitation in tough Arctic conditions, sanctions regime imposed by the Western powers on Russia as also the dropping oil prices which may negatively influence the Arctic energy projects implementation. The predictions concerning undiscovered Arctic oil and gas resources have a significant margin of uncertainty and it may be prudent

---

[10] Third Pole Environment, accessed at http://tpe.ac.cn/about/giance/201910/t20 191029_221836.html. Accessed on 02 August 23.

[11] Arctic Circle.org, accessed at https://www.arcticcircle.org/forums/arctic-circle-abu-dhabi-forum. Accessed on 02 August 23.

[12] Ministry of external affairs, https://mea.gov.in/Speeches-Statements.htm?dtl/36560/remarks+by+secretarywest+at+the+national+conference+on+polar+sciences+organised+by+national+centre+for+polar+and+ocean+researchncpor+vasco+da+gama+goa. Accessed on 02 August 23.

[13] Nikhil Pareek, supra note 142 in Chapter 4.

from the Indian perspective to participate in such projects in Africa, South East Asia, or Latin America which have a greater degree of certainty on the likely outcomes. India's position on hydrocarbon exploitation will also define and clarify her position as a responsible state committed to stand by its promise of preventing further environmental damage, pollution, and potential fight for resources in the sensitive Arctic region.[14] Since India has not charted out its position on the issue of resource exploration in the Arctic, its policy document and vision will convey the long-term engagement plan in the region.

Around 80% of India's s energy imports are from the Middle East region and logically India must diversify its supplies to insure against any future disruptions. Though the oil and gas from the Arctic region are lucrative, yet for optimally utilising the benefits of NSR, the areas best suited are those lying North of Hong Kong. The areas South of Hong Kong or beyond may have an equal or perhaps more benefit from the present Southern routes in terms of time, cost, seaborne threats, marine insurance, and so on. Thus given India's Geophysical location, it will not benefit directly from the Arctic shipping routes. Also, India has no claims to the hydrocarbon resources in the Arctic region, and it will have to collaborate with the other Arctic member states to fulfil its energy aspirations so as to provide concrete benefits both to her and the supplier thereof.

The comprehensive political and economic approach of the Republic of India has still not been carved out. The involvement and participation in scientific research in the fields of Oceanography, Climatology, Glaciology, etc., have been furthered but no so in the case of political, economic, and strategic engagement. To prevent any disruption in energy supplies and aggravation during times of conflict, there is a requirement to have maritime agreements on logistics services and hence inter-regional partnerships will ensure a steady flow of hydrocarbon resources. International cooperation will be at the forefront in establishing a commonly agreed to a framework for Arctic shipping lanes as well as SLOCs which will be essential for ease of traffic movement, regulation of shipping traffic, and prevent any conflict situations.

---

[14] Ibid.

Counterbalance/Co-opt China

China is emerging a global disruptionary force and is demanding its transitioned new place, which is also threatening the global order. The periods of power transition have been conflict-ridden and peaceful management of China's rise has to be handled sensitively and deftly by all stakeholders.

NATO, for the first time in the history of the alliance, formally acknowledged the "opportunities and challenges" posed by China's increasing global role. As per the NATO statement released in 2019, it was stated that 'We have now, of course, recognised that the rise of China has security implications for all allies. They recently displayed a lot of new modern capabilities, including long-range missiles able to reach all of Europe, United States.'[15] Also, in Halifax International Security Forum which was held in Canada in late November 2019, similar views were aired on Chinese growing posturing and the perceived threat in the Arctic region. The USA had also voiced its reservations of Chinese intervention in the Arctic on two occasions in 2019 and echoed similarly in the Halifax conference. These malignant fears of the Chinese offer a contrarian advantage to India provided it projects itself as a serious partner in the economic, cultural, and scientific fields and uses this to her advantage. India by its policies of cooperation and joint confidence-building has been a preferred and trusted ally of the Arctic nations. However, in the event of growing scepticism by Arctic nations in the wake of certain aggressive policies of others, India may also be made to pay the price. China holds the key to this discourse in the wake of certain statements by Arctic 8 leaders criticising China's overly ambitious policies. India must draw out lessons from the Chinese experiment in the Arctic, where there is scepticism of its policies and interests in the Arctic, visible by the testimony of Stephanie Pezard before the House of Commons of Canada on November 26, 2018, in which it was projected that increasing Chinese investments and economic diplomacy may be a precursor to some form of military presence which will manifest later to secure these projects. Many in the Arctic view the economic diplomacy by China as a precursor to military manoeuvring which is viewed with greater suspicion and scepticism.

---

[15] Dw.com, 2019, accessed on 12 December 2019 from https://www.dw.com/en/nato-recognizes-china-challenges-for-the-first-time/a-51519351.

Both India and China have been vying for resources, especially hydrocarbons and there is a risk that the quest between these two may also hamper the multilateral engagement in the Arctic at a later date. Both have a history of escalation for squaring off oil resources in the South China Sea earlier, hence a mature and considered approach should be adopted. The presence of China in the Arctic region is fraught with risks of militarisation, especially for the protection of its commercial assets. India realises that the intra-Asia competition pits her against its main regional rival, China, and calculated and measured attempts by India will go a long way in propelling India's ambitions in the Arctic.

A lot of posturing has been done by China, which makes a case for India, as a mature democracy to align its interests with those of the Arctic states to avoid any embitterment and preserve the successful Arctic diplomatic model. China's focus on energy is no surprise, as it seeks to ensure an adequate supply of oil and gas to fuel its growing economy while looking beyond traditional Middle Eastern suppliers. India has to its benefit enjoyed the support of countries in the High North on critical issues, including its permanent membership to UNSC and other areas. India should draw out a clearly defined strategy to tap the close relations it enjoys with technologically inclined northern European economies in various sectors like clean energy, communications, and defence. India should focus and energise its efforts to make ubstantial and fast pace progress in the International North–South Transport Corridor (INSTC) which will be far much more beneficial to South Asia in access to Arctic resources. However, this will require increased trade and commerce with the small Nordic and Other Arctic littoral countries for mutual benefit. The opening of NSR and China accessing oil from the North will also deprive India (and the USA) of the strategic leverage on choking/ controlling the Malacca and other Southern straits.

On the other hand, it is acknowledged in international affairs that mutually beneficial economic cooperation can assuage strained relations between mature nations. Both India and China are accorded observer status which entitles them to know the policy and direction of the deliberations of the AC member states. The concerted and joint interaction will logically not only assist both countries in the Arctic region but also serve to reduce tensions elsewhere. Thus India must have a strategic understanding of energy with China too since both are major energy consumers seeking energy from the same sources. India has a long tradition of public debate and intellectual pluralism. Addressing complex problems through reasoned dialogues and accommodating conflicting views and perspectives are ingrained in Indian culture, which results in constructive debate and dialogue.[16] Given the stated Indian position of non-hegemonic and non-aggressive stance, it may be worth consideration to co-opt China and progress not only the scientific but eco-strategic dimension of the changes in the Arctic region. Unlike Japan and ROK, India does not view China as the key to tilting the North-East Asian regional balance by extensive Sino-Russo alliance.

Bilateral and Multilateral Means of Engagement

The Indian diplomacy has to its credit few attributes like being non-hegemonic, non-prescriptive, and non-intrusive in the affairs of other states. The Chinese on the other hand practice aggressive economic diplomacy backed by strategic and geopolitical calculations which have made the Chinese endeavours quite suspicious in the Arctic region and India can deftly utilise its strengths. India has chosen not to be overly and overtly assertive in its dealings and statements, which are also in contrast to Chinese attempts. There is an immense possibility to build on this benign and mellow approach as being friendly and alive to the local issues and not resource hungry to the detriment of the Arctic 8. Indian views on issues like access to the region, constructive dialogue, SAR, fisheries management, climate change, and maritime EEZ claims, etc., are sought so that there is benefit from mutuality and joint synergies.

Considering the geographical distances and network of legal regimes, it will be prudent for India to take the path of cooperation with the coastal Arctic states in exploiting the energy and other resources located within their uncontested EEZs. As an observer nation, India must advance the Council's work by financing select projects and contributing India's expertise on issues affecting the region. The role that can be played by India in formulating strict methodologies to fight climate change by instituting measures like the recent initiative to ban single-use plastic, Swachh Bharat (prevent open defecation), etc., will go a long way in articulating India's position.

---

[16] NMF, National Maritime Foundation, India and China, Exploring convergences in Asia, accessed on 10 October 2019 from http://www.maritimeindia.org/View%20Profile/Book%20NMF%20AWW%20Dialogue%202.pdf.

Some portions of Indian studies have placed Indian bets in the Arctic to its Russian proximity. Russia-India collaboration in the region will not only strengthen the mutual friendship but also counterbalance the forming of Russia-China cooperation in the High North. The time-tested Russia-India bilateral can be extended to other spheres too for mutual benefit. Since the AC governing rules impose restrictions on participation by the observers and there are curbs on even funding of expert groups, the means of engaging in meaningful dialogue and collaboration with the member states on a bilateral basis will prove to be more effective.

India will have to route its strategic ambitions in a veil of economic diplomacy employing bilateral arrangements. Countries like Norway, Sweden, Russia, and the USA among the Arctic states and Japan, Singapore, and South Korea among the non-Arctic states are significant players in providing India a foothold in strategic calculations. The FTAs and trade talks with these countries should be enlarged to include maritime logistics agreements, maritime transport, and technologies. India should reaffirm its commitment to the sovereignty of the Arctic nations and build mutual trust employing compliance with international law and mechanisms to redress any differences and conflicts. India needs to become diplomatically active by forging alliances to become a reckonable force. The key for India lies in non-military cooperation in fields like scientific and cultural with the Arctic states and assumes a leadership role to fight climate change.[17] Another beginning can be participation in SAR/marine rescue exercises, to develop military contacts with the Arctic states. It is prudent and advisable for India to incorporate the Arctic nations in joint ventures with a fair degree of transparency and following commercial contracts to indulge in resource extraction including metals, minerals, and oil and gas. This will not only ensure compliance with local and regional laws and parameters but also allow progressing commercial diplomacy.

Other Measures

(a) Role of Indian Navy (IN): The IN has been involved in securing the sea lanes of communication (SLOCs) in the IOR, and with the Indian Energy supplies shifting, though marginally, to the Arctic will expose the trade to the newer dimension of security risks.

---

[17] Nikhil Pareek, supra note 142 in Chapter 4.

Because of reduced Chinese reliance on Southern straits, the IN will have to seek newer avenues of incorporating and formulating a role in the Arctic routes. The efforts of IN in piracy control in the Arabian Sea and Africa have won accolades and even if NSR and Arctic shipping becomes voluminous, it will not diminish the potential of traditional Europe-Asia route and with US and China playing out in the Indo-Pacific, the role of Indian Navy is well charted out.[18] In light of the increasing usage and reliance on the shorter Polar Sea lanes of communication (SLOC), the Indian Navy will also be required to equip and adapt itself for enforcement of rules-based order as defined in the UNCLOS mechanism.

India should aim to build its naval capability for foraying in the Arctic region, as this will broaden the maritime view as it also demonstrates India's commitment and interest to Arctic affairs. Also, the PRV programme should be expedited, preferably with a partnership with an Arctic 8 partner to obtain geo-economic and geopolitical leverage. India should realise that the development of PRV is the first step to make its icebreaker, in the times to come. India also does not possess any ice-class vessels, until now.

(b) Observers' Decision making: Mild and veiled calls for a revision in the decision-making process of the Arctic Council by giving increased rights to observers should be advanced by the observer states including India. This is going to be a very difficult path that will encounter stiff resistance by Arctic states including Russia, yet the same has to be developed incrementally. The reactions of the Baltic States to begin must be obtained during bilateral visits and exchanges, and based on assured support, the path must be treaded. Norway and Finland were the ones who had advance India's proposal for the Observer and this path should be trodden carefully.

The Arctic coastal states are inclined to view their national rights and obligations under the UNCLOS, while the non-Arctic states are viewing

---

[18] Ibid.

theirs from the perspective of high seas, freedom of navigation, and bilateral agreements with the terrestrial states. There has to be alignment between these two divergent views on mutually agreed and acceptable terms for solutions for mankind/international interests.

(c) Cooperation and Partnerships: Towards the goal of making India self-reliant in its energy requirements, an ambitious goal is to switch over to renewable energy. The leadership position enjoyed by Nordic states in geothermal energy should be leveraged to build and develop India's geothermal plants. At this juncture, it is vital to note that though such cooperation has figured in the official deliberations but on the contrary, Sino Petroleum Corp (Sinopec) of China and Iceland's Arctic Green Energy Corporation (AGEC) have developed geothermal projects in 40 Chinese cities. This shows that the progress undertaken by the Indian side is rather a snail-paced and must be developed expeditiously to engage the Nordic partner commercially on a bilateral basis.

(d) Manpower: India should exploit the demographic dividend of a large qualified and skilled workforce to assist in projects to develop ports and extract minerals from the rich Barents and circumpolar regions. A large number of Indians are employed in skilled engineering and navigation duties on-board ships and this should be extended to the Arctic region too. This has already been discussed and agreed during the Vladivostok Eastern Economic Forum plenary and has to be developed further.

(e) Division: India should also take a cue from its recent addition of a separate Division, NEST (New, Emerging and Strategic Technologies) in the MEA and set up either a separate Division or amalgamate the function of the existing Americas, Central Europe, and Eurasia divisions to leverage and decipher the Arctic issues with precision. The existing disconnect between these three divisions does not provide a single point and seamless understanding of the complex Arctic issues and the creation of an umbrella subunit will offer better and precise inputs that will enlarge India's engagement.

(f) Funds: Polar logistics, including maintenance of research Stations and launching of expeditions, takes a maximum share of the budget of the National Programmes. Matching financial support for the advancement of scientific research, by involving more and more universities and institutions, is need of the hour.

(g) Ambassador: In the Arctic Circle assembly of 2019, India was the only exception that didn't depute any Ambassador/Special Representative like China, Japan, and Korea. It is vital to have a benign and responsible face of a person, committed to climate change goals and with established and respected credentials to portray India's position. The Arctic ambassador will be the Indian voice of Arctic at unrepresented fora like SAARC, BIMSTEC, IBSA, etc., to garner the attention of these multinational fora and also emerge as a strong voice for Arctic affairs and thereby gain the trust of the Arctic nations.

Prologue

India by virtue of certain parameters like its size, democratic and inclusive society, vibrant multi ethno cultural social fabric, and soft power makes it a candidate to aspire for great power status. Yet, there are several obstructions to this aspiration for assuming global leadership. In the current era of global politics, which is witnessing the third era of transformation since the 1987 Murmansk speech, namely the period of the post-cold war peace, the era of a unipolar world under the USA, and the current era of growing challenges to the world order by demanding global leadership by Russia and China.

India has been seen to be adopting a middle ground by employing multiple strategies like limited hard and economic balancing, greater cooperative strategies with Japan, USA, Australia, ASEAN, and so on, and limited engagement with the potential adversary, China. Thus the Indian strategy so far has been of having multi-alliance to act as a hedging safeguard for unforeseen situations, which again is possible till such times that there is no static world order, after which one will have to choose among the partners in a bipolar world. The India-US equation, for instance during the cold war years, had very limited potential, as India had aligned with the USSR, notwithstanding the underlying theme of NAM.

The Arctic region which has already witnessed the presence of all contenders of great power status and to carve out a strategy for India requires deliberate forethought. In light of the acute discrepancies in the Indian state capacity and stated objective as a major power, the world community is noticing the differential between the rhetoric and concrete actions. It is also established that mere soft power is not enough to any claims for global/major power and the Indian strategy has to have a multi-pronged approach to carve out a niche role in the Arctic affairs. In the recent past, India has been plagued by vocal internal strife, withdrawal from trade arrangements, and history of delayed implementation of projects. In light to effectively engage with the Arctic states bilaterally, India has to sort these matters urgently. Since the Arctic can be a playground to outsmart China, India will have to soft balance with others to develop and present a viable alternative to China.

The Arctic states and the AC along with its associated fora have been successful, especially in times where great power rivalry and inter-regional manoeuvrings were rampant in isolating and insulating the region from these dynamics. This speaks a lot about the farsightedness in evolving AC with considerable clout in Arctic affairs and binding the Arctic 8 in areas of mutual interest. These efforts must be reinvigorated and emphasised so as let AC be a torchbearer in regional leadership and a cooperative framework and a model to emulate. India, by its democratic heritage and collaborative lineage, fits the requirements of an external observer state and must continue to build on its strengths for mutual betterment.[19]

---

[19] Ibid.

Annexure A: Republic of India's Observer Report

(Submitted by Ministry of External Affairs, Room no. 1033, A—block, Jawaharlal Nehru Bhavan, 23-D, Janpath, New Delhi 110011 on 18 May 2018 to ARCTIC COUNCIL)

Ever since India's induction as an Observer to the Arctic Council, several projects were implemented in line with the objectives of various Arctic Council working groups. Given below is a background brief of the projects implemented by India which are being dovetailed to the activities of the respective working groups/project steering group.

The Arctic Contaminants Action Program (ACAP): Coinciding with the goal of ACAP viz. to reduce emissions of pollutants into the environment and the identified pollution risks, encourage national actions for Arctic State Governments to take remedial and preventive actions relating to contaminants and other releases of pollutants, etc., India is implementing following projects:

A. Mercury Geochemistry in the Sediments of Kongsfjorden, Ny-Ålesund, Arctic: The main aim of this project theme is to create background information on the geochemistry and bioavailability of mercury in the sediments of Kongsfjorden, an Arctic fjord. The approach includes physical and chemical speciation; and fractionation of mercury in the sediments and its geochemical relation with the physicochemical parameters like sulphur, iron, organic carbon, humic acids, pH, and temperature in the sediments of Kongsfjorden. This project is being implemented since 2013.

B. Investigations of atmospheric aerosols and their characterization over the Arctic during summer season: Arctic atmosphere is impacted by long range transport of dust and also from the emissions from mid latitude regions. Despite the increase in our understanding of the polar aerosols, information based on measurement data is scarce and validation of model results is a challenge. The projects envisages quantification of the physical and optical properties of the aerosols and associated processes during the summer season by using different aerosol instruments and using them to estimate the aerosol radiative forcing over that region. This study would be critical in assessing long range transport of pollutants. This project is being implemented since 2009. In addition, NCAOR has established a dedicated facility (Gruvebadet lab) in Ny-Ålesund for conducting studies pertaining to pollution, gas fluxes, and precipitation. The lab is in operation since the summer of 2015. Radiometer Profiler, Micro Rain Radar, Ceilometer, etc., are being operated from the station nearly round the year.

Arctic Monitoring and Assessment Programme (AMAP): In consideration of goal of AMAP viz. providing reliable and sufficient information on the status of, and threats to, the Arctic environment, and providing scientific advice on actions to be taken in order to support Arctic governments in their efforts to take remedial and preventive actions relating to contaminants, India has mounted the following projects:

A. Long-term monitoring of Kongsfjorden system of Arctic region for climate change studies: The Kongsfjorden, an Arctic fjord acts as a natural laboratory to study the climatic impacts of global warming. The fjord is influenced by both climatically important Atlantic and Arctic signals. Freshening of Arctic waters could also modulate the physical linking between the Atlantic Multi-decadal oscillation and the multi-decadal variability in Indian summer monsoon rainfall. This project is being implemented since 2010. NCAOR has deployed in 2014 a multi-sensor mooring in Kongsfjorden which measures currents, temperature, salinity, dissolved oxygen, fluorescence, dissolved carbon dioxide, etc., on real time basis.

The mooring is currently operational and serviced every year. This mooring could be a part of the Arctic Ocean Observing Networks and will provide much impetus to scientific collaborations and discussions with countries deeply involved in Arctic research.

B. Monitoring of Arctic Precipitation: Mass balance of polar ice sheets is one of the crucial points for the calculation of global sea level rise. One of the important parameters controlling the mass balance of ice sheets is the precipitation. Rising global temperatures over the next few decades are likely to increase evaporation and accelerate the global hydrological cycle which may cause drying of subtropical areas and increase precipitation at higher latitudes. Precipitation is measured using a Micro Rain Radar coupled to measurement of temperature and humidity profiles using a Microwave Radiometer Profiler. The project is implemented since 2013.

C. Integrated Monitoring of Glaciers in Ny-Ålesund, Svalbard, Arctic: The focus of this study is to understand glacier fluctuation by monitoring mass budget, snout and dynamics of Vestre Broggerbree and Feringbreen glaciers in Ny-Ålesund. The network of stakes over glacier surface and their timely monitoring in addition with climate data are very useful to understand glacier climate inter-relationship. Attempt is being made to address accumulation/ablation and mass balance of these during summer and winter. Researchers have also conducted DGPS and GPR surveys on the glaciers. This project is being implemented since 2012.

Conservation of Arctic Flora and Fauna (CAFF): CAFF serves as a vehicle to cooperate on species and habitat management and utilization, to share information on management techniques and regulatory regimes, and to facilitate more knowledgeable decision-making. Brief details of projects implemented by India at Svalbard which could contribute to CAFF are given below:

A. Bacterial diversity in various niches around Ny-Ålesund, Svalbard: This study on diversity of heterotrophic bacteria in the Kongsfjorden has clearly revealed entry of mesophilic health significant bacteria into this environment. The entry is through two possible routes such as Atlantic warm water influx from lower latitudes during summer and through migratory birds such as

Barnacle goose. Apart from the harsh physico-chemical conditions, other factors such as competition from autochthonous counterparts in the Arctic environments, predation by protozoans, Bdellovibrios, and bacteriophages also play crucial role in their survival. However, our research so far indicate considerable presence of diverse Escherichia coli serotypes in the tundra environment and mesophilic health significant bacteria such as Enterobacter ludwigii and Stenotrophomonas maltophilia in the water from Kongsfjorden. Since most of thesemesophilic health significant bacteria are from areas in the tropics/sub-tropics which are anthropogenically influenced and organically polluted, the prevalence of antibiotic resistance among them is relatively high. Migratory birds such as Arctic terns and Barnacle goose which have major presence in the Arctic, especially Svalbard region, act as potential carriers of such health significant mesophilic bacteria. These mesophilic intruders when co-exist with autochthonous bacteria of the Arctic region, horizontal gene transfer mechanisms could promote dissemination of antibiotic resistant genes into the pristine arctic environment, which could pose potential danger to living forms here. India hosted 41st Ny-Ålesund Science Managers Committee (NySMAC) meeting in Goa, India during 6th–7th November, 2014 and Ny-Alesund Atmosphere Flagship Gap Analysis workshop in Goa, India during 4th–5th November, 2014. India has bilateral collaboration with Research Council of Norway.

India commits to have focussed research initiatives and looks forward to cooperation from permanent participants to expand the research themes with wider geographic coverage. One of the thrust areas of the Indian Arctic Program is to conduct long-term monitoring of the Arctic fjords and the Ocean. This is planned to understand the impact of climate and its further tele-connection with tropical processes like Indian monsoon. India has been monitoring a couple of fjords in the Svalbard for understanding the variability in hydrographic parameters and to delineate its forcing on the biogechemical cycles. It is anticipated that a pan-Arctic approach will be required in the immediate future to strengthen the scientific understanding of the processes and to derive tangible benefits for mankind. In this scenario close scientific and logistic collaborations with permanent will provide much needed momentum for pan-Arctic measurements. This could involve formulation of joint programs, field campaigns, data sharing, etc., which is also one of the key mandates of the IASC and Arctic council. India is looking forward to continuation of its collaboration with Research Council of Norway and new collaboration with Russia. Indian plans to (a) Extend ocean observations and modelling in the Arctic-North Atlantic region (b) Deploy and service deep sea moorings in Arctic Ocean (c) Set-up molecular & proteomics facilities in NCAOR (d) Train and generate specialised manpower for more focussed research (e) National collaborations among research and academic institutes for research in Arctic (f) International scientific collaborations to achieve pan-Arctic mission.

India setup a permanent research base named 'Himadri' located at the International Arctic Research base, NyÅlesund, Svalbard, Norway. Himadri provides extensive field and laboratory support required for pursuing research activities in the Arctic.

India's Gruvebadet atmospheric laboratory at Ny-Ålesund is dedicated to understand the various atmospheric parameters like monitoring clouds, precipitation, humidity profiles etc. The facility houses instruments like Micro Rain Radar, Ceilometer, Radiometer Profiler, etc., which are being operated continuously streaming in data to NCAOR. In addition, this laboratory also provides support to campaigns studying aerosols and black carbon. The laboratory is equipped with Nephelometer, Aethalometer, Multistage impactor, etc.

The 'IndARC' India's multi-sensor oceanographic subsurface mooring was deployed by India in cooperation with Norwegian Polar Institute in the transition zone of Kongsfjorden in July 2014. The mooring which is 180 m long hosts an array of sensors for measuring temperature, salinity, dissolved oxygen, currents, fluorescence, nutrients, etc. Over 100 scientists/researchers from 25 research and educational institutes in India have visited the Indian Research station 'Himadri.' More than 40 research publications have been published by Indian researchers based on their scientific studies in the arctic.

India is member of the Ny-Ålesund Science Managers Committee (NySMAC) and International Arctic Science Committee (IASC).

Annexure B: Select Questions in the Parliament on India's Polar Research

1. **Question No. 3991**, August 06, 2014, Lok Sabha, Unstarred Question No. 3991, to be Answered on 06 August 2014: Arctic Council[1]

   Question: Will the Minister of External Affairs be pleased to state:
   (a) the details of objectives and functions of the Arctic Council along with the names of member countries therein;
   (b) The position of India vis-à-vis other member countries in this council;
   (c) The details of challenges confronting the Arctic Council along with the number of discussions held and outcome thereof during the last three years; and
   (d) The benefits likely to be accrued to India in this regard?
   Answer: Scientific and expert-level exchanges about the ongoing changes in the Arctic region, its implications and experiences, and best practices to manage these will help India better understand the climate processes of its own region and its environmental and economic impact in this region.

---

[1] Ministry of External Affairs, Government of India, accessed on 20 December 19 from https://www.mea.gov.in/lok-sabha.htm?dtl/23837/q+no3991+arctic+council.

2. **Question No. 2380**, February 13, 2014, Rajya Sabha, Unstarred Question No. 2380, to be Answered on 13 February 2014: Permanent Observers in Arctic Council[2]

Question: Will the Minister of External Affairs be pleased to state:
(a) Whether India along with China and Japan has asked to be Permanent Observers in the Arctic Council of eight countries that have Arctic Territory; and
(b) If so, the details thereof?
Answer: The minister of state in the Ministry of External Affairs (Shri E. Ahamed)
(a) (a) & (b) Yes. India, along with China, Japan, Republic of Korea, Italy, and Singapore, was granted Observer status in the Arctic Council during its Ministerial Meeting held in Kiruna, Sweden on May 15, 2013.

(b) The Arctic Council now is composed of 8 member states (Canada, Denmark, Finland, Iceland, Norway, Russia, Sweden, and the USA), 6 Permanent Participants, 12 Observer states (France, Germany, Netherlands, Poland, Spain, UK, China, India, Italy, Japan, Republic of Korea and Singapore). Besides, 9 inter-governmental and interparliamentary organisations and 11 non-governmental organisations have been accorded Observer Status.

3. **Question No. 2005**, March 09, 2016, Lok Sabha, Unstarred Question No. 2005, to be Answered On 09 March 2016[3]

Question: Will the Minister of External Affairs be pleased to state:
(a) the details of India's current stand on the territorial claims of various countries on the polar regions of the Earth;
(b) Whether India has made any claim over any territory in the Arctic and Antarctic;
(c) If so, the details in this regard;
(d) Whether any deliberations have been held among various countries in this regard; and
(e) If so, the details and outcome thereof?

---

[2] Ministry of External Affairs, Government of India, accessed on 20 December 19 from https://www.mea.gov.in/rajya-sabha.htm?dtl/22918/Q+NO+2380+PERMANENT+OBSERVERS+IN+ARCTIC+COUNCIL.

[3] Ministry of External Affairs, Government of India, accessed on 20 December 19 from https://www.mea.gov.in/lok-sabha.htm?dtl/26494/.

Answer: The Minister of State in the Ministry of External Affairs, [GEN. (DR) V. K. SINGH (RETD)]

(a) India is a party to the Antarctic Treaty of 1959 and abides by the provisions of the Treaty, under which all territorial claims stand frozen. India enjoys an Observer status in the Arctic Council, which was formally established by the Ottawa Declaration of 1996. The Arctic Ocean does not belong to any country and is governed by the 1982 United Nations Convention on the Law of the Sea, to which India is a party.

(b) No. India has not made any claim over any territory in the Arctic or the Antarctic.

(c) Not applicable.

(d) India has not held any deliberations with any country with regard to any territorial claims on the Polar Regions.

(e) Not applicable.

4. **Question No: 4883**, August 13, 2014, Lok Sabha, Research Stations in Arctic and Antarctica[4]

Question: Will the Minister of Earth Sciences be pleased to state:-

(a) Whether the Government proposes to set up more research stations in Arctic and Antarctica;

(b) If so, the details thereof;

(c) If not, the reasons there for;

(d) Whether India has ice-breakers for exploration and research in the above places;

(e) If not, the reasons there for; and

(f) The steps contemplated by the Government for the manufacture of indigenous ice-breakers?

Answer: Minister for Ministry of Science and Technology and Ministry of Earth Sciences (Independent Charge) (Dr. Jitendra Singh)

(a) No Madam.

(b) Does not arise.

(c) India presently has two research stations at Antarctica namely 'Maitri' and 'Bharati.' New station 'Bharti' has been constructed and

---

[4] Press Information Bureau, Government of India, accessed on 21 November 19 from https://pib.gov.in/newsite/PrintRelease.aspx?relid=98006.

established in March 2013. At both stations, research and investigations are undertaken to understand the Polar processes and phenomenon. Observations and studies are carried out in atmospheric, biological, geological, ecological sciences, etc. Maitri station has been in operation since 1989. Indian Arctic station 'Himadri' is located at Ny Alesund, Spitsbergen Island, Norway, and serves as a hub of Indian scientific investigations since 2008.

(d) No Madam.

(e) In Antarctica, scientific studies and investigations are undertaken on the continental part and contiguous shelf ice part. Observations in the ocean in summer months are made during the voyage to 'Maitri' and 'Bharati' on board the chartered vessel hired for transport of material and personnel to these stations. At the Arctic, also meteorological, biological, glaciological, and past climate studies are undertaken in the vicinity of the station 'Himadri.' Local boats are hired for marine research. Chartered ice-breaker ship along with Cargo vessel was used during the construction of the 'Bharati' station in Larsemann Hills, East Antarctica. Chartered ice-class cargo vessel is presently used for transporting personnel and material for the 'Maitri' and 'Bharti' stations.

(f) The acquisition/construction of Polar Research Vessel is under consideration.

5. **Question 988**, 02 March 2016, Lok Sabha, Research in Polar Regions[5]

Question: Will the Minister of Earth Sciences be pleased to state:-

(a) Whether the Government proposes to focus in the Arctic region for more research and studies about climate changes

(b) If so, the details thereof

(c) Whether the Government proposes to purchase ice breakers and polar vessels for more exploration in both North and South Pole regions;

(d) If so, the details thereof, and the funds allocated by the Government for the purpose?

Answer: The Minister of State for Ministry of Science and Technology and Ministry of Earth Sciences (Shri. Y. S. Chowdary)

---

[5] Ministry of Earth Sciences, Government of India, accessed on 11 November 19 from https://www.moes.gov.in/previous-sessions?theme=moes.

(a) Yes, Madam.

(b) Considering the need for trans-hemispheric studies focussing on climate variability and change, in 2007 the Ministry of Earth Sciences decided to dovetail the country's scientific endeavour in the Antarctic region with some major long-term scientific initiatives in the Svalbard area of the Arctic. Many long-term scientific programmes in the frontier areas of climate change, glaciology, terrestrial and aquatic ecology, and atmospheric sciences have been initiated by the Indian scientists in the Arctic region. To facilitate the studies, a permanent station "Himadri" was set up at the International Arctic Research facilities at Ny-Ålesund on the Spitsbergen island of Svalbard, Norway. A research project for 'Long –term monitoring of Kongsfjorden system (Ny-Alesund, Svalbard, Norway) of Arctic region for climate change studies' was initiated and multi-sensor mooring system in the Arctic at a water depth of 190 m in the Kongsfjorden has been deployed.

(c) Yes, Madam.

(d) The first tender process for identification of shipbuilder could not be concluded into a contract and the re-tender process has been initiated. Earlier, the Cabinet Committee on Economic Affairs (CCEA) in its meeting held on 29th October 2014 approved the acquisition of a Polar Research Vessel at an estimated expenditure of Rs. 1051.13 crore.

6. **Question 6595**, 06 May 2015, Lok Sabha, Polar Research Vessel[6]

Question: Will the Minister of Earth Sciences be pleased to state:-

(a) Whether the construction of a Polar Research Vessel as announced in 2008–2009 has been facing delay over the years

(b) If so, the details thereof along with the reasons therefore; and;

(c) The time by which the Polar Research Vessel is likely to be built/commissioned and objectives thereof?

Answer: Minister of State for Ministry of Science and Technology and Ministry of Earth Sciences (Shri Y. S. Chowdary)

(a) & (b) The proposal for acquisition of Polar Research Vessel was earlier approved at an estimated cost of Rs. 490 crore in June 2010.

---

[6] Ministry of Earth Sciences, Government of India, accessed on 12 October 19 from https://www.moes.gov.in/writereaddata/files/LS_US_6595_06052015.pdf.

The process leading to agreement with the shipyard involves various time-consuming steps with detailed consultations with Project Monitoring and Coordination Committee at every stage viz. preparation of requirements, the appointment of the consulting firm to prepare a detailed specification of the vessel, finalization of detailed specifications prepared by a consulting firm, preparation and floating of Expression of Interest, technical evaluation of bids and short-listing of bidders, preparation of a comprehensive document for Request for Proposal, pre-bid meeting with bidders, receipt of bids, technical analysis of received bids and seeking clarifications from bidders before opening the financial bids, clearances for the signing of agreement and finalization of the agreement. A Consulting firm was appointed for working out detailed specifications as per requirement in October 2010 after following the tender process. Final design specifications and provisional cost estimates were prepared in consultation with the Project Monitoring and Coordination Committee by the Consulting firm upon discussion within January 2011. In July 2011 expression of interest was finalized after working out detailed drawing for shipbuilding, propulsion system, icebreaking capability, etc. In December 2011, a request for a proposal was issued to the shortlisted shipyards whose bids underwent detailed technical evaluation thereafter. The financial bids were opened in March 2013. A Standing Committee constituted to examine the cost reasonableness submitted its report in September 2013 and recommended the revised cost of Rs. 1051 crores as reasonable. The proposal of the Revised Cost Estimate was prepared which was recommended by the Expenditure Finance Committee in March 2014 for the approval of the Cabinet Committee on Economic Affairs (CCEA). The proposal was approved by the CCEA in October 2014. Presently, the agreement with the shipbuilder is under finalization and the necessary clearances in this regard, are under process. (c) The Polar Research Vessel is likely to be built in 34 months after signing of an agreement with the following major objectives.

(i) Launching of scientific expedition to Antarctica for transfer of personnel and material for two Antarctic Indian stations—Maitri and Bharati, and (ii) undertaking scientific research & investigations in Antarctic, Arctic, and the Indian Ocean.

7. **Question 1495**, 04 March 2015, LOK SABHA, POLAR RESEARCH VESSEL[7]

Question: Will the Minister of Earth Sciences be pleased to state:-
(a) Whether the Government has acquired or proposed to acquire Polar Research Vessel;
(b) If so, the details in this regard and the present status of such proposal; and
(c) The manner in which the country will be benefited by such an acquisition in their research mission?

Answer: Minister for Ministry of Science and Technology and Ministry of Earth Sciences (Dr. Harsh Vardhan)
(a) Yes, Madam. It is proposed to acquire Polar Research Vessel. (b) The Cabinet Committee on Economic Affairs (CCEA) in its meeting held on 29th October 2014 approved the Revised Cost Estimates (RCE) for the acquisition of a Polar Research Vessel (PRV) at an estimated expenditure of Rs. 1051.13 crore. An administrative order in favour of the implementing agency National Centre for Antarctic & Ocean Research (NCAOR), Goa for the acquisition of PRV has been issued on 14th November 2014.

(b) The vessel will help in sustaining two Indian research bases in Antarctica (Maitri and Bharti); dovetail research initiatives in the Southern Ocean domain with those in the proximal regions of the Antarctic continent; widen the thrust on Arctic research disciplines, undertaken through Indian Station Himadri; and will also provide a suitable research platform for other ocean programmes.

8. **Question 240**, 23 March 2017, Rajya Sabha, Research on climate change in Northern Pole[8]

Question: Will the Minister of Earth Sciences be pleased to state:-
(a) Whether the Government proposes to conduct research on climate change in the northern pole;

---

[7] Ministry of Earth Sciences, Government of India, accessed on 02 December 19 from https://www.moes.gov.in/previous-sessions.

[8] Ministry of Earth Sciences, Government of India, accessed on 02 December 19 from https://moes.gov.in/writereaddata/files/RS_S_240_hindi_23032017.pdf.

(b) If so, the details thereof;
(c) The details of expenditure likely to be incurred on such research;
(d) Whether any agreement has been signed with any other country for collaboration in this regard; and
(e) If so the details thereof?

Answer: Minister for Ministry of Science and Technology and Ministry of Earth Sciences (Dr. Harsh Vardhan)

(a)–(e): A statement is laid on the Table of the House.

Statement Referred to in Reply to Parts (a)–(e) of the Rajya Sabha Starred Question No *240 Regarding Research About Research on Climate Change in Northern Pole: For Answer on 23rd March 2017

(a) Yes Sir.

(b) The National Centre for Antarctic and Ocean Research (NCAOR), Ministry of Earth Sciences has a long-term programme of monitoring one of the major fjords at Ny-Ålesund (1200 km to the south of the North Pole) on the Svalbard archipelago in the Arctic region to understand how it may respond to changing climate. The main objective of the project is to establish a long-term comprehensive physical, chemical, biological, and atmospheric measurement programmes to study:

- The variability in the Arctic/Atlantic climate signal.
- The winter convection and its role in biogeochemical cycling.
- The trigger mechanism of spring bloom and its temporal variability and biomass production.
- The production and export of organic carbon in the fjord.

The scientific challenges associated with the cryospheric changes in the Arctic to climate variability are also addressed at the Centre for Climate Change Research, Indian Institute of Tropical Meteorology, Pune.

(b) An expenditure of around Rs. 45 crores is likely to be incurred during the next 3 years (2017–2020).

(c) Yes Sir. NCAOR, Goa, an autonomous institute of MoES has entered into an MOU with the Norwegian Polar Institute (NPI) for scientific and logistic cooperation in the Arctic.

(d) A wide range of scientific activities concerning climate response of the Polar and Himalayan Cryosphere are being carried out at NCAOR, Goa.

9. **Question No. 1365** to be Answered on 3rd March, 2011, expedition to Arctic[9]

Question: Will the Minister of Earth Sciences be pleased to state:
(a) Whether the first Indian expedition to the Arctic has been launched;
(b) If so, the composition of the expedition team and its objectives;
(c) Whether the team is likely to work in cooperation with other countries;
(d) If so, the details thereof;
(e) Whether the Government proposes to set up a permanent station for research in the Arctic;
(f) If not, the reasons therefore; and
(g) The time by which the results achieved by the expedition are likely to be known?

Answer: Minister of State in the Ministry of Planning, Minister of State in the Ministry of Parliamentary Affairs, Minister of State in the Ministry of Science and Technology and Minister of State in the Ministry of Earth Sciences (Shri Ashwani Kumar)

(a) Yes, Madam.

(b) India launched its first scientific expedition to Ny-Alesund on the Spitsbergen island of Norway in August 2007 to mark the beginning of long-term scientific research by Indian scientists through global scientific endeavour in the Arctic region. The five-member inter-disciplinary and inter-institutional team of scientists of the first Arctic Expedition were drawn from National Centre for Antarctic & Ocean Research (NCAOR), Goa; Centre for Cellular & Molecular Biology (CCMB), Hyderabad; Indian Institute of Tropical Meteorology (IITM), Pune; and Lucknow University. The objectives of the Indian Arctic programmes during XI plan period are: (i) The characterization of sea ice in the Arctic using satellite data from Indian/foreign satellites to estimate the effects of global warming in the northern polar region; (ii) Comprehensive glaciological studies of the Arctic that will involve not only satellite data but also ground truth measurements; (iii) Research on the dynamics and mass budget of Arctic glaciers. The focus would be on the effect of glaciers

---

[9] Ministry of Earth Sciences, Government of India, accessed on 02 October 19 from https://www.moes.gov.in/previous-sessions?theme=moes.

on sea-level change and on the freshwater input into fjords and embayments; (iv) Comprehensive assessment of the flora & fauna of the Arctic vis-a-vis their response to anthropogenic activities and a comparative study of the life forms from both the Polar Regions in terms of the environment; (v) Study of sea ice microbial communities; (vi) To carry out detailed isotopic, chemical and micropaleontological studies on the sediments from the Arctic Ocean to decipher their response and feedback to past climate changes; (vii) Measurement of atmospheric aerosols and ions; (viii) Snowpack production of carbon monoxide and its variabilities (ix) Carbon cycling in the near shore environments; (x) To ensure a perceptible and influential presence of India in the Arctic and to uphold the country's strategic interests in the Polar Regions and the surrounding oceans.

(c) & (d) Yes, Madam. An MoU has been signed on 1st July 2008 between the National Centre of Antarctic & Ocean Research (NCAOR), an autonomous agency of the Ministry and Norwegian Polar Institute (NPI) on Cooperation in Polar Research.

(e) & (f) A research station at Arctic namely 'Himadri' was launched at Ny-Alesund in the Svalbard region on 1st July 2008. Research in various disciplines, i.e. glaciology, Palaeoclimate, microbiology, atmospheric science, etc., during different seasons in a year have since been undertaken in the region around the Ny-Alesund. The nature of research, which is in phases, does not necessitate all-year-round-presence presently. Since 2007, four expeditions (interdisciplinary and comprising of multi-institutional team of scientists) to the Arctic have been undertaken.

(g) The results of the first Arctic expedition to the Ny-Alesund region indicate the following: (i) The total number, concentration and size distributions of aerosols in the Ny-Ålesund show good correlation with wind speed and wind direction; (ii) The electrical conductivity does not show any diurnal variation as the ionization due to cosmic radiation is abundant during the Arctic summer period; (iii) Sediment and water samples from the Midtre Lov'enbreen glacier have bacteria from four phyla namely Actinobacteria, Bacilli, Flavobacteria, and Proteobacteria, and bacterial abundance is more at the convergence point of glacial melt and the sea. The studies at the Arctic are aimed at understanding the processes and phenomena in such a cold climate and their link if any, and importance in the overall understanding of the litho, hydro, and atmosphere.

10. Question No. 6875, May 17, 2012, exploration of Arctic regions[10]

Question: Will the Minister of Earth Sciences be pleased to state:
(a) The steps/initiatives taken up to explore the Arctic regions;
(b) The total budgetary allocation for the same during the last three years; and
(c) The result achieved so far in respect of exploration of Arctic regions?

Answer: Minister of State in the Ministry of Planning, Minister of State in the Ministry of Science and Technology and Minister of State in the Ministry of Earth Sciences (Dr. Ashwani Kumar)

(a) Madam, India began its scientific endeavours in the Arctic in 2007 when a team of five scientists visited the International Arctic Research Facilities at Ny-Ålesund on the Svalbard archipelago in Norway to initiate studies in the fields of Arctic microbiology, atmospheric sciences, and geology. Following the success of this initial step, the Ministry embarked on a long-term programme of regular scientific activities in the Arctic. To date, over 60 scientists from 18 national institutions, organisations and universities have participated in the Indian Arctic Programme, which is being coordinated and implemented by the Goa-based National Centre for Antarctic and Ocean Research (NCAOR), an autonomous institution of the Ministry. At Ny-Ålesund, Indian scientists are engaged with the frontier areas of sciences relevant to the Arctic realm, such as glaciology, atmospheric science, biology, and climate change. To facilitate the Indian activities, a station building at Ny-Ålesund has been taken on lease to serve as India's Research Base in the Arctic. This station building christened "Himadri" has adequate living and workspace for a total of 8 scientists.

(b) Madam, the budgetary allocation for the last three years from 2009 to 2012 was 13.33 crores. Year-wise budgetary allocation for the Indian Arctic Programme for the past three years is as below: 2009–2010: 2.60 crores 2010–2011: 1.94 crores 2011–2012: 8.79 crores.

(c) Madam, salient features of the studies carried out by Indian scientist are as given below: Atmospheric Sciences: The studies of atmospheric

---

[10] Ministry of Earth Sciences, Government of India, accessed on 23 October 19 from https://www.moes.gov.in/writereaddata/files/LU6875_10_15_2012.pdf.

aerosols, quantification of their physical and optical properties and estimating the aerosol radiative forcing over Arctic region are among the ongoing long-term investigations by the Indian scientists from the Space Physics Laboratory (SPL), Trivandrum, Indian Institute of Tropical Meteorology (IITM), Pune and NCAOR, Goa. A study carried out involved the simultaneous measurements of an atmospheric electrical field, conductivity, the concentrations and size distribution of atmospheric aerosols over Ny-Alesund. The total number of concentration and size distributions of aerosols observed shows a good correlation with wind speed and wind direction. Snow-pack production of carbon monoxide and its diurnal variability at the Arctic: Photochemical reactions in snow have recently witnessed an unprecedented surge of interest. Recent investigations have shown production and significant release of CO flux from the snow-covered region. On the basis of measurements made at Maitri, Antarctica, and at Ny-Alesund, Arctic, a group of researchers from the National Physical Laboratory has observed a systematic diurnal cycle in the snow-pack production of carbon monoxide coinciding with the diurnal cycle of solar radiation. This variation implies that the photochemical production of CO is active in the snow-covered regions of Antarctica and Arctic. Glaciological Studies: A major multi-institutional programme has been mounted by scientists from NCAOR, GSI, and JNU for long-term measurements of snow ablation/accumulation on the Vestre Broggerbreen glacier. The glaciological studies also comprise a detailed chemical analysis of snow/ice. Preliminary snow ablation/accumulation measurements reveal that the observed short-term ablation/accumulation, especially in the higher and middle reaches of the glacier, is mainly attributed to the wind deflation rather than melting. The biogeochemical studies programme has been undertaken in the Kongsfjorden system is being implemented by NCAOR. The first phase of studies has focussed on the plank tonic studies in the fjord while the second phase concentrated on nitrogen cycling. Biological Sciences: Scientists from various institutions and Universities have participated in the biological programmes being mounted in the Kongsfjorden system. Broad-scale changes to Arctic ecosystems and communities illustrate the sensitivity of these systems to changing conditions, both natural and human-induced.

Annexure C: Engagement of Indian Leaders with Arctic Leaders on Arctic Issues

(a) **Valdai Discussion Club 27 August 2019: Indian External Affairs Minister (EAM)**

"I think again part of the exploration of greater maritime opportunities would also arise from what is happening in with reference to the Arctic. The **possibility of new maritime routes** opening up."

(b) **Meeting of PM Modi with Vladimir Putin, President of Russian Federation on the margins of 11th BRICS Summit: November 13, 2019**

President Putin highlighted the potential of Arctic region in natural gas and invited India to invest in the region.

(c) **External Affairs Minister's Speech at the 4th Ramnath Goenka Lecture, November 14, 2019**

The **global commons is also more in disputation** as multilaterism weakens. Even climate change is a factor, contributing to geopolitics among others by the opening of an Arctic passage. In short, change is upon us as never before.

(d) **Press Statement by President on His State Visit to Iceland: September 10, 2019**

President Johannesson and I discussed in detailed our global partnership. I congratulated him on Iceland assuming the chair of the Arctic Council and conveyed India's desire to meaningfully contribute to its deliberations and outcomes.

(e) **Transcript of Media Briefing by Secretary (West) on Upcoming Visit of President to Iceland, Switzerland, and Slovenia: September 07, 2019**

India is an observer in the Arctic Council and we are looking to be very active in the work of the council. There is a lot of interest in such areas as geothermal energy, fisheries, tourism, cultural cooperation. So these are some of the areas with Iceland, they are extremely relevant and important and the desire to work with us closely and we share similar approaches in many ways.

(f) **India-Russia Joint Statement During Visit of Prime Minister to Vladivostok, September 05, 2019**

"REACHING NEW HEIGHTS OF COOPERATION THROUGH TRUST AND PARTNERSHIP"

1. Prime Minister of the Republic of India H.E. Narendra Modi paid an official visit to the Russian Federation on September 4–5, 2019 on the invitation of President of the Russian Federation H.E. Mr Vladimir Putin. The 20th India-Russia Annual Summit was held in Vladivostok. H.E. Mr Narendra Modi also participated in the 5th Eastern Economic Forum as the Chief Guest.
2. At the jubilee 20th Annual Summit, both leaders noted progressive development of the Special and Privileged Strategic Partnership between India and Russia. These relations are unique, confiding, and mutually beneficial by nature, encompassing all possible areas of cooperation. They are based on similar civilizational values, time-tested friendship, mutual understanding, trust, common interests, and proximity of approaches to the fundamental

issues of development and economic progress. Regular meetings of the leaders of the States, including those on the sidelines of various international fora and growing momentum of bilateral contacts at all levels are a vivid proof of this Partnership.

3. India-Russia ties have successfully coped with the turbulent realities of the contemporary world. They have never been and will not be susceptible to outside influence. Development of the entire gamut of India-Russia relations is a foreign policy priority for both countries. The leaders agreed to facilitate, in all possible ways, exploring the impressive potential of our strategic partnership to the full, demonstrating its special and privileged nature which has emerged as an anchor of stability in a complex international situation.

4. Both Sides welcomed intensive cooperation between their parliaments and noted the importance of interparliamentary interaction as a valuable component of their bilateral relations. They highlighted the visit of the Chairman of the State Duma to India in December 2018 and look forward to the visit of the Speaker of the Lok Sabha to Russia later in 2019.

5. Both Sides prioritise strong, multifaceted trade, and economic cooperation as the foundation for further expanding the range of India-Russia relations.

6. The Leaders highly appreciated the work of the India-Russia Intergovernmental Commission on Trade, Economic, Scientific, Technological, and Cultural Cooperation which ensures progressive development of bilateral cooperation in various areas.

7. The Sides expressed satisfaction with the stable mutual growth of trade turnover. To bring it to USD 30 billion by 2025, they agreed to more actively engage the impressive resource and human resources potential of India and Russia, enhance industrial cooperation, create new technological and investment partnership, especially in advanced high-tech areas, and find new avenues and forms of cooperation.

8. Both Sides expressed their interest in expanding the participation of Russian business in "Make in India" program and that of Indian companies in investment projects in Russia. In this context, they agreed to speed up preparations for signing of the India-Russia Intergovernmental Agreement on Promotion and Mutual Protection of Investments.

9. The Sides agreed to intensify joint work towards eliminating barriers in mutual trade, including protective measures, customs, and administrative barriers, to further consider reducing restrictive measures through bilateral dialogue. This would be facilitated, inter alia, by the proposed Trading Agreement between the Eurasian Economic Union (EAEU) and the Republic of India.
10. They agreed to improve the structure of trade in goods and services, environment for entrepreneurial activities and investment, harmonise and refine relevant import and export procedures, streamline and standardise technical, sanitary, and phytosanitary requirements.
11. The work on promoting mutual settlements of payments in national currencies will be continued.
12. The office of the Russian export support group established in Mumbai on the platform of the Russian Trade mission to India jointly with the Russian Export Center to promote bilateral trade and economic relations was welcome. The Sides also noted the continued facilitation of Russian investments in India provided by the Russia Plus Desk of Invest India.
13. The Sides noted the contribution of the St. Petersburg International Economic Forum and the India-Russia Business Dialogue that took place on its sidelines this year to enhanced trade, economic, and investment cooperation.
14. The two Leaders welcomed the holding of the 2nd edition of the India-Russia Strategic Economic Dialogue on 10 July 2019 in New Delhi. The Strategic Economic Dialogue has emerged as a promising mechanism aimed at promoting cohesive and mutually beneficial economic cooperation across core sectors by way of structured and continuous interaction between our two countries. A comprehensive Action Strategy for advancing bilateral Trade-Economic and Investment Cooperation has been developed and adopted in 2018–2019 based on the work of the Dialogue.
15. The Leaders expressed satisfaction with the cooperation between New Delhi and Moscow in the sphere of the development of the Russian Far East. Several Indian companies have been successfully set up in the Far East region, such as M/s KGK in Vladivostok in the field of diamond cutting and M/s Tata Power in Krutogorovo in Kamchatka in coal mining. The Russian Side welcomed the

intent of the Indian Side to expand its economic and investment presence in the Far Eastern region and Siberia.

16. India is making efforts at enhancing cooperation with the Russian Far East. As a first step, for the first time ever a delegation of four Chief Ministers of Indian states led by the Commerce and Industry Minister of India visited Vladivostok on 12–13 August 2019 to explore avenues of greater bilateral engagement in targeted sectors. Both Sides also look forward to exploring cooperation on temporary placement of skilled manpower from India to Far East Russia.
17. India looks forward to cooperate with Russia in the Arctic. India has been following the developments in the Arctic region with interest and is also ready to play a significant role in the Arctic Council.
18. Russia on its part, expressed its readiness to participate in major infrastructural and other projects in India. Both Sides welcomed the recent opening of the Far East Investment and Export Agency's office in Mumbai and looked forward to its contribution to the development of bilateral trade and economic relations with regard to the Russian Far East.
19. The energy industry has traditionally been a key area of interaction between the two countries—this is an area where Indian and Russian economies complement each other beneficially. Civil nuclear cooperation between India and Russia is an important component of strategic partnership. The Sides noted the pace of progress achieved in the construction of the remaining four of the six nuclear power plants at Kudankulam. Both Sides engaged in discussion on the second site and welcomed continuation of technical discussions on the VVER 1200 of the Russian design and joint manufacturing of equipment and fuel.
20. The Sides highlighted successful cooperation in the construction of the Rooppur NPP in Bangladesh and expressed their readiness to expand similar cooperation in third countries.
21. The leaders note immense potential of cooperation in the field of non-nuclear fuel and energy. India and Russia welcome the success of interaction between JSC Rosneft Oil Company and Consortium of Oil and Gas Public Sector Undertakings in implementing the Vankorneft and Taas-Yuryakh Neftegazodobycha projects, the work of the Nayara Energy Limited oil refinery, cooperation in

extracting hydrocarbon resources over the last two decades as well as the timely delivery of liquefied natural gas under the agreement between Gazprom and GAIL India. The Sides agreed to cooperate in supply of coking coal from Russian Far East to India.

22. The leaders are determined to forge cooperation in geological exploration and joint development of oil and gas fields in Russia and India, including offshore fields. They will continue their work to develop the ways of delivering energy resources from Russia to India, including a long-term agreement for sourcing Russian crude oil, the possible use of the Northern Sea Route and a pipeline system. They noted the prospects of Nayara Energy Limited increasing the capacity in Vadinar oil refinery. India and Russia agreed to consider the prospects for expanding cooperation in hydro and thermal power, energy efficiency as well as for designing and constructing facilities that generate energy from non-conventional sources.

23. With the signing of the Roadmap for cooperation in Hydrocarbons for 2019–2024 during the Summit, both Sides expect bilateral cooperation in this sector to touch new heights in the next five years.

24. To promote further development of trade and economic ties between India and Russia, the Sides intend to work on improving the transport infrastructure. They attach great importance to the development of the International North–South Transport Corridor (INSTC). The major thrust in the INSTC is to secure freight volumes, upgrade and improve the transport and logistics services provided, simplify document workflow and switch to electronic document workflow, introduce digital technologies and satellite navigation into the transportation process.

25. Both Sides foresee good potential in establishing cooperation in the sphere of railways. They expressed satisfaction with the progress of the feasibility study for raising the speed of the Nagpur-Secunderabad Section and noted the interest of Russian Government to participate in the implementation of that development project. The Sides will continue to actively engage in this regard.

26. The Sides agreed to review possibility of expanding direct passenger and cargo flights including flights between various regions of both the countries.

27. They intend to further cooperate in transport education, professional training, and scientific support for the infrastructure transport projects.
28. The Sides emphasised the importance of joint research in science and technology. They are committed to intensify development of high-tech products in such spheres, as telecommunications, robotics, artificial intelligence, nanotechnologies, pharmacy, and others. To this end, the leaders appreciated signing of the MoU between Department of Science & Technology of the Republic of India and Ministry of Economic Development of the Russian Federation for cooperation in the field of Innovation.
29. The Russian Side hailed results of the 2018 All India Tiger Estimation, which established that India was home to 75% of the global tiger population with 2967 tigers. Indian Side welcomed the Russian Side's initiative to hold the Second International Tiger Conservation Forum in 2022 (also called the Second Tiger Summit, the first Summit was held in Saint-Petersburg in 2010). Acknowledging their leadership role in tiger conservation efforts, both Sides agreed to hold a HighLevel Tiger Forumin India in 2020, involving tiger range countries, conservation partners, and other stakeholders.
30. Promising areas of cooperation include aviation and space. The Sides agreed to explore the prospects of establishing joint ventures in India for the development and production of civil aircraft.
31. The Sides welcomed the increased cooperation between the State Space Corporation "Roscosmos" and the Indian Space Research Organization, including the human spaceflight programs and satellite navigation. The Sides agreed that it was necessary to exploit to a greater extent potential of India and Russia in launch vehicles development, construction, and utilization of spacecraft for different applications, as well as research and use of outer space for peaceful purposes, including planetary exploration.
32. The Sides welcomed the active work carried out within the framework of the signed MoU on support of the Russian Side for India's first manned mission "Gaganyaan."
33. Both Sides intend to strengthen cooperation within the UN Committee on the Peaceful Uses of Outer Space (UN COPUS), including guaranteeing long-term sustainability of outer space

activities and developing "Space 2030" Agenda and implementation plan.
34. They attach high importance to cooperation in the diamond industry. The successful activity of the PJSC ALROSA office in India was noted by the Sides. They declared their interest in enhancing rough diamonds trading system and exploring ways to further improve the regulatory environment in this field with the aim of protecting the equity of natural diamonds.
35. The Sides acknowledged the opportunities to increase bilateral trade in the sphere of agriculture. They expressed their intent to take specific steps to enhance legal framework in this sector and harmonise phytosanitary standards, develop logistics, find new ways to promote agricultural commodities in our countries' markets and study the capacities and needs of each other more carefully. Green Corridor mechanism envisages pre-arrival exchange of information between two Customs administrations. This would help faster clearance to goods, through enhanced risk management. It would thus significantly improve trade facilitation.
36. India-Russia close cooperation in military and military-technical fields is a pillar of their bilateral Special and Privileged Strategic Partnership. The Sides expressed their satisfaction with regular military contacts and joint exercises of the Armed Forces of the two countries. They welcomed the successful implementation of the 2011–2020 Long-Term Program for Military and Technical Cooperation. They agreed to speed up elaboration of a new long-term plan of interaction in this area.
37. The Sides expressed their commitment to upgrading their defence cooperation, including by fostering joint development and production of military equipment, components and spare parts, improve the after-sales service system and continue holding regular joint exercises of the Armed Forces of the two countries.
38. Both Sides agreed to take forward ongoing engagement to encourage joint manufacturing in India of spare parts, components, aggregates, and other products for maintenance of Russian origin Arms and defence equipment under Make-in-India program through transfer of technology and setting up of joint ventures.
39. The Sides aspired to create favourable conditions for further development of bilateral cooperation between their Armed Forces and recognised the requirement of an institutional arrangement for

reciprocal provision of logistic support and services for the Armed Forces. It was agreed to prepare a framework for cooperation on reciprocal logistics support.
40. Both Sides reaffirmed their commitment to enhance military to military cooperation through military political dialogues, joint military exercises, staff-talks, training in each other's military institutions and through other mutually agreed area of cooperation. Sides noted that this year, second Joint Tri-Services Exercises INDRA-2019 will be carried out in India.
41. The Sides commended the implementation of the bilateral Cultural Exchange Program, which directly helps bring the peoples of the two countries together. They agreed to continue the successful practice of holding reciprocal festivals of the Russian culture in India and of the Indian culture in Russia, as well as of Russian film festivals in India and of Indian film festivals in Russia. Both Sides welcomed that Russia will be the Partner Country in the 50th International Film Festival to be held in Goa on November 20–28, 2019. It was agreed that there is a need for geographical expansion of cultural exchanges and greater involvement of the youth and folk art groups and to further promote the Russian language in India and Hindi in Russia comprehensively, including by developing contacts between relevant educational institutions.
42. The Sides welcome intensification of cooperation in the sphere of education. They will continue to promote establishment of direct contacts between universities and educational institutions. Bilateral intergovernmental agreements on mutual recognition of academic credentials will give impetus to these activities. They also agreed to expedite work on preparation of the agreements.
43. The Sides emphasised the importance of promoting cooperation between the states/union territories of the Republic of India and entities of the Russian Federation and stated their intention to organise a forum between them coordinated by their respective Ministries. The Sides agreed to establish exchanges of cultural and business missions between the states of India and the regions of Russia. They agreed to further develop the twin cities format to give a fresh impetus to the existing ties and create new ones.

44. India-Russia tourism ties have been developing vigorously and serve to further reinforce the relations of the Special and Privileged Strategic Partnership and mutual understanding. Both Sides agreed to continue to deepen cooperation in this area.
45. Both Sides welcomed progressive simplification of visa formalities, in particular, further extension of duration of e-Visa facility for business and tourism purposes to one year including for Russian nationals and the introduction of free electronic visas for Indian nationals to visit the Kaliningrad region and Vladivostok. They agreed to continue the work on simplification of the visa regime in future.
46. Both Sides noted the high level of political dialogue and cooperation between our countries, including at the UN, and agreed to deepen it further.
47. Both Sides stressed the imperative of further strengthening of multilateralism, including the central coordinating role of the United Nations in world affairs. The Sides underlined the primacy of international law and emphasised their commitment to the purposes and the principles stated in the UN Charter including the inadmissibility of interference in the internal affairs of Member States.
48. Both sides shared the view that implementation in good faith of genuinely universally recognised principles and rules of international law excludes the practice of double standards or imposition of some States of their will on other States and considers that imposition of unilateral coercive measures not based on international law is an example of such practice.
49. Both Sides called for reform of the UNSC to reflect contemporary global realities and to make it more representative, effective, and efficient in dealing with issues of international peace and security.
50. Russia will continue to support India's candidacy for the permanent membership of a reformed UN Security Council.
51. Both Sides reiterated their commitment to strengthen multi-sectoral partnership within BRICS and agreed to extend full support to the success of the 11th BRICS Summit to be held in Brazil in November 2019.
52. India and Russia unanimously recognise the effectiveness and great potential of the Shanghai Cooperation Organization. India and Russia will increase their interaction, including in the framework

of Russia's SCO Presidency in 2019–2020, to further strengthen the Organization as an important pillar of the emerging multi-polar world order based on equal and indivisible security.
53. The Sides intend to focus particularly on increasing the effectiveness of countering terrorism, extremism, drug trafficking, cross-border organised crime, and information security threats, in particular by improving the functionality of the SCO Regional Anti-Terrorist Structure.
54. The Sides will promote expansion of economic cooperation within the SCO, primarily in transport and logistics, infrastructure, science, technology, and innovation to build a greater, equitable, open, and mutually beneficial cooperation in the Eurasian space. We are determined to deepen cultural and humanitarian ties within the SCO format.
55. The Sides support increased role of the SCO in international affairs, comprehensive development of the Organization's contacts with the UN and its specialised agencies, the CSTO, the CIS, ASEAN, and other multilateral organizations and associations. In this context, they support the establishment of official ties between the SCO and Eurasian Economic Union.
56. The Sides intend to intensify cooperation within the RIC framework, consistently promote common approaches to pressing issues on the global and regional agenda with a focus on upholding international law, countering the expansion of protectionism and unilateral sanctions, and combating terrorism and other new threats and challenges. Regular meetings in this format at the level of Heads of State/Government, foreign ministers and, if necessary, between heads of other agencies, will continue.
57. We agreed to improve coordination within the G20 and other international organizations and fora with a view to facilitate the early resolution of key international issues. Both Sides reaffirmed their commitment to deepen cooperation on issues of global and mutual interest in G20 and international fora.
58. The leaders strongly condemned terrorism in all its forms and manifestations and called on the international community to set up a united front to fight against this evil. They reaffirmed their commitment to undertake all measures to prevent and combat terrorism. They welcomed the Bishkek Declaration of the Shanghai Cooperation Organization's Heads of State Council Meeting.

They insisted on the inadmissibility of double standards in countering terrorism and extremism, as well as of the use of terrorist groups for political ends. Both leaders called for enhanced coordination of our states' efforts within the framework of international counter-terrorism cooperation, including by strengthening the fight against the use of information and communication technologies for terrorist purposes. They agreed to intensify counter-terrorism cooperation in bilateral and multilateral formats and called for early finalisation of the Comprehensive Convention on International Terrorism. The Sides reaffirmed their mutual commitment to strengthening the current inter-state drug control regime based on the three relevant United Nations conventions. Today no country is aloof from the shadow of terrorism. India and Russia need to be united in their counter-terrorism efforts. Russia noted India's proposal to organise a global anti-terrorism conference.

59. The Sides appreciated the level of interaction between our countries on Cooperation in the field of Security in the Use of Information and Communication Technologies, including at multilateral specialised negotiating platforms, primarily at the United Nations. It was noted that based on the outcomes of the 73rd session of the UNGA, a set of international rules, norms, and principles of responsible behaviour of States has been adopted by the UN General Assembly in December 2018, and a wide discussion on information and communication technologies (ICTs) security including countering the use of ICT for criminal purposes has been launched.

60. They emphasised the need to establish a framework for cooperation among BRICS countries in the sphere of security in the use of ICTs, including through concluding relevant intergovernmental agreement between the association's member-states.

61. The Sides reaffirmed the commonality of approaches to provision of security in the use of ICTs and willingness to strengthen bilateral inter-agency practical cooperation through realization of the India-Russia intergovernmental agreement on cooperation in Security in the use of ICTs.

62. They resolved to take necessary steps to enhance bilateral cooperation in accordance with the Plan to implement the main directions of cooperation between India and Russia on the security in the

use of Information and Communication Technologies for 2019–2020. Both sides stressed the need to continue efforts aimed at improving the international security environment, as well as to work consistently with a view to increasing the level of inter-state trust and strengthening global and regional stability in all its aspects as a basis for ensuring lasting peace founded on the principle of equal and indivisible security for all, while respecting the interests and concerns of all states.

63. They agreed to maintain intensive contacts on the entire range of security issues through the National Security Council Secretariat and the Security Council of the Russian Federation.

64. Both sides expressed concern over the possibility of an arms race in outer space and outer space turning into an arena for military confrontation. It was reaffirmed that the prevention of an arms race in outer space (PAROS) would avert a grave danger to international peace and security and that they intended to continue to make efforts in this direction. They stressed the paramount importance of strict compliance with existing international legal agreements providing for the peaceful uses of outer space including the support to international peace and stability, promotion of international cooperation, and mutual understanding.

65. The sides supported negotiation of a multilateral, legally binding instrument to establish reliable guarantees for non-placement of any weapons in the Earth orbit. They reaffirmed that the Conference on Disarmament is the only forum for holding multilateral negotiations on an international agreement (or agreements) on the prevention of an arms race in outer space in all its aspects.

66. It was agreed that universal, non-discriminatory, and practical transparency and confidence building measures can play complementary role to a legally binding instrument on PAROS.

67. The sides supported strengthening of the Biological and Toxins Weapons Convention (BTWC) including by adopting a protocol to the Convention providing for, inter alia, an international, non-discriminatory, and effective compliance verification mechanism. They reaffirmed that BTWC functions, including in what concerns the UN Security Council, should not be duplicated by other mechanisms.

68. Both sides reaffirmed support to the Organization for the Prohibition of Chemical Weapons (OPCW), which has contributed

to effective implementation of the provisions of the Chemical Weapons Convention (CWC). They reaffirmed their determination to support efforts and initiatives aimed at preserving the role of the CWC, and preventing the politicization of the activities of the OPCW. They called on the States Parties to the CWC to stand united and engage in a constructive dialogue with a view to restoring the spirit of consensus in the OPCW in order to preserve the integrity and sanctity of the Convention.
69. To address the threat of chemical and biological terrorism, both sides emphasised the need to launch multilateral negotiations on an international convention for the suppression of acts of chemical and biological terrorism at the Conference on Disarmament.
70. Both sides reiterated their commitment to further strengthen global non-proliferation. Russia expressed its strong support for India's membership of the Nuclear Suppliers Group.
71. India and Russia support all efforts for an inclusive peace and Afghan-led and Afghan-owned reconciliation in Afghanistan. The Sides expressed their commitment to an early peaceful settlement in Afghanistan, their determination to achieve this goal by continuing cooperation within the SCO-Afghanistan Contact Group and other internationally recognised formats, and their support for the intra-Afghan dialogue launched in Moscow in February 2019. The Sides will continue intensive discussions on Afghanistan. They encouraged all interested States in their efforts to make peace process in Afghanistan broad based, preserve the constitutional order, bring durable peace and to turn Afghanistan into a peaceful, secure, stable, and independent state. They called for immediate cessation of violence.
72. The sides welcomed the stabilization of the situation in Syria. They insisted on the need to respect Syria's sovereignty and territorial integrity and called for the settlement of the Syrian crisis exclusively through political and diplomatic means.
73. They emphasised the importance of combating terrorist organizations in Syria, as defined by the United Nations Security Council. They agreed to continue to step up assistance to Syria with a view to reconstruction, including the creation of conditions for the return of refugees and temporarily displaced persons. The sides insisted on the need for strict compliance with the principles of international humanitarian assistance laid down in United Nations

General Assembly resolution 46/182, which gives the key role in defining the parameters of humanitarian assistance to the Government of the affected country in order to respect the national sovereignty of the affected country.
74. Both sides recognised the importance of full and effective implementation of the Joint Comprehensive Plan of Action on the Iranian Nuclear Programme (JCPOA) in the context of securing regional and international peace, security, and stability and reaffirmed their full commitment to the United Nations Security Council resolution 2231. Issues around it should be resolved peacefully and through dialogue. Both sides expressed their determination to continue mutually beneficial and legitimate economic and commercial cooperation with Iran.
75. Both Sides stressed the importance of continued peaceful dialogue among all parties concerned in order to realise lasting peace and stability in a denuclearised Korean Peninsula. In this regard, they urged all parties concerned to work together towards this goal.
76. It was agreed to explore mutually acceptable and beneficial areas of cooperation in third countries especially in the Central Asia, South East Asia, and Africa.
77. The Sides agreed on the need to preserve and strengthen the role of the World Trade Organization for upholding a transparent, non-discriminatory multilateral trading system. The Sides intend to work together to shape a fair and open global economy.
78. Both sides emphasised the importance of deepening regional economic cooperation to ensure sustainable socio-economic development and the implementation of the 2030 Agenda, including the expansion of cooperation within the framework of the United Nations Economic and Social Commission for Asia and the Pacific in such key areas as transport, energy, and trade.
79. The Sides reaffirmed their commitment to building an equal and indivisible security architecture in Asia and the Pacific region. They support the development of multilateral dialogue on this topic within the framework of the East Asia Summits and other regional platforms. They agreed that initiatives aimed at strengthening the regional order should be based on the principles of multilateralism, openness, inclusiveness, and mutual respect and should not be directed against any country. India and Russia as

stakeholders in this common space agreed to intensify consultations on complementarities between integration and development initiatives in greater Eurasian space and in the regions of Indian and Pacific Oceans.

80. The Sides were satisfied to note the significant similarity in approaches to their foreign policy priorities and stressed the importance of further development of the India-Russia Special and Privileged Strategic Partnership, both in the context of the current bilateral relations and in addressing regional and international issues. They expressed their mutual intention to strengthen and expand their bilateral relations for the benefit of the peoples of India and Russia.

81. Prime Minister Narendra Modi thanked President Vladimir Putin for the gracious hospitality extended to him and his delegation in Vladivostok. He invited President Vladimir Putin to visit India next year for the 21st India-Russia Annual Summit.

(g) **Translation of Prime Minister's Press Statement During His Visit to Vladivostok, September 04, 2019**

A 5-year roadmap for cooperation in this sector, and cooperation in the search for Hydro-Carbon and LNG in Far East and the Arctic have been agreed. Whenever the need arises, India and Russia work together not only in ordinary places of the world but in Antarctica and Arctic also.

(h) **Transcript of Media Briefing by Foreign Secretary on the Bilateral Meeting Between India and Russia on the Sidelines of SCO Summit 2019 in Bishkek, June 13, 2019**

A new area of focus that was identified by both leaders is Arctic region oil & gas. Prior to that the Deputy Prime Minister and the Special Representative of President Putin for the Arctic region in the Far East, Deputy Prime Minister Trutnev will visit India in June and we are also planning for the possibility of the India-Russia Inter-Governmental Consultation which is headed by the External Affairs Minister on our side to also be held, if we can, before September before the annual summit. Nor was any discussion on any regional or international issues because the focus was entirely on how to make the Prime Minister's visit for the next Annual Summit successful and what we need to do in this new area, new dimension of cooperation in the Russian Far East and the Arctic.

(i) **Visit of Minister of Foreign Affairs of Iceland to India, December 07–14, 2018**

The two Ministers also discussed the possibility of enhanced cooperation in the Arctic Council, an inter-governmental Forum of Arctic states where India has an Observer status.

(j) **India–Russia Joint Statement During Visit of President of Russia to India, October 05, 2018**

The Sides expressed interest in the development of mutually beneficial cooperation in the Arctic, inter alia in the sphere of joint scientific research. The Sides expressed their support to companies from both sides for development of cooperation and exploring opportunities for joint development of oil fields in the Russian territory, including in the Arctic shelf of Russia and joint development of projects on the shelf of the Pechora and Okhotsk Seas.

(k) **India–Canada Joint Statement During State Visit of Prime Minister of Canada to India, February 23, 2018**

To enhance geo-spatial collaboration and to consider Indian participation in Canadian Arctic research.

(l) **Prime Minister's Statement on the Subject "Creating a Shared Future in a Fractured Word" in the World Economic Forum, January 23, 2018**

The first threat is of Climate Change. Glaciers are shrinking, the ice at Arctic is melting and many islands have either submerged or are on the verge submersion.

(m) **English Translation of Speech by External Affairs Minister at the Inauguration of Eastern Economic Forum in Vladivostok, September 06, 2017**

Rich natural resources of this region and its unique geographical location of providing passage to both Arctic and Pacific Ocean fills it with unlimited opportunities.

(n) **Statement by M.J. Akbar, Minister of State for External Affairs at UNGA's Ocean Conference, New York, June 08, 2017**

Indian scientists today collaborate in research stations on the Arctic Ocean studying its links with climate in our own region.

(o) **Saint Petersburg Declaration by the Russian Federation and the Republic of India: A Vision for the Twenty-first Century, 01 June 2017**

We are interested in launching joint projects on exploration and exploitation of hydrocarbons in the Arctic shelf of the Russian Federation.

(p) **Transcript of Media Briefing by JS (XP) and JS (ERS) on Ongoing Visit of Prime Minister to Russia, June 01, 2017**

The two leaders actually had great discussion in the aspect of the energy collaboration, the energy bridge between the two countries which is being set and as a contour of that they referred to obviously nuclear, six units of which are up and running including today the fifth and sixth one supplemented by the hydrocarbon investment which had happened last year and actually they added to that as we all know it has happened in the Sakhalin and Vankor but this time they had indicated that they desire to actually go beyond that to also do joint exploration and exploitation of hydrocarbons in the Arctic area of the Russian Federation.

(q) **India–Russia Joint Statement During the Visit of President of the Russia to India: Partnership for Global Peace and Stability**

With the aim of further strengthening oil and gas cooperation the Russian Side expressed its interest in attracting Indian oil companies to participate in joint projects in the offshore-Arctic fields of the Russian Federation. Recognising the importance of the Arctic and given that Russia is a member of the Arctic Council and India is an observer since May 2013, the Sides agreed to facilitate scientific cooperation to study the challenges (like melting ice, climate change, marine life and biodiversity), facing the rapidly changing Arctic region.

(r) **Opening Remarks by External Affairs Minister at the Opening Plenary During the Second India-US Strategic and Commercial Dialogue (S&CD) in New Delhi, August 30, 2016**

India will take part in the Arctic Science Ministerial being hosted by the White House as well as in Our Ocean Conference that you are hosting next month.

(s) **India-Iceland Joint Statement During the Visit of Foreign Minister of Iceland to India, April 05, 2016**

The Ministers discussed the challenges of climate change for the Arctic and the Himalayan regions and the importance of continued scientific cooperation aimed at understanding better the implications of climate change for the ice covers and glaciers in the two regions.

(t) **India-Finland Joint Statement During the Visit of Prime Minister of Finland to India, February 13, 2016**

The Prime Minister of India thanked Finland for its support for India becoming an observer in the Arctic Council.

(u) **Joint Statement Between the Russian Federation and the Republic of India: Shared Trust, New Horizons, December 24, 2015**

The Russian Side welcomes the interest and involvement of Indian partners with regard to cooperation in joint projects stipulating the possibility of LNG supply to India from JSC NOVATEK project Arctic LNG on the resource base of the fields located on the Gydan Peninsula and partly in the Gulf of Ob. Considering Russia's status as a member of the Arctic Council (AC) and India's observer status at this organization since 2013, the Sides emphasised the importance of joint activities in the framework of the Arctic Council. They acknowledged the potential for the development of joint scientific research in the Arctic region, particularly the Russian Scientific Center on Spitsbergen (Svalbard) archipelago.

(v) **5th Session of India-Norway Joint Commission Meeting: 02 November 2015**

Bilateral collaboration in education spans joint research and higher education at post graduate level in diverse fields including energy, climate change, ocean and Arctic/polar research, public health, and information security; urban planning and development; environment; biotechnology and the medical sciences; marine sciences; innovation and geo-hazards.

(w) **President's Banquet Speech in Stockholm, June 01, 2015**

We are grateful for your endorsement of India's rightful claim to Permanent Membership of the United Nations Security Council and for your proactive efforts that helped India achieve Observer status in the Arctic Council during the period of Sweden's Chairmanship.

(x) **Transcript of Media Briefing on President's Forthcoming Visit to Sweden and Belarus, 30 May 2015**

Incidentally Sweden has supported India's application for becoming Observer to the Arctic Council two years ago, and for that we are very appreciative.

(y) **Transcript of Media Briefing by Foreign Secretary on President's Ongoing Visit to the Russian Federation, May 09, 2015**

On energy cooperation it was noted that ONGC's investment in Sakhalin-1 had been very successful. Its MoU with Rosneft for exploration on the Arctic Shelf is being progressed. GAIL's contract for LNG supply to India has entered into force.

(z) **What's in it for Canada? Lots: April 15, 2015**

Canada's leadership secured India its observer status in the Arctic Council.

(aa) **Druzhba-Dosti: A Vision for Strengthening the Indian-Russian Partnership over the Next Decade'—Joint Statement During the Visit of President of the Russian Federation to India: 11 December 2014**

India and Russia recognise the importance of the Arctic and the contributions in promoting cooperative activities to address Arctic issues by the Arctic Council, given that Russia is a member and India has joined as an observer in May 2013. The sides agreed to facilitate scientific cooperation to study the challenges (like melting ice, climate change, marine life and biodiversity), facing the rapidly-changing Arctic region.

(ab) **Transcript of President's Onboard Media interaction Enroute from Rovaniemi to New Delhi: October 17, 2014**

Question: Sir, my question is related to the Arctic Council. India is a permanent observer, when you were discussing with the two main Scandinevian countries, what has India got in commitment that in future India would be playing a greater role in the Arctic Council?
President: We are already playing an important role because I made it quite clear in my speech even today in the Business meeting that our research is not meant for merely India's interest. Our global and glacial research by our scientists in Himadri research station in North Pole is meant for the whole world and we would like to complement the efforts made by other states also. Therefore, we are fully involved in Arctic Council and also in the polar research, glacial research, climate research—as all these are interlinked.

(ac) **Address by President to the Parliament of Finland: October 16, 2014**

India will continue to deploy its significant polar research capabilities and scientific understanding for strengthening the work of the Arctic Council.

(ad) **President's Speech at the State Banquet hosted by His Majesty, the King of Norway: 13 October 2014**

We are grateful for your endorsement of India's rightful claim to Permanent Membership of the United Nations Security Council and for your proactive efforts that helped India achieve Observer status in the Arctic Council.

(ae) **Transcript of Media Briefing by Secretary (West) and Official Spokesperson (October 10, 2014)**

I must mention in this regard here that, as many of you would recall, in May 2013 India became permanent observer to the Arctic Council and Norway was one of the countries which gave us unconditional support within the Arctic Council to breakthrough, so to speak. And the earth sciences collaboration because of our station in Himadri and other areas has been expanding before and even more so since the fact that we became members of the Arctic Council. This is something which we are looking at going further. The tremendous interest in earth sciences comes from the fact that whatever happens in the Arctic affects us immediately in terms of climate change, in terms of predictability of monsoons, in terms of various other natural phenomena which happen up there and have to researched. We have recently put up a deep-sea probe up beyond towards the North Pole which is playing a very critical role in this research.

Question: This question is to Navtej. Presently India's interest in the Arctic region so far is scientific research, etc. But now many countries have become permanent observers. They are not looking at only on the scientific issues, rather they are exploring the possibility of extracting the resources from the Arctic region. How is India looking at the Arctic region's possibilities in future? Is India competing with those countries or will India's interests be limited to only scientific exploration?

Secretary (West): I certainly would not foreclose any possibilities in regard to whatever benefits the Arctic might offer to the world. At the same time, we really do not believe in entering organisations or situations like this with an avowed objective of exploiting resources. So, I think we have to work very carefully in the Arctic Council. It is a very delicate, fragile environment. We have to work with full sensitivity to the people of the countries of the Arctic Council who are the Arctic members. It is not only the states that are involved, there are also the various indigenous populations in the Arctic who are permanent participants as against observers in the Arctic Council. We have to keep their interests in mind. So, certainly we will go along with the Arctic Council as it opens up different areas, as different possibilities open up.

(af) **Joint Statement on the 14th India-Russia Annual Summit: Deepening the Strategic Partnership for Global Peace and Stability: October 21, 2013**

The Indian side expressed OVL's interest in participating along with Russian companies in exploration for hydrocarbons in the Arctic region.

(ag) **Transcript of Media Briefing by Foreign Secretary and India's Ambassador to Russia on Prime Minister's Visit to Russia, October 21, 2013**

On hydrocarbons, we are cooperating in many parts of Russia. There is the OVL, Sakhalin, Arctic, there is Imperial Energy, Tomsk. We are even thinking in terms of a pipeline that will connect ultimately from Russia to India. This might well be some years in the future but still we have a vision. And I think that it is important to have something that you work towards with your trusted strategic partners. And something like this when implemented will be truly transformational.

(ah) **Transcript of Media Briefing by Foreign Secretary on Prime Minister's Forthcoming Visits (October 18, 2013)**

Question: Madam, you are talking about cooperation with Russia in hydrocarbons. Do you expect any new agreements during the visit in this regard?

Foreign Secretary: Russia is a major energy producer while India is one of the fastest-growing energy consumers. ONGC Videsh Limited has large investments in Sakhalin-1 and Tomsk, and is considering new investment opportunities in oil and gas, in projects in Siberia, in Russia's Far East and in the Arctic Shelf with companies such as Rosneft, Gazprom and Novatech. And we are hoping to have successful conclusion of these endeavours when the time is right. So, energy cooperation whether it is nuclear energy or oil and gas sectors are an important dimension of our strategic partnership. In the oil and gas sectors, cooperation has been progressing very well. But newer areas definitely need to be explored. We have brought to the Russian side's attention OVL's keen interest in newer projects including joint exploration of the Russian Arctic zone which is very rich in minerals.

Annexure D: Memorandum of Understanding (MOU) Signed with Arctic Countries

(a) **List of MoUs/Agreements Signed During State Visit of President to Slovenia: September 17, 2019**

Sl. No	Name of agreement/MoU	Indian signatory	Slovenian signatory
1.	Programme of Scientific and Technological Cooperation between the Ministry of Science and Technology of India and the Ministry of Education, Science, and Sport of Slovenia for the period 2020–2022	Mr. Param Jit Mann Ambassador of India to Slovenia	Dr. Jernej Štromajer, State Secretary, Ministry of Education, Science, and Sport
2.	MoU on Cooperation in the field of Sport between the Ministry of Youth Affairs and Sports of India and the Ministry of Education, Science, and Sport of Slovenia	Mr. Param Jit Mann Ambassador of India to Slovenia	Dr. Jernej Štromajer, State Secretary, Ministry of Education, Science, and Sport
3.	Programme of Cooperation in the fields of Culture, Arts, Education, Sports, and Mass Media	Mr. Param Jit Mann Ambassador of India to Slovenia	Dr. Jernej Štromajer, State Secretary, Ministry of Education, Science, and Sport

(continued)

(continued)

Sl. No	Name of agreement/MoU	Indian signatory	Slovenian signatory
4.	Programme of Cooperation between the Bureau of Indian Standards (BIS) and the Slovenian Institute for Standardization (SIST) on Technical Cooperation in the field of Standardization	Mr. Param Jit Mann Ambassador of India to Slovenia	Ms. Marjetka Strle Vidali General Director Slovenian Institute for Standardization
5.	MoU between Invest India and SPIRIT Slovenia	Mr. Deepak Bagla MD & CEO Invest India	Ms. Ajda Cuderman, Director of SPIRIT Slovenia—Public Agency for Entrepreneurship, Internationalization, Foreign Investments, and Technology
6.	Memorandum of Understanding between IIT Kanpur (for Ganga/India) and VGB (Slovenia)	Dr. S. Ganesh Dean Research & Development IIT Kanpur	MSc. Smijan Juvan, CEO VGB
7.	Memorandum of Understanding between IIT Kanpur (for cGanga/India) and Space-SI (Slovenia)	Dr. S. Ganesh Dean Research & Development IIT Kanpur	Dr. Tomaž Rodič Director Spare-SI
8.	Cooperation Agreement Between Chamber of Commerce and Industry of Slovenia (CCIS) and the Associated Chambers of Commerce and Industry of India (ASSOCHAM)	Ms. Sonja Šmuc, Director General CCIS	Mr. Kishor Kumar Sharma, Chairman National Council of Arbitration ASSOCHAM

(b) List of Documents Signed During the State Visit of Hon'ble President to Norway (from October 12–14, 2014)

S. No	Details of the agreement/ MoU	Signatories	Purpose
In the meeting between the President and the Prime Minister			
1.	Agreement on exemption of visa requirement for holders of diplomatic and official passports	Ambassador Browne of India and Director General Tore Hattrem, Norwegian MFA	This Agreement will help to promote bilateral relations by facilitating the travel of diplomatic and official passport holders to the territory of the two countries
At Munch Museum			
2.	MoU between Indian Ministry of Culture and Munch Museum, Norway	Prof Rajeev Lochan, Director National Gallery of Modern Arts and Mr Stein Olav Henrichsen, Director, Munch Museum	The MOU aims to inspire the mutual desire of institutions to strengthen and enhance friendly cultural relations between the two countries, deepen mutual understanding of their peoples and promote cultural co-operation and exchanges
At Confederation of Norwegian Enterprise (NHO)—High Level Plenary			
3.	MoU between Ministry of Earth Sciences (MoES) and Research Council of Norway (RCN) in the field of Earth System Sciences	Secretary Shailesh Nayak, MoES, and Mr. Arvid Hallén, Director General of RCN	The purpose of this MOU is to facilitate arrangements and understanding that lead to India-Norwegian cooperation and coordination of activities and progress in Earth System Sciences. Its objective is to allow exchange of scientific resources, personnel, and technical knowledge to support the improvement and development of progress in Earth Sciences and services

(continued)

(continued)

S. No	Details of the agreement/MoU	Signatories	Purpose
4.	MoU between IIT Kanpur and NTNU	Director Prof Indranil Manna, IIT Kanpur, and Pro-Rector Professor Johan Hustad, NTNU	This MOU aims to facilitate further cooperation between IIT Kanpur and NTNU in research and education. This MOU is a statement of intent to foster genuine and mutually beneficial collaboration and seeks to promote mobility of students and faculty/staff, joint research activities and publications, exchange of academic materials, and special short-term academic programs
5.	MoU between IISER, Thiruvananthapuram and SINTEF Materials and Chemistry	Director Prof. V. Ramakrishnan, IISER, and Prof. Duncan Akporiaye, Vice President Research of SINTEF	The purpose is to enhance relations between the two institutions and to develop academic and cultural interchange in the areas of education, research and other activities and to cooperate and work towards internationalization of higher education. The institutions will promote and cooperate academic exchange, R&D collaborations, training and teaching, collaborative research, exchange of information regarding business ideas, product innovation, and commercialization

(continued)

(continued)

S. No	Details of the agreement/ MoU	Signatories	Purpose
6.	MoU between University of Oslo and University of Hyderabad	Vice-Chancellor Dr. R. Ramaswami, University of Hyderabad and Ole Petter Ottersen, Rector at UiO and Head of the Board of the Norwegian Association of Higher Education Institutions	The MOU will enhance relations between the two Universities and develop academic and cultural interchange in areas of education, research and other activities and work towards internationalization of higher education. The parties will promote and cooperate in activities including academic exchange and collaborations, training and teaching, collaborative research, and exchange of information
7.	Statement of Intent (SoI), between DRDO, MoD of India and Norwegian Defence Research Establishment (FFI), MoD of Norway	Dr Sudershan Kumar, DRDO, and John-Mikal Størdal, Director General of FFI	This declares the intent of both institutions to explore opportunities for cooperation in research and development programs in the field of defence research and development through organization of seminars, conferences, workshops, and exchange of relevant information
	At Confederation of Norwegian Enterprise (NHO)—Thematic Sessions		

(continued)

(continued)

S. No	Details of the agreement/ MoU	Signatories	Purpose
8.	MoU between IISER Thiruvananthapuram and Institute of Energy Technology	Director Prof. V. Ramakrishnan, IISER and Research Director Dr. Arve O Holt, IET	The two institutions have agreed to establish a framework for scientific collaboration with the aim to enhance relations to develop academic and cultural interchange in the areas of research and development by identifying collaboration opportunities in relation to academic exchange and R&D collaborations in areas of mutual interest
9.	MoU between University of Oslo and IIT Kanpur	Director Prof. Indranil Manna, IIT Kanpur and Ole Petter Ottersen, Rector at UiO and Head of the Board of the Norwegian Association of Higher Education Institutions	The MOU will **promote cooperation in academic education and research between the Institutions including activities of collaborative research, lectures and symposia, exchange of scholars, researchers, students, and exchange of information and materials in fields which are of interest to both parties**

(continued)

(continued)

S. No	Details of the agreement/ MoU	Signatories	Purpose
10.	MoU between Council for Scientific and Industrial Research CSIR—SINTEF	DG CSIR Dr. P. S. Ahuja and Ernst Kristiansen, Executive Vice President of SINTEF	This MOU will support promotion and extension of cooperation in "Scientific Research and Technology Development" in the fields of mutual interest of both sides. The cooperation will include exchange of scientists, research scholars, scientific and technical information, joint identification of science and technical problems, formulation and implementation of a joint research program in area of *Building & Infrastructure, Materials & Chemistry and Technology & Society* as well as exchange of knowledge, expertise and know-how resulting from the joint collaborative program

(continued)

(continued)

S. No	Details of the agreement/ MoU	Signatories	Purpose
11.	MoU between Indian Council for Medical Research ICMR and Research Council of Norway (RCN)	Ambassador Browne of India and Mr. Arvid Hallén, Director General of RCN	The main purpose of this MOU is to establish a health research relationship for encouraging research in a range of health-related areas of mutual interest, including human vaccines, infectious diseases and antimicrobial resistance. The agreement shall promote direct cooperation within the field being organised through joint calls and funding for research proposals/projects as well as facilitating exchange of scientists and scientific information
12.	MoU between IIT Kanpur and NILU	Director Prof. Indranil Manna, IIT Kanpur and Dr. Kari Nygaard, Managing Director, NILU	Through this MOU both institutes agree to develop collaborative activities in the academic areas of mutual interest taking the forms of research and development projects and collaboration on education and training programs through project funding
13.	MoU between University of Hyderabad and University of Bergen	Vice-Chancellor Dr. R. Ramaswami, University of Hyderabad and Prof. Anne Chr. Johannessen, Vice Rector, University of Bergen	The MOU aims to enhance relations between the two Universities and to develop academic and cultural interchange in areas of education, research, and other activities and agree to work towards internationalization of higher education

(continued)

(continued)

S. No	Details of the agreement/ MoU	Signatories	Purpose
	On the Sidelines of the State Visit		
14.	MoU between University of Hyderabad and NTNU	Vice-Chancellor Dr. R. Ramaswami, University of Hyderabad and Prof. Gunnar Bovim, Rector of NTNU	The MOU aims to enhance relations between the two Universities and to develop academic and cultural interchange in areas of education, research, and other activities and agree to work towards internationalization of higher education
15.	MoU between Indira Gandhi National Tribal University and University of Agder	Vice-Chancellor Prof. T. V. Kattimani, IGNTU, and Professor Mohan Kolhi, Dept. Engineering, University of Agder	

(c) **List of Agreements/MoUs Signed During the State Visit of President to Sweden: June 01, 2015**

S. No	Agreement/MoU	About the agreement/MoU	Indian signatory	Swedish signatory
1.	MoU on Cooperation in the field of Sustainable Urban Development	This MoU aims at closer and long term cooperation between India and Sweden in the field of sustainable development and protection of the environment. The areas of cooperation include dialogue and interaction on global sustainable urban development issues, exchange of knowledge, institutional cooperation including capacity building, research and development, and commercial relations regarding sustainable urban development	Ambassador of India to Sweden, Ms. Banashri Bose Harrison	Minister for Housing, Urban Development and Information Technology, Mr. Mehmet Kaplan

(continued)

(continued)

S. No	Agreement/MoU	About the agreement/MoU	Indian signatory	Swedish signatory
2.	MoU between the Ministry of Micro, Small and Medium Enterprises of the Republic of India and the Ministry of Enterprise and Innovation of the Kingdom of Sweden on cooperation in the field of Micro, Small, and Medium Enterprises	This MoU aims at promoting partnership projects, institution to institution and enterprise to enterprise cooperation relating to MSMEs, encourage exchange of information and experiences in policy setting and research on the development of MSMEs in areas of mutual interest, stimulating the development of industrial potential surveys and feasibility studies to identify thrust areas and opportunities for development of MSMEs and facilitating exchange of business mission to held initiate technology transfer and sustainable business alliances	Ambassador of India to Sweden, Ms. Banashri Bose Harrison	Minister of Enterprise and Innovation, Mr. Michael Damberg
3.	Agreement on Visa Exemption for diplomatic passports	This agreement will facilitate the entry of citizens of India and Sweden who are holders of diplomatic passports into their respective countries with the aim to strengthen the friendly relations	Ambassador of India to Sweden, Ms. Banashri Bose Harrison	Minister for Justice and Migration, Morgan Johansson

(continued)

(continued)

S. No	Agreement/MoU	About the agreement/MoU	Indian signatory	Swedish signatory
4.	Letter of Intent between Earth System Science Organisation (ESSO), Ministry of Earth Sciences of Government of India and the Swedish Polar Research Secretariat (SPRS) on Collaboration in Polar and Ocean Research	This LoI is to encourage collaboration in the areas of Polar (Antarctic and Arctic) and Ocean Research by enhancing scientific capabilities, conducting joint research and survey activities, exchange of informational material on education, training and research matters, etc.	Ambassador of India to Sweden, Ms. Banashri Bose Harrison	Director General, Swedish Polar Research Secretariat (SPRS), Dr. Björn Dahlbäck
5.	Memorandum of Intent between the Indian Council of Medical Research (ICMR) and the Swedish Research Council for Health Working Life and Welfare (FORTE)	This agreement records the intention of both institutions to cooperate in the field of ageing research and health	Ambassador of India to Sweden, Ms. Banashri Bose Harrison	Director General, Swedish Research Council for Health Working Life and Welfare (FORTE), Ms. Ewa Ställdahl

(continued)

(continued)

S. No	Agreement/MoU	About the agreement/MoU	Indian signatory	Swedish signatory
6.	Memorandum of Intent between the Central Drugs Standard Control Organization (CDSCO) of the Republic of India and the Swedish Medical Products Agency (MPA)	This agreement, complimentary to the ongoing cooperation between India and Sweden covering the area of health, is for increasing bilateral cooperation in the fields of pharmacovigilance, electronic submissions in related matter, clinical trials, drugs, medical devices and diagnostic kits, cosmetic and hygiene products and for exchange of information, and experiences regarding good manufacturing practice	Ambassador of India to Sweden, Ms. Banashri Bose Harrison	Director General, Swedish Medical Products Agency (MPA), Ms. Inger Andersson

(d) List of Documents Signed During the State Visit of President to Finland (October 14–16, 2014)

S. No.	Name of agreement/MoU	Signatory from India	Signatory from Finland	Remarks
Signed before the President				
1.	MoU between the Indian Institutes of Technology and Consortium of Finnish Higher Education Institutions, Finland	Indranil Manna Director, IIT, Kanpur	Tuula Teeri President Aalto University	The MoU encourages direct contact and cooperation between faculty and staff, departments and research institutions. The cooperation would be pursued through visits and interchange of faculty, staff and students, exchange of materials, publications, joint education and research activities and joint research seminars, and conferences
2.	Partnership Agreement between Chempolis Oy and Numaligarh Refinery Ltd. (NRL)	Mr. Puthiya Padmanabhan, Managing Director, Numaligarh Refinery Ltd	Mr. Pasi Rousu, President, Chempolis Asia & Pacific and Americas	The purpose of the MoU includes Partnership agreement and Joint Venture Agreement to establish a long term partnership to build first BioRefinery in India

(continued)

(continued)

S. No.	Name of agreement/MoU	Signatory from India	Signatory from Finland	Remarks
3.	MoU between the Department of Bio Technology, GOI and Tekes, Finnish Funding Agency for Innovation for Cooperation in the field of Biotechnology	Dr. K. Vijayraghavan Secretary	Pekka Soini Director General	The MoU shall help collaborate in the areas of diagnostics in health and well-being. Other fields of life science industry, especially health and well-being, food and nutrition, and environmental, and energy applications of bio technology through joint funding of collaborative projects and workshops, seminars, visits, and knowledge transfers

(continued)

(continued)

S. No.	Name of agreement/MoU	Signatory from India	Signatory from Finland	Remarks
4.	Arrangement for cooperation between the Atomic Energy Regulatory Board of India and the Radiation and Nuclear Safety Authority of Finland	S. S. Bajaj Chairman	Petteri Tiippana Director General	The arrangement is for cooperation in the field of nuclear and radiation safety regulation concerning exchange of information and personnel related to the peaceful use of nuclear energy and radiation related to nuclear installations, radiation and nuclear safety including radioactive waste management, safety-related issues and research, radiation safety, emergency preparedness, and radioactive waste management associated with the operation of nuclear power plants

(continued)

(continued)

S. No.	Name of agreement/MoU	Signatory from India	Signatory from Finland	Remarks
5.	MoU on Renewable Energy Cooperation between the Ministry of New and Renewable Energy of the GOI and the Ministry of Employment and the Economy of the Government of the Republic of Finland	Ashok Kumar Sharma Ambassador	Jan Vapaavuori Minister of Economic Affairs of Finland	The objective of the MoU is to establish the basis for an institutional cooperation in order to encourage and promote bilateral cooperation on new and renewable energy issues. Cooperation will take place in the fields of new and renewable technologies related to among others solar wind and bio-energy, biomass, as also solar projects for solarisation of non-electrified areas, waste-to-energy and efficient energy technologies. This would be done by sharing experiences, joint projects, facilitating creation of joint commercial and non-commercial activities, etc.

Announcement Made Before President

(continued)

(continued)

S. No.	Name of agreement/MoU	Signatory from India	Signatory from Finland	Remarks
6.	Memorandum of Understanding between Indian Institute of Science Education and Research (IISER), Bhopal, and CLEEN Ltd	Prof. Vinod K. Singh, Director, IISER, Bhopal	Dr. Tommy Jacobson, CEO, CLEEN Ltd.	The MoU aims at cooperating in the fields of Renewable and Sustainable energy development, integrated treatment and disposal of hazardous waste, water and waste water systems, air pollution, science and engineering, conservation of energy and environment, environmental change and sustainable development, and soil system

(continued)

(continued)

S. No.	Name of agreement/MoU	Signatory from India	Signatory from Finland	Remarks
7.	Agreement on Scientific, Educational and Cultural Cooperation between Indian Institute of Science Education and Research, Bhopal, India (IISER Bhopal) and University of Turku, Finland	Prof. Vinod K. Singh, Director, Indian Institute of Science Education and Research, Bhopal	Prof. Kalervo Väänänen, Rector, University of Turku	The objective of this agreement is to encourage cooperation and exchanges between the two universities in all academic fields and activities as well as among their related faculties and schools through exchange and collaboration of researchers and faculty, exchange of students organization of joint academic programmes and other forms of knowledge exchange, exchange of literature, conducting combined research projects, and exchange of expertise
8.	Agreement on co-operation in science and education between Indian Institute of Science Education and Research (IISER), Bhopal and Lappeenranta University of Technology (LUT)	Prof. Vinod K. Singh, Director from IISER, Bhopal	Dr. Juha-Matti Saksa, Provost, Lappeenranta University of Technology (LUT)	The MoU aims at cooperating in the fields of Renewable and Sustainable energy system development, air pollution, science and engineering, conservation of energy and environment, environmental change and sustainable development, waste management, and water treatment

(continued)

(continued)

S. No.	Name of agreement/MoU	Signatory from India	Signatory from Finland	Remarks
Signed in Smolna, Helsinki				
9.	Agreement on Scientific, Educational and Cultural Cooperation between Indian Institute of Science Education and Research Thiruvananthapuram (IISER TVM), India and University of Turku, Finland	Prof. V. Ramakrishnan, Director, IISER TVM	Prof. Kalervo Väänänen, Rector, University of Turku	The objective of this agreement is to encourage cooperation and exchanges between the two universities in all academic fields and activities as well as among their related faculties and schools through exchange and collaboration of researchers and faculty, exchange of students organization of joint academic programmes and other forms of knowledge exchange, exchange of literature, conducting combined research projects, and exchange of expertise

(continued)

(continued)

S. No.	Name of agreement/MoU	Signatory from India	Signatory from Finland	Remarks
10.	Memorandum of Understanding between University of Hyderabad, India and University of Eastern Finland, Joensuu, Finland	Dr. R. Ramaswamy, Vice-Chancellor, University of Hyderabad	Prof. Jukka Mönkkönen, Academic Rector, University of Eastern Finland	The MoU aims to enhance relations between the two universities and to develop academic and cultural interchange in the areas of education, research, and other activities and to work towards internationalization of higher education. The areas of collaboration would include academic exchange in the disciplines of natural sciences and social sciences, R and D collaborations, training and teaching, collaborative research and organization of national and international symposia and conferences

(continued)

(continued)

S. No.	Name of agreement/MoU	Signatory from India	Signatory from Finland	Remarks
11.	Memorandum of Understanding between Indian Institute of Science Education and Research (IISER) Thiruvananthapuram and Abo Akademi University (AAU)	Prof. V. Ramakrishnan, Director from IISER, Thiruvananthapuram	Prof. Jorma Mattinen, Rector, Abo Akademi University (AAU)	The MoU will enhance relations by developing relations between the two universities and to develop academic and cultural interchange in the areas of education, research and other activities and to work towards internationalization of higher education. The areas of collaboration would include academic exchange, R and D collaborations, training and teaching and student exchange, collaborative research and organization of national and international symposia and conferences, exchange of information regarding business ideas, product innovation and commercialization

(continued)

(continued)

S. No.	Name of agreement/MoU	Signatory from India	Signatory from Finland	Remarks
12.	Memorandum of Understanding between Indira Gandhi National Tribal University (IGNTU), Amarkantak (M.P.), India and University of Turku, Finland	Prof. T. V. Kattimani, Vice-Chancellor, Indira Gandhi National Tribal University (IGNTU), Amarkantak (M.P.), India	Prof. Kalervo Väänänen, Rector, University of Turku, Finland	The role of the cooperation is to foster collaboration, provide opportunity for global experience, and to facilitate advancement of knowledge, best efforts and frequent interactions. The modes of collaboration include exchange of information on research, teaching, learning materials, joint organisations of seminars, conferences and engagement in teaching or training programmes sponsored by funding agencies

(continued)

(continued)

S. No.	Name of agreement/MoU	Signatory from India	Signatory from Finland	Remarks
13.	Memorandum of Understanding between University of Hyderabad and University of Helsinki	Dr. R. Ramaswamy, Vice-Chancellor, University of Hyderabad	Prof. Jukka Kola, Rector, University of Helsinki	The MoU aims to enhance relations between the two universities and to develop academic and cultural interchange in the areas of education, research and other activities and to work towards internationalization of higher education. The areas of collaboration would include academic exchange in the disciplines of natural sciences and social sciences, R and D collaborations, training and teaching, collaborative research and organization of national and international symposia and conferences

Commercial Agreements signed on sidelines

S. No.	Name of agreement/MoU	Signatory from India	Signatory from Finland	Remarks
14.	Memorandum of Understanding between Labsystems Diagnostics Oy, DesignInnova, Kaivogen Oy and University of Turku, Finland, Translational Health Science and Technology (THSTI) Institute	Mr. Dinesh Kumar, Director, DesignInnova, India Dr. G. Balakrish Nair, Executive Director, Translational Health Science and Technology Institute (THSTI), India	Mrs. Leena Kokko, Director, Kaivogen, Finland Prof. Kalervo Väänänen, Rector, University of Turku, Finland Dr. G. S. K. Velu, Chairman and Managing Director, Trivitron Healthcare Ltd., Chairman, Labsystems Diagnostics Oy	

(continued)

(continued)

S. No.	Name of agreement/MoU	Signatory from India	Signatory from Finland	Remarks
15.	Memorandum of Understanding between Trivitron Healthcare Ltd. and University of Turku, Finland	Dr. G. S. K. Velu, CEO, Trivitron Healthcare Ltd., India	Prof. Kalervo Väänänen, Rector, University of Turku, Finland	
16.	Memorandum of Understanding between Nordic Institute of Dental Education (NIDE) and Trivitron Healthcare Pvt Ltd.	Dr. G. S. K. Velu, CEO, Trivitron Healthcare Ltd., India	Mr. Jouko Nykänen, Vice President, Planmeca Oy Mrs. Jenni Pajunen, CEO, Nordic Institute of Dental Education Oy	

(e) **List of MoUs/Agreements Exchanged During Visit of Prime Minister to Vladivostok: September 04, 2019**

1. Joint Statement "Reaching New Heights of Cooperation through Trust and Partnership."
2. Joint Strategy for the Enhancement of India–Russia Trade and Investments.
3. Agreement between the Government of the Republic of India and Government of the Russian Federation and on the cooperation in the production of spare parts for Russian/Soviet military equipment.
4. Agreement between the Government of the Republic of India and the Government of the Russian Federation on Cooperation in Audiovisual Co-production.
5. Memorandum of Understanding between the Ministry of Road Transport and Highways of the Republic of India and the Ministry of Transport of the Russian Federation on bilateral cooperation in the road transport and road industry.
6. Memorandum of Intent between the Ministry of Shipping of the Republic of India and the Ministry of Transport of the Russian Federation on the Development of Maritime Communications between the Port of Chennai, Republic of India and the Port of Vladivostok, Russian Federation.
7. Plan for cooperation between the Central Board of Indirect Taxes and Customs, Ministry of Finance, Republic of India and the Federal Customs Service (Russian Federation), for combating customs violations in 2019–2022.
8. Memorandum of Understanding between the Ministry of Energy of the Russian Federation and the Ministry of Petroleum and Natural Gas of the Republic of India on the use of Natural Gas for Transportation.
9. Program between the Ministry of Petroleum and Natural Gas of the Republic of India and the Ministry of Energy of the Russian Federation on expansion of cooperation in oil and gas sector.
10. Memorandum of Understanding between Coal India Limited and Far East Investment and Export Agency to cooperate in coking coal mining projects implementation in the Russian Far East.

11. Cooperation Agreement between Invest India and the Russian Direct Investment Fund for Investment Collaboration.
12. Cooperation agreement between the Federation of Indian Chambers of Commerce and Industry the Roscongress Foundation.
13. Memorandum of Understanding between the Federation of Indian Chambers of Commerce and Industry and the Autonomous Non-profit Organization Agency for Strategic Initiatives to promote New Projects.
14. Memorandum of understanding between the Joint Stock Company NOVATEK and PETRONET LNG Limited on cooperation with respect to the joint development of downstream LNG Business and LNG supplies.
15. Agreement on Cooperation between Joint-Stock Company Rosgeologia and Srei Infrastructure Finance Limited;

List of Commercial Documents signed by various Russian and Indian Entities on the Sidelines of the Prime Minister's Visit to Vladivostok: September 06, 2019

1. Memorandum of Understanding for the Manufacture and Assembly of Primary Trainer Aircraft, DAKSH between Yakovlev Design Bureau and Bharat Earth Movers Limited.
2. Memorandum of Understanding between Zarubezhneft and Sungroup Enterprises Pvt. Ltd.
3. Memorandum of Understanding between Far Eastern Mining Company and the State Trading Corporation of India Ltd.
4. Cooperation Agreement between Far Eastern Mining Company and SUN Gold Eurasia.
5. Memorandum of Understanding between Autonomous Non-Profit Organization 'Agency for Strategic Initiatives' and the Global Education and Leadership Foundation.
6. Memorandum of Understanding between the Skolkovo Foundation and the Global Education and Leadership Foundation.
7. Memorandum of Understanding between National Skill Development Corporation and Manav Rachna Vidyantariksha Pvt. Ltd. and JSC ROBBO.
8. Letter of Intent 'Communicating Culture. Consolidating Relationships' between Federal State Unitary Enterprise 'Rossiya

Segodbya,' International Information Agency, founder of the Russian Media Outlet "Sputnik Information Agency" and Zee Media Corporation Limited's entity WION.
9. Memorandum of Understanding between Invest India and Skolkovo Foundation.
10. Cooperation Agreement and Collaboration between RUS Education Pvt. Ltd., Far East Federal University, and Far East Investment and Export Agency.
11. Cooperation Agreement between autonomous non-commercial organization Far East Investment and Export Agency and S A S Fininvest LLP.
12. Cooperation Agreement on the implementation of investment project between autonomous non-commercial organization Far East Investment and Export Agency and KGK Sudima Evergreen Pvt. Limited and the Government of Zabaikalsky Krai.
13. Agreement for the Establishment of the Mahatma Gandhi Centre between Far East Federal University, Nand & Jeet Khemka Foundation and the Global Education & Leadership Foundation.
14. Cooperation Agreement between LLC RITE and Star Overseas Ltd.
15. Memorandum of Understanding between National Skill Development Corporation, Magic Billion and LS-Ruspacific Co. Ltd.
16. Memorandum of Understanding between Magadan Region Government and LLC SUN Eurasia.
17. Memorandum of Understanding between National Mineral Development Corporation and Limited Liability Company Far East Mining Company.
18. Cooperation Agreement between NLC India Ltd. and Far East Mining Company.
19. Cooperation Agreement between Far East Mining Company and Steel Authority of India Limited.
20. Cooperation Agreement between Far East Mining Company and MMTC Ltd.
21. Cooperation Agreement between Limited Liability Company Far East Mining Company and Khanij Bidesh India Ltd.
22. Cooperation Agreement between Far East Mining Company and Coal India Limited.

23. Cooperation Agreement between Russian Direct Investment Fund and UPL Limited on Joint investments in agriculture and crop protection market in Russian Federation.
24. Memorandum of Understanding on mutual business collaboration (Financial Cooperation initiative for development of the Russian Far East and State of Tamil Nadu, India) between Joint Stock Company "The Far East and Baikal Region Development Fund" and Tamil Nadu Infrastructure Fund Management Corporation.
25. Memorandum of Understanding between H-Energy Global Ltd and Joint Stock Company NOVATEK for cooperation in LNG sphere.
26. Memorandum of Understanding between Far East Federal University (Vladivostok, Russian Federation) and Pandit Deendayal Petroleum University (Gandhinagar, Gujarat, Republic of India).
27. Agreement of Intent on the implementation of the investment project of LLC KGK DV in Primorsky Territory.
28. Agreement between Volzhsky Abrasive Works and Murugappan Group.
29. Cooperation Agreement between Limited Liability Company "RITE" and Rooman Technologies Pvt. Ltd.
30. Memorandum of Understanding to explore the possibilities of developing renewable energy projects between State Development Corporation VEB.RF, Joint Stock Company Zarubezhneft, Havel Limited Liability Company, Indian Oil Corporation Limited, and Sungroup Enterprises Private Limited.
31. International Memorandum of Understanding between Amity Universities & Institutions, India and Ministry of Investment Development of Zabaikalski Krai, Russia.
32. Memorandum of Understanding between Government of Chukotka autonomous Region (Anadyr, Russian Federation) and Amity University (New Delhi, Republic of India).
33. Memorandum of Understanding between FEFU Technology Entrepreneurship Fund (Russky Technopark) and Amity University.
34. Agreement on operating in an Advanced Special Economic Zone between JSC Far East Development Corporation and Limited Liability Company Far Eastern Natural Resources Limited (100% subsidiary of the Tata Power Co. Ltd.).

35. Agreement of Intent on implementation of project on the territory of the Republic of Buryatia between the Government of the Republic of Buryatia and Star Overseas Ltd.

(f) **Documents Signed/finalised in the Run upto the Visit of Prime Minister of India to the US: June 07, 2016**

S. No.	Title	Description	Signatories	Date/place of signature
1.	Arrangement between the Multi-Agency Centre/Intelligence Bureau of the Government of India and the Terrorist Screening Center of the Government of the United States of America for the exchange of Terrorist Screening Information	As per this Arrangement, India and the US shall provide each other access to terrorism screening information through the designated contact points, subject to domestic laws and regulations. The Arrangement would enhance the counter terrorism cooperation between India and the US	**India:** Shri Rajiv Mehrishi, Union Home Secretary **US:** Mr. Richard Verma, Ambassador of the United States of America to India	Signed in New Delhi on 2 June 2016
2.	Memorandum of Understanding (MoU) between the Government of India and the Government of the United States of America to enhance cooperation on Energy Security, Clean Energy and Climate Change	The objective of the MoU is to enhance cooperation between India and the US on energy security, clean energy and climate change through increased bilateral engagement and further joint initiatives for promoting sustainable growth	**India**: Shri P. K. Pujari, Secretary, Ministry of Power, Government of India **US**: Mr. Richard R. Verma, Ambassador of the United States of America to India	Signed in New Delhi on 2 June 2016

(continued)

(continued)

S. No.	Title	Description	Signatories	Date/place of signature
3.	Memorandum of Understanding (MoU) between Government of India and Government of the United States of America to enhance co-operation on Wildlife Conservation and Combating Wildlife Trafficking	The MOU seeks cooperation in areas such as Wildlife Forensics and Conservation Genetics; Natural World Heritage Conservation and Nature Interpretation; and Conservation Awareness, between India and the US for wildlife conservation and management and combating wildlife trafficking	**India**: Shri Arun K. Singh, Ambassador of India to the United States of America **US**: Ms. Catherine A. Novelli, Under Secretary of State for Economic Growth, Energy and the Environment	Signed in Washington DC on 2 June 2016
4.	Memorandum of Understanding (MoU) between Consular, Passport and Visa Division of the Ministry of External Affairs, Government of India and US Customs and Border Protection, Department of Homeland Security of the United States for the Development of an International Expedited Traveler Initiative (the Global Entry Programme)	The Global Entry is a US Customs and Border Protection programme, which allows expedited clearance for pre-approved, low-risk travelers upon arrival in the United States. After joint scrutiny and clearance by both countries, the approved Indian travellers will be extended the facility of expedited entry into the United States through automatic kiosks at select airports	India: Shri Arun K. Singh, Ambassador of India to the United States of America **US**: Mr. Kevin K. McAleenan, Deputy Commissioner, US Customs and Border Protection, Department of Homeland Security	Signed in Washington DC on 3 June 2016

(continued)

(continued)

S. No.	Title	Description	Signatories	Date/place of signature
5.	Technical Arrangement between the Indian Navy and the United States Navy concerning Unclassified Maritime Information Sharing	The Arrangement would allow sharing of unclassified information on White Shipping between India and the US as permitted by respective national laws, regulations and policies, and provides a framework for mutually beneficial maritime information	India: Vice Admiral Karambir Singh, Deputy Chief of Naval Staff **US**: Vice Admiral Ted N. Branch, Deputy Chief of Naval Operations for Information Warfare	Signed through Diplomatic Channels on 26 May 2016
6.	Memorandum of Understanding (MoU) between the Ministry of Petroleum and Natural Gas, Government of India and the Department of Energy of the United States of America for Cooperation in Gas Hydrates	The MOU aims to increase the understanding of the geologic occurrence, distribution, and production of natural gas hydrates along the continental margin of India and in the US	**India:** Shri Arun K. Singh, Ambassador of India to the United States of America **US:** Christopher A. Smith, Assistant Secretary for Fossil Energy, Department of Energy	Signed in Washington DC on 6 June 2016

Documents finalised

(continued)

(continued)

S. No.	Title	Description	Signatories	Date/place of signature
7.	Information Exchange Annex (IEA) between the Ministry of Defence, Government of India and the Department of Defense of the United States of America to the Master Information Exchange Agreement concerning Aircraft Carrier Technologies	IEA is aimed to enhance data and information sharing specific to aircraft carriers technology between India and the US		
8.	Logistics Exchange Memorandum of Agreement between the Ministry of Defence, Government of India and the Department of Defense of the United States of America	The agreement is aimed at facilitating mutual logistic support between India and the US for authorised port visits, joint exercises, joint training and HA-DR (humanitarian assistance and disaster relief)		

(g) List of Agreements/MoUs Signed During the Visit of Prime Minister to Russia (December 24, 2015)

S. No.	MoU/agreement/contract

Joint Statement Between India and Russia: Shared Trust, New Horizons

1.	Protocol amending the agreement between the Government of the Republic of India and the Government of the Russian Federation on simplification of requirements for mutual travels of certain categories of citizens of the two countries 21 December 2010
2.	Protocol amending agreement between the Government of the Republic of India and the Government of the Russian Federation on mutual travel regime for holders of Diplomatic & Official Passports of 3 December 2004
3.	Agreement between the Government of the Republic of India and the Government of the Russian Federation on Cooperation in the field of Helicopter Engineering
4.	Plan for Cooperation between the Federal Customs Service of the Central Board of Excise and Customs, Department of Revenue, Ministry of Finance, Republic of India and the Russian Federation for combating Customs violations in 2015–2017
5.	Programme of Action Agreed Between The Department of Atomic Energy of India And The Russian State Atomic Energy Corporation "Rosatom" for Localization of Manufacturing in India for Russian-Designed Nuclear Reactor Units
6.	Memorandum of Understanding between the Ministry of Railways of the Republic of India and the Joint Stock company "Russian Railways" on technical cooperation in railway sector
7.	MoU between Solar Energy Corporation of India and Russian Energy Agency regarding construction of solar energy plants in the Republic of India
8.	MoU for cooperation between HEC & CNIITMASH for development of Centre of Excellence for heavy engineering design at HEC
9.	MoU for cooperation between HEC & CNIITMASH for upgradation and modernization of HEC's manufacturing facilities
10.	Memorandum of Understanding Between Prasar Bharati and Digital Television Russia on Cooperation in the field of Broadcasting
11.	Tripartite Memorandum of Understanding between Centre for Development of Advance Computing (C-DAC), Indian Institute of Science Bangalore (IISc) and Lomonosov Moscow State University (MSU)
12.	Tripartite Memorandum of Understanding between Centre for Development of Advance Computing (C-DAC), OJSC "GLONASS" and GLONASS Union
13.	MoU in the field of investment cooperation in the Russian Far East between The Tata Power Company Limited and Ministry for Development of the Russian Far East
14.	MoU for Cooperation for geologic survey, exploration and production of hydrocarbons onshore and on the continental shelf of the Russian Federation
15.	Confirmation of successful completion of the first stage pre-completion actions in relation to the creation of a Joint Venture in JSC VankorNeft

(continued)

(continued)

S. No.	MoU/agreement/contract
16.	MoU for Cooperation for geologic survey, exploration and production of hydrocarbons onshore the Russian Federation between Rosneft oil company, Oil India Limited and Indian Oil Corporation Limited
17.	Agreement between Central Council for Research in Ayurvedic Sciences, Republic of India and Peoples' Friendship University of Russia (PFUR) on Cooperation in the field of Ayurveda

(h) MoU Signed During the State Visit of Prime Minister of Norway to India: January 08, 2019

S. No.	MoU	Signed on the Indian side by	Signed on the Norway side by
1	MoU between the Ministry of External Affairs, Government of India and the Ministry of Foreign Affairs, Government of Norway on India–Norway Ocean Dialogue	Sushma Swaraj, External Affairs Minister	Ine Eriksen Søreide, Minister of Foreign Affairs

(i) List of Documents Signed During the Visit of Minister for Foreign Affairs of Denmark to India: December 17, 2018

S. No.	Agreements/MoUs	Signed/exchanged on the Indian side by	Signed/exchanged on the Danish side by
1	Protocol on Consultations between the Foreign Ministries of India and Denmark	Sushma Swaraj, External Affairs Minister	Anders Samuelsen, Minister of Foreign Affairs

(continued)

(continued)

S. No.	Agreements/MoUs	Signed/exchanged on the Indian side by	Signed/exchanged on the Danish side by
2	MoU between National Institute of Wind Energy of India and Denmark Technical University	Dr. K. Balaraman, Director General of the National Institute of Wind Energy	Eric Laursen, Head of Department for Asia, Oceania and Latin America

(j) List of Agreements/MoUs Exchanged Between India and Russia During Visit of President of Russia to India: October 05, 2018

Sl. No.	Name of the MOU/ Agreement/Treaty	Exchanged on the Russian Federation side by	Exchanged on the Indian side by
1.	Protocol for Consultations between the Ministry of Foreign Affairs and MEA for the period 2019–2023	H. E. Mr. Sergey Lavrov Minister of Foreign Affairs of Russian Federation	Smt. Sushma Swaraj External Affairs Minister
2.	Memorandum of Understanding between the Ministry of Economic Development of the Russian Federation and the National Institution for Transforming India (NITI Aayog)	H. E. Mr. Maxim Oreshkin, Minister of Economic Development of the Russian Federation	Dr. Rajiv Kumar VC, NITI Aayog
3.	Memorandum of Understanding between Indian Space Research Organization (ISRO) and the Federal Space Agency of Russia 'ROSCOSMOS' on Joint Activities in the field of Human Spaceflight Programme	Mr. Dmitriy Rogozin Director of ROSCOMOS	Shri Vijay Gokhale Foreign Secretary

(continued)

(continued)

Sl. No.	Name of the MOU/Agreement/Treaty	Exchanged on the Russian Federation side by	Exchanged on the Indian side by
4.	Memorandum of Cooperation between the Indian and Russian Railways	Mr. Oleg Belozerov, CEO-Chairman of JSC Russian Railways	Shri Vijay Gokhale Foreign Secretary
5.	Action Plan for Prioritization and Implementation of Cooperation Areas in the Nuclear Field	Mr. Alexi Likhachev, DG, Rosatom	Shri K. N. Vyas Secretary, DAE
6.	Memorandum of Understanding between the Russian Ministry of Transport and Indian Railways in the Development Cooperation in Transport Education	H. E. Mr. Nikolay Kudashev, Ambassador of the Russian Federation to India	Shri D. B. Venkatesh Varma Ambassador of India to Russia
7.	Memorandum of Understanding between the National Small Industries Corporation (NSIC), of India and the Russian Small and Medium Business Corporation (RSMB), on Cooperation in the field of Micro, Small and Medium Enterprises	Mr. Alexander Braverman, Director General, Russian Small and Medium Business Corporation	Shri D. B. Venkatesh Varma Ambassador of India to Russia
8.	Cooperation Agreement in the Fertilizers Sector between the Russian Direct Investment Fund ("RDIF"); PJSC Phosagro (PhosAgro) and Indian Potash Limited (IPL)	Mr. Kirill Dmitriev, Director general of the Russian Direct Investment Fund **Andrey Guryev**, CEO for PhosAgro	Shri D. B. Venkatesh Varma Ambassador of India to Russia

(k) List of MoUs/Agreements Signed During the State Visit of Prime Minister of Canada to India (February 23, 2018)

S. No.	Name of MoUs/ agreements	Indian side	Canadian side
1.	Joint Declaration of Intent Between the Ministry of Electronics And Information Technology of the Republic of India and The Department of Innovation, Science and Economic Development of Canada on Cooperation in the Field of Information Communications Technology and Electronics	Shri Ravi Shankar Prasad, Minister Law & Justice, Electronics & Information Technology	Mr. Navdeep Bains, Minister of Innovation, Science and Economic Development
2.	Terms of Reference for the India-Canada Ministerial Energy Dialogue Between the Ministry of Petroleum and Natural Gas of the Republic of India and The Department of Natural Resources of Canada	Shri Dharmendra Pradhan, Minister for Petroleum and Natural Gas	Ms. Chrystia Freeland, Minister of Foreign Minister
3.	Memorandum of Understanding Between the Ministry of Youth Affairs & Sports of the Republic of India and The Department of Canadian Heritage (Sport Canada) on Cooperation in Sport	Col. Rajyavardhan Singh Rathore, Minister of State (Independent Charge), Ministry of Youth Affairs and Sports	Ms. Kirsty Duncan, Minister of Sports and Persons with Disabilities

(continued)

(continued)

S. No.	Name of MoUs/ agreements	Indian side	Canadian side
4.	Memorundum of Understanding Between the Department of Industrial Policy and Promotion, Ministry of Commerce and Industry, Government of Republic of India and The Canadian Intellectual Property Office Concerning Cooperation on Intellectual Property Rights	Shri Ramesh Abhishek, Secretary (Industry Policy and Promotion)	Mr. Nadir Patel, High Commissioner of Canada to India
5.	Memorundum of Understanding Between the Government of the Republic of India and The Government of Canada Concerning Cooperation in Higher Education	Shri R. Subrahmaniam, Spl Secretary, Dept of Higher Education, MHRD	Mr. Nadir Patel, High Commissioner of Canada to India
6.	Memorandum of Understanding Between the Department of Atomic Energy of The Republic of India and The Department of Natural Resources of Canada Concerning Co-Operation in the Fields of Science, Technology and Innovation	Dr. Sekhar Basu, Chairman AEC and Secretary DAE	Mr. Nadir Patel, High Commissioner of Canada to India

(1) List of Documents Signed During the Official Visit of President of Russian Federation to India (December 10–11, 2014)

Sl. No.	Name of the document	Details/scope	Indian signatory	Russian signatory
1. Inter-Governmental Documents				
1.	Protocol for consultations between the Ministry of External Affairs & Ministry of Foreign Affairs of Russia for the period 2015–2016	Envisages close consultation between the two Foreign Ministries on as many as 17 issues, ranging from Asia-Pacific to West Asia to West Europe to Latin America as also at various multilateral for a like UN, G20, BRICS, SCO, RIC	Sushma Swaraj, External Affairs Minister	Sergey Lavrov, Foreign Minister
2.	Agreement for Training of Indian Armed Forces Personnel in the Military Educational Establishments of the Defence Ministry of the Russian Federation	Lays down provisions and procedures for training courses in military educational and training establishments. Will facilitate better understanding between the two defence forces	Radha Krishna Mathur Secretary, Ministry of Defence	A Bakhin, First Deputy Minister of Defence
3.	Strategic Vision for Strengthening Cooperation in Peaceful Uses of Atomic Energy between the Republic of India and the Russian Federation	Envisages roadmap of bilateral cooperation in the civil nuclear energy sector for the next two decades	Ratan Kumar Sinha, Secretary, Department of Atomic Energy	Sergey Kirienko, Director General, ROSATOM
4.	Provisions for the Technical Data and Information Nondisclosure in the framework of cooperation in the field of Peaceful Use of Nuclear Energy	Envisages provisions/terms of information exchange between the nuclear agencies of both the countries. Will provide an impetus to scientific and technological cooperation in the peaceful use of nuclear energy	Ratan Kumar Sinha, Secretary, Department of Atomic Energy	Sergey Kirienko, Director General, ROSATOM

(continued)

(continued)

Sl. No.	Name of the document	Details/scope	Indian signatory	Russian signatory
5.	Programme of Cooperation (POC) under Framework of Inter-governmental Agreement for Enhancement of Cooperation in Oil & Gas in 2015–2016	Sets out a concrete programme for cooperation, envisaging projects including joint exploration and production of hydrocarbons, long term LNG supplies and joint study of a hydrocarbon pipeline system connecting Russia with India	Dharmendra Pradhan, MoS (I/C), MoP&NG	Alexander Novak, Minister of Energy
6.	MoU between Quality Council of India (QCI) and Federal Accreditation Service of Russian Federation on technical cooperation on accreditation	Aims at development of accreditation systems, sharing of information, recognition of test reports, and creation of conditions for the elimination of technical barriers in trade and economic cooperation	Adil Zainulbhai, Chairman, Quality Council of India	Savva Shipov, Head of Federal Accreditation Service
7.	Memorandum of Understanding between the Indian Council of Medical Research (ICMR) and the Russian Foundation for Basic Research (RFBR) on cooperation in Health Research	Envisages programme of cooperation in specific areas of health research such as oncology, bioinformatics & bioimaging, neurosciences, new generation vaccine research and research in HIV/AIDS	Dr. V. M. Katoch, Secretary & DG, Indian Council of Medical Research	Vladislav Panchenko, Chairman, RBFR Board
2. Commercial Contracts				
8.	MoU between TATA Power and Russian Direct Investment Fund (RDIF)	Describes cooperation in exploring investment opportunities in the energy sector across the Russian Federation	Krishna Kumar Sharma, Executive Director & CEO, Coastal Gujarat Power Limited	Kiril Dmitriev, General Director, RDIF

(continued)

(continued)

Sl. No.	Name of the document	Details/scope	Indian signatory	Russian signatory
9.	MoU between ACRON of Russia and NMDC of India (consortium leader) to implement the understanding reached to acquire stake in a potash mine in Russia	Envisages acquisition of stakes by a consortium of Indian companies in a US$ two billion project of ACRON, a Russian fertiliser company	Narendra Kothari, Chairman & MD, NMDC	Alexander Popov, Senior Vice President, ACRON
10.	MoU between VTB (Vneshtorgbank) of Russia and ESSAR Group	Envisages finance arrangement of US$ one billion to ESSAR by VTB for general corporate purpose	Shashi Ruia, Chairman, ESSAR	Andrey Kostin, Chairman, VTB
11.	MoU between IDFC (Infrastructure Development Finance Corporation Ltd) and RDIF (Russian Direct Investment Fund) on a co-investment opportunity up to US$ one billion	Describes terms and conditions on creation of a fund for investments in India and Russia	Dr Rajiv Lall, Executive Chairman, IDFC	Kiril Dmitriev, Chairman, RDIF
12.	MoU between 'Oil India Limited' and 'Zarubezhneft'	Envisages cooperation in joint search and evaluation of new hydrocarbons exploration, production, and transportation projects. Will facilitate technological association on hydrocarbon projects in India	Sunil K Srivastava, Chairman, OIL	S. I. Kudryashov, Director General, Zarubezhneft
13.	MoU between FICCI and Delovaya Rossiya	Aims at broadening and strengthening economic ties and identifying new areas of economic cooperation. Will facilitate exchange of information and support to enterprises in both countries	Sidharth Birla President, FICCI	Alexey Repik, President, Delovaya Rossiya

(continued)

(continued)

Sl. No.	Name of the document	Details/scope	Indian signatory	Russian signatory
14.	MoU between news agencies PTI and TASS	Envisages cooperation on exchange of news and the right to use news items. Aims at exchange of expertise and technical assistance through contacts between editorial staff, experts, journalists, press photographers and senior managers	Maharaja Krishna Razdan, Editor-in-Chief of PTI	Sergey Mikhailov, Director General, ITAR-TASS
15.	MoU between Electronics and Software Export promotion Council of India (ESEPCI) and Skolkovo Foundation of Russia	Describes support to companies in the Information Technology and 'innovation' sectors in their efforts to enter new markets by means of joint ventures, strategic alliances and in joint research and development	Deepak Kumar Sareen, Executive Director, ESEPCI	Victor Vekselberg, President, Skolkovo Foundation
16.	MoU between ESSAR and ROSNEFT for long-term supply of crude oil	Envisages ten year supply and purchase by India of crude oil and feed stocks/products	Shashi Ruia, Chairman, ESSAR	Igor Sechin, President ROSNEFT
17.	Supplement to the General Framework Agreement (GFA) for Units 3 and 4 of Kudankulam Nuclear Power Project between Nuclear Power Corporation of India Limited (NPCIL) and ATOMSTROYEXPORT (ASE)	Will operationalise the General Framework Agreement (GFA) and Technical Commercial Offer (TCO) signed in April 2014, for the implementation of Kudankulam Nuclear Power project (KKNPP) Units 3 and 4	Kailash Chandra Purohit, Chairman, NPCIL	Valery Limarenko, President, NIAEP (Company of ATOMSTROYEXPORT)
18.	Contract between Nuclear Power Corporation of India Limited (NPCIL) and ATOMSTROYEXPORT (ASE) for unit 3 and 4 of Kudankulam Nuclear Power Plant	Will mark the commencing of the implementation of the Units 3 and 4 of Kudankulam Nuclear Power with supply of some major equipment by ATOMSTROYEXPORT	Roopak Kumar Gargaye, Director (Projects), NPCIL	Andrey Lebedel, Vice President, NIAEP (Company of ATOMSTROYEXPORT)

(continued)

(continued)

Sl. No.	Name of the document	Details/scope	Indian signatory	Russian signatory
19.	MoU between Gamesa Wind Turbine Pvt Ltd. of India and ROTEK of Russia	Will facilitate cooperation between the two companies in wind power equipment	Ramesh Kaymal, Chief Executive Director, Gamesa Pvt Ltd.	Mikhail Lifshitz, Director General, ROTEK
20.	MoU between EIRENE SYSTEMS and GLONASS Union	Envisages a joint venture to market GLONASS technologies and solutions in India. Will contribute to joint development and implementation of projects like 'Navigation Platform' and 'Geographical Information System' in India	Subodh Agarwal, Director, Eirene Systems Private Limited	Alexander Gurko, President, GLONASS Union

(m) **List of Documents Signed During the State Visit of Governor General of Canada (February 24, 2014)**

S. No.	Title	Signatory from India	Signatory from Canada	Remarks
1.	India-Canada Audio-Visual Co-production Agreement	Shri Bimal Julka, Secretary, Ministry of Information and Broadcasting, Government of India	H. E. Mr. Stewart Beck, High Commissioner of Canada to India	This Agreement between Ministry of Information and Broadcasting and Heritage Canada will open doors for wide ranging audio-visual collaborations between our two countries; notably these co-production will receive national treatment in India as well as Canada
2.	Programme of Cooperation on collaboration between Department of Biotechnology and Grand Challenges Canada to address health and development need	Dr. T. S. Rao, Senior Advisor to Department of Biotechnology, Government of India	Mr. Peter Singer, CEO of Grand Challenges Canada	This Programme of Cooperation will pave a collaborative roadmap for addressing global health challenges, especially relating to women and child health, early child development, global mental health, scaling of innovations at proof of concept stage, and point of care diagnostics

(continued)

(continued)

S. No.	Title	Signatory from India	Signatory from Canada	Remarks
3.	MoU between National Skill Development Corporation [NSDC] and Association of Canadian Community Colleges [ACCC]	Mr. Dilip Chenoy, MD & CEO, National Skill Development Corporation	Ms. Denise Amyot, President and CEO, Association of Canadian Community Colleges	This MoU will facilitate exchange and learning between NSDC and ACCC in best practices in training, transnational standards, and certification, which will go a long way in creating a workforce that can serve global needs

(n) **List of Documents Signed at the 13th India-Russia Annual Summit: December 24, 2012**

S. No.	Name of the document	Details	Indian signatory	Russian signatory
1.	Protocol on Foreign Office Consultations 2013–2014	The Protocol is an instrument to continue the tradition of close political consultations between the two Foreign Offices. The current Protocol outlines seventeen different broad themes for such exchanges. The bi-annual Protocol mechanism enables frequent contacts and promotes broad-based understanding between the various wings of the two Foreign Offices	Shri Salman Khurshid, External Affairs Minister	Mr. S. Lavrov, Minister for Foreign Affairs
2.	Memorandum on Cooperation between the Ministry of Science & Technology, Government of India and the Ministry for Education and Science of the Russian Federation in Science, Technology & Innovation	The Memorandum shall facilitate deepening cooperation in the field of innovation and S&T, through implementation of joint programs or projects involving educational, R&D and industrial institutions. It also stipulates formation of a Working Group to implement the provisions of this MoC	Shri Jaipal Reddy, Minister for Science & Technology	Mr. Dmitry Livanov, Minister for Education and Science

(continued)

(continued)

S. No.	Name of the document	Details	Indian signatory	Russian signatory
3.	Cultural Exchange Programme between the Ministry of Culture of the Republic of India and The Ministry of Culture of the Russian Federation for the Years 2013–2015	The document envisages enhancing bilateral cultural contacts through exchanges in performing arts, films, archives, museums and conservation, literature and language and through organization of reciprocal Festivals. It is in continuation to the previous CEP 2009–2012. It also aims to preserve and promote the legacy of the Roerich Estate in Kullu (Himachal Pradesh), an important icon of cultural cooperation between the two countries	Smt. C. K. Katoch, Minister of Culture	Mr. Vladimir Medinsky, Minister of Culture

(continued)

(continued)

S. No.	Name of the document	Details	Indian signatory	Russian signatory
4.	Memorandum of Understanding to Promote Direct Investment between Russia and India	MoU envisages investments upto US$2 billion in important bilateral projects or companies, privatization and other opportunities RDIF is a US$10 billion sovereign-backed Russian private equity fund established by the Russian Government to co-invest alongside global institutional investors. Since its inception in 2011, it has led investments totalling US$1.5 billion in Russian companies together with some of the largest asset managers in the world	Shri Pratip Chaudhuri, Chairman, State Bank of India	Mr. Kirill Dmitriev, Director-General, Russia Foundation for Direct Investments

(continued)

(continued)

S. No.	Name of the document	Details	Indian signatory	Russian signatory
5.	Memorandum of Understanding between Bharat Sanchar Nigam Ltd., New Delhi, India & Mahanagar Telephone Nigam Ltd., New Delhi, India and NIS-GLONASS, Russia for conducting the proof of concept through pilot project for providing the Satellite based navigation services	The MoU envisages a pilot project to assess the usage of the Russian Global Navigation Satellite System (GLONASS—the Russian equivalent of GPS) using the capabilities of BSNL/MTNL ground infrastructure. Success of the pilot project may provide insights for wider applicability of GLONASS signals in the future in areas such as disaster management, telephony and long-distance communications	Shri R. K. Upadhyay, Chairman & Managing Director, Bharat Sanchar Nigam Ltd., & Shri A. K. Garg, Chairman & Managing Director, Mahanagar Telephone Nigam Ltd	Mr. Alexander Chub, Director-General, OAO "NIS"

Military-Technical Contracts

6	Contract for Delivery of 71 Mi-17V-5 helicopters	An order for procurement of 59 Mi-17 v5 MLH was agreed to in February 2010, which was subsequently increased to 71. The current contract is in context of the order
7	Contract for Delivery of 42 technological kits for SU-30MKI aircraft licensed production	The Protocol-II on licensed manufacturing of additional 42 SU-30MKI aircraft units was signed during Annual Summit 2011. The current contract is a follow up to this Protocol

Business Level Contracts

8	Strategic Cooperation Agreement between Tata Consultancy Services Ltd. and Joint Stock Company "Navigation Information Systems" (NIS) of Russia	The Agreement shall establish and strengthen technology partner relations between the two enterprises in software development, systems integration, product engineering, professional services for and marketing of NIS products and TCS Solution frameworks. The areas of cooperation visualised concern sectors such as information technology enabled services, telecommunication systems, manufacturing, etc
9	Joint Venture Agreement between Elcom Systems Private Ltd. and OAO "Vertoleti Rassi" (JSC "Helicopters Russia")	The joint venture aims to set up in India, a modern industrial facility for manufacturing of Russian models of helicopters (Ka- and Mi-brands). The JV will serve as an industrial base for hi-tech rotorcraft products from Russia to India and shall contribute to the development of the domestic aerospace industry. The enterprise will be eligible for implementing offset projects under various procurement tenders in India. JSC "Russian Helicopters" is a leading player in the global helicopter industry engaged in the business of modern civilian and military helicopters and training of aviation personnel. Elcom Systems is an established entity in the Indian telecommunications, security and navigation sectors
10	Memorandum of Understanding for Joint Venture arrangement between Elder Pharmaceuticals Ltd., Mumbai and Pharm Eco of Russia	The joint venture company will engage in the manufacturing, marketing and distribution of pharmaceuticals in Russia and other countries and envisages an investment of at least US$100 million. PharmEco will have 51% stake in the joint venture while Elder Pharmaceuticals will own 49% in the joint venture company

(o) **List of Documents Signed During the State Visit of Prime Minister of Canada: November 06, 2012**

Document/MoU	Indian signatory	Canadian signatory	Synopsis
Agreement on Social Security	Shri Vayalar Ravi, Minister of Overseas Indian Affairs	Mr. Edward Fast, Minister of International Trade and Minister of Asia Pacific Gateway	The Agreement, signed between Ministry of Overseas Indian Affairs and Department of Human Resources and Skills Development Canada, provides for avoidance of double social security contributions by detached workers (employed persons who are subject to the legislation of a country and who are sent by their employers to work in the territory of another country) from the host country legislation, portability of contributions at the time of relocation, and totalization of the periods of contribution for determining eligibility to a benefit

(continued)

(continued)

Document/MoU	Indian signatory	Canadian signatory	Synopsis
MOU on cooperation in Information Communication Technology and Electronics	Smt Preneet Kaur, Minister of State for External Affairs	Mr. Edward Fast, Minister of International Trade and Minister of Asia Pacific Gateway	The MOU, signed between Ministry of Communications and Information Technology and Department of Industry Canada, will provide the necessary framework for cooperation in the Information Communication Technology and Electronics (ICTE) sector between the two countries for establishing a strong and effective business to business partnership and cooperation; raising awareness among private and public sector stakeholders on ICTE opportunities in Canada and India; and establishing an ICTE Working Group to engage in a wide variety of ICTE Sector related issues

(continued)

(continued)

Document/MoU	Indian signatory	Canadian signatory	Synopsis
MOU between DRDO and York University, Canada for cooperation in the areas of Joint Research and Development in Defence Science & Technology	Dr. V. K. Saraswat, Scientific Advisor to Raksha Mantri	Dr. Robert Hache, Vice-President, Research & Innovation, York University, Canada	The MOU will establish a framework for cooperation and identify opportunities for collaboration in the areas of joint research and development in defence science and technology through information and personnel exchanges

Annexure E: Emails by Various Working Groups/PPs

1. PAME

<soffia@pame.is> 18 Dec 2019
Dear Nikhil,

Thanks for this information and the response to your questions is as follows:
(a) proposals submitted, proposal accepted, outcomes
   None
(b) funding assistance
   None
(c) papers etc. submitted which were accepted and published by PAME
   None
(d) any citation/reward/acknowledgement of prolific scientific work by India
   None
(e) any other information on India's endeavours

India has participated in <u>one PAME Meeting</u> since it became an Arctic Council Observer. It also participated in a workshop on how to <u>systematically engage with Observers in PAME's shipping work.</u>

Kind regards,

Soffia Gudmundsdottir

2. Gwich'in Council

GCIadmin <GCIadmin@gwichin.nt.ca>   Wed, Dec 18, 2019, 1:44 AM
to me

Hi,
I don't believe there have been any specific contributions to GCI, but you could look at contributions to the Arctic Council.
Mahsi'

Devlin

3. NAMMCO

Nammco-sec <nammco-sec@nammco.org>   Dec 17, 2019, 4:57 PM
to me

Dear Nikhil
India is not an observer country to NAMMCO and has never participated nor contributed in any way to the work of NAMMCO.
Kind regards/mvh

Charlotte Winsnes

Deputy Secretary
  NAMMCO—North Atlantic Marine Mammal Commission
POB 6453, N-9294 Tromsø, Norway, +47 77 68 73 71,

charlotte@nammco.org, www.nammco.org, www.facebook.com/nammco.org/

4. EPPR

FMN-JPH Holst-Andersen, Jens Peter <JPH@fmn.dk>   Tue, Dec 17, 2019, 12:43 PM
to me, eppr@arctic-council.org

RELEASABLE TO INTERNET TRANSMISSION
Dear Nikhil
Thank you for your email.
India has not been an active part of the work in EPPR the last 5 years and has therefore not submitted any proposals.

Best regards
Jens Peter Holst-Andersen

Chair, Emergency Prevention, Preparedness and Response Working Group, Arctic Council
Danish Ministry of Defence
Holmens Kanal 9, DK-1060 Copenhagen K
Phone: +45 2092 6217
E-mail: jph@fmn.dk
Web: Arctic Council EPPR/**@EPPR_Arctic**

5. Saami Council

Samiraddi Saami Council <saamicouncil@saamicouncil.net>   Fri, Dec 20, 2019, 4:19 PM
to me

Dear Nikhil,
The answer to all of your questions is zero.

Yours sincerely,

Áile Jávo, Saami Council

6. ACAP

Kseniia Iartceva <Kseniia@arctic-council.org>   Thu, Jan 2, 6:24 PM
to ijw@kld.dep.no, Nina, Joël, me, Acap

Dear Mr. Pareek,

Thank you for your message. With reference to your inquiry, India has not been actively involved in the work of the ACAP Working Group during the last 5 years.

In November 2018, a representative of the Indian National Center for Polar and Ocean Research (NCPOR) attended the ACAP Working Group meeting in Reykjavik, Iceland. However, this is the only example of India's participation in ACAP's activities.

There is one contribution by India I am aware of, but it is not connected to ACAP's work, though it is related to the problem of short-lived climate pollutants. India provided data for the Summary report by the Arctic Council's Expert Group on Black Carbon and Methane (2017). I have attached the report hereto for your information.

I hope this was helpful.
Best regards and Happy New Year!
Kseniia Iartceva,
ACAP Executive Secretary

7. OSPAR Commission

Secretariat—OSPAR <secretariat@ospar.org>   Mon, Jan 6, 3:13 PM
to me

Dear Nikhil

India is not a Contracting Party to the OSPAR Commission.

You may need to contact Arctic Council for answers to your questions

Kind regards

8. AMAP

AMAP <amap@amap.no>   Wed, Jan 15, 12:11 AM
to me

Dear Nikhil Pareek,

Reference is made to your below e-mail request. We apologise for the somewhat late response!

This is to inform you that for the 5 last years there have been no contribution nor participation from India to AMAP in regards to item listed under (a)–(d) included. As for your request under item (e) you will find a direct link on AMAP website (https://www.amap.no/about/organisational-structure) that will direct you to the list of all Arctic Council observers, including India on the following item: "the Arctic Council Observing Countries and Organizations." Observers to the Artic Council are automatically also observers to its working group, including AMAP.

Best regards,

Arctic Monitoring and Assessment Programme (AMAP) Secretariat
  Visiting: Hjalmar Johansens gate 14, 9007 Tromsø
  Postal: The Fram Centre, Box 6606 Langnes, 9296 Tromsø
  Norway

9. CAFF

Courtney Price <courtney@caff.is>   Thu, Jan 16, 9:02 AM
to Tom, Kári, me

Hello Nikhil,

Answers a–d were unanswered because there have been none to date. My answer to e can be found in my last email. India is an active and interested partner in developing cooperation through CAFF's AMBI.

I trust I have answered this request.

Courtney

Courtney Price <courtney@caff.is> Wed, Jan 15, 7:53 PM
to Tom, Kári, me

Hello Nikhil,

Thank you for the information.

Recently CAFF has had good cooperation and discussions with India about deepening our partnership through CAFF's Arctic Migratory Birds Initiative (AMBI). In December 2018 a representative of the Bombay Natural History Society attended our AMBI technical workshop in Hainan, China to help finalise our AMBI Work Plan 2019–2023. In November 2019 the AMBI Chair and AMBI Global Coordinator attended the CWAMWAF conference in Lonavala at the invitation of the Bombay Natural History Society. AMBI staff gave two plenary addresses, participated in panels, and hosted a special session to further present and discuss AMBI implementation actions of relevant to the Central Asian Flyway. In addition, AMBI staff were invited to Delhi to meet with relevant Ministerial staff to discuss further partnerships and AMBI implementation. There was keen interest to partner further. Further events and discussions are planned for February 2019 at the CMS COP13 in Gandhinagar, India.

If you have any additional information that you can share on your project that would be of help to us.

Hope this helps,
Courtney

10. Aleut International

Liza Mack <liza.mack@aleut-international.org> Fri, Jan 17, 7:01 AM
to me

I am not aware of any contributions from India to Aleut International Association or our research efforts.

Thank you.
Sincerely,
Dr. Liza Mack

11. Sustainable Development Working Group (SDWG)

Jeniffer Spence secretariat@sdwg.org   Jan 15 2020
Dear Nikhil,

Thank you for your message. The SDWG secretariat is a small body. We do not have the capacity to collect and organise the information requested. I encourage you to visit the SDWG website and the Arctic Council public archive to retrieve publicly available information related to your topic.

Best of luck with your research.
Jennifer

Bibliography

Primary Sources

Reports/Annual Reports

Annual Report 2018–2019, NCPOR, National Centre for Polar and Ocean Research, Ministry of Earth Sciences, Government of India.

Annual Report 2017–2018, NCAOR, National Centre for Antarctic and Ocean Research, Ministry of Earth Sciences, Government of India.

Annual Report 2016–2017, NCAOR, National Centre for Antarctic and Ocean Research, Ministry of Earth Sciences, Government of India.

Annual Report 2015–2016, NCAOR, National Centre for Antarctic and Ocean Research, Ministry of Earth Sciences, Government of India.

Annual Report 2018–2019, Ministry of Earth Sciences, Government of India.

Annual Report 2017–2018, Ministry of Earth Sciences, Government of India.

Annual Report 2016–2017, Ministry of Earth Sciences, Government of India.

Annual Report 2015–2016, Ministry of Earth Sciences, Government of India.

Annual Report 2018–2019, GAIL, Gas Authority of India Limited, Ministry of Petroleum and Natural Gas, Government of India.

Annual Report 2017–2018, GAIL, Gas Authority of India Limited, Ministry of Petroleum and Natural Gas, Government of India.

Annual Report 2016–2017, GAIL, Gas Authority of India Limited, Ministry of Petroleum and Natural Gas, Government of India.

Annual Report 2015–2016, GAIL, Gas Authority of India Limited, Ministry of Petroleum and Natural Gas, Government of India.

Annual Report 2018–2019, ONGC, Oil and Natural Gas Corporation, Ministry of Petroleum and Natural Gas, Government of India.
Annual Report 2017–2018, ONGC, Oil and Natural Gas Corporation, Ministry of Petroleum and Natural Gas, Government of India.
Annual Report 2016–2017, ONGC, Oil and Natural Gas Corporation, Ministry of Petroleum and Natural Gas, Government of India.
Annual Report 2015–2016, ONGC, Oil and Natural Gas Corporation, Ministry of Petroleum and Natural Gas, Government of India.
Hydrocarbon Vision 2015, Ministry of Petroleum and Natural Gas, Government of India.
India's Observer Report 2017–2019, Ministry of External Affairs, Government of India.
Annual Report 2018–2019, Ministry of Petroleum and Natural Gas, Government of India.
Annual Report 2017–2018, Ministry of Petroleum and Natural Gas, Government of India.
Annual Report 2016–2017, Ministry of Petroleum and Natural Gas, Government of India.
Annual Report 2015–2016, Ministry of Petroleum and Natural Gas, Government of India.
Annual Report 2018–2019, OIL, Oil India Limited, Ministry of Petroleum and Natural Gas, Government of India.
Annual Report 2017–2018, OIL, Oil India Limited, Ministry of Petroleum and Natural Gas, Government of India.
Annual Report 2016–2017, OIL, Oil India Limited, Ministry of Petroleum and Natural Gas, Government of India.
Annual Report 2015–2016, OIL, Oil India Limited, Ministry of Petroleum and Natural Gas, Government of India.
Annual Report 2018–2019, Petronet LNG Limited, Ministry of Petroleum and Natural Gas, Government of India.
Annual Report 2017–2018, Petronet LNG Limited, Ministry of Petroleum and Natural Gas, Government of India.
Annual Report 2016–2017, Petronet LNG Limited, Ministry of Petroleum and Natural Gas, Government of India.
Annual Report 2015–2016, Petronet LNG Limited, Ministry of Petroleum and Natural Gas, Government of India.
Annual Report 2018–2019, Indian Oil Limited, Ministry of Petroleum and Natural Gas, Government of India.
Monthly Reports January 2019 to December 2019, Directorate General of Foreign Trade, Ministry of Commerce and Industry, Government of India.
Monthly Reports January 2018 to December 2018, Directorate General of Foreign Trade, Ministry of Commerce and Industry, Government of India.

Monthly Reports January 2017 to December 2017, Directorate General of Foreign Trade, Ministry of Commerce and Industry, Government of India.
International Energy Agency Report, Gas 2018: Analysis and Forecasts to 2023.
Annual Report 2018, Novatek Corporation, Russia.
Annual Report 2017, Novatek Corporation, Russia.
Annual Report 2018, Gazprom Corporation, Russia.
Annual Report 2017, Gazprom Corporation, Russia.
Annual Report 2018, Rosneft Corporation, Russia.
Annual Report 2017, Rosneft Corporation, Russia.
Population of Overseas Indians, Ministry of External Affairs, Government of India.

Treaties and Legal Context

Maritime Jurisdiction and Boundaries in the Arctic Region http://www.dur.ac.uk/ibru/resources/arctic/Map and Briefing notes produced by International Boundaries Research Unit, Durham University.
Rothwell, D. (1996). The Polar Regions and the Development of International Law. Cambridge: Cambridge University Press. London Reference Collection: YC.1996.b.8815 DS Shelfmark: 98/09848.
The United Nations Convention on the Law of the Sea (a historical perspective), http://www.un.org/Depts/los/convention_agreements/convention_historical_perspective.htm#Historical%20Perspective.
UN. (1983). The Law of the Sea: Official Text of the United Nations Convention on the Law of the Sea with Annexes and index. London Reference Collection: UNA 287/193.
UN Division for Ocean Affairs and The Law of the Sea. (1997). The Law of the Sea: official texts of the United Nations Convention on the Law of the Sea of 10 December 1982, and of the agreement relating to the implementation of part XI ... with index and excerpts from the final act of the Third United Nations Conference on the Law of the Sea. London reference collection: UNA.287A/394 Part XI refers to management of resources at or under the seabed, and establishes the International Seabed Authority.
Adede, A. O. (1987). The System for Settlement of Disputes Under the United Nations Convention on the Law of the Sea: A Drafting History and Commentary. Dordrecht: Nijhoff. London Reference Collection: YC.1988.b.5763.
Anderson, D. (2008). Modern Law of the Sea: Selected Essays. Leiden: Martinus Nijhoff. London Reference Collection SPIS: 341.45.
Miles, E. (1998). Global Ocean Politics: The Decision Process at the Third United Nations Conference on the Law of the Sea, 1973–982. The Hague: Martinus Nijhoff. London Reference Collection: YC.2000.a.9337.

Nordquist, M. H., Heidar, T. H., and Moore, J. N. eds. (2010). Changes in the Arctic Environment and the Law of the Sea. Boston: Martinus Nijhoff. DS Shelfmark: 3113.144070 no. 14.

Suarez, S. V. (2008). The Outer Limits of the Continental Shelf: Legal Aspects of Their Establishment. Berlin: Springer. DS shelfmark: 1878.768000 Band 199 (2008).

SECONDARY SOURCES

Aki Tonami. (2014). "The Arctic Policy of China and Japan: Multi-layered Economic and Strategic Motivations," *The Polar Journal* 4, no. 1 (July), 119, https://doi.org/10.1080/2154896X.2014.913931.

Anderson, A. M. (2009). After the Ice: Life, Death, and Geopolitics in the New Arctic. New York: Smithsonian Books London Reference Collection: m10/.14674 DSC.

Arvind Gupta. (2009). "Geopolitical Implications of Arctic Meltdown," *Strategic Analysis* 33, no. 2, 175, https://doi.org/https://doi.org/10.1080/09700160902775101.

Bates, P. ed. (2009). Climate Change and Arctic Sustainable Development: Scientific, Social, Cultural and Educational Challenges. Paris: UNESCO. London Reference Collection: YD.2010.a.1805.

Berkes, F. et al. (2005). Breaking Ice: Renewable Resource and Ocean Management in the Canadian north. Calgary: University of Calgary Press. DS Shelfmark: 6151.014270V no. 7.

Bravo, M. and Sörlin, S. eds. (2002). Narrating the Arctic: A Cultural History of Nordic Scientific Practices. Carleton, MA: Science History Publications. London Reference Collection: Maps 234.a.82 DS Shelfmark: m02/40854.

Bratspies, R. M. (n.d.). *Human Rights and Arctic Resources*. 15, 33.

Burn, C. R. (2014). "Five Hundred Meetings of the Arctic Circle," *Arctic*, 67, no. 2, 266–268. Retrieved from http://www.jstor.org/stable/24363711.

Byers, M. (2017). "Crises and International Cooperation: An Arctic Case Study," *International Relations*, 31, no. 4, 375–402. https://doi.org/10.1177/0047117817735680.

Cabbarov, S. (n.d.). *Emerging Trans-Regional Corridors: South and Southeast Asia*. ISBN: 978-81-86818-26-8.96.

Canada, G. A. C.-A. Mondiales. (2017, April 12). Canada and the Circumpolar Arctic. Retrieved 30 November 2019, from GAC website: https://www.international.gc.ca/world-monde/international_relations-relations_internationales/arctic-arctique/index.aspx?lang=eng.

Chater, A. (2016). "Explaining Non-Arctic States in the Arctic Council," *Strategic Analysis*, 40, no. 3, 173–184. https://doi.org/10.1080/09700161.2016.1165467.

Chaturvedi, S. (2014). "India's Arctic Engagement: Challenges and Opportunities," *Asia Policy*, *18*, no. 1, 73–79. https://doi.org/10.1353/asp.2014.0037

Chaturvedi, S., Khare, N. and Pandey, P. C. (2005). India in the Antarctic: Scientific and Geopolitical Perspectives. New Delhi: South Asia Publishers (in association with National Centre for Antarctic and Ocean Research, and Centre for the Study of Geopolitics). DS Shelfmark: m08/.26151.

Chaturvedi, S. (1996). Polar Regions: A Political Geography. Chichester: Wiley. London Reference Collection: YC.1996.b.3467 DS Shelfmark: 97/26798.

Child, J. (1988). Antarctica and South American geopolitics: frozen lebensraum. London: Praeger. London Reference Collection: YC.1988.b.6268.

Dodds, K. (1997). Geopolitics in Antarctica: Views from the Southern Oceanic Rim. Chichester: Wiley. London Reference Collection: YC.2000.a.9593.

Dodds, K. (2002). Pink Ice: Britain and the South Atlantic Empire. London: I. B. Tauris. London Reference Collection: YC.2004.a.4548.

Depledge, D., Kennedy-Pipe, C., and Rogers, J. (2019). *The UK and the Arctic: Forward Defence*. 9.

Didenko, N. I., & Cherenkov, V. I. (2018). "Economic and Geopolitical Aspects of Developing the Northern Sea Route," *IOP Conference Series: Earth and Environmental Science*, *180*, 012012. https://doi.org/10.1088/1755-1315/180/1/012012.

Elliott, L. M. (1994). *International Environmental Politics: Protecting the Antarctic*.

EDOCS-4033-v1-2016-12-16_India_Observer_activity_report.pdf. (n.d.).

Egilsdottir, A. M. (n.d.). *Agreement Between Iceland and Norway on the Continental Shelf Between Iceland and Jan Mayen*. 82.

Filimonova, N. (2015). "Prospects for Russian–Indian Cooperation in the High North: Actors, Interests, Obstacles," *Maritime Affairs: Journal of the National Maritime Foundation of India*, *11*, no. 1, 99–115. https://doi.org/10.1080/09733159.2015.1025537.

Filimonova, Nadezhda and Krivokhizh, Svetlana. (2016). "How Asian Countries Are Making Their Way into the Arctic," *The Diplomat*, October 29, 2016, https://thediplomat.com/2016/10/how-asiancountries-are-making-their-way-into-the-arctic/.

Galt, Jerry A., Lehr, William J. and Payton, Debra L. (1991). "Fate and Transport of the Exxon Valdez Oil Spill: Part 4," *Environmental Science and Technology* 25, no, 2 (February), 202. https://doi.org/10.1021/es00014a001.

Geopolitics and Security in the Arctic: Regional Dynamics in a Global World, 1st Edition (Hardback)—Routledge [Text]. (n.d.). Retrieved 29 November 2019, from Routledge.com website: https://www.routledge.com/Geopolitics-and-Security-in-the-Arctic-Regional-dynamics-in-a-global-world/Tamnes-Offerdal/p/book/9780415734455.

Gjørv, G. H., and Hodgson, K. K. (2019). *"Arctic Exceptionalism" or "Comprehensive Security"? Understanding Security in the Arctic.* 13.

Global Greenhouse Gas Emissions Data | Greenhouse Gas (GHG) Emissions | US EPA. (n.d.). Retrieved 28 November 2019, from https://www.epa.gov/ghgemissions/global-greenhouse-gas-emissions-data.

Goodsite, M. E., Bertelsen, R. G., Cassotta Pertoldi-Bianchi, S., Ren, J., van der Watt, L.-M., & Johannsson, H. (2016). "The Role of Science Diplomacy: A Historical Development and International Legal Framework of Arctic Research Stations Under Conditions of Climate Change, Post-Cold War Geopolitics and Globalization/Power Transition," *Journal of Environmental Studies and Sciences*, 6, no. 4, 645–661. https://doi.org/10.1007/s13412-015-0329-6.

Goh Sui Noi, "China's Polar Ambitions Cause Anxiety," *The Straits Times*, February 20, 2018, https://www.straitstimes.com/asia/eastasia/chinas-polar-ambitions-cause-anxiety.

Greaves, W. (2019). *Arctic Break Up: Climate Change, Geopolitics, and the Fragmenting Arctic Security Region.* 17.

Gu, Liping, "China's Xuelong Ice Breaker Sets Out for Arctic Expedition," *Ecns.cn*, July 22, 2018, http://www.ecns.cn/news/scitech/2018-07-22/detail-ifywhfmh2716468.shtml.

Guy, E., and Lasserre, F. (2016). "Commercial Shipping in the Arctic: New Perspectives, Challenges and Regulations," *Polar Record*, 52, no. 3, 294–304. https://doi.org/10.1017/S0032247415001011.

Haglund, D. G. ed. (1989). The New Geopolitics of Minerals: Canada and International Resource Trade. Vancouver: UBC Press. London Reference Collection: YA.1994.b.5337.

Hall, C. M. and Johnston, M. E. (1995). Polar Tourism: Tourism in the Arctic and Antarctic Regions. Chichester: Wiley. London Reference Collection: YC.1995.b.2198 DS Shelfmark: 96/04387.

Huebert, R. (2019). *A New Cold War in the Arctic?! The Old One Never Ended!* 4.

Hunter, T. (2017). "Russian Arctic Policy, Petroleum Resources Development and the EU: Cooperation or Coming Confrontation?" In Liu, N., Kirk, E. A., & Henriksen, T. (eds.), *The European Union and the Arctic*. https://doi.org/10.1163/9789004349179_008.

Hydrocarbon Vision. (2015). Ministry of Petroleum and Natural Gas, Government of India.

Ibsen, Thórir. (2018). "The Arctic Cooperation, a Model for the Himalayas—Third Pole?" In Goel, Prem Shankar, Ravindra, Rasik and Chattopadhyay, Sulagna (eds.) Science and Geopolitics of the White World: Arctic-Antarctic-Himalaya. Switzerland: Springer, pp. 3–16.

India in the Arctic: A multidimensional approach. (2019). "Vestnik of Saint Petersburg University," *International Relations*, 12, no. 1. https://doi.org/10.21638/11701/spbu06.2019.107..

India's Observer Report 2017–2019, Ministry of External Affairs, Government of India.

Ingenfeld, E. (2010). "'Just in Case' Policy in the Arctic," *Arctic*, 63, no. 2, 257–259. Retrieved from http://www.jstor.org/stable/27821977.

International Energy Agency Report, Gas 2018: Analysis and Forecasts to 2023.

Jason S FN OSD OUSD POLICY (AS), H. (n.d.). *2019-DOD-Arctic-Strategy*. 19.

Joshi, A. D. (n.d.). *NMF Annual Maritime Conference—2015*. 7.

Keskitalo, E. C. H. (2004). Negotiating the Arctic: the Construction of an International Region. London: Routledge. London Reference Collection: YC.2005.a.7816 DS Shelfmark: m04/23102.

Kriwoken, L. K. et al. eds. (2007). Looking South: Australia's Antarctic Agenda. Leichhardt, New South Wales: Federation Press DS Shelfmark: m08/.34659.

Koivurova, T. (n.d.). *International Environmental Governance*. 15.

Kupriyanov, A., & Korolev, A. (n.d.). *The Eurasian Chord and the Oceanic Ring*. 19.

Lanteigne, Marc. (2014). "China's Emerging Arctic Strategies: Economics and Institutions," *Institute of International Affairs: The Centre for Arctic Policy Studies*, 13, https://brage.bibsys.no/xmlui/bitstream/handle/11250/285164/ChinasEmergingArcticStrategiesPDF_FIX2.pdf?sequence=3&isAllowed=y.

Lanteigne, M. (2015). "The Role of China in Emerging Arctic Security Discourses, *Sicherheit & Frieden*, 33, no. 3, 30–35. https://doi.org/10.5771/0175-274X-2015-3-30

Lasserre, F. (2011). "Arctic Shipping Routes: From the Panama Myth to Reality," *International Journal*, 66, no. 4, 793–808. Retrieved from http://www.jstor.org/stable/23104393

Lindholt, L. (n.d.). *3. Arctic Natural Resources in a Global Perspective*. 14.

Lück, M. et al. eds. (2010). Cruise Tourism in Polar Regions: Promoting Environmental and Social Sustainability? London: Earthscan. London Reference Collection SPIS: 338.479198.

MacDonald, A. P. (2019). *Precarious Existence or Staying the Course? The Foundations and Future of Arctic Stability*. 29.

McGhee, R. (2004). The Last Imaginary Place: A Human History of the Arctic World. Oxford: Oxford University Press. London Reference Collection: YC.2007.a.6737 DS Shelfmark.

Monthly Bulletin on Foreign Trade Statistics. (2019). 81.

Olafsson, R. H. (n.d.). *UNDERSTANDING_THE_ARCTIC_COUNCIL*. 19.

Rajan, H. P. (2014). The Legal Regime of the Arctic and India's Role and Options," *Strategic Analysis* 38, no. 6 (November), 904–912. https://doi.org/10.1080/09700161.2014.9.

Stokke, Olav Schram. (2013). "The Promise of Involvement: Asia in the Arctic," *Strategic Analysis* 37, no. 4 (August), 476, https://www.tandfonline.com/doi/abs/https://doi.org/10.1080/09700161.2013.802520.

Stokke, Olav Schram. (2015). "Can Asian Involvement Strengthen Arctic Governance," In Leiv, Lunde, Jian, Yang and Iselin, Stensdal (eds.), Asian Countries and the Arctic Future. Singapore: World Scientific Publishing, p. 52.

Tseng, Po-Hsing and Cullinane, Kevin. (2018). "Key Criteria Influencing the Choice of Arctic Shipping: A Fuzzy Analytic Hierarchy Process Model," *Maritime Policy and Management* 45, no. 4 (June), 422–438. https://doi.org/10.1080/03088839.2018.1443225.

Pezard, S. (2018). *The New Geopolitics of the Arctic: Russia's and China's Evolving Role in the Region*. https://doi.org/10.7249/CT500..

Pham, T. B. V., & Miltiadis, A. (n.d.). *Feasibility Study on Commercial Shipping in the Northern Sea Route*. 123.

Population of Overseas Indians, Ministry of External Affairs, Government of India.

Rnadall, R. E., & Jin, C. K. (n.d.). *Challenges of Dredging in the Arctic and Other Deep Ocean Locations*. 16.

Rothwell, D. R. (n.d.). *Australian National University*. 16.

Sakhuja, D. V. (n.d.). *India and the Arctic: Beyond Kiruna*. 5.

Chaturvedi, Sanjay. (2013). "China and India in the 'Receding' Arctic: Rhetoric, Routes and Resources," *Jadavpur Journal of International Relations* 17, no. 1 (June), 62, https://doi.org/10.1177/0973598414524126.

Sikri, R. (n.d.). *The Geopolitics of Energy Security and Implications for South and Southeast Asia*. 28.

Sørensen, C. T. N. (2019). *Intensifying U.S.-China security dilemma dynamics play out in the Arctic: Implications for China's Arctic strategy*. 15.

Tianming, G., & Erokhin, V. (2019). *China-Russia Collaboration in Shipping and Marine Engineering as One of the Key Factors of Secure Navigation Along the NSR*. 20.

Sinha, Uttam Kumar and Gupta, Arvind. (2014). "The Arctic and India: Strategic Awareness and Scientific Engagement," *Strategic Analysis* 38, no. 6 (November), 875, https://doi.org/10.1080/09700161.2014.952945.

Wing, Winnipeg. (2010). The Future Security Environment, 2008–2030. Part 1, Current and Emerging Trends. Ottawa: Chief of Force Development London Reference Collection: OPF.2010.x.55.

Xie, K. (n.d.). *Developing Powers Look North*. 5.

Websites

http://csis.org/region/arctic.
http://law.emory.edu/.
http://pib.nic.in.
http://www.arctic.au.dk.
http://www.arcticinfo.eu.
http://www.iarc.uaf.edu.
http://www.icwa.in.
http://www.idsa.in/.
http://www.ifpa.org/.
http://www.islandstudies.ca.
http://www.maritimeindia.org/.
http://www.mea.gov.in/.
http://www.ncaor.gov.in.
http://www.sipri.org/.
http://www.tandfonline.com.
http://www.uarctic.org/.
https://en.wikipedia.org/wiki.
https://un.org.
https://www.arcus.org.
https://www.usnwc.edu/.
https://loksabha.nic.in/.
https://www.cbc.ca/.
https://www.theguardian.com/.
http://www.voiceof.india.com/.
https://aleut-international.org/.
https://Arcticathabaskancouncil.com/.
https://gwichincouncil.com/.
https://www.inuitcircumpolar.com/.
http://www.raipon.info/en/.
http://www.saamicouncil.net/en/.
http://www.dnaindia.com/.
https://thewire.in/.
http://www.imo.org
https://www.barentscooperation.org/.
https://Arcticportal.org.
https://www.clingendael.org/.
https://www.Arcticfrontiers.com.
http://www.Arcticcircle.org/.
https://Arcticeconomiccouncil.com/.
https://oaarchive.Arctic-council.org/.
https://www.Arcticcoastguardforum.com/.

https://www.theArcticinstitute.org/.
https://www.apan.org/.
https://Arcticyearbook.com/.
http://norden.diva-portal.org/.
https://www.whitehouse.gov/.
https://www.vocativ.com/.
www.utu.fi.
https://archive.usgs.gov/.
https://pubs.usgs.gov/.
https://pdfs.semanticscholar.org.
https://www.sciencedirect.com/.
https://www.Arcticphoto.com/.
https://www.dailymail.co.uk/.
https://cambridge.org.
https://Arctic-lio.com/.
http://www.arctis-search.com/.
https://www.spri.cam.ac.uk/.
https://pame.is/.
https://www.Arctic.ac.uk.
http://www.defense.gov/.
https://media.defense.gov/.
http://www.parl.gc.ca/.
http://www.Arctic-office.de.
http://www.oceanlaw.org/.
http://international.gc.ca.
https://www.mfa.is/.
http://www.openaid.se/.
http://english.www.gov.cn/.
http://thediplomat.com/.
https://www.hindustantimes.com/.
https://www.moes.gov.in/.
http://www.ncaor.gov.in/.
https://www.maritime-executive.com.
https://www.ongcvidesh.com.
http://petroleum.nic.in/.
https://www.oil-india.com.
https://dgft.gov.in.
https://gailonline.com/home.html.
https://www.petronetlng.com/.
www.iea.org.
https://oilprice.com/.
https://www.gazprom.com/.

https://www.rosneft.com/.
https://www.total.com/.
http://www.novatek.ru/en/.
http://www.dgciskol.gov.in.
https://www.mosaic-expedition.org/.
https://www.npr.org/.
https://dst.gov.in/.
https://www.state.gov.
https://www.amap.no/.
https://www.jstor.org.
https://climatetippingpoints.info/.
http://nsidc.org/.
https://www.unenvironment.org/.
http://academicworks.cuny.
https://www.rand.org/.
https://projekter.aau.dk.
https://www.dur.ac.uk/.
https://www.researchgate.net/.
https://www.livemint.com/.
https://www.ongcindia.com/.
https://forumvostok.ru/en/about-the-forum.
www.oceanlaw.org/.
https://www.nato.int.
https://www.washingtonpost.com/.
https://www.navy.mil/.
https://ee.usembassy.gov/.
https://www.eurasiareview.co.
https://www.indepthnews.net/.
https://www.government.is/.
https://www.highnorthnews.com/.
https://www.newsweek.com.
https://nationalinterest.org/.
https://uk.usembassy.gov/.
https://www.stripes.com.
https://fas.org.
https://www.pmel.noaa.gov/.
https://www.equinor.com.
https://Arcticwwf.org.
https://www.huffpost.com/.
https://www.csis.org/.
https://www.newscientist.com/.
https://climateactiontracker.org/.

http://www.business-standard.com/.
http://sdg.iisd.org/.
https://strategicstudyindia.blogspot.com/.
http://english.itpcas.cas.cn/.
https://www.wsws.org/.
https://www.dw.com/.

Index

A
Academic pursuits, 175
Accidents, 261
Advisory Committee on Protection of the Sea (ACOPS), 17
Aleut, 44
Aleut International Association (AIA), 11
Alliance of Small Island States (AOSIS), 244
Ambassador, 327
Antarctic, 25
Antarctic Treaty, 113
Arctic, 1
Arctic Athabaskan Council (AAC), 13
Arctic Bridge route, 59
Arctic Circle, 6, 34, 45
Arctic Climate Impact Assessment (ACIA), 204
Arctic Coast Guard Forum (ACGF), 36, 247
Arctic Contaminants Action Program (ACAP), 15
Arctic Council (AC), 11, 37
  limitations of, 232
Arctic disequilibrium, 274
Arctic Economic Council, 35
Arctic Eight, 242
Arctic Environmental Protection Strategy (AEPS), 9, 235
Arctic Frontiers, 34
Arctic glaciers, 103
Arctic governance, 4, 303
Arctic Home in the Vedas, The, 102
Arctic Human Development Report, 44
Arctic Institute of North America (AINA), 17
Arctic Migratory Birds Institute (AMBI), 194
Arctic Military Code of Conduct (AMCC), 254
Arctic Monitoring and Assessment Programme (AMAP), 6, 15
Arctic Policy Directive, 82
Arctic Research and Policy Act (ARPA), 81
Arctic security, 220

Arctic Ship Traffic Data (ASTD), 71
Arms control treaties, 249
Asian partnership, 318
Association of World Reindeer Herders (AWRH), 18
Atlantification, 212

B
Baltic Sea, 252
Barents Euro-Arctic Cooperation (BEAC), 11
Barents Sea Boundary Treaty, 73
Bastion, 251
Bay of Bengal Initiative for Multi-Sectoral Technical and Economic Cooperation (BIMSTEC), 140
Bazaar Governance, 235
Beaufort Sea, 213
Belt and Road Initiative (BRI), 94
Bering Sea Treaty, 73
Bhabha Atomic Research Centre, 314
Bharati, 107
Blue economy, 36

C
Canada, 2, 162
Canada–Denmark Boundary Treaty, 72
Central Arctic Ocean (CAO), 52, 231
Central North-Atlantic, 51
Centre for Cellular and Molecular Biology, 314
Chairmanship, 19
China, 2, 92
China Communication Construction Company Ltd, 80
China-Iceland Aurora Observatory (CIAO), 128
China-Nordic Arctic research centre (CNARC), 96

Chukchi, 44
Circum-Arctic Resource Appraisal (CARA), 47
Circumpolar Conservation Union (CCU), 18
Climate change, 317
CO_2 emissions, 292
Cold Response, 254
Cold War, 230
Commission on the Limits of Continental Shelf (CLCS), 3, 214, 247
Common heritage of mankind, 137, 270
Communities, 209
Community of Common Destiny, 255
Conference for Security and Cooperation in Europe (CSCE), 236
Conference of Parties, 131
Conflict, 3
Conservation of Arctic Flora and Fauna (CAFF), 15
Contiguous Zone, 29
Continental, 41
Convention for the Protection of the Marine Environment of the North-East Atlantic (OSPAR), 33
Crude oil, 42

D
Democracy, 301
Denmark, 159
Department of Ocean Development (DOD), 105
Destination traffic, 62
Diaspora, 175, 187
Directorate General of Foreign Trade, 169

E

Eastern Bering Sea, 51
Economic and Social Council for Asia and Pacific (ESCAP), 119
Economic interests, 1
Emergency Prevention, Preparedness, and Response (EPPR), 15
Environmental interests, 1
Environmental problems, 200
Eurasia, 309
European Union (EU), 2, 83
Evenk, 44
Exceptionalism, 229
Exclusive economic zone (EEZ), 29
Extended Bastion, 251
External Affairs Minister (EAM), 307

F

Feedback loop, 207
Finland, 2, 159
Finnish Meteorological Institute (FMI), 133
First Defence Strategy, 251
Fishing, 51
Floating Nuclear Power Plant (FNPP), 227
Food shortages, 126
Forestry, 56
France, 22
Freedom of Navigation Operations (FONOPS), 265

G

Gandhi, Indira, 304
Gas Authority of India Limited (GAIL), 148
Gas hydrates, 45
Gas reserves, 43
Gazprom, 157
Geo-economic role, 3
Geological Survey of India (GSI), 314
Geopolitical implications, 243
Geopolitics, 1, 140
Geostrategic role, 3
Geothermal energy, 58
Germany, 2
GLACIER (Global Leadership in the Arctic Cooperation, Innovation, Engagement and Resilience) conference, 291
Glaciers, 2
Global commons, 137
   disputation of, 284
Global Environment Facility (GEF), 119
Graded Response Action Plan (GRAP), 289
Great Powers, 277
Greenhouse gases (GHGs), 206
Greenland, 2
Greenland–Svalbard Boundary Treaty, 73
Gross domestic product (GDP), 128, 301
Gwich'in Council International (GCI), 13

H

Hambantota, 310
Hans Island, 213
Himadri, 5, 102
Himalayas, 307
Hormuz, 309
Hydrocarbon, 2, 45

I

Ice cover, 2, 201
Iceland, 2, 159
ICEX, 254
Imperial energy, 144, 277
IndARC, 110

India, 2
India Meteorological Department (IMD), 106
Indian Institute of Tropical Meteorology (IITM), 106
Indian Navy (IN), 324
Indian Ocean Region (IOR), 118
India's Regional Navigation Satellite System (IRNSS), 116
Indigenous people, 4
Indigenous population, 315
INF treaty, 228
International Arctic Research Base, 102
International Arctic Science Committee (IASC), 9, 18
International Centre for Integrated Mountain Development (ICIMOD), 119
International Convention for the Prevention of Pollution from Ships (MARPOL), 3
International Convention for the Safety of Life at Sea (SOLAS), 31
International Council for the Exploration of the Sea (ICES), 16
International Federation of Red Cross & Red Crescent Societies (IFRC), 16
International Maritime Organisation (IMO), 16, 247
International Network for Terrestrial Research and Monitoring in the Arctic (INTERACT), 84
International North-South Transport Corridor (INSTC), 195
International Pacific Halibut Commission, 52
International Solar Alliance (ISA), 289
International Tribunal for the Law of the Sea (ITLOS), 30
International Union for Circumpolar Health (IUCH), 18, 235
International Union for the Conservation of Nature (IUCN), 16
International Work Group for Indigenous Affairs (IWGIA), 18
Inuit, 44
Inuit Circumpolar Council (ICC), 13
Italy, 22

J
Jan Mayen Treaties, 73
Japan, 22, 85
Jurisdiction, 23

K
Khanij Bidesh India Ltd (KABIL), 168
Khanty, 44
Kirkenes Declaration, 32
Kiruna Ministerial Meeting, 20
Kola Peninsula, 3
Kyoto Protocol, 130, 290

L
Left-Green Movement (LGM), 225
License 61, 150
Lincoln Sea, 75
Liquefied natural gas, 152
Liu Xiaobo, 314
Lombok, 309
Lomonosov Ridge, 271

M
Maitri, 107
Malaccan Straits, 67
Marine environment, 206
Maritime boundaries, 138

Maritime boundaries and agreements, 72
Micro plastics, 263
Mineral resources, 2
Minerals, 53
Ministerial meeting, 247
Ministry of Earth Sciences (MoES), 105
Ministry of Environment, Forest and Climate Change (MoEFCC), 119
Ministry of External Affairs (MEA), 117
Ministry of Science and Technology (MoST), 119
Ministry of Tribal Affairs (MoTA), 119
Multidisciplinary Drifting Observatory for the Study of Arctic Climate (MOSAiC) expedition, 82, 169

N

Namimi Gange (Clean Ganga), 289
National Centre for Earth Science Studies (NCESS), 106
National Centre for Medium-Range Weather Forecasting (NCMRWF), 106
National Centre for Polar and Ocean Research (NCPOR), 104
National Geophysical Research Institute, 314
National Institute of Ocean Technology (NIOT), 106
National Institution for Transforming India (NITI), 129
National Polar Data Centre (NPDC), 110
National Security Council Secretariat (NSCS), 311
Natural calamities and disasters, 5
NDC, 292
Near-Arctic, 302

Nenets, 44
Netherlands, 2
New, Emerging and Strategic Technologies (NEST), 140
Non-Arctic state Observer, 237
Non-resident Indians (NRIs), 187
Nordic Council of Ministers (NCM), 16
Nordic Environment Finance Corporation (NEFCO), 16
North American Aerospace Defence Command (NORAD), 255
North Atlantic Marine Mammal Commission (NAMMCO), 16
North Atlantic Treaty Organisation (NATO), 33, 92, 226
North-East Atlantic, 51
North East Passage (NEP), 59, 64
Northern Dimension, 32
Northern Forum (NF), 18
Northern Strategy, 251
North Pacific Anadromous Fish Commission (NPAFC), 52
North Pole, 302
North West Passage (NWP), 59
Norway, 2, 159
Norwegian Polar Institute (NPI), 111
Norwegian Sea, 252
Novatek, 156
Ny-Ålesund Science Managers Committee (NySMAC), 104

O

Observer Report, 190
Observers, 11
Observers crisis, 240
Observer status, 5
Oceana, 18
Oil and Natural Gas Commission (ONGC), 143
ONGC Videsh Limited (OVL), 143

OSPAR Commission, 16
Ottawa Declaration, 9

P
Pacification, 212
Pacific Islands Forum (PIF), 244
Pacific Regional Environmental Protection Programme (PREP), 244
Pacific Small Island Developing States (PSIDS), 244
Permafrost, 2, 36
Permanent Participants, 6
Persian Gulf, 309
Persistent Organic Pollutants (POPS), 83
Petronet LNG Ltd (PLL), 150
Polar Code, 31
Polar Research Vessel (PRV), 170
Polar Silk Road (PSR), 94, 260
Polar vortex, 212
Policy documents, 77
Political discourse, 175
Political interests, 1
Pollution, 261
Positive feedback, 211
Power of Siberia, 308
Protection of the Arctic Marine Environment (PAME), 15
Public health, 209

R
Realist, 234
Research Council of Norway (RCN), 111
Research in Svalbard (RiS), 133
Rules-based order, 302
Russia, 1, 165
Russian Arctic Zone (RAZ), 47
Russian Association of Indigenous Peoples of the North (RAIPON), 14
Russian Marine Doctrine, 86, 250
Russian Optical Trans-Arctic Submarine Cable System (ROTACS), 59

S
Saami, 44
Saami Council (SC), 14
Sakhalin-1, 143, 278
Science, Technology and Innovation (STI), 119
Scientific diplomacy, 313
Sea ice, 203
Sea-level, 104, 208
Search and Rescue (SAR), 31
Security interests, 1
Senior Arctic Official (SAO), 11
Sever, 254
Shipping routes, 59
Short-term climate pollutants, 211
Singapore, 22
Smart Cities Mission, 289
South Asian Association for Regional Cooperation (SAARC), 119
South China Sea (SCS), 224
South Korea, 22
Sovereignty, 23
Sovereign Wealth Fund, 197
Space Applications Centre, 314
Spain, 2, 22
Spitsbergen Treaty, 4, 102
Standing Committee of the Parliamentarians of the Arctic Region (SCPAR), 17, 235
St Petersburg Declaration, 134
Strait of Malacca, 309
Strategic rivalry, 308
Sub-Arctic, 1, 302

Submarine cables, 58
Sunda, 309
Sustainable, 4
Sustainable Development Goals (SDGs), 244
Sustainable Development Working Group (SDWG), 15
Sustainable economic development, 36
Svalbard Islands, 4, 75
Swachh Bharat (Clean India), 289
Sweden, 2, 159

T
Taas-Yuryakh, 150
Terra nullius, 233
Third Pole vision, 318
Thule, 253
Tourism, 57
Trans Arctic Passage, 59
Transatlantic, 252
Transit traffic, 61
Transpolar route, 69
Treaty, 26
Trident Juncture, 252, 254
Tsentr, 254
2008 Ilulissat Declaration, 27

U
Ujala Yojana (focus on energy-saving lighting), 289
Ujjawala Yojana (clean cooking scheme), 289
United Kingdom, 22
United Nations Conference on Environment and Development (UNCED), 119
United Nations Convention on the Laws of the Sea (UNCLOS), 3
United Nations Declaration on the Rights of Indigenous Peoples (UNDRIP), 119
United Nations Development Programme (UNDP), 17
United Nations Economic Commission for Europe (UN-ECE), 235
United Nations Environment Programme (UNEP), 17
United Nations Framework Convention on Climate Change (UN FCCC), 310
United Nations Security Council (UNSC), 22
United States Geological Survey (USGS), 6
University of the Arctic (UArctic), 18
USA, 2, 78, 162
U.S. Geological Survey (USGS), 45

V
Vankor, 144
Vankorneft, 149
Voting rights, 23

W
Warming, 200
Water stress, 126
Western Bering Sea, 51
West Nordic Council (WNC), 17
Winter whiplash, 208
Working Groups, 6
World Health Organisation (WHO), 129, 288
World Meteorological Organisation (WMO), 17
World Wide Fund for Nature-Global Arctic Programme (WWF), 19

X

Xuelong, 293

Y

Yamal, 157
Yiwu-London rail link, 309
Yupik, 44